INCREASING STUDENT ENGAGEMENT AND RETENTION USING CLASSROOM TECHNOLOGIES: CLASSROOM RESPONSE SYSTEMS AND MEDIATED DISCOURSE TECHNOLOGIES

CUTTING-EDGE TECHNOLOGIES IN HIGHER EDUCATION

Series Editor: Charles Wankel

Recent Volumes:

Volume 1: Educating Educators with Social Media – Edited by Charles Wankel

Volume 2: Higher Education Administration with Social Media: Including Applications in Student Affairs, Enrollment Management, Alumni Relations, and Career Centers – Edited by Laura A. Wankel and Charles Wankel

Volume 3: Teaching Arts and Science with the New Social Media – Edited by Charles Wankel

Volume 4: Transforming Virtual World Learning – Edited by Randy Hinrichs and Charles Wankel

Volume 5: Misbehavior Online in Higher Education – Edited by Laura A. Wankel and Charles Wankel

Volume 6A: Increasing Student Engagement and Retention Using Online Learning Activities: Wikis, Blogs and Webquests – Edited by Charles Wankel and Patrick Blessinger

Volume 6B: Increasing Student Engagement and Retention Using Social Technologies: Facebook, E-Portfolios and Other Social Networking Services – Edited by Laura A. Wankel and Patrick Blessinger

Volume 6C: Increasing Student Engagement and Retention Using Immersive Interfaces: Virtual Worlds, Gaming, and Simulation – Edited by Charles Wankel and Patrick Blessinger

Volume 6D: Increasing Student Engagement and Retention Using Mobile Applications: Smartphones, Skype and Texting Technologies – Edited by Laura A. Wankel and Patrick Blessinger

CUTTING-EDGE TECHNOLOGIES IN HIGHER EDUCATION VOLUME 6E

INCREASING STUDENT ENGAGEMENT AND RETENTION USING CLASSROOM TECHNOLOGIES: CLASSROOM RESPONSE SYSTEMS AND MEDIATED DISCOURSE TECHNOLOGIES

EDITED BY

CHARLES WANKEL

St. John's University, New York, USA

PATRICK BLESSINGER

St. John's University, New York, USA

IN COLLABORATION WITH

JURATE STANAITYTE

NEIL WASHINGTON

Created in partnership with the Higher Education Teaching and Learning Association

Higher Education Teaching & Learning

http://hetl.org/

Emerald

United Kingdom – North America – Japan

India – Malaysia – China

Emerald Group Publishing Limited
Howard House, Wagon Lane, Bingley BD16 1WA, UK

First edition 2013

British Library Cataloguing in Publication Data
A catalogue record for this book is available from the British Library

ISBN: 978-1-78190-511-1
ISSN: 2044-9968 (Series)

ISOQAR
REGISTERED
ISOQAR certified Management System, awarded to Emerald for adherence to Environmental standard ISO 14001:2004.

Certificate Number 1985
ISO 14001

INVESTOR IN PEOPLE

CONTENTS

PART II: APPLICATION OF CLASSROOM RESPONSE SYSTEMS AND MEDIATED DISCOURSE TECHNOLOGIES

LIST OF CONTRIBUTORS

Anthony 'Skip' Basiel	Adobe Systems Ltd., UK
Patrick Blessinger	St. John's University, Queens, NY, USA
Leonardo Caporarello	Università L. Bocconi, Milan, Italy
Marija Cubric	University of Hertfordshire, Hatfield, UK
Elizabeth Dell	Rochester Institute of Technology, Rochester, NY, USA
Antonella Esposito	University of Milan, Milan, Italy
Iris Fischlmayr	Johannes Kepler University Linz, Linz, Austria
Robert Garrick	Rochester Institute of Technology, Rochester, NY, USA
Sarah Gilbert	University of British Columbia, Vancouver, British Columbia, Canada
Lauren Miller Griffith	Central Michigan University, Mount Pleasant, MI, USA
Mark J. Hager	Menlo College, Atherton, CA, USA
Rhiannon Hart	Rochester Institute of Technology, Rochester, NY, USA
Michael Howarth	University College London, London, UK
Amanda Jefferies	University of Hertfordshire, Hatfield, UK
Tine Köhler	The University of Melbourne, Parkville, Victoria, Australia
Timo Lainema	Turku School of Economics, University of Turku, Turku, Finland
Brian Lukoff	Harvard University, Cambridge, MA, USA

Eric Mazur	Harvard University, Cambridge, MA, USA
Ferdinando Pennarola	Università L. Bocconi, Milan, Italy
Brian A. Roberts	Central Michigan University, Mount Pleasant, MI, USA
Cristina Rubino	California State University, Northridge, CA, USA
Mark Russell	King's College London, London, UK
Eeli Saarinen	Turku School of Economics, University of Turku, Turku, Finland
Julie Schell	Harvard University, Cambridge, MA, USA
Lorn Sheehan	Dalhousie University, Halifax, Nova Scotia, Canada
Lois M. Shelton	California State University, Northridge, CA, USA
Binod Sundararajan	Dalhousie University, Halifax, Nova Scotia, Canada
Larry Villasmil	Rochester Institute of Technology, Rochester, NY, USA
Charles Wankel	St. John's University, Queens, NY, USA
Christa L. Wilkin	California State University, Northridge, CA, USA
Deone Zell	California State University, Northridge, CA, USA
Tarek Zoubir	Middlesex University, London, UK

PART I
ADOPTION OF CLASSROOM RESPONSE SYSTEMS AND MEDIATED DISCOURSE TECHNOLOGIES

CREATIVE APPROACHES IN HIGHER EDUCATION: AN INTRODUCTION TO USING CLASSROOM-MEDIATED DISCOURSE TECHNOLOGIES

Patrick Blessinger and Charles Wankel

INTRODUCTION

The chapters in this book focus on using different types of mediated discourse technologies such as classroom response systems and class replay systems to create technology-rich social learning environments within the classroom. Improvements in low-cost, ubiquitous digital technologies and development of modern learning theories are rapidly changing the manner in which we teach and learn in the postindustrial age. These transformative advancements are also refining our views of what it means to teach and learn in a globalized world. At both the individual and group levels, mediated discourse technologies are becoming more prevalent in higher education as teaching and learning tools across a wide range of disciplines to better engage students and create more participatory and engaging learning environments. Using these technologies in a purposeful manner

Increasing Student Engagement and Retention using Classroom Technologies: Classroom Response Systems and Mediated Discourse Technologies
Cutting-edge Technologies in Higher Education, Volume 6E, 3–16

ISSN: 2044-9968/doi:10.1108/S2044-9968(2013)000006E003

also has the potential of creating more interesting and enjoyable social learning environments for both instructors and students.

When coupled with germane teaching and learning methods such as peer instruction, these technologies have the potential to enhance or transform a classroom, make learning more meaningful and interesting, and increase academic achievement. So, it is important to use these technologies in such a way that is appropriate to the context of the learning environment (e.g., the type and nature of the course, the grade level, the learning objectives of the course, learning needs of the students) and the pedagogical approach of the instructor. For instance, research carried out by Gok (2011) showed that tools such as "clickers" (i.e., classroom response systems or student response systems) are viewed as one tool among many at the disposal of instructors to support their effort to increase student learning in the classroom. Gok noted that increased student participation, the ability to solicit real-time student feedback, increased motivation to attend class, and an easy way to collect data for formative assessment purposes were cited by instructors and students as reasons that led to greater student engagement. Gok also noted that this technology also has the potential to be used across a range of inquiry (from basic to advanced) and across a range of courses (from large introductory courses to small advanced courses).

Increased participation alone is unlikely to yield more effective learning if these tools, as with any tool, are not used contextually and in a purposeful manner. In other words, success depends, in large part, on how instructors use these technologies to fit the learning objectives of their course and how they are specifically used to mediate classroom learning activities. For instance, at one end of the continuum a simple use of these technologies could be to promote the comprehension and recall of foundational knowledge such as facts and concepts (e.g., as one might expect in a large, introductory undergraduate course) and, at the other end of the continuum, they can also be used to cultivate deep, holistic learning (e.g., as one might expect in a small, advanced course). So, the tool should be adjusted to fit the requirements of the course (e.g., by the type and the manner in which questions are structured and posed).

There is not simply one right way to use mediated technologies for all courses. Each instructor must figure out for himself/herself how to appropriately use these technologies depending on the context of his/her course. As such, these classroom-mediated technologies provide educators with many new possibilities and opportunities to either enhance or transform how instructors interact with students and how students interact with each other. They provide instructors with another means to enlarge our views of teaching and learning but, at the same time, they allow us to do so while maintaining the core ideals of the academy (e.g., academic freedom, pedagogical pluralism, academic rigor).

Classroom-mediated discourse technologies can be defined as a set of technologies that facilitate student participation in learning activities in the classroom. As such, they can be viewed as participatory tools that mediate discourse in the classroom. This broad definition can serve as a good starting point for drilling down into the specifics of who, what, where, when, why, and how of mediating technologies in an educational context. So, regardless of whether these technologies are used at the undergraduate level or postgraduate level, or whether they are used in a physics class or a philosophy class, the notion of facilitation to foster more effective learning is important since it connotes the notion that these technologies are enablers used to generate new teaching and learning possibilities. This broad definition connotes the idea that better learning (i.e., more enriched, more meaningful, more purposeful, more authentic) is the main outcome of their use. To that end, these mediating technologies open up new possibilities to enhance or transform existing instructional methods.

Mediated discourse tools are being used together with a broader set of teaching and learning tools and strategies to (1) increase student participation and motivation through more effective ways that engage and interest students, (2) create a social learning environment through meaningful classroom discussions, and (3) provide a mediated means to assess in real-time (as well long-term) the students' understanding of the lecture material. The power of using these tools resides in their ability to create agile, real-time formative assessment opportunities (and long-term summative assessments of the group's progress) that can gauge more precisely the effectiveness of the learning that is occurring in the classroom. Using mediated technologies expands and makes more flexible traditional teaching and learning boundaries (Francis & Raftery, 2005). Technology-mediated discourse environments provide both the instructor and students another way to cultivate a more dynamic and meaningful teaching and learning environment.

However, it should be noted that the novelty alone or the technical sophistication of these technologies is not sufficient to engage and retain learners. As with any technologies, these tools must be used in a purposeful and meaningful way and integrated within a relevant theoretical framework that is appropriate to the teaching and learning context (e.g., institutional mission, educational level, type of course, course objectives, learning outcomes). Thus, knowledge of the technology must be integrated with the relevant pedagogical and content knowledge in a purposeful manner. Using valid and reliable pedagogical methods and learning principles and theories is key. Again, as with all technologies, in addition to relevant and established theory, it is also imperative to be cognizant of the epistemological, ontological, and phenomenological basis that are germane to utilizing such technologies.

ADOPTION PRINCIPLES

Two key principles emerge from the findings of the chapters in the adoption section of the book that help to frame the content of the book and this specific set of technologies:

1) Technology-mediated discourse environments should be viewed as social learning communities and participatory systems in which inquiry is fostered at all levels and within all contexts as a means to discuss and assess knowledge, query students' perspectives, solve problems, and think more critically and collaboratively about course concepts.
2) Building social learning communities within the classroom has the potential to foster a greater sense of belonging, interactivity, and group cohesiveness which are important factors in student motivation and their willingness to participate in such communities.

These principles are indicative of the growing emphasis on student-centeredness, authentic learning, contextual/situated learning, integrative learning, developing advanced problem-solving abilities, developing portable skills that can be used in any context/situation, and developing learners who are critically engaged in all aspects of the learning process (Dangle & Wang, 2008). Authentic learning involves aligning the course objectives with meaningful, real-life learning activities. Contextual learning occurs by the complex interplay of situated interactions. Integrative learning involves the ability to connect concepts and meanings across courses and life experiences. These skills and abilities are reflective of the growing importance of living and working in a postindustrial, globalized world where interconnectedness and interdependence are growing in importance. All else being equal, it follows that students will be more motivated to engage more passionately in learning activities that are more authentic and meaningful to their personal life-worlds.

These technologies are not limited to simple ask–respond scenarios. They can be tailored to work in any course in any discipline and be used at any level on Bloom's taxonomy of learning objectives, from simple recall of facts and conceptual understanding (knowledge and comprehension) to problem solving (application, analysis, synthesis) to the more challenging critical assessment and value-based judgments (evaluation). Also, all these approaches can be used within a single course or single class session in a scaffolded way that continually and gradually builds students' higher order thinking skills. The idea is to pinpoint any difficulties that students may have with lower level knowledge and concepts that may be preventing them from progressing up the cognitive levels toward increasingly more challenging and critical thought processes, skills, and abilities in an integrative and contextualized manner. Therefore, the types of queries asked should mirror the learning objective sought.

Participation with these technologies should aim to provide a means for students to feel more comfortable in engaging with the class in a more low-risk way compared to, for instance, calling out students by name. For instance, these technologies may provide introverted students, who may not be inclined to speak out in front of their classmates for fear they may give the wrong answer, a relatively low-risk way to engage with the rest of the class. This helps create a social presence in the classroom without inadvertently embarrassing students by putting them on the spot in front of their peers. This anonymity also allows the instructor to be more efficient and effective with his/her use of time and puts the focus on the learning needs of the students and not so much on personality differences. Again, used appropriately and in a purposeful manner, these technologies can produce several positive effects in the classroom.

APPLICATION BENEFITS

As illustrated in the book chapters in the application section, these types of learner-centered technology-mediated social learning environments support:

1) relatively non-obtrusive and efficient forms of classroom monitoring,
2) real-time queries and responses to match the topic being covered to identify problem areas (formative assessments) that may be an impediment to students in developing higher order thinking,
3) audience-paced instruction and peer-based instruction that fosters collaborative and social learning,
4) anonymity of responses that provides students and instructors with a potentially less threatening way to assess the readiness of the students to progress forward, and

5) collection and analysis of responses over longer terms in order to summatively and longitudinally assess the progress of the group (Deal, 2007).

If designed properly and integrated into the course in a purposeful manner, mediated discourse technologies have the potential to better engage learners by fostering a participative social learning classroom environment and creating a sense of belonging, group cohesiveness, and more personalized learning. According to Lave and Wenger (1991) learning involves enculturation into the practices of a community. These tools help to foster such communities in the micro-sociological world of the classroom. In short, the question becomes: how can we use these promising technologies to transform simple facts into requisite knowledge, and knowledge into synthesis, and synthesis into evaluative ethical judgment making.

THEORETICAL FRAMING

Through varied approaches, the authors in this volume operationalize the use-mediated discourse technologies' tools in the spirit of cognitive and social constructivism, which are supported by the learning theories of Piaget, Vygotsky, and Bandura. Constructivism can be broadly defined as cognitive and social learning wherein the learner constructs new knowledge and meaning based on his/her contextualized, situated, and authentic experiences. Thus, constructivism provides a plausible framework for designing mediated learning contexts that support engaging students in classroom discussions.

Based on the principles of Vygotsky (1978), knowledge is constructed socially in a cultural-historical context through one's personal interactions with other people and then individually. Core constructivist philosophy holds that learning is first constructed in a social context and then situated at the individual level (Eggen & Kauchak, 2006). The constructivist view thus suggests that learners continually seek to understand their life-world through meaningful interactions with their life-worlds and through meaningful interactivity with others. Mediated discourse technologies can be integrated with content and pedagogy to enhance learning (Mishra & Koehler, 2006). Thus, the challenge is not so much cost or access to technology in the classroom but how best to use the technology in a way that is most appropriate to the context of the course and the class and that suits the pedagogical preference of the instructor. For instance, Dangle and

Wang (2008) provide a useful theoretical framework for designing courses using classroom response systems but could potentially be applied to other forms of mediated discourse technologies as well. This framework overlays Bloom's Taxonomy with Chickering and Gamson's (1987) seven principles of good practice in undergraduate education.

TECHNOLOGY

The tools discussed in this book are especially useful as ancillary tools to support those instructors who may be more comfortable with traditional teaching methods such as lecture. So, these tools do not necessarily require or ask instructors to radically change the teaching methods they may be most comfortable with but, rather, they provide a relatively easy and flexible way to improve the learning environment depending on the learning needs of the students and the pedagogical preferences of the instructor. In this way, these tools support the ideas of meaningful learning and pedagogical pluralism. As such, these tools should be viewed as another means by which instructors can enhance their own teaching methods and improve student learning by increasing student engagement and participation.

This book presented several studies that illustrated how these classroom-mediating technologies are being used in a variety of educational courses as active-mediated discourse learning tools. As such, technology-mediated instruction can support instructors in creating higher quality of interaction and more meaningful learning activities because the students collaborate with the instructor to control the pace and development of the course. So, the pace of the course occurs in a more conscious manner and is based on the learning needs of the students and the learning objectives of the course. The locus of control for the progress of the class is therefore more distributed between students and instructor. Thus, these technologies have the potential to support more democratic, more flexible, and more self-regulated forms of learning.

CHAPTER OVERVIEWS

In "Enhancing Learning and Teaching Using Electronic Voting Systems – The Development of a Framework for an Institutional Approach for Their Introduction," by Amanda Jefferies, Marija Cubric, and Mark Russell, the authors examine the introduction of Electronic Voting Systems (EVS) at a

UK university to support the student learning experience and the factors involved in moving from an "ad hoc" and individual basis for their use at local and school level to offering support for using and developing EVS on a wider institutional basis. The authors propose the development of a framework for introducing technologies to support learning, such as the EVS after reviewing current technology adoption models. Their framework incorporates a three-way focus on the development of a sound technology infrastructure, the provision of support and training for those using the new technologies, placed within the context of sound change management principles and thus supported by the research into all these areas.

In "Using The Phoebe Pedagogic Planner to Enhance Student Learning and Engagement in Undergraduate Psychology Courses," by Mark J. Hager, Anthony 'Skip' Basiel, Michael Howarth, and Tarek Zoubir, the authors discuss a question posted to the LinkedIn user group "Technology-using professors": Do your students Facebook or text while you're lecturing? This case study explores how we co-opted social media technologies toward educational ends; informally exchanging ideas could occur in Google groups or a Moodle discussion board, and text messages became classroom response technology providing data for discussions and assessment. A majority of faculty instructing online or blended courses seek guidance on appropriate instructional technology integration. We examine a year applying the Phoebe pedagogic planner to enhance student learning and engagement in undergraduate psychology courses. The Phoebe planner provides guidance on learning design and appropriate technology use, and it is strengthened when used in combination with current research, as done here, to evaluate interactive media options while planning instructional engagement in and out of class. We highlight challenges such as planning time and resource needs faculty can encounter when planning for and introducing instructional technology. Numerous lessons were learned for faculty development and institutional development of a culture of e-learning. Motivation plays a key role in faculty adoption of instructional technology. Faculty may be motivated by their desire to master new technology; they also may be motivated by institutional factors such as rewards and recognition for engaging in the extra demands of developing and refining e-learning pedagogies. Systemic institutional planning and learner-centered collaboration among faculty, researchers, and administrators can shape and improve student engagement and are crucial to developing institutional cultures of e-learning.

In "Where Technologies Collide: A Technology Integration Model," by Christa L. Wilkin, Cristina Rubino, Deone Zell, and Lois M. Shelton, the authors explain how educators need to be fluent in content, pedagogical, and technological knowledge domains so that they can increase student learning and engagement. They state that educators' primary focus ought to be on the entire set of knowledge domains that teachers need to incorporate technology into their classrooms; this knowledge is known as "TPACK" or *technological, pedagogical, and content knowledge*. This knowledge varies by instructor, which suggests that there are individual characteristics that influence instructors' TPACK. Additionally, although educators may possess TPACK, this does not necessarily translate into the effective integration of technology in the classroom. Factors such as organizational and classroom context likely influence the extent that instructors use technology. These factors are a key motivation as to why we need to extend the current TPACK model because knowledge alone is insufficient. We extend the TPACK framework by proposing a theoretical model that examines precursors to TPACK (e.g., educators' experience and attitudes) and educator, student, and school outcomes of using technology (e.g., educator satisfaction, student engagement and satisfaction, school resources). We also include several boundary conditions for these relationships in the proposed model. Specifically, we argue that developing TPACK and technology use is context-bound by environmental factors such as the classroom environment, the availability of technology, and students' needs and learning styles.

In "The Networked Faculty and Student Engagement: The Case of Microblogging to Support Participation in a Human Resources Management Postgraduate Course," by Antonella Esposito, the author contends that issues of student engagement in higher education in the social media age have to be treated as evolving modes of knowledge production and distribution both by faculty and students. Faculty are considered in their emerging practices as networked researchers, which are likely to also affect their behaviors as teachers. On the other hand, beyond the generational claims, the author holds that digital literacy is to be thought of as a key attribute for higher education students, as situated in a specific disciplinary culture. Both faculty and students are dealing with a diverse typology of online engagement required by the social Web, in which also the propensity to build one's own digital identity is at work. Microblogging is here examined as a significant example of engagement in social media that is contributing to change style and modes of academic discourse, whereas the prevailing type of online engagement by the participants, the topic object of study, the educational approach, and the affordances of the communication tool are aligned. The potential niches of coevolution of learning and research practices that are likely to be developed through the close collaboration between faculty and students need to be grounded in a more participatory notion of student engagement, enabling a continuing negotiation of meanings and sustainability among professors, learners, and institutions.

In "Enhanced *Class Replay*: Will This Turn into Better Learning?," by Ferdinando Pennarola and Leonardo Caporarello, the authors explore how technology development and diffusion have significantly influenced the evolution of educational paradigms. A number of experiments and studies have been conducted, in particular, over the last years in this field. Nevertheless, it seems much has to be done, as a consolidated education model, which includes the effective use of technology, is still not here. There are a high number of variables that influence and determine the successful use of technology for educational purposes. The authors focus their attention on a specific classroom lecture recording system, a service technology that records lectures and makes them available on dedicated online channels as video files or audio podcast. The technology is currently being deployed in a leading Italian university, and its innovative aspect relies on the possibility of decoupling two sources: the video/audio recording and the PC stream recording. The user has the possibility of reviewing separately, but synchronously, the two sources with equal quality, say anything shown by the lecturer from the classroom PC with the video/audio of the lecturer. The system produces a unique sequential output (multimedia file) to be posted on the online university's learning portal, at the end of the day. No post-production will be necessary. The authors argue that to improve service and impact on effective learning, a social tagging must enrich the technology platform: contextual tags should be either provided by the lecturer during the recording, or by the students while reviewing the multimedia files online. This will re-create the classroom experience in full, and allow learners to effectively integrate the multimedia resource with other provided learning material like readings and exercises. A technology-mediated learning model is proposed and a number of research hypotheses are explored to help check the validity of the initial assumptions.

In "Bringing the World into Our Classrooms: The Benefits of Engaging Students in an International Business Simulation," by Tine Köhler, Iris Fischlmayr, Timo Lainema, and Eeli Saarinen, the authors contend that without concrete experiences, it is difficult for university students to acquire the skills and awareness necessary to function as part of an international team, working on a task that is highly interdependent and complex. VIBu – Virtual Teams in International Business – is the name of a training concept, aimed at familiarizing participants with collaborating in a virtual, networked business environment. In VIBu participants are assigned to multicultural virtual teams that represent different manufacturing companies. These companies are either competing or collaborating with each other. Interaction and negotiation are required throughout the whole simulation. The main challenge in the environment is that participants are located in different countries and time zones all over the world. Given current work trends, students need to learn how to navigate in global teams before they leave university as they are bound to become involved in organizational global teamwork sooner rather than later. The business simulation provides students with learning experiences that they need to use in constructing their own insights and learning. The sociocultural approach of constructivism is used in this chapter to describe how students learn from participation in business simulations. We provide examples from student reflections that support the ideas of constructivism. In other words, we highlight the potential for learner engagement that the simulation gaming approach offers. Furthermore, we direct the reader's attention to ways in which the simulation can be used for research purposes, interuniversity collaborations, and multidisciplinary research on teaching practices and engaged learning.

In "Mediated Discourse in Higher Ed Classrooms Using Text Messaging," by Binod Sundararajan, Lorn Sheehan, and Sarah Gilbert, the authors explore the efficacy of text messaging (texting) as a supplementary teaching tool in higher education classrooms. The mixed methods study looks at groups of students using three forms of communication: face-to-face (control group), instant messenger (positive control), and texting to discuss questions based on lecture material. Using a thematic referential coding scheme and the concept of conversational maxims, the content analysis of the text and instant messenger (IM) conversations indicates that the participants were able to discuss points using a standard model of argumentation, and reach consensus on the topics discussed. Participants found texting (and IM) fairly useful for discussing subject matter, learning new and conceptual knowledge, and keeping them focused on the task. The chapter also presents network diagrams of the thematic referential codes to indicate the close connections and alignment of specific code categories like claims, rebuttals, evidence and consensus, providing further evidence that these IM and text conversations are quite similar to face-to-face conversations. Based on the results of the content analysis, the authors propose a modified thematic referential coding model that can be used to study texting and instant messenger communications, in both learning environments and in broader contexts.

In "Catalyzing Learner Engagement Using Cutting-Edge Classroom Response Systems in Higher Education," by Julie Schell, Brian Lukoff, and Eric Mazur, the authors introduce a new technology for facilitating and measuring learner engagement. The system creates a learning experience for students based on frequent feedback, which is critical to learning. We open by problematizing traditional approaches to learner engagement that do not maximize the potential of feedback and offer a research-based solution in a new classroom response system that two of the authors developed at Harvard University – Learning Catalytics. The chapter includes an overview of cognitive science principles linked to student learning and how those principles are tied to Learning Catalytics. We then provide an overview of the limitations of existing classroom response systems and describe how Learning Catalytics addresses those limitations. Finally, we describe how we used Learning Catalytics to facilitate and measure learner engagement in novel ways, through a pilot implementation in an undergraduate physics classroom at Harvard University. This pilot was guided by two questions: How can we use Learning Catalytics to help students engage with subject matter in ways that will help them learn? And how can we measure student engagement in new ways using the analytics built into the system? The objective of this chapter is to introduce Learning Catalytics as a new instructional tool and respond to these questions.

In "Creating Technology Rich Learning Environments for the Classroom," by Robert Garrick, Larry Villasmil, Elizabeth Dell, and Rhiannon Hart, the authors review student engagement and learning over a six-year study period (>500 students) in a technology-rich learning environment. The overall objective of this environment is immersive visualizations. This objective was to allow the students and instructor to visualize new items previously hidden. The technology-rich learning environment in this project consists of tablet PCs for each student (1:1 environment), three projection screens, and collaborative digital inking software. This chapter reviews the education problem being addressed, and the learning theory used as a lens to focus specific active learning pedagogical techniques to address the educational problem. From this problem-based, learning theory-grounded approach, the features desired in a technology-rich learning environment were developed. The approach is shared in this chapter to allow others to implement technology-rich learning environments with active learning pedagogical approaches to address specific education problems in their institution. The technology-rich learning environment implemented and studied includes multiple hardware/software pieces to create a system-level solution versus a single device or single application solution. The results shared indicate that the technology-rich interactive learning environment improves student grades, especially those students who are academically at risk (GPA < 3.0 out of 4.0).

In "Learning Tool or Distraction: Student Responses to the Use of iOS Devices," by Lauren Miller Griffith and Brian A. Roberts, the authors argue that, in an age when "technology" seems to be everywhere, effective integration of technology into an educational environment demands that faculty and administrative staff understand the importance of (re)designing a course in accordance with sound pedagogical practices. This is the only way to ensure a positive impact on our students' learning. Just because students are surrounded by technology does not mean that they truly understand how to use it to enhance their learning. We must be the ones to coach students in educationally appropriate and value-added uses of the devices they may already be using. This chapter takes a critical stance toward the pros and cons of using iOS devices in the classroom. We approach this subject from multiple vantage points including that of faculty, support staff, and students. Our conclusions are drawn from an ethnographic study of a large, introductory course. The authors share what worked, what didn't, and provide recommendations to others who are considering a similar undertaking with a course of their own.

CONCLUSION

In this collection of chapters, we have presented different perspectives on how to use mediated discourse technologies in order to more fully engage learners. Current research suggests that these enabling technologies have the potential to increase engagement and retention but it should be remembered that technology is but one piece of the learning puzzle. If the course is designed based on sound pedagogical principles and grounded in appropriate learning theories and sound content knowledge, the mediated discourse technologies presented in this book have the potential to provide a more effective way to encourage student participation and foster a more meaningful sense of belonging and community. Mediated discourse technologies can provide an important means to motivate students (extrinsically and intrinsically) and to increase competence levels in a more socially enabled way. Compared with pure passive methods of learning (e.g., pure lecture, videos), mediated discourse environments are potentially better at enabling students to more actively participate in the classroom environment.

Regardless of the technology used, education should be a place where self-regulated learning is fostered and where students begin to take on the attitudes and values that are necessary to become self-regulated lifelong learners. In this sense, the classroom therefore becomes an incubator where the necessary higher order thinking skills, attitudes, and values are fostered, and not just a place to acquire foundational knowledge. These technologies should not be viewed as passing technology fads but rather as opportunities for educators to better connect with students and as an opportunity for educators to reframe what it means to teach and learn in the postindustrial age. Please join us in exploring the innovative use of these tools as we explore new ways to better engage students.

REFERENCES

Chickering, A. W., & Gamson, Z. F. (1987). Seven principles for good practice in undergraduate education. *The Wingspread Journal*, *9*(2), 1–16.

Dangle, H., & Wang, C. (2008). Student response systems in higher education: Moving beyond linear teaching and surface learning. *Journal of Educational Technology Development and Exchange*, *1*(1), 93–104.

Deal, A. (2007). *A teaching with technology white paper: Classroom response systems*. Retrieved from http://www.cmu.edu/teaching/technology/whitepapers/ClassroomResponse_Nov07.pdf

Eggen, P., & Kauchak, D. (2006). *Educational psychology: Windows on classrooms* (7th ed.). Upper Saddle River, NJ: Prentice Hall.

Francis, R., & Raftery, J. (2005). Blended learning landscapes. *Brookes eJournal of Learning and Teaching*, *1*(3), 1–5.

Gok, T. (2011). An evaluation of student response systems from the viewpoint of instructors and students. *The Turkish Online Journal of Educational Technology*, *10*(4), 67–83.

Lave, J., & Wenger, E. (1991). *Situated learning: Legitimate peripheral participation*. Cambridge: Cambridge University Press.

Mishra, P., & Koehler, M. J. (2006). Technological pedagogical content knowledge: A new framework for teacher knowledge. *Teachers College Record*, *108*(6), 1017–1054.

Vygotsky, L. S. (1978). *Mind in society*. Cambridge, MA: Harvard University Press.

ENHANCING LEARNING AND TEACHING USING ELECTRONIC VOTING SYSTEMS – THE DEVELOPMENT OF A FRAMEWORK FOR AN INSTITUTIONAL APPROACH FOR THEIR INTRODUCTION

Amanda Jefferies, Marija Cubric and Mark Russell

ABSTRACT

This chapter examines the introduction of Electronic Voting Systems (EVS) at a UK university with the aim of promoting and supporting the student learning experience and moving from an 'ad hoc' and individual basis for the use of EVS at the local school level to offering support for using and developing their use on a wider institutional basis. Following discussion of the research into EVS adoption and use, the authors propose a framework to be used by those academics and managers in higher education institutions (HEI) who are interested in introducing specific

Increasing Student Engagement and Retention using Classroom Technologies: Classroom Response Systems and Mediated Discourse Technologies
Cutting-edge Technologies in Higher Education, Volume 6E, 17–45

ISSN: 2044-9968/doi:10.1108/S2044-9968(2013)000006E004

technologies to support learning, such as the EVS. The framework incorporates a three-way focus on the development of a robust technology infrastructure, the provision of support and training for those using new technologies, placed within the context of sound change management principles and thus supported by the research into these areas. Previous studies in Europe, the United States and Canada into the use of EVS as, for example, in the REAP (Re-Engineering Assessment Practices) project (Nicol & Draper, 2009) have indicated that students are enthusiastic about their use in the lecture hall and seminar room and that the creative use of EVS by academics enhances their use to stimulate and support a number of classroom interactions. To date, however, there has been a lack of research studies on institutional deployment of EVS. This work is intended to outline the salient issues and start that conversation.

INTRODUCTION

This chapter discusses the institutional approaches that were adopted for introducing large-scale Electronic Voting System (EVS) use, and the change management factors for a major project in an academic institution, with the introduction of EVS handsets across eight academic schools to 3,845 students. The aim of the project was to promote and encourage the use of EVS to help reduce the overall assessment workload on academics and to increase student learning and engagement. Developing an institutional approach to technology adoption ensured training and support could be organised centrally, instead of locally for each school, resulting in cost and time savings. In exploring the issues concerning the institution-wide introduction of EVS presented in this chapter, one clear difference between local and institution-wide introduction of EVS technology was the strategic decision to organise the technology introduction and support for academics and students at the institutional level. The importance of personal local support for both academic staff and students is explored as are the levels of student satisfaction and engagement with their learning and the pedagogic changes that the use of EVS introduced.

The rest of the chapter is organised as follows. Firstly there is a discussion on the background of EVS and their introduction into higher education. This is followed by an introduction to technology adoption models and an exploration of the case study in question and its environment of use.

The authors then introduce their own framework for technology introduction; this is based on their experiences of change management and institutional adoption of technology and the experience of 'early adopters' at the University of Hertfordshire, and then they discuss the issue of moving forward once technology has been adopted to consider the embedding of technology in the culture of an institution.

A REVIEW OF THE RECENT ADOPTION OF EVS IN HE

Electronic Voting Systems (EVS) have become a popular medium for encouraging student engagement in class-based activities and for enabling prompt feedback in formative and summative assessments. Systems similar to EVS, such as groupware products (VisionQuest™ from Intellect Corp and GroupSystems™ from Ventana Corp) that support brainstorming in which every student's anonymous response to a question is shown on a large display, were used back in 1995 (Shneiderman, Alavi, Norman, & Borkowski, 1995), but more widespread adoption of EVS started in early 2000 in the United States, United Kingdom, Australia, and Canada (see examples given below and also Mulye & Westberg, 2009). Characterised by the use of a personal handset they allow the user or a group of users to press one or more buttons to indicate their choice of answer from a given set of choices or to insert a text answer. EVS have been marketed and described in a number of different ways, which are generally reduced to a three-letter acronym based on the local name for them. Thus they are typically known as Personal Response Systems (PRS) (Draper & Brown, 2002, 2004), Group Response Systems (GRS) (Cutts, Kennedy, Mitchell, & Draper, 2004), Audience Response Systems (ARS) (Caldwell, 2007), 'clickers' and handsets (Caldwell, 2007; Simpson & Oliver, 2007), Student Response Systems (Bunce, VandenPlas, & Havanki, 2006) and Electronic Voting Systems (EVS) (Cutts et al., 2004). Their initial popularity with students in the secondary and tertiary classrooms has also been ascribed to their introduction and use on popular television programmes including 'Who wants to be a Millionaire?' in the United States and the United Kingdom. These quiz programmes were among the earliest to offer the studio audience an opportunity to give an opinion or to respond to a question by choosing electronically from the choices available and thus afford a level of personal interaction in the recorded action, which had previously been absent. In the authors' own experiences of introducing EVS to students for the first time, it is commonplace for the students to suggest a link to the TV programmes, thus creating positive expectations from students on using familiar technology. In this chapter the term 'Electronic Voting Systems' (EVS) will be used.

There are a number of competing EVS available commercially and internationally for the education market but they all typically comprise four elements for working effectively:

- a hand-held remote device (the 'handset') allocated per student or group of students,
- a Radio Frequency (RF) receiver (or similar) to capture responses from the individual handsets,
- lecture presentation software into which questions can be embedded, typically based around the use of applications such as Powerpoint™ or Excel™ and with the facility to collate and present the responses in a variety of graphical ways,
- associated hardware to present the questions, which would typically comprise a computer and digital projector.

In the earliest examples of EVS the handsets were bulky and often egg-shaped (e.g. Promethean acti-Vote™) to fit into the user's hand comfortably. They typically only offered up to six buttons corresponding to letters or numbers and they could be used for simply choosing a single answer for a set of multiple choice questions (Poulis, Massen, Robens, & Gilbert, 1998). The display allowed only one digit to be shown at a time. Later styles of handsets (2012) are most likely to resemble thin mobile phone devices in shape and size and to offer an array of buttons, perhaps a small screen and to present the options for text input as well as single or multiple digit answers (Barber & Njus, 2007). The latest development of EVS handsets to resemble mobile phone devices is not accidental, although their use is far less sophisticated than the latest mobile technology particularly when compared with the interface of a 'smart phone' such as the iPhone™. The use of the EVS texting facility with the currently available EVS handsets, for example, TurningTechnologies NXT™ or Promethan's ActiveExpression™ is similar to the process of using a 2G mobile phone. For many students the texting software is rather slow and awkward when they have become more accustomed to the touch screens and onscreen keyboards of their phones and personal computers. The discussion in current research into the practice of using EVS versus mobile telephony in the classroom situation has centred around the speed with which EVS can be used in the classroom setting (and thus teachers and students can gain feedback) and their relative accessibility throughout the institution, when mobile and wireless networks do not always extend to each teaching room. The response time for in-class use of EVS is virtually instantaneous, when compared with the authors' experiences of the slowness and the unreliability of the mobile network when used inside large lecture theatres. However, it is to be expected that the future may well incorporate greater advances in the use of mobile apps for promoting interactivity in class – see for example, the work of Koos, Beldhuis, and Heutink (2011) from University of Groningen in Netherlands on the use of SMS to increase learner engagement in large-scale lectures.

It is not solely predicated on the design of the handsets that EVS has grown in importance for its place in the classroom. The evidence for the academic use of EVS indicates that it is not confined to the didactic nature of the lecture hall but instead there are increasing examples of its use in workshops and tutorials (D'Inverno, Davis, & White, 2003) to support co-operative learning through peer instruction (Nicol & Boyle, 2003), facilitating student debates (Thornton, 2009) and promoting 'deep learning' via interactive teaching and Mazur's concept tests (Mazur, 1997). Its growing relevance is noted especially for its encouragement of the adoption of a constructivist pedagogy in the classroom (Mayes & de Freitas, 2008) through a greater use of conversation and interaction. Draper and Brown (2004) refer to Laurillard's encouragement of 'dialogue' in the classroom because it is such a crucial component of learning and was promoted through the use of Laurillard's 'conversational framework' (Laurillard, 1993). The importance of EVS proposed by Draper and Brown (2004) for learning in Highter Education (HE) as they discuss it and with which the authors concur is in its use for increasing the level of dialogue in large and small group teaching and for facilitating the outcome of the students' focussed discussions. The EVS can thus be used to enable a number of classroom dialogues:

1. Between the students and the teacher
    - i. By answering questions via EVS
    - ii. By receiving a response or feedback from the teacher
    - iii. Through the teacher's understanding of the level of knowledge acquisition by the students
2. Between one student and other students
    - i. By comparing their own responses to those of others
    - ii. By discussing their results with others

The progressive adoption of the EVS technology for use in education has typically followed in line with Moore's earlier categorisation of technology adoption (Moore, 1991, developed from Rogers, 1995). Initially the literature indicates that there were a number of 'early adopters' who widely researched the use of EVS both in their own classrooms and among other colleagues. This was followed by a steady series of reports into the use of EVS across different disciplines and a variety of institutions. Many of these early researchers and writers such as D'Inverno et al. (2003) and Draper and Brown (2002) demonstrated their personal ease and enthusiasm at introducing new technologies into the HE classroom, of which EVS was one among a number of significant advances in the use of learning technologies that have been evidenced in the past 15 years. More recently there has been a spread of EVS use into the areas other than natural sciences of the school and university curriculum such that a technology which started in the Physics classroom has now been used across virtually all the academic disciplines (Caldwell, 2007; Lorimer & Hilliard, 2010). This can create a new challenge that of writing good quality questions especially in less-exact disciplines where questions are often open-ended such as in Humanities and Business inter alia.

TECHNOLOGY ADOPTION MODELS

Technology adoption has been studied from a variety of different perspectives both inside and outside the business and management disciplines, and the related body of work spans over several academic disciplines including information systems and technology (IS/IT), human computer interaction (HCI), innovation/change management, psychology and sociology. This has resulted in several theoretical models that consider how best to instigate the process of technology adoption on a personal as well as an organisational level. These include, for example, the theory of reasoned action (Fishbein, 1967), the theory of planned behaviour (Ajzen, 1991), the technology acceptance model (Davis, 1989) and diffusion theory (Rogers, 1995). Research into technology adoption identifies important individual factors that affect behavioural intentions and actual usage of technology and the authors suggest the factors should be considered in any institutional adoption of technology.

More recent work by Venkatesh, Morris, Davis, and Davis (2003) has led to the proposal of a Unified Theory of Acceptance and Use of Technology (UTAUT) theory, which has been formulated as an attempt to unify different technology acceptance models and theories and provide decision makers with a useful tool for assessing the likelihood of success for new technology introduction and help them in devising the strategies and interventions for wider technology adoption. The UTAUT theory proposed by Venkatesh and colleagues has been empirically validated and found to outperform all of the original eight models researched.

UTAUT identifies four significant factors, which act as direct determinants of behavioural intentions and thus the actual personal usage of technology. These are

- performance expectancy,
- effort expectancy,
- social influence and
- facilitating conditions.

Performance expectancy is defined as the 'degree to which an individual believes that using the system will help him or her to attain gains in their work'. It is related to the attributes from other models, such as perceived usefulness, job-fit, extrinsic motivation, relative advantage and outcome expectations. In brief, it is a determination as to whether using the technology will make the adopter's working life easier or not. Effort expectancy is defined as the 'degree of ease associated with the use of the system', and it includes ease of use and complexity of the technology. Social influence is defined as the 'degree to which an individual perceives that important others believe that he or she should use the new system', and relates to social factors, image and subjective norms. Facilitating conditions are defined as the 'degree to which an individual believes that an organizational and technical infrastructure exists to support use of the system' and is linked to perceived behavioural control and compatibility.

UTAUT states that performance expectancy, effort expectancy and social influence are direct determinants of behavioural intentions to use the system; these in turn, together with facilitating conditions are direct determinants of actual usage of the system.

Furthermore, UTAUT identifies four moderating variables (age, gender, experience and voluntariness of use) which increase the causal relationship between the four factors and usage of the technology. Thus, for example, effects of performance expectancy on behavioural intentions are found to be stronger for men and younger workers, while effects of effort expectancy are found to be stronger for women, older workers and those with limited experience.

In the context of the University of Hertfordshire's institutional deployment of EVS systems, as will be noted below, the factors such as Performance and Effort Expectancy were well understood and appropriate strategies were embedded in the institutional implementation through staff training and workshops. These sessions were meant to provide potential 'early adopters' with 'hands-on' experience, demonstrating the 'ease of use' (effort expectancy). Equally important was educating staff on specific usage examples and related pedagogical benefits (performance expectancy). The social influence factor was less exploited, as the 'important others' (e.g. line managers, subject experts) had not been directly targeted in the EVS introduction campaign.

Similarly, facilitating conditions that are meant to enable the move from 'behavioural intentions' to 'actual usage' of the system have been supported only partially through the identification of local EVS champions and the central Help Desk system support. Equally and more importantly, however, is the 'compelling value' (Geoghegan, 1994) that EVS adds to the individual staff teaching practice as well as the institutional commitment to the technology. At the University of Hertfordshire that institutional commitment can be assessed through close integration with the institutional managed learning environment (MLE). Later in this chapter, the authors will comment on the relationship between the UTAUT and the proposed framework.

THE CASE STUDY ENVIRONMENT – EXPLORING A CULTURE OF ENCOURAGING TECHNOLOGY ADOPTION ACROSS THE UNIVERSITY POPULATION OF STAFF AND STUDENTS

The University of Hertfordshire (UH) is located in southern England, some 30 kilometres north of central London. The total campus-based student body numbers in excess of 24,500, including more than 2,000 international students from over eighty five different countries. The university has been keen to embrace the use of technology to enhance the student learning experience and developed its own MLE called StudyNet. This system was introduced across all campuses in 2001 and resulted in UH being one of the first universities in the United Kingdom to offer a personal online study portal to all staff and students.

In terms of increasing the use of technology to enhance learning experience there has been an internal policy of top-down encouragement for local and institutional technology adoption since before the start of the current century. This pre-dated the introduction of a centralised university group in 2005, the Blended Learning Unit (BLU). Supported by UK national funding as a Centre for Excellence in using technology to enhance learning (HEFCE, 2005) the BLU over the next five years was committed to promoting and supporting the use of all types of technology to enhance learning and to researching and developing the pedagogic literature for academic practitioners.

The authors have documented the acceptance of institutional technologies over the past several years and in the case of EVS the move from its adoption by colleagues, since 2002 in a diverse set of disciplines; these included Engineering, Radiography, Physiotherapy, Pharmacy, Business, Computer Science and Biology. This local ad hoc adoption was described as somewhat akin to a 'cottage industry' (Jefferies, 2011) since enthusiastic colleagues were generally using locally purchased school class sets of the student 'handsets', which were handed out for single occasion in-class use. There was initially some variety in the types of handsets used locally as they were purchased from different manufacturers and designed for use in individual classrooms with a single local receiver on a laptop. There were also a few sets available for pre-booking by academics on a day-to-day basis from the UH Learning Resources Centres. At this initial stage of 'personal adoption' of the technology there was no strategic organisation of classroom support for the use of EVS and the specialist software and receivers were pre-installed onto a laptop, which could be borrowed on a session-by-session basis. This localised set-up was typical of the systems seen in various HEIs, as evidenced in the research literature by, for example, Draper working at the University of Glasgow and Davis and White at the University of Southampton.

Research into the experience of EVS at the University of Hertfordshire from 2004 had been carried out as action research by individual lecturers within their own academic schools, see for example Russell (2006) and Lorimer and Hilliard (2008, 2009). At the start of the University's engagement with EVS, teachers would book and use a centrally managed system. Following experience of the initial uses of EVS some five schools took the local decision to purchase cohort-sized sets of receivers and handsets for academics to use with small groups of mainly undergraduate students. In this initial trial scenario, which was also replicated across other institutions in the United Kingdom (JISC, 2009), the handsets were still being distributed at the start of a teaching session and collected in again at the end of it. In some regards, as helpful as this pilot EVS activity was, EVS was still primarily being used by enthusiasts and the so-called early adopters (Moore, 1991).

Local, practical, pedagogic and technical support was developed and encouraged as a result of the BLU's training sessions which shared examples of good practice in EVS use (Lorimer & Hilliard, 2009). This overall situation of small-scale adoption of EVS technology changed dramatically in 2010 when it was proposed that a much wider take-up of EVS should be encouraged across the whole university. This recommendation was based on largely positive experience of the 'early adopters' with the use of technology, in addition to the increasing body of literature reporting on successful use of EVS in a classroom. There was also a perceived need to address findings from the UK National Students' Survey (NSS) where students generally were requesting more feedback and improvements in assessment approaches. These were the starting points for a University-wide Assessment and Feedback project, which included the decision to promote and create situations in which EVS could be deployed more widely.

Funding was provided centrally and eight academic schools opted to take part in the university-wide project which involved 3,850 students in the initial year (2010/11) and was then planned to roll out the adoption of the EVS technology gradually across the University's remaining 21,000 plus campus-based students in succeeding years. Funding was subsequently provided in September 2011 by the Joint Information Systems Committee (JISC) to support the evaluation of the institutional deployment of EVS at the University of Hertfordshire, known as the Evaluating EVS project (EEVS, 2012). By January 2012 nearly 5,000 undergraduate and postgraduate students had been issued with a personal EVS handset and additional handsets were available to academics for ad hoc use. This is described in more detail in the next section and in Fig. 1. Unlike the situation in some other HEIs (Twetten, Smith, Julius, & Murphy-Boyer 2007), a single supplier was now contracted to provide and support the

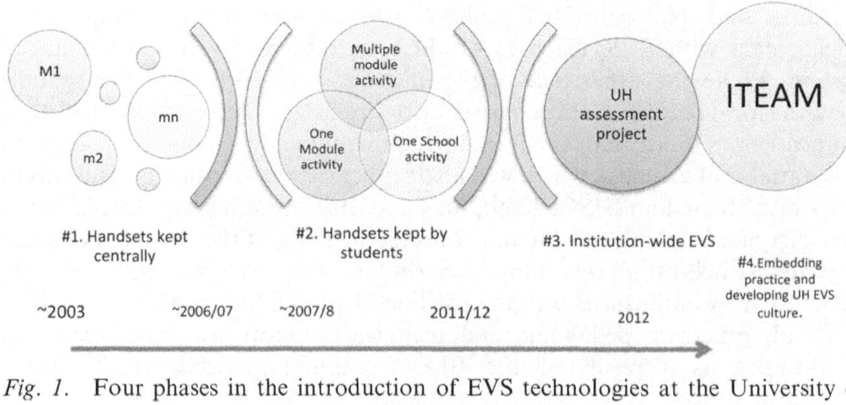

Fig. 1. Four phases in the introduction of EVS technologies at the University of Hertfordshire.

handsets and receivers with supporting software that was easily downloadable to the personal computers of each academic using it.

Discussion with colleagues from across the United Kingdom indicates that the University of Hertfordshire's EEVS project (EEVS, 2012) is probably one of only a handful of research projects currently investigating a whole-institution approach to the adoption of EVS, although the use of EVS is flourishing in many pockets of adoption. One important reason for the enthusiasm for using EVS in classroom-based teaching as reported in the research literature has been the continuing popularity of EVS use among students. This may be because of the general ease of use of EVS as perceived by students and confirmed in a recent survey at the University of Hertfordshire. In a survey of student use of EVS and their attitudes, 87% of participants ($n = 590$) agreed that EVS are easy to use and 69% agreed or strongly agreed that they liked using them and the way they are being used to change interaction in classrooms.

Students were also asked to reflect on the use of EVS at the University of Hertfordshire and whether they liked using EVS. They commented on the changing style of the class that:

> Definitely, it makes them [lectures] more fun. The more interactive a lecture is, the more likely I am to find it interesting and enjoyable. (Humanities student, Female)
>
> I do think that this subject fits well into using EVS for consolidation, practice, clarity and even assessments every now and then. Due to the scope of the topics and the course, EVS can be used to gain further insight into a whole topic or even just case analysis. (Law student, Female)
>
> If you get a correct answer you know you are on the right track; you learn from mistakes. (English Language Student, Male)

Caldwell had noted that: 'Most reviews agree that "ample converging evidence" suggests that EVS generally causes improved student outcomes such as improved exam scores or passing rates, student comprehension and learning and that students like clickers.' (Caldwell, 2007, p. 13). The recent evidence at the University of Hertfordshire suggests that their use is still popular among students when they are used in class and this may have contributed to a broader change in pedagogy by those academics and teachers who have thoughtfully adopted their use. Some researchers assert that their use has increased attendance especially where their use becomes an integral part of the grade awarded and that the students' concentration in class had improved (Burnstein & Lederman, 2001; Cutts et al., 2004). This is comparable to the responses from the UH students where over 75% agreed that 'Using EVS allows problem areas to be identified' and over 80% agreed that 'Viewing EVS responses gives me an idea of how I am doing in relation to others.'

From among academic colleagues in this institution, Lorimer and Hilliard have reported from their own work in Radiography that the use of EVS to support lectures and tutorials was almost universally popular with their students (Lorimer & Hilliard, 2009) and Robins noted that large cohorts of Business school students were also keen to use the EVS because of the interaction which their use afforded in class (Robins, 2011). Other investigations indicate that formative assessment which will indicate how much a student knows about a topic and which can be tested through informal regular testing has proved encouraging to students. In an internal report to colleagues in the university, Willis (2009) from the school of Life Sciences identifies the typical positive student reaction to the use of EVS in a class of 150 students (Table 1).

On the other hand, Simpson and Oliver (2007) have cautioned that while the popularity of EVS with students is not usually in doubt, so far the existing research has not been systematic enough to allow scientific conclusions to be drawn about the underlying cause of the benefits. Is it due to student motivation, a change in the perceptions of assessment approaches or a change in pedagogic approach or a combination of all of these factors? The continuing research at Hertfordshire intends to offer further contribution to this discussion in the future.

THE BACKGROUND TO THE TECHNOLOGY INTRODUCTION FRAMEWORK

In reflecting on the initial adoption of EVS in their own institution, the authors consider it can now be seen as a microcosm of the widespread introduction of EVS in terms of the move to an environment where EVS hardware and software is readily available in each classroom and each

Table 1. Usefulness of EVS as Assessed by Level 4 students ($n = 150$).

Question	1	2	3	4	5
EVS helps me compare with my peers how much I understand the material	22%	50%	22%	1%	4%
EVS would help the lecturer know how much the whole class understood	32%	47%	12%	5%	4%
I enjoy the session more if the lecturer uses EVS	25%	42%	26%	5%	3%

1 = strongly agree; 2 = agree; 3 = neutral; 4 = disagree; 5 = strongly disagree.

student is issued with and takes responsibility for their personal handset. Their own framework has been developed from the widespread sharing of good practice (from external and internal sources). In drawing up their proposals for the development of the elements of an institutional framework for introducing technologies such as EVS, the authors have drawn on research in different areas.

In addition to considering the 'change management' literature, they have reviewed the practice and research from other institutions. Their methodology included reviewing quantitative and qualitative survey data from their own institution, gathered from the school reports from the local project leaders in 2010–2011 and interviews with a range of local stakeholders, staff and students. The need for their model is justified on the basis that while there is much benefit to be gained from applying the breadth of Venkatesh's work on the UTAUT, this model is simpler and seeks to offer a practical means to review the institutional processes required for the introduction and ongoing support of learning technologies. Before describing the model in more detail the authors outline the different stages in the adoption of EVS technology in their own institution.

In Fig. 1 the University of Hertfordshire's own adoption of technologies to enhance learning is shown. It demonstrates the progression over a period of seven years, via a series of local and institutional initiatives and projects, including the JISC-funded iTEAM project (JISC, 2011), indicating how the student learning experience has been impacted through the introduction of technology to enhance learning and documenting the gradual changes in technology adoption for EVS.

The figure identifies four separate phases in the adoption of EVS technologies, which are described below in relation to UH.

Stage 1

At stage #1, c.2003 onwards, the handsets were kept centrally:

- The handsets and associated equipment (receiver, software and laptop) were kept centrally and delivered to the classroom following a booking by an academic.
- A small number of staff were using EVS to good effect and demonstrating its likely benefit.
- EVS use by students was initially anonymous unless individual handsets were checked out and matched to students via a class list.

- There were some minor frustrations for academics regarding the reliability of the delivery of equipment to classrooms.

Stage 2

At stage #2, from 2006 to 2009, the handsets were kept by students:

- The BLU purchased a set of handsets to be loaned to students to 'own' for the duration of a semester.
- The 'student owned' model influenced thinking and the development of EVS use in the School of Life Sciences.
- The School of Life Sciences then purchased handsets and issued them to all members of their undergraduate student cohort.
- Students in the School of Life Sciences were now experiencing a multi-module EVS experience and the academic staff were receiving considerable local support and direction.
- Initiatives in the Business School and the School of Computer Science saw the increased use of EVS with undergraduate and postgraduate students and handsets being kept locally in the school.

Stage 3

At stage #3, during 2010–2011, eight schools were supported in developing EVS use as part of the UH Assessment and Feedback project:

- The University was being made 'EVS ready'.
- Related activity was commenced with supporting areas of the University (Disability Services, The University Students' Union and Information Hertfordshire) as well as with support from local champions and deployment leads.

In Table 2 the schools which participated in the UH 2010/11 assessment project are identified with the number of handsets provided to students.

Stage 4

By stage #4 in 2012, there was ongoing work into the development of the next stage of the institutional adoption of technologies for learning, a 'student dashboard', through the UH iTEAM project (JISC, 2011), into which results from the use of EVS for summative testing inter alia will be fed

Table 2. Distribution of handsets across the University (2010/11) on a school by school basis when eight out of fourteen potential schools opted in for this project funding.

Academic School	2010/11	Handset Type (Turningpoint™)
Psychology	500	LCD RF
Computer Science	320	XR
Humanities	575	XR
Business	1000	LCD RF
Education	260	LCD RF
Law	450	LCD RF
Life Sciences	420	LCD RF
Physics, Astronomy, Maths	320	LCD RF

back directly through the MLE to be viewed from the students' personal StudyNet portals. The anticipated conclusion of iTEAM is 2013.

INTRODUCING EVS ON A LARGE SCALE IN THE HE INSTITUTION: DEVELOPING THE FRAMEWORK IN PRACTICE

The issues to consider for employing EVS on a wider scale are similar to those which relate to the successful introduction and ongoing use with the large-scale adoption of other technologies in any large organisation. They will typically include the adoption of a suitable strategy for change management (Burnes, 2011) and skilful infrastructure project management. At the University of Hertfordshire the institutional issues to address included:

- The change management issues – moving from a culture of local 'early adopters' to supporting mainstream adoption by a majority of academics.
- The facilitation issues of support and training which surround large-scale technology adoption.
- The technical issues of deployment of the technology infrastructure. This was based around the institutional strategy for the support and management of IS/IT through the extension and maintenance of the institutional information systems infrastructure to support the adoption of EVS technology.

Underlying these issues was the need to reflect on the benefits of using EVS at the local and institutional levels and a consideration of the pedagogical changes which had been documented for some years by the researchers. The latter supported a shift to a classroom environment which encouraged greater student engagement and the development of constructivist approaches to learning, as previously referred to above by Lorimer and Russell and others including Mayes and De Freitas.

The authors first constructed a graphical representation of the interaction of the three key institutional issues to consider shown in Fig. 2. An equilateral triangle is used to indicate that each point is vitally linked to the successful provision of the others if the technology is to be successfully adopted and embedded. The three areas are interlinked and mutually supportive since while there may be a clear willingness and impetus for change, this cannot fully occur across the institution unless the technological infrastructure is satisfactorily in place and there is sufficient current and future support for the users. Similarly, there may be sufficient support and adequate infrastructure but in the absence of a planned management of the changes needed to embed the changing culture the benefits are likely to be short-lived. Likewise, there may be an excellent infrastructure but if there is little appetite for supporting change from the top-down and no support for developing pedagogy in place, the process of technology introduction may well stall and remain as a series of local initiatives instead of an

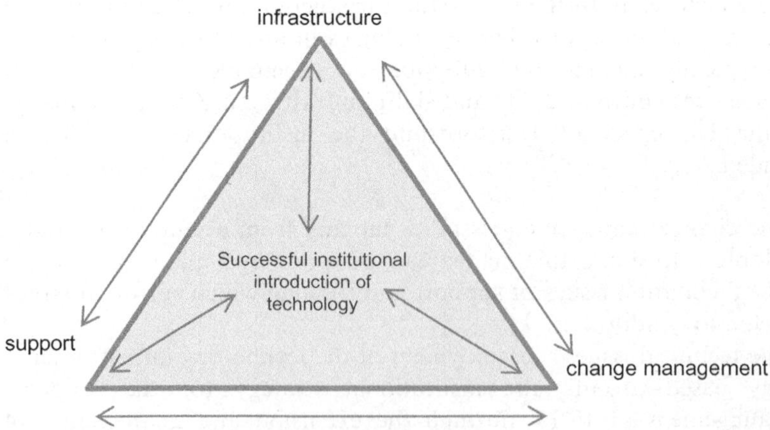

Fig. 2. The interrelationship of the three key issues to support successful institutional introduction of technology.

institution-wide success. The authors propose therefore that all three elements are critical to the successful introduction and embedding of technology in the institution, at HE level both in general, and for EVS specifically.

The Importance of User Training and Support

The facilitation, support and training for technology adoption are first considered before reviewing the generic issues related to infrastructure development. Support for the academic user of EVS in the broader institutional context at Hertfordshire developed from what was previously available at a local level and comprised both pedagogical support and technology support. The aim of the increased use of EVS was to move beyond the realm of merely encouraging the 'early adopters' (Moore, 1991), and towards promoting, supporting and encouraging a far-wider take-up by academics, of the opportunities afforded by adopting EVS technology. The result would lead to the adoption of the technology by Moore's so-called 'early majority' of users (1991). The strategy had been previously demonstrated at the University of Hertfordshire in the introduction and subsequent development of the institution's MLE, StudyNet. A process for the introduction of the MLE technology was developed which had top-down involvement from the University's Vice Chancellor and his senior management team and was accompanied by widespread technical support provided at institutional and local levels (Bricheno, Higgison & Weedon 2004; Thornton, Jefferies, Alltree, Jones & Leinonen 2004; Jefferies, 2004). In line with good practice for the adoption of technology, the process was gradual and not all academic staff were required to adopt the technology immediately to use for their teaching.

The ultimate aim for the introduction of the MLE had been the embedding of the technology into the academic staff and student culture within a period of three years. Research undertaken at the time (Jefferies, 2004; Thornton et al., 2004) indicated a swifter adoption by students to access their learning via the MLE technology and a slower adoption by staff to a changing pedagogy (Bullen, 2004). This latter adoption by academics took approximately five years to settle in, until the point was reached where it had been embraced by the general majority of academics and was used as an integral part of all their teaching. Use of the University of Hertfordshire MLE has continued to increase as it has been further enhanced annually with new features and in the 2010–2011 academic year a total in excess of 10 million annual log-ins to the MLE by staff and students was recorded.

The key lesson learnt about support for introducing learning technology to academics from the earlier experience was that in the initial stages plenty of technical and pedagogic support should be available in a variety of forms which were readily accessible to academics. This is further supported by research conducted by Venkatesh et al. (2003) in their discussion of technology adoption by individuals. Examples of support and training included the early appointment of local school-based champions and personal as well as online guidance for academics through the processes of uploading materials in addition to regular institutional-wide workshops and training for administrative staff.

The same pattern has now been followed with the large-scale EVS expansion, with the provision of funding for additional, local 'hands-on' support for new users and a variety of frequent training and support workshops over several years. As the introduction of EVS progressed into a second year in September 2011, an annual conference and workshop was introduced to showcase examples of using EVS with students, in order to build on the previous examples of good practice at local level and to provide an institutional forum for sharing ideas. This served to encourage the 'enthusiasts' and early adopters and provided additional support for the slower adopting 'majority'.

The workshop programme developed through the first year of the EVS introduction had two aims. The first aim was to support users with adopting their technology use and the management of the EVS process. The second aim was to develop skills in designing 'objective tests'. Many academics had previously developed these skills through the continuing professional development programmes at the university so the workshops served as refresher courses for them alongside acquiring the easy technical skills required. In addition to the local schedule of regular support, there was a '*getting going*' institutional training schedule led by a core team from the School of Life Sciences who were able to draw upon their own experience of embedding EVS in their school over the previous three years. This training schedule was in turn supported by the school-based EVS champions who provided support for colleagues. This allowed discipline-relevant questions to be asked and further introduced the concept of mutual support for module teams who were teaching together. The training workshops started the process of facilitating the sharing of the question banks that academics were preparing. These were seen as part of an iterative development process so that academics did not consider their training was a one-off but a progression through the development of the EVS and objective testing skills.

Table 3. Seven Actions for Supporting EVS Adoption into Academic Practice.

Seven Actions to Incorporate into Facilitation and Support	Rationale
1. Separate out the 'technology support' from the 'pedagogical support'	This shows academic staff why they might wish to engage with EVS in addition to learning how to use the technology
2. Establish pedagogy workshops	Ensures the pedagogy support includes describing good objective testing, good uses of EVS, as well as the management of the EVS process
3. Identify local champions and technology mentors	Local champions provide context-relevant help to their colleagues and allow staff to access one-to-one support
4. Establish a 'getting going' training schedule	Keeps the sessions school-based to help with the EVS discussions to include discipline-relevant support
5. Introduce 'EVS for existing users' training sessions	More functionality can be introduced here, and a review of how the system is currently being used; enables a fast response to emerging questions/ issues
6. Use existing central Help Desk system for technical support	An institutional endeavour requires a sustainable and adequately provisioned Help system
7. Ensure inclusive practice	Ensures that the University-wide endeavour does not inadvertently disadvantage any student groups

The development of the key areas and actions for institution-wide support and their rationale are summarised in Table 3.

Developing the Technology Infrastructure

The importance of the use of an equilateral triangle to model the framework shown in Fig. 2 is that each point is of equal importance and is supportive of the others. The institutional technical infrastructure was already well developed at the University of Hertfordshire when the decision was taken to introduce EVS on a wider basis. An ongoing strategic information plan was already in place. This had previously ensured that all academic staff had access to their personal online portals on StudyNet and access to email from their desktop for some years. There was an easily accessible wireless connection throughout the two primary campuses of the university and a recent upgrading of the teaching rooms had meant that these were already equipped to a high standard for delivering learning. These essential component factors together promoted the aim of minimising and removing barriers (Burnes, 2011), which was deemed to be highly important to move the widespread use of EVS beyond the 'early adopters' and 'enthusiasts'. Thus it was a relatively small organisational step to then ensure that the computers in the teaching rooms were ready for the use of EVS with the software pre-loaded and the receivers pre-installed. These actions removed the previous requirement for staff to either make a booking for the teaching room equipment in advance, or to take a personal laptop and receiver to each class. Academics were now able to turn up for their classes with their objective tests/quizzes/questions pre-loaded onto, for example, a USB stick to run their EVS activities. Alternatively, because the teaching room PCs were all networked, it was now also possible to download a presentation or a formative/summative assignment immediately from StudyNet.

Probably one of the most critical points of moving from a local focus to an institutional focus in the use of EVS was the issue of student responsibility for their personal handset. In the earlier scenarios described above the students had kept the handsets only for the class in question. The decision to have an institution-wide strategy for student ownership required additional technical development so that students could be issued with their personal handset on an annual basis. Some institutions for example the University of Surrey (2012) have preferred to delegate this activity to their library sector, and the handsets have been treated in the same way as a book, which could be loaned and then returned electronically according to its unique barcode. Alternatively, the handsets may be purchased from the central bookstore on campus (Twetten et al., 2007). The University of Hertfordshire opted instead for a central facility for monitoring EVS handset usage and was keen to ensure that each student retained their own unique handset so that use of the handset could be logged for both objective tests and student attendance. A database was designed and written with an easily accessible interface for academics and professional staff to use via their StudyNet log in. This database linked the ownership of the handset to a student's identity card number. As a result of this academics could now check which handset belonged to a student and download a centrally held and managed weekly or monthly class list. This would show not only which students were registered for their module but the number of the handset issued to them. The class list could be downloaded from the module area in the MLE in a format which was then readable as the Participant List in TurningPoint™. This was facilitated for the University of Hertfordshire through the manufacturers of TurningPoint, whose software they had purchased

The recording of student ownership could thus be organised through any member of academic or professional staff with access to the MLE for a student's modules. Moreover, the student who mislaid their handset could quickly enquire from an administrator or module leader what the personal handset number was. Any handsets that were mislaid and handed in centrally could be swiftly returned to their owners, whichever school they were attached to, once the ownership had been established online. A protocol was drawn up which allowed those students who did mislay or severely damage their handsets to pay for another one through the Student Finance Office and have the new number promptly recorded on the central EVS database. This removed the need for students to order another handset online and potentially be without a handset for a week or more. An alternative would have been for the university bookshop to stock them but the handset still needed to be recorded against the student modules online so that their forthcoming test results would not be lost. A similar protocol was drawn up which allowed students whose handsets were faulty to replace them; this occurrence was extremely rare in practice. Students were responsible for replacing the batteries on an annual basis as they would have been for a calculator or similar equipment.

As part of the infrastructure support for developing the use of EVS, the university was now able to organise the central purchasing of handsets on an annual basis, a firm recommendation from the work of Twetten et al. (2007) reviewing the adoption of EVS in four universities in the United States The current scenario at the University of Hertfordshire is one where individual schools can still determine which type of handset can be purchased from within the manufacturer's range. This allows for choice at the school level, as some academics prefer the opportunity for texting answers or the optional homework modules on certain handsets. This variety of handset type is manageable at the local level and supports the preferred autonomy of the academic body, but only so long as the display consoles in each classroom with their computers, projectors and pre-installed EVS receivers are managed and maintained centrally.

The initial installation of the computer software and hardware to support the use of EVS was probably the most significant task to be undertaken in the first year of the institutional decision to make EVS use more widespread across the university. It depended on careful project management and forward planning for ensuring classrooms were free for the planned changeover to upload the software and install the receivers during the teaching week, unless all maintenance and installation can be undertaken during weekends, evenings and vacation times. When classrooms were in

Table 4. Six Stages for Ensuring the Institution-wide Infrastructure Can Support the Use of EVS.

Six Stages for Ensuring the Infrastructure Can Support the Adoption of EVS	Rationale
1. Organise the single issuing of handsets to students on either an annual or semester basis or for a semi-permanent loan for 3 years	This saves time by removing the need to issue and collect handsets in at the end of each class
2. Centralised ordering of equipment and contracting of customer support	More cost-effective to contract the supply for large quantities
3. Ensure a robust system for recording the students' personal handset	A centralised database or similar allows all staff with permissions to check handset ownership easily
4. Link handset ownership through a central information system such as the MLE	This allows academics to easily download class lists and maintain student records for students across multiple Schools
5. Install the hardware and software into classrooms through a centralised process	This ensures that teaching staff are assured that they can enter the room ready to teach and use EVS
6. Establish protocols for: i) students to replace handsets ii) staff to access student details iii) maintenance of the classroom equipment which include the EVS systems	This clarifies the responsibility for different areas of IT supply and support across the university

constant use for up to 11 hours per day, this required a willing and agile workforce to work around the daily academic routines.

The six recommended stages for the infrastructure support for EVS technologies are summarised in Table 4 with their associated rationales to show how the technical support was planned for and provided in a relatively short space of time.

Change Management for Embedding an Institutional Framework for Using Technology

The third point of the triangle in Fig. 2 indicates the need for robust change management. This does not stand in isolation as an issue but links closely to both the requirements for institutional pedagogical support and a sound infrastructure. Robust change management strategies will ensure that the training, support and infrastructure are in place and that adequate preparations have been made prior to the introduction of a new technology. In higher education the provision of an MLE or similar for allowing access to student materials online is no longer perceived as an option by senior managers since most students will have already experienced this in their earlier study at school or college. Other educational technologies such as EVS may not yet be an essential part of the student experience at HE but they are being chosen as an integral part of promoting and supporting successful student learning and engagement. Institutions may choose not to include them in their portfolio of available technologies but the benefits of the use of objective testing and the clear benefits reported from the use of EVS for academics and students cannot be ignored. Gaining the confidence and goodwill of users is important at the outset as noted by Venkatesh et al. (2003) and careful management of expectations can ensure a smoother transition to technology use.

Much has been written about the importance of having a clear and agreed strategy for managing the changes which will be introduced following the decision to install new technologies. Burnes (2011, p. 316) identified a number of strategies for managing the changes which adopting new technologies will bring and noted that:

> Perhaps the only factor common to all organisations is change … It is now generally accepted that the ability to manage change effectively is a crucial component of an organisation's ability to compete successfully.

Pettigrew and Whipp (1993, p. 6) have additionally proposed that managing change involves 'linking people at all levels of the business', rather than having universal rules with regards to leading change and suggested a model for successfully managing strategic and operational change with five interrelated factors. At UH this was achieved through a synchronised approach using the Learning and Teaching Institute, the central unit responsible for Learning and Teaching policy, Information Hertfordshire, the central unit responsible for the technical infrastructure and support and the local school project leads and Champions.

Additionally, Kanter et al's well-known '10 Commandments for Executing Change' (Kanter, Stein, & Jick, 1992, p. 382–383) which explore the ways that organisations can introduce change at a strategic level informed the debate. These have been referenced widely in change management literature.

Kanter has explored extensively two approaches to conducting major strategic change in organisations with her comparison between 'The Long March', which involved planning for a long-term period of change for the introduction of technologies and adaptation of the organisational culture, and 'Bold Strokes', where change was introduced for a rapid and clear impact. Kanter has argued that while organisations may favour one approach over the other, both have their benefits and dangers and the best solution may be to use them in a complementary way. If the University of Hertfordshire's earlier introduction of their MLE from 2001 was viewed in terms of being a 'Long March' to embed the technology in the culture and the pedagogy of the university, their swifter changeover in the 2010–2011 academic year from pockets of local adoption of EVS to a widespread institutional use of EVS might be considered in Kanter's terms as a 'Bold Stroke'.

The earlier introduction of the MLE at the University of Hertfordshire can be clearly defined as a 'Long March' type of change process since it was introduced with management support through an initial pilot project over one year and then successively introduced across all the campus-based programmes in succeeding years. On reflecting back over the introduction of the MLE technology which would radically change the university's approach to supporting and engaging students, there are clear examples of how academic staff were engaged through: 'Creating a shared vision and a common direction' and ultimately through 'Reinforcing and Institutionalising change'. The more recent introduction of EVS built on the experiences of the MLE adoption but once the decision was taken to introduce it university wide in a short time period (nearly 4,000 handsets within a semester) as a 'large-scale' investment then it became a 'Bold Stroke' innovation. The technology introduction in this case was possible because many of the processes identified by Kanter were already in place as a scaffolding and the time was perceived to be right by the senior management to proceed with the major change within a relatively short timescale.

DISCUSSION

The importance to academics and students of a reliable and successful technology on their first encounter lays the basis for confidence in its future regular use. This is then supported by peers for both the students and academic staff and a task-relevant situation in class in which to use the EVS. While incentives have not been discussed above specifically, one of the main drivers for the increasing use of EVS at UH has been the speed with which students can receive results from assessment conducted through EVS use and the associated reduction in the marking burden for academics. These tie in additionally with Wilson, Ryder, McCahan, and Sherry's (1996) set of technology adoption principles for staff and students within the context of the introduction of networked learning environments. These can be seen to have applied to the diffusion of EVS learning technology as it became institution wide:

- First-time success
- Ongoing peer support
- Real task activities (responding to real needs)
- Variety of incentives

A technology adds a 'compelling value' if it performs an existing task in a better way, or it performs a new task in a way that adds a major benefit (Geoghegan, 1994). While a number of academics have praised the use of EVS for adding a significant pedagogical value in the areas of deep learning, feedback and engagement, there is still a significant portion of staff unwilling to engage with the new technology, suggesting that the 'compelling value' factor is more difficult to assess as it depends not only on personal needs, but also on the quality of previous experience with new technologies. Indeed, a negative experience with the introduction of a new technology could significantly diminish the 'compelling value'. The continuing research of the authors intends to include further contributions in the area of correlating the 'compelling value' with some of the individual characteristics such as experience and risk-taking attitude, as well as more testing of the value of the UTAUT in the context of EVS adoption at University of Hertfordshire.

CONCLUSION

In this chapter, the authors have proposed a three-way model as a framework for developing and embedding learning technology use in HE and have taken the specific example of adopting EVS technology to demonstrate how the framework relies on its three central tenets of a sound technical infrastructure, focussed support and appropriate training for users directed by a commitment to tried, tested and successful change management approaches.

Moving on from the local adoption of technology such as EVS for an HEI towards its large-scale adoption requires the community of 'early adopters' to expand to embrace and mentor the 'early majority' and in time to draw in the 'later majority' as well. This has been seen over the period of some years at the University of Hertfordshire with the introduction and embedding of the MLE into the staff and student learning culture. The same process is now in place for the more widespread adoption of EVS technology with the aim of enhancing the student learning experience and providing support for reviewing and refining the assessment and feedback side of their learning. In the process of acceptance and adoption by academics of associated EVS pedagogies it is intended that this will then lead to the widespread adoption of more socially constructivist approaches to learning as identified by inter alia Mayes and de Freitas (2008). These approaches have been proposed as more conducive to student engagement and understanding in a digital age, where the importance of social media and the choice of being always online now dominates the personal and study lives of many students (Jefferies, Bullen, & Hyde, 2009; White & Le Cornu, 2011). Building further on this work the authors anticipate developing a set of critical success factors for the institutional introduction of technologies to enhance learning and using academic staff and student opinions to reflect on whether technology introduction is best effected through the use of a 'Bold Stroke' or a 'Long March' approach.

EVS technology is here proposed as a means to greatly enhance and support the student learning process in an information-rich society rather than as the sole motivator for future change. When adopted and supported thoughtfully across the institution, technology should become an important integral element of the learning process for students in higher education and subsequently to enhance their engagement with lifelong learning.

ACKNOWLEDGEMENTS

The authors gratefully acknowledge the support of their colleagues and students at the University of Hertfordshire, especially those who have worked alongside them in the Blended Learning Unit and the Learning and Teaching Unit and on the EEVS and iTEAM projects.

REFERENCES

Ajzen, I. (1991). The theory of planned behavior. *Organizational Behavior and Human Decision Processes*, *50*(2), 179–211.

Barber, M., & Njus, D. (2007). Clicker evolution: Seeking intelligent design. *CBE- Life Sciences Education*, *6*, 1–8.

Bricheno, P., Higgison, C., & Weedon, E. (2004, October). The impact of networked learning on education institutions - INLEI Project. Paper presented at the Fourth Networked Learning Conference, Bradford University, Bradford, UK.

Bullen, P. (2004). Application to HEFCE for funding of a CETL for the Blended Learning Unit. Available at http://www.hefce.ac.uk/learning/tinits/cetl/final/show.asp?id=11

Bunce, D., VandenPlas, J., & Havanki, K. (2006). Comparing the effectiveness on student achievement of a student response system versus online WebCT quizzes. *Journal of Chemical Education*, *83*(3), 488–493.

Burnes, B. (2011). *Managing change: A strategic approach to organisational dynamics*. Harlow, UK: Prentice Hall.

Burnstein, R. A., & Lederman, L. M. (2001). Using wireless keypads in lecture classes. *Physics Teaching*, *39*, 8–11.

Caldwell, J. E. (2007). Clickers in the large classroom: Current research and best-practice tips. *CBE˙Life Sciences Education*, *6*, 9–20.

Cutts, Q., Kennedy, G., Mitchell, C., & Draper, S. (2004). *Maximising dialogue in lectures using group response systems*. Paper presented at 7th IASTED International Conference on Computer and Advanced technology in Education 2004, Hawaii. Retrieved from http://www.dcs.gla.ac.uk/˜quintin/papers/cate2004.pdf

Davis, F. D. (1989). Perceived usefulness, perceived ease of use, and user acceptance of information technology. *MIS Quarterly*, *13*(3), 319–339.

D'Inverno, R., Davis, H., & White, S. (2003). Using a personal response system for promoting student interaction. *Teaching Mathematics and Its Applications*, *22*(4), 163–169.

Draper, S. W., & Brown, M. I. (2002). *Use of the PRS handsets at Glasgow University*. Interim Evaluation Report: March 2002. Retrieved from http://www.psy.gla.ac.uk/˜steve/evs/interim.html

Draper, S. W., & Brown, M. I. (2004). Increasing interactivity in lectures using an electronic voting system. *Journal of Computer Assisted Learning*, *20*(2), 81–94.

Fishbein, M. (1967). Attitude and the prediction of behavior. In M. Fishbein (Ed.), *Readings in attitude theory and measurement* (pp. 477–492). New York: Wiley.

Geoghegan, W. H. (1994). What ever happened to instructional technology? Paper presented at the 22nd Annual Conference of the International Business Schools Computing Association. Baltimore, MD. Available at http://eprints.soton.ac.uk/260144

HEFCE. (2005). Centres for Excellence. Retrieved from http://www.hefce.ac.uk/whatwedo/It/enh/cetl/

Jefferies, A. (2004). Impact of StudyNet on student learning: Preliminary outcomes of a LTDF project. *Journal for the Enhancement of Learning and Teaching*, *1*(1), 40–41.

Jefferies, A. (2011). Introducing and using electronic voting systems in a large scale project with undergraduate students: Reflecting on the challenges and successes. In S. Greener & A. Rospigliosi (Eds.), *Proceedings of 10th European Conference for E-Learning* (pp. 319–325). Brighton, UK: API.

Jefferies, A., Bullen, P., Hyde, R. (2009). *Researching learners' journeys - STROLL: A JISC funded project (Student reflections on lifelong e-learning)*. Retrieved from http://www.jisc.ac.uk/media/documents/programmes/elearningpedagogy/strollanalysis.pdf

JISC. (2009). *Effective practice in a digital age: A good practice guide in designing for learning*. Bristol, UK: JIS.

JISC. (2011). *JISC i-TEAM*. Retrieved from http://www.jisc.ac.uk/whatwedo/programmes/elearning/assessmentandfeedback/iTeam.aspx

Kanter, R. M., Stein, B. A., & Jick, T. D. (1992). *The challenge of organizational change*. New York, NY: Free Press.

Koos, W., Beldhuis, H., & Heutink, J. (2011). Reaction lecture - SMS to increase learner engagement in large scale lectures. In S. Greener & A Rospigliosi (Eds.), *Proceedings of the 10th European Conference on e-Learning ECEL-2011*. Brighton, UK: ACI Reading UK.

Laurillard, D. (1993). *Rethinking university teaching: A framework for the effective use of educational technology*. London: Routledge.

Lorimer, J., & Hilliard, A. (2008). What is your response? It's time to get personal. In D. Remenyi (Ed.), *Proceedings of the 7th European Conference on E-Learning, 2008*, Aghia Napa, Cyprus. ACI Reading UK.

Lorimer, J., & Hilliard, A. (2009). Use of a electronic voting system (EVS) to facilitate teaching and assessment of decision making skills in undergraduate radiography education. In D. Remenyi (Ed.), *Proceedings of the 8th European Conference on e-Learning*, Bari, Italy. ACI Reading UK.

Lorimer, J., & Hilliard, A. (2010). *How applications of a Personal response System (PRS) may be integrated into Teaching to enhance the Student's Learning (Research Briefing Paper)*. York, UK: HEA EvidenceNet.

Mayes, J. T., & de Freitas, S. (2008). Learning and e-learning: The role of theory. In H. Beetham & R. Sharpe (Eds.), *Rethinking pedagogy for a digital age* (pp. 13–25). Abingdon: Routledge.

Mazur, E. (1997). *Peer instruction: A user's manual*. Upper Saddle River, NJ: Prentice-Hall.

Moore, G. A. (1991). *Crossing the chasm*. New York, NY: Harper Business.

Mulye, R., & Westberg, K. (2009). Mobile phone clickers in the classroom: Experiences from a large introductory marketing class. *The World University's Forum*, *2*(5), 109–121.

Nicol, D., & Boyle, J. T. (2003). Peer instruction versus class-wide discussion in large classes: A compariosn of two interaction methods in the wired classroom. *Studies in Higher Education*, *28*(4), 457–473.

Nicol, D., & Draper, S. (2009). A blueprint for transformational organisational change in higher education: REAP as a case study. In T. Mayes, D. Morrison, H. Mellar, P. Bullen & M. Oliver (Eds.), *Transforming higher education through technology-enhanced learning* (pp. 191–207). York, UK: The Higher Education Academy.

Oliver, M. (2006). New pedagogies for e-learning? *ALT-J: Research in Learning Technology*, *14*(2), 133–134.

Pettigrew, A. M., & Whipp, R. (1993). Understanding the environment. In C. Mabey & B. Mayon-White (Eds.), *Managing change* (2nd ed.). London: The Open University/Paul Chapman Publishing.

Poulis, J., Massen, C., Robens, E., & Gilbert, M. (1998). Physics lecturing with audience paced feedback. *American Journal of Physics*, *66*(5), 439–441.

Robins, K. (2011). *EVS in the business school*. University of Hertfordshire Internal Report. Hatfield, UK.

Rogers, E. M. (1995). *Diffusion of innovations* (4th ed.). New York, NY: Free Press.

Russell, M. B. (2006). Preliminary explorations into just-in-time teaching. *Journal for the Enhancement of Teaching and Learning*, *3*(2), 29–37.

Shneiderman, B., Alavi, M., Norman, K., & Borkowski, E. (1995). Windows of opportunity in electronic classrooms. *Communications of the ACM*, *38*(11), 19–24.

Simpson, V., & Oliver, M. (2007). Electronic voting sytems for lectures then and now: A comparison of research and practice. *Australasian Journal of Educational Technology*, *23*(2), 187–208.

Thornton, H. A. (2009). *Undergraduate physiotherapy students' choice and use of technology in undertaking collaborative tasks*. Open University, UK, Milton Keynes.

Thornton, M., Jefferies, A., Alltree, J., Jones, I. & Leinonen, E. (2004). Changing pedagogy: Does the introduction of networked learning have an impact on teaching? *Proceedings of 4th International Conference on Networked Learning, Lancaster, 2004*. Retrieved from http://www.networkedlearningconference.org.uk/past/nlc2004/proceedings/contents.htm

Twetten, J., Smith, M. K., Julius, J., & Murphy-Boyer, L. (2007). Successful clicker standardization, good ideas. *EDUCAUSE Quarterly*, *30*(4), 63–67.

University of Surrey. (2012). *Electronic voting handsets*. Retrieved from http://www.surrey.ac.uk/library/resources/borrowing/evh/

Venkatesh, V., Morris, M. G., Davis, G. B., & Davis, F. B. (2003). User acceptance of information technology: Toward a unified view. *MIS Quarterly*, *27*(3), 425–478.

White, D., & Le Cornu, A. (2011, September 5). Visitors and residents: A new typology for online engagement. *First Monday [Online]*, *16*(9). Retrieved from http://firstmonday.org/htbin/cgiwrap/bin/ojs/index.php/fm/article/view/3171/3049

Willis, J. (2009). *Using EVS in the school of life sciences*. University of Hertfordshire Internal Report. Hatfield, UK.

Wilson, B., Ryder, M., McCahan, J., & Sherry, L. (1996). Cultural assimilation of the Internet: A case study. In M. Simonson (Ed.), *Proceedings of Selected Research and Development Presentations*. Washington, DC: Association for Educational Communications and Technology.

USING THE PHOEBE PEDAGOGIC PLANNER TO ENHANCE STUDENT LEARNING AND ENGAGEMENT IN UNDERGRADUATE PSYCHOLOGY COURSES

Mark J. Hager, Anthony 'Skip' Basiel,
Michael Howarth and Tarek Zoubir

ABSTRACT

This chapter presents a case study of the ways the Phoebe pedagogic planner assists faculty to design and select e-learning technology because "it's not the technology, but the [quality] of the educational experience that affects learning" (Seltz, 2010, p. 1). Faculty applied guidance from Phoebe to evaluate various interactive media options for undergraduate psychology courses to enhance student learning and engagement. The authors discuss the application of instructional technology in Introduction to Psychology, Cross-cultural Psychology, and Human Motivation and Emotion courses. These projects were prompted by earlier work (Hager & Clemmons, 2010) that explored collaboration to promote integration of technology in traditional courses. The new technologies include discussion

Increasing Student Engagement and Retention using Classroom Technologies: Classroom Response Systems and Mediated Discourse Technologies
Cutting-edge Technologies in Higher Education, Volume 6E, 47–79

ISSN: 2044-9968/doi:10.1108/S2044-9968(2013)000006E005

forums; online simulations, cases and assessments; text-to-poll; and the Moodle learning management system (LMS). Current theories of e-learning are applied to analyze and critique these projects, concluding with recommendations for future research, practice, and faculty development to incorporate learning technologies. The authors demonstrate how learner-centered collaboration among faculty, researchers, and administrators can shape and improve student engagement and develop institutional cultures of e-learning.

INTRODUCTION

A recent post to the LinkedIn user group "Technology-using professors" queried: Do your students Facebook or text while you are lecturing? Howe and Strauss (2000) coined the term "millennials" to describe the generation born between 1981 and 2000. As college students, they are digital natives (see, for example, Prensky, 2001), born into a world of highly integrated personal technology and adept with social media. Social networks, mobile devices, and instant communications are instruments and practices in their educational, social, and professional toolboxes; they expect them in their learning environments (Champion & Novicki, 2006; Wankel, 2009). Yet, they and faculty must learn how to appropriate social and instructional media to educational ends. As Cameron (2008a) asked, "in what contexts and for what purposes are [learning technologies] best used?" (p. 504).

The authors take Cameron's (2008a) query as the driving research question and propose the cases described here as ways to answer it within the context of a small college actively pursuing a higher level of blended learning activities. One tool available to assist faculty in that pursuit is a pedagogic planner, a system to evaluate teaching and learning options to select the most appropriate pedagogical activities and tools to achieve curricular goals (Cameron, 2008b). The cases present a year applying the online Phoebe pedagogic planner ("Phoebe," n.d.) to design course activities integrating learning technology into blended instruction undergraduate psychology courses. The Phoebe planner was selected to provide guidance on learning design and appropriate technology use (Cameron, 2008b; Masterman, 2008). To complement Phoebe, the case study emphasizes the application of research on blended instruction and e-learning to enhance student learning and engagement and simultaneously promote faculty development of greater fluency and sophistication selecting and using e-learning pedagogy. Because "it's not the technology, but the [quality] of the educational experience that affects learning" (Seltz, 2010, p. 1), faculty using such a planner and relevant pedagogical research can evaluate various interactive media options when planning instructional engagement in and out of class. Applying guidance from Phoebe, students' skills with and preferences for social media websites and texting were translated to exchanging ideas in a Google group discussion board and "text-to-poll" electronic voting activities to provide data for discussions as these technologies were co-opted toward educational ends. Learning technology was integrated into the following courses: Cross-cultural Psychology, Introduction to Psychology, and Human Motivation and Emotion.

This year of exploration was prompted by earlier work (Hager & Clemmons, 2010) proposing faculty and IT (Information Technology) collaboration to promote faculty integration of technology in traditional courses – blended learning (Lim & Morris, 2009). Applying the Phoebe pedagogic planner first as a planning tool and then a catalyst to enhance teaching and student learning and engagement, the authors explore current theories of e-learning to analyze and critique these applications. Acknowledging barriers that may hinder faculty adoption and institutional development of a culture of e-learning, the chapter concludes with recommendations for future research and practice to support faculty development incorporating appropriate technology into teaching and learning. These projects demonstrate how learner-centered collaboration among faculty, information technologists, researchers, and administrators can shape and improve student engagement and achievement while developing an institutional culture of e-learning.

CONTEXT

Menlo College is a small, private undergraduate business college in the heart of the Silicon Valley. Faculty and students enjoy small classes and the personalized attention to teaching, learning, and mentoring relationships its small size affords. At the time of this case study, the College CIO had launched an ambitious plan to revitalize campus learning technologies, introducing the college's first learning management system (LMS), the open source e-learning platform Moodle, and inviting faculty to expand their pedagogical repertoire to include appropriate learning technologies. During the summer 2010, the first author (Hager) received a summer research fellowship to study technologically enhanced teaching and learning at

Harris Manchester College, Oxford. The goals of the research were to enhance e-learning at Menlo College and create a series of pilot tests of blended learning experiences for students as the College rolled out new technologies.

Colleagues at Middlesex University and Oxford University's Technology Assisted Lifelong Learning unit shared a wealth of research on e-learning pedagogy, including that sponsored and compiled by the Joint Information Systems Committee in the United Kingdom. This research, coupled with guidance from Oxford University Computing Services and the Learning Design Support Environment, guided the exploration of the Phoebe Pedagogic Planner (Masterman, 2008; "Phoebe," n.d.) and provided the theoretical framework against which this case study was designed and analyzed (JISC, 2004, 2008, 2009). Collaboration internally and across institutions contributed two influential elements the College later would learn are important contributors to successful e-learning innovations. It established a network of professional peers on whom to draw for guidance and a framework on which to build a library of e-learning resources (Covington, Petherbridge, & Warren, 2005). In total, almost 80 empirical, theoretical, and practitioner papers were gathered and analyzed for these projects.

Early in the fall 2010 term, an informal group of faculty and students discussed questions related to faculty use of technology: What kinds of technology do faculty use in class? What kinds of technology would students like them to use? Why? Their answers were not surprising. PowerPoint was unimpressive, especially as a flat delivery system used without the more innovative and eye-catching features that it and other presentation software packages offer. Students acknowledged some faculty used YouTube videos to enhance discussions. The Microsoft Office suite was mentioned. They also discussed, and were most curious about, Moodle and how the College was rolling it out the following semester.

Those who were taking courses pilot testing Moodle were excited for what it would do: discussions, electronic submissions, resources collected in one place and available when they wanted them. Discussing e-learning activities, students knew they did not want class Facebook pages. Echoing some of the ambivalence in the research on academic uses of personal social networking sites (Roblyer, McDaniel, Webb, Herman, & Witty, 2010), "I don't want my teachers in my Facebook" was a common reaction. Google discussion groups, email, and Moodle were more appropriate academic communication environments to this small group of students. Electronic voting systems (see in this volume Jeffries, Cubric, & Russell, in press) and online case simulations and psychological assessments raised their excitement for the e-learning possibilities on the horizon. One student whose faculty used PowerPoint and Excel reflected the enthusiasm of the others, "I wish my teachers were doing some of this stuff."

The technologies applied here were selected for this case study based on faculty discussions of generational strengths among NetGen students and their engagement with social media and technology (Worley, 2011). Research supported the assertion that these tools afforded opportunities to enhance student engagement and learning while capitalizing on their desire for technologically mediated learning (Reeves & Ho, 2007). The Phoebe pedagogic planner helped connect technology selection with course goals and student learning outcomes (see Table 1).

PHOEBE PEDAGOGIC PLANNER

The Phoebe pedagogic planner (Manton, 2008; Masterman, 2008) provides a number of useful resources for designing curriculum and planning the use of technology in teaching and learning, including a framework from which a variety of technologies may be evaluated as appropriate to achieve key student learning outcomes. Using the lesson planner and the library of technological resources, faculty may plan a lesson for students to debate a psychological theory and select blogs, wikis, or mashups for students to compile their arguments and collaborate among team members. The lesson planner template within Phoebe provides a basic framework with which faculty can design the lesson, including: contextual information such as the target project; curriculum aspects driven by student learning outcomes; the teaching resources and learning activities to achieve them; and student assessment and instructor reflection (see Fig. 1). These elements are useful for planning individual projects and larger course goals.

The most salient components of the Phoebe pedagogic planner to this case study are the reference materials in the teaching and technology guidance, including "the e-learning advantage," a guide to selecting appropriate technologies for creating learning activities to achieve particular learning outcomes. Prompted in one of two ways, faculty may enter the advantage from the perspective of an existing activity that could be enhanced with technology, "what can I use technology for…?" Or, faculty may have a specific technology in mind, such as discussion forums, and they may access "what can I do with…?" to gain guidance on structuring them effectively or the practicalities of student engagement in discussions online (see Figs. 2 and 3).

Table 1. Technologies Used and Their Learning Outcomes.

New Technology	Course	Instructional Goals	Learning Outcomes
Phoebe pedagogic planner	Cross-cultural Psychology; Introductory Psychology; Human Motivation and Emotion	Organizer of plans and opportunities for e-learning	Varied; enhance student performance and engagement
Discussion boards (e.g., Google Groups, LMS)	Cross-cultural Psychology	Promote independent reflection on course content; provide opportunities for thoughtful response to class and online discussion prompts; enhance classroom participation by building on discussion board posts; provide "safe space" for less vocal students to contribute to class discussion	Students would be able to post thoughtful discussion and reflection points to extend class discussions; students would demonstrate enhanced engagement in course content
Online simulations of psychological case diagnostics and assessment practices (PsykTrek)	Introductory Psychology	Have students apply theories and definitions to psychological issues and practices; independent and private practice with diagnostics; promote class discussion of (in)correct diagnostics	Students would apply developing understanding of psychological theories and concepts to real world situations; students would share individual diagnostic reasoning to achieve greater understanding of psychological assessment
Text-to-poll; electronic voting systems (e.g., proprietary clickers, Poll everywhere)	Introductory Psychology; Motivation and Emotion	Comprehension check; respond to sensitive topics; provide opportunities to voice opinions anonymously; frame discussions of common assumptions and stereotypes	Students would demonstrate collective understandings of key topics for expansion and analysis in class discussion; more students would participate than can do so in traditional discussion format sessions
Learning management system (LMS) or Virtual learning environment (VLE) (e.g., Moodle, Blackboard CT)	Learning and Cognition; Motivation and Emotion; Senior Thesis	File sharing; discussions; independent student access to course content; running peer/faculty feedback; enhanced in-class participation	As noted above

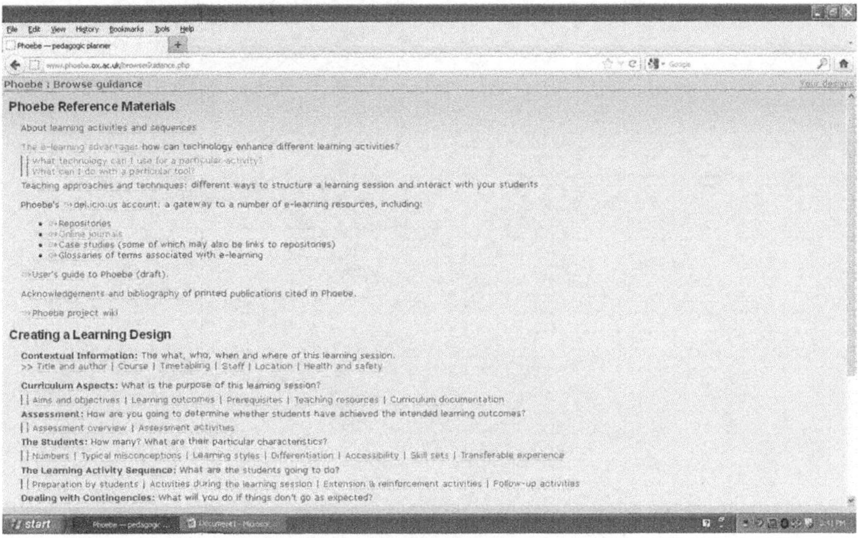

Fig. 1. Phoebe Reference Materials.

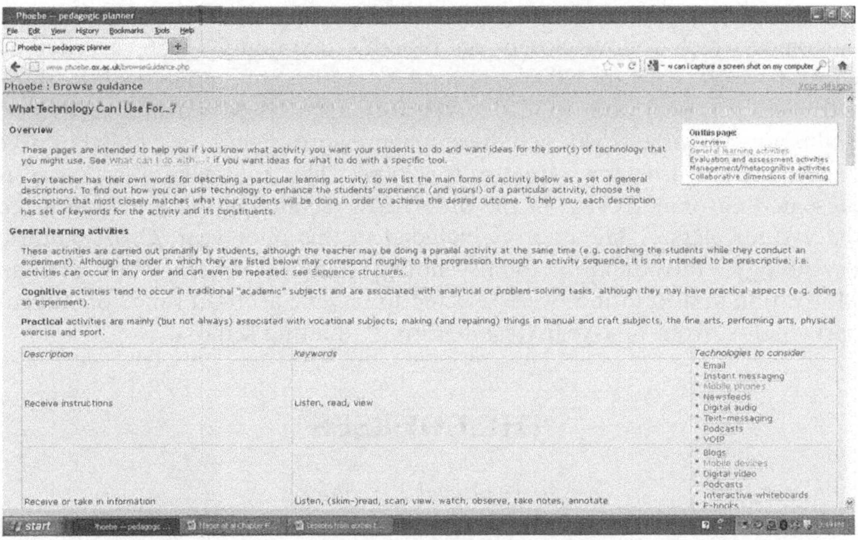

Fig. 2. Phoebe: What Technology Can I Use For …?

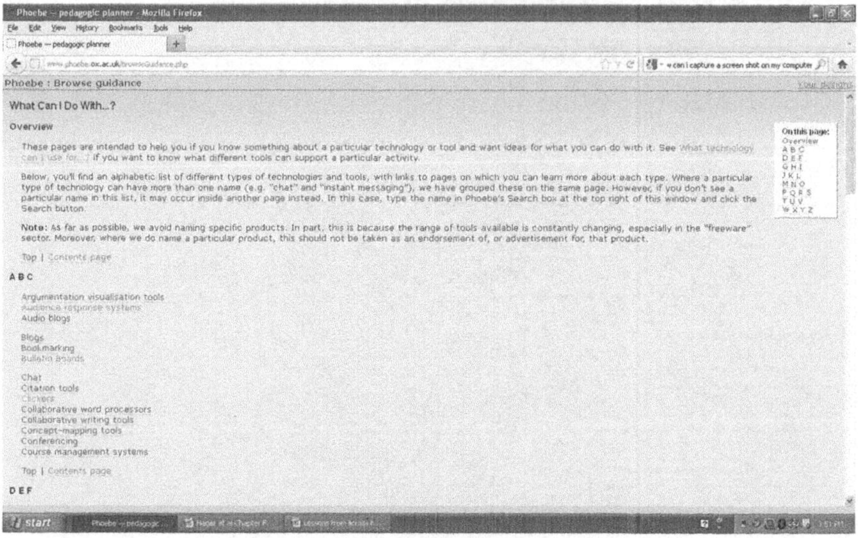

Fig. 3. Phoebe: What Can I Do With ...?

In both cases, relevant technologies are meant to support driving learning activities and outcomes as organized in Phoebe – activities and learning outcomes which follow closely on Bloom's taxonomy (1956, as cited in Crossgrove & Curran, 2008): general cognitive and analytical learning activities; practical and applied or performance based learning activities; evaluation and assessment activities; meta-cognitive activities; collaborative dimensions of learning (Heathcote, 2006). The following discussion is presented chronologically, in the order each technology was introduced to the various classes. The courses included in this pilot year, Cross-cultural Psychology, Introduction to Psychology, and Psychology of Human Motivation and Emotion, were selected to include a broad range of student participants, from first-year freshmen to graduating seniors.

THE COURSES

Cross-cultural Psychology

The first pilot course, Cross-cultural Psychology ($N = 9$), was selected because of its small enrollment of upper division students, affording greater time for the faculty to prepare and trouble-shoot potential student difficulties. Discussion boards, or forums, were selected as they were tools embedded in the coming Moodle LMS. The faculty decided to assess student engagement with the discussion boards in order to refine activities that would be available the following semester in Moodle. Assessment at this early stage included counts of student posts, correlations of posting activity with student performance, and "depth" of student posts based on a minimum standard of one sentence responses to more involved paragraph-length comments. The Google group discussion board yielded mixed results and prompted Dr. Hager's research focus on technologically mediated teaching and learning while at Oxford. The research uncovered during the fellowship led to greater attention to data-driven innovations in Introductory Psychology and Human Motivation and Emotion.

Introductory Psychology

The second e-learning application was conducted in Introductory Psychology (*N* = 50; two sections of 25 students) because of the College's goals to align the course more purposefully with American Psychological Association guidelines (APA, 2007) for undergraduate competencies and learning outcomes. PsykTrek online psychological simulations were selected because simulations can enhance real world applications and increase the integration of information and technological literacy within psychology – two driving undergraduate guidelines (APA, 2007). This exploratory pilot was assessed correlating students' self-reported use of the online simulations with their final course grades. Classes also were surveyed at the end of the term for their engagement and satisfaction with the technology.

Human Motivation and Emotion

The electronic voting system, Poll Everywhere (2011), was integrated into Introductory Psychology and Psychology of Human Motivation and Emotion (*N* = 27) after studying research and cases on the Phoebe site and the EDUCAUSE Learning Initiative that pointed to the efficacy of "clickers" to encourage student participation. Using informal polling to guide discussions "in vivo" with live student-generated data can demonstrate collective understanding and shared misconceptions (ELI, 2005; Simpson & Oliver, 2006; Zhu, 2007). Participation in the polling activities

Table 2. Course Descriptions and Participants.

	Cross-cultural Spring '10	Introductory Fall '10	Motivation and emotion Spring '11
Course level	Upper division elective	Lower division general education option or elective	Upper division elective
Students	Juniors and seniors; $N=9$	First year students; two sections of 25 students each	Juniors and seniors; $N=27$
Majors	Psychology, business, liberal arts	Psychology, business, liberal arts, undeclared	Psychology, business

was assessed formally using students' comments on an end of the year survey and informally by comparing the numbers of students who shared their ideas or opinions via text survey with those who typically raised their hands or spoke out during class. Table 2 describes the courses and student participants in each class.

DISCUSSION BOARDS

Goals and Application

Engaging students in their preferred modes of asynchronous and technologically mediated communication (Sharpe, Benfield, & Francis, 2006) extends and blurs the boundaries of formal teaching and learning as faculty have traditionally designed them (Francis & Raftery, 2005). Discussion boards and forums provide an online and out of class opportunity for students to launch, continue, or expand classroom discussions in blended courses ("Phoebe," n.d.). Faculty integrating online discussion boards often seek – and students demonstrate – greater depth of participation and engagement with course materials (Wang, 2011). Discussion boards provide numerous benefits from both course management and student engagement perspectives:

- Convenience: Students and faculty post to the thread at times that make sense for them. Students can "lurk" in the discussion, reading colleagues' posts, and reply as they have time (Dennen, 2008).
- Confidence: Students can take time to think through a response to a prompt or peer's earlier post without the instantaneous pressures of classroom discussion. This especially helps those learners who take more

time to digest class topics or who want to contribute more thoughtfully than a quick reply in class (Baglione & Nastanski, 2007).

- Privacy: Students who are shy speaking in public may find the online environment more conducive to self-expression (Ramli, 2010).

The driving learning objective for using Google groups to promote discussion in Cross-cultural Psychology was for students to contribute thoughtful comments to community posts, thereby extending course discussions and identifying areas of mastery and misconception. The discussion board was intended to provide students the necessary developmental time to reflect and think more critically about course content than may happen in a typical class period ("Phoebe," n.d.). Each week a student discussion leader posted three questions about the week's readings. Other students in the class were required to respond to at least two of the posted questions or to another peer's responses. Responses could take the form of critique or extension via personal example or outside reading.

Outcomes

The pilot was simultaneously a success and failure, providing us with motivation to continue, barriers to overcome, and lessons to learn. While there was a positive correlation between quantity and depth of postings (Pearson's $r = .798$; $p < .01$), discussion board activities had no significant relationship with final grades. The successes were almost expected. As prior research has shown (Wang, 2011), those students who engaged more often and more rigorously in class discussion posted the most elaborate questions or responses; those who participated less in the class posted less often and with less depth. The initial failures were in the open-ended structure and in faculty presumptions that students would post because it was a course requirement. The lack of detailed structure for peer responses may have contributed to student posts typical of earlier research. Students frequently described or paraphrased the reading and were not often critical; only occasionally did students extend the conversation or challenge their peers (Finegold & Cooke, 2006; Lu & Jeng, 2006/2007; Maurino, 2007).

Wise and Chiu (2011) have shown students can post thoughtful critical comments that extend discussions, promote deeper processing, and enhance their intellectual engagement when there is sufficient scaffolding from the instructor. The intersection of the bricks and mortar classroom with the online forum provided the venue for promoting more critical responses and more interactive discussions. In this pilot, the quality of student discussion posts changed when prompted by the instructor for critiques or greater depth. Sometimes those prompts came from class discussion; other times an encouraging post from faculty on the discussion board was sufficient to increase participation levels. For example, the following faculty post encouraged students and asked them to connect back to the course theme before continuing an online discussion of moral reasoning. "You are posting some interesting reflections. Keep it up, and remember as we go on to include cross-cultural reflections as well. What do you think about how our answers [to a moral reasoning survey] would appear to another culture?" This discussion thread was the most successful of the semester in terms of quantity of posts and depth of student comments. All nine students and two external guests posted online, and the discussion continued later in class. Further research would be necessary to determine whether the prompt or the topic influenced participation more.

Mager (2012) demonstrated that clearly articulated faculty expectations and pedagogical posts to the online discussion enhanced student performance and critical thinking. Yet, while this example is optimistic, it should be noted that in the present case study faculty scaffolding in class or online enhanced contributions for only some students. Over the course of the semester, more capable students (earning A or B grades) posted significantly lengthier and more involved or critical comments more often, but the weakest students (earning D or F grades) required greater individualized attention to improve the quantity and depth of their online contributions.

The classroom also provided the setting for another type of discussion of the online community – lurking. Several students in the pilot were reticent to post but not to read (Dennen, 2008). The same pressures that online discussion boards alleviated for some were magnified for others when they considered their peers reading and analyzing each posting. In class discussion, those few felt they were most likely to post when they were comfortable with their level of content mastery (Du, Zhang, Olinzock, & Adams, 2008). They claimed they gained sufficiently from reading posts to participate in class if not online, as if they were the quiet students in class listening to their more vocal peers (Wise, Hsiao, Marbouti, Speer, & Perera, 2012).

Lessons

Several lessons can be drawn from this first activity, all of which can be guided by a pedagogic planner and informed by current e-learning research.

Cases and examples on Phoebe helped to shape goals for using the technology: increased time for students to reflect and craft their responses and greater participation from quieter students. Current research pushed the faculty member to recognize the need for better articulated scaffolding of student participation.

Detail and structure are necessary to scaffold students successfully to richer and more meaningful posts. Instructors or tutors must provide prompts in class and online to scaffold students in the online discussion forum. Faculty should clarify expectations of student roles and responsibilities and assign facilitating roles to initiate a thread and elaborate or extend discussions with outside resources. With sufficient scaffolding, students can provide clarifying comments to summarize and integrate the discussion at key points (Wise & Chiu, 2011).

Faculty must incorporate the online discussion with classroom activities, purposefully demonstrating and modeling integration of the two settings. Bringing student posts into the classroom conversation demonstrates the importance of the "extra" work done out of class, and it provides students the opportunity to assimilate the material into the meaningful whole of the course (Suler, 2004). Using this approach as the semester progressed fostered deeper discussions in class and online, as shown by a trend to longer and more frequent posts, and provided opportunities to clarify and extend students' understanding. Students replied to their peers in both settings, continuing class discussions via discussion posts days after the "official" discussion had ceased.

The lessons of scaffolding in the online environment and intentional integration of the online discussion with the physical classroom were applied in the next level of incorporating technology, the use of online diagnostics and simulations in Introductory Psychology. An even stronger lesson centered on the use of current pedagogical research to plan how to use the new technology. Cases can successfully model "real world" issues and theories via text, video, audio, role-play, etc. (Blumenfeld, Soloway, Marx, Krajcik, Guzdial, & Palincsar, 1991) to help students model authentically situated practice. The use of interactive online diagnostic simulations extends the power of cases to provide immediate feedback to students (Raisinghani & Vinaja, 2006). However, faculty must guide students in their strategic use and benefits, and to do so requires thoughtful preparation appropriating relevant pedagogical research and sharing knowledge among technology-using peers. Moving from discussion boards to online simulations highlighted the necessity of faculty motivation to learn and use new technology (Georgina & Olson, 2008) and to develop a key professional skill, technological pedagogical content knowledge (TPACK) – the intersection of technological savvy with one's ability to teach one's content area (Koehler, Mishra, & Yahya, 2007).

ONLINE SIMULATIONS

Goals

Simulations afford psychology faculty and students a unique opportunity to test theories and apply practical diagnostic strategies in a safe environment which would be "hard or impossible to engage with in real life" ("Phoebe," n.d., Modeling Tools and Simulations, para. 2). While students may read about and practice assessment and analytical strategies using traditional course texts and empirical research, the addition of online simulations provides immediate feedback on the outcomes of their decisions. With the immediate response, students may critique their decisions and recommendations, weighing new options in light of success or failure.

As in other health sciences, in the field of psychology, the safety of the online simulation is that there will be no real impact on a client presenting a mental health concern; students are free to develop these "soft" interpersonal analytical skills without fear that mistakes will harm a client (Dagger et al., 2008). The feedback about diagnostics or assessments can be incorporated as students advance through an assessment or as they repeat one due to errors, refining their understanding of key concepts and diagnostic processes. This is especially important in survey courses such as the Introductory Psychology class. Students are exposed to a different field of psychology each week and expected to master basic concepts and be exposed to modes of mature practice (Lave & Wenger, 1991) as they are enculturated into the practices of the field.

The Introductory Psychology course text used at Menlo College (Rathus, 2011) includes PsykTrek online support, of which several units are diagnostic simulations. These diagnostic cases have multiple goals:

- Help students to apply theories and definitions when analyzing psychological issues and practices;
- Develop technological and information literacy;
- Provide for independent and private practice with diagnostics;
- Promote class discussion of (in)correct diagnoses;
- Enhance student learning and achievement "in vivo";

- Increase student engagement with course content and the field of psychology by engaging in guided practices.

Of these, the overall learning objectives were increasing student learning and engagement, achieved via the targeted learning outcomes of each activity (APA, 2007; "Phoebe," n.d.). Three sections of the Introductory Psychology course were instructed by two faculty; one pair of classes required completion of the PsykTrek online modules while the other made them optional. Students in the sections requiring PsykTrek were assigned one online module weekly. Some were informational with individualized tutorials and quizzes, such as units on Freudian theory and Humanistic psychology. Other activities simulated professional practices like decision making or clinical diagnosis of obsessive-compulsive disorder or schizophrenia.

Application

Guidance from the Phoebe planner and related pedagogical research shaped introduction, enactment, and follow-up activities related to the online simulations. The sections requiring the online components integrated those activities into class discussion and homework sets to show their relevance to real world psychological diagnostics; course assessments were designed to give students an interactive medium to demonstrate their understanding, in line with APA undergraduate guidelines (APA, 2007; US Department of Education, 2009). To build confidence with each analysis or activity, the students participated in a portion of the assignment in class through an anonymous login prior to each independent online activity. Inviting students to participate in class highlighted differences in engagement with the technology. Those who participated most during the preview sessions also reported greater usage of the online modules more routinely and ultimately achieved better performance in both online activities and in class assessments.

Outcomes and Lessons

Based on this enhanced and more purposeful integration, student learning and engagement outcomes were vastly different from the Google group activity of a semester earlier. Student achievement was assessed in two ways.

Final grades were correlated with self-report Likert scale surveys of students' level of engagement and usage of the online resources. Correlations between earned grades and self-reported PsykTrek usage were moderate and very significant for assigned use (Pearson's $r = .391$; $p < .05$) and for independent use (Pearson's $r = .351$; $p < .05$). Students who used the simulations regularly as assigned performed significantly better than those who did not. Those who used them independently also performed significantly better than their non-using peers.

Aggregate outcomes were shared with the classes, and individual results were discussed with students in one-to-one advising sessions. The discussions showed the informational units were not popular, and students described them as traditional and didactic, but interactive, homework. Students were most engaged by the simulation activities. Modeling strategic decision making and clinical diagnostics were simultaneously challenging and rewarding in nontraditional ways. In an end of the year discussion, students said simulations forced them to "think like a psychologist" applying novel and abstract concepts to make recommendations and diagnoses (Lim & Morris, 2009). They said they had room to explore and to make decisions and mistakes (Adams, Reid, LeMaster, McKagan, Perkins, Dubson, & Wieman, 2008).

Diagnosis of obsessive-compulsive disorder was the most challenging activity of the semester. Top students often missed key characteristics and required multiple attempts. Two students attempted diagnoses 17 and 21 times, respectively. At first it may appear they were not taking the activity seriously; however, to the contrary, they were very serious and engaging the simulation in its intended manner. In class discussion, those students acknowledged the safety they felt applying different characteristics to test multiple hypotheses about the case until they felt secure in their diagnoses. Their extreme experiments led the class to discuss the value of the simulations: independent time practicing the concepts, immediate feedback, and opportunities to apply different ideas and theories without severe consequences. As one suggested "better now than when I'm with a patient."

Incorporating online diagnostic simulations and assessments, Introductory Psychology students could work through analytical processes used in various fields of psychological research and practice – with the added benefits of immediate feedback and no negative consequences – experiencing and learning from the real world application and integration of relevant information technology emphasized in the APA guidelines for undergraduate learning (APA, 2007; "Phoebe," n.d.). Students reported greater interest and independence with individual access points and times (JISC,

2009) and immediate feedback. The results of the PsykTrek simulations indicated students who were more engaged and used the online simulations more frequently also performed better on objective assessments of their mastery of course content. Positive correlations of students' performance and participation in online simulations are in line with recent U.S. Department of Education suggestions that online simulations have a moderately positive effect on performance (2009) and Stark-Wroblewski and her colleagues' (2008) finding that psychology students' learning increased with virtual experiences of various diagnostic and treatment approaches. Students' comments reinforce Lim and Morris' (2009) findings that applicability of the activity, in this instance decision processes and diagnosing mental illness from clinical interviews, may have enhanced their engagement with the technology.

Some students reported greater initiation of group work or peer-led tutorials to work on the simulations. While they may have been capitalizing on social networking and collaborative skills that are reported hallmarks of Net Generation students (Howe & Strauss, 2000; Jones & Ramanau, 2009), collaboration on these activities was neither preferred nor dominant in this case and was often related to general information sharing to solve a problem or clarify terms but not to higher level analysis. Future research should investigate the purposes for students' collaboration in the online environment to better delineate which student learning outcomes are achieved and how. Electronic voting systems (classroom response technology) are additional e-learning tools that have been shown to enhance student collaboration and participation when purposefully integrated into lectures and discussions (Draper & Brown, 2004; Masıkunas, Panayiotidis, & Burke, 2007). The introduction of a classroom response system to Introductory Psychology and Human Motivation and Emotion culminated the year of pilot tests with more informed preparation and application of the technology.

TEXT-TO-POLL ELECTRONIC VOTING SYSTEM

Goals

Prior collaboration at the College (Hager & Clemmons, 2010) had identified "clickers" and in-class polling (electronic voting systems, classroom response systems) as hot technology and engaging to millennial students seeking greater interaction in class (Stowell & Nelson, 2007). Most electronic voting systems involve proprietary handsets and technology, tools that can be expensive and involved to purchase, set up, and maintain (see in this volume Jeffries, Cubric, & Russell, in press). A simpler, more universal and similar resource is also available: text-to-poll ("Poll Everywhere," 2011). Similar to clickers, text-to-poll may act as an opinion poll or a snapshot of a class's aggregate understanding before a new unit or after a particularly challenging discussion (ELI, 2005). The discussion leader – faculty, tutor, or peer – creates a poll at an online site, and students text their responses to register their opinions or answers; they may also log into the website directly via smart phone or computer to answer. Responses are tallied in the moment, as they are with proprietary classroom response systems. Used prior to a class discussion, instructors can assess preliminary understandings and misconceptions based on independent preparation. Used during or after a unit, the same brief survey allows students to demonstrate their collective understanding (Draper, 2005; "Phoebe," n.d.). However the responses turn out, discussion can ensue to clarify and elaborate the content.

The JISC guide to innovative digital practices (JISC, 2009) and the EDUCAUSE Learning Initiative (ELI, 2005) suggest classroom response systems can enhance student participation; recent research has supported increased student engagement (Draper & Brown, 2004) and performance (Campbell & Mayer, 2009; Shapiro, 2009). The pedagogical argument for incorporating text-to-poll activities in the Introductory Psychology classes was two-fold: to enhance student participation in a non-threatening and anonymous way and to assess student preparation (preliminary readings, online interactive activities) to target lecture and discussion at the start of new units of instruction (Draper, 2002; Gauci, Dantas, Williams, & Kemm, 2009; "Phoebe," n.d.).

Application

The first text-to-poll activity was an extension of the informal student lunch poll to verify those results with two sections of Introductory Psychology. Students in each class were asked to identify the types of technology their faculty used to teach: PowerPoint; digital media, audio and video; MS Office Suite; online discussions; online quizzes; other. The most common technologies were PowerPoint and digital media, each 43%. In discussion, students said faculty incorporated YouTube videos to present historic and contemporary content, for example, archival footage of a psychology experiment or a current affairs analysis of marketing and promotional media. None had been assigned online discussions or quizzes, and among first-year students, relatively few reported using any of the MS Office suite in class. Juniors and seniors reported using Excel and other analytical software. Of greater note, though, were the students' responses to the activity. Being asked to use their phones in class was novel, and watching the votes tally led to lively discussions during the voting: "Does anyone do that?" and "How does that work?" were common questions about the two online choices. The students' increased animation was in line with Draper and Brown's (2004) research showing students are more engaged when classroom response systems are used.

The first academic unit selected for a text-to-poll activity in Introductory Psychology presented the concept of performance or test anxiety. This unit was selected because of adjustment issues first-year college students often experience around academic standards and performance (Davis, DiStefano, & Schutz, 2008). Prior to the session, students read research about test anxiety and the idea that one's arousal levels may go so high during assessment situations that performance is hindered. The class discussed the concept and various social, academic, athletic, and professional contexts where it might occur. The goal of the text-to-poll was to frame the follow-up discussion of applications and interventions (Gauci et al., 2009), so an opinion poll aggregating students' personal feelings was conducted. Almost two-thirds of the students (61%) reported tests in general were threatening, while only 30% considered them a challenge for which they were routinely prepared. The remaining students reported they were relaxed with testing situations (see Fig. 4).

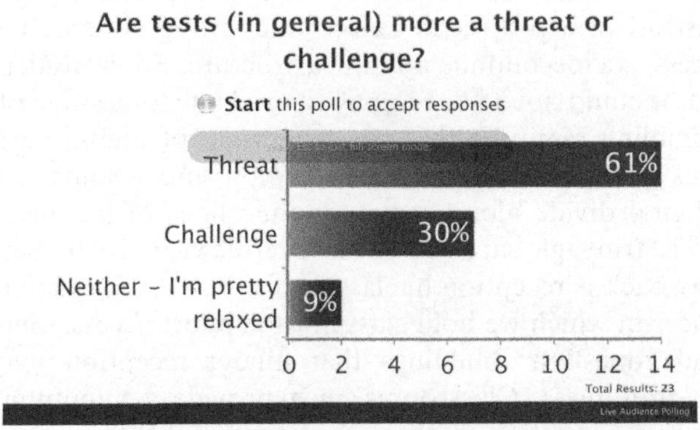

Fig. 4. Text to Poll: Test Anxiety.

Unlike the earlier poll, students were quieter as the results tallied, watching and nodding, or commenting "I thought so." The results provided the necessary launch into causes and effects of test anxiety and interventions clinicians, instructors, and individuals can use. Students said they felt their anxiety was validated because they learned the majority of their peers, anonymously, reported the same stress.

Outcomes and Lessons

These two text-to-poll activities and subsequent polls in Introductory Psychology and Human Motivation and Emotion on paired associate learning, gestalt principles of perception, motivation, and marketing psychology all benefited from increased participation as compared to traditional class discussion. Students engaged the process of anonymous disclosure differently from the more traditional lecture and discussion format with raised hands or answers called out. Since most students participated in most of the activities, more students shared their answers, albeit anonymously and with less depth, than usually spoke out in class (Gauci et al., 2009).

Future research should evaluate the relationship between the text-to-poll topics and students' success with targeted items on subjective and objective assessments, as recent research has shown that students in classes which regularly incorporate this technology outperform their peers in similar courses without it (Mayer et al., 2009).

While more students may have participated via text responses than did in traditional discussions, challenges can arise incorporating cell phone text messages instead of a proprietary electronic voting system. Two concerns relate to access: socioeconomic and infrastructure. Some students said they did not want or could not afford to pay to send a text message often in class. This is a humbling reminder that the generation of digital natives is not a homogeneous group with equal social capital and resources for web 2.0 lives. The digital divide along socioeconomic lines of income, access, and opportunity is truly global (Brown & Czerniewicz, 2010; Selwyn, 2004). Another drawback is reception in classrooms. For texting activities to work well, the spaces in which we hold class must support access. Geographic cell phone "dead zones" or buildings that hinder reception may limit this technology's usefulness. Classrooms must provide a minimum of internet connectivity and projection to share the results publicly.

SUMMARY AND SYNTHESIS: A CALL TO ACTION

Create a Foundation for E-Learning Activities

Much of the empirical and theoretical research incorporated here confirmed increased student engagement and learning when appropriate technology was introduced in classroom instruction and out-of-class coursework (e.g., Price & Kirkwood, 2011; US Department of Education, 2009). The teaching cases provide examples that both succeeded and disappointed yet were instructional and developmental nonetheless, each highlighting the utility of both the Phoebe pedagogic planner and the vast research resources appropriated to plan and enact these projects.

The Phoebe pedagogic planner affords faculty a structure within which to explore, critique, and adopt e-learning pedagogies to construct teaching and learning environments. Be they synchronous bricks and mortar, asynchronous and virtual, or blended as in these cases – each can serve as spaces of heightened student engagement and learning, depending on their design and enactment within a learning community. By providing an extensive library of resources paired with learning activities, Phoebe prompted critical reflection not only on particular technologies but also on their pedagogical utility (Masterman, 2008). Accessing the research and scholars in the field of learning technology highlighted additional contributions institutional support and interested peers can make to faculty adoption of e-learning strategies.

Challenges and Evolution

The initial disappointment of the Google group discussions was due to an overly simplified application of the technology and demonstrated the opportunity, and necessity, for increased faculty development. It opened a conversation among faculty and IT professionals and challenged faculty to elaborate pedagogy enhanced by technology. It was these initial challenges that brought Phoebe's usefulness to the fore. Greater reliance on the reference and planning resources highlighted the need for more purposeful faculty guidance in the discussion boards and in later implementations of online simulations and electronic voting systems. One of the strengths of the Phoebe pedagogic planner is having models of best practices and lessons learned (Masterman, 2008).

Students' participation in, and learning from, the online simulations and text-to-poll activities in subsequent classes benefited from the lessons of the earlier but less successful application of the discussion board technology in Cross-cultural Psychology. The more strategic integration of the online simulations was facilitated by the earlier presumptions and corrections derived from the in vivo experiences and reflections with students about their learning with discussion boards along with critiques informed by e-learning research and practitioner reports in Phoebe. The online simulations were more carefully scaffolded and more intentionally integrated into the daily work of the class and into homework and assessment activities that bridged the two learning environments, effectively "bookending" them "with teaching, providing proper context, focus and review" ("Phoebe," n.d., Modeling Tools and Simulations, para. 2) to facilitate student learning and engagement.

Similar lessons were applied when electronic polling was introduced. From the initial poll on faculty technology use to those closely integrated with disciplinary content, the polls were purposefully incorporated into class activities to demonstrate shared conceptions and prompt discussions targeted at enhancing student understanding and engagement. Phoebe and research on electronic voting systems and "clickers" (e.g., ELI, 2005; Mayer et al., 2009) helped to shape the pedagogy, including the structure of the class discussions before and after the polls.

All of the lessons learned – whether via Phoebe, e-learning research or the cases – were not without difficulties. The challenges and evolution of planning and implementation reminded faculty and academic technologists that e-learning is "enhanced learning" and demonstrated "it is the pedagogy, not the tool, that comes first" (JISC, 2008, p. 17). An important element of determining what technology is appropriate to enhance learning is understanding which technologies work best with which student learning objectives and pedagogical techniques – key strengths of the Phoebe pedagogic planner (Masterman, 2008). According to a recent survey (Taylor & McQuiggan, 2008), a majority of university faculty, 55.9%, desired assistance selecting from among the wealth of technological options available to enhance their courses when designing for online learning. The Phoebe pedagogical planner provided the framework within which to explore different technologies and their integration:

- *Analyzing* the *context* of the target project
- *Determining curricular* aspects including prerequisite knowledge, aims for teaching, student learning outcomes, and the resources necessary to

achieve them: personnel, technological, web 2.0, print, and TPACK (Mishra & Koehler, 2006)

- *Planning activities* to achieve desired learning outcomes
- *Selecting* appropriate technology to achieve particular learning outcomes and creating activities around available technologies (the e-learning advantage within the Phoebe site)
- *Designing assessment* to demonstrate student achievement in terms of learning and engagement

Institutional Support

This process was supported by cross-departmental and cross-functional collaboration. Faculty and staff motivation to explore e-learning was supported institutionally by the campus CIO and her team along with the administration's goals to increase technological support for teaching and learning. Institutional support and faculty curiosity unearthed a wealth of research on technologically enhanced teaching and learning to facilitate the pedagogical evolution shown across these projects.

As this chapter demonstrates, successful IT integration revolves around collaboration and thoughtful faculty development to create venues and spaces for faculty and student e-learning. The Phoebe planner and access to research and training facilitated the faculty's development of TPACK (Mishra & Koehler, 2006). Developing TPACK provided language and background to understand how technology could enhance teaching and learning and how to scaffold student contributions and engagement in the activities.

The Phoebe planner supplied a structure within which to design learning activities and a library of technologies to select or reject various media for different educational goals. Phoebe further connected technology to learning activities, so a faculty member desiring students to synthesize content across units might select appropriate technologies from several that support integration and synthesis of ideas. Argumentation visualization and concept mapping tools, wikis, discussion forums, blogs, and conferencing technology could enhance students' synthesis of new learning and their ability to demonstrate it. These tools, in conjunction with research on their application and outcomes, strengthened technological pedagogical skills for the faculty to contribute to student learning and engagement, important aspects of building an institutional culture of e-learning.

Faculty Motivation to Design for E-Learning

To develop a culture of e-learning, including blended pedagogy as presented here, faculty and administration should engage many facets of intrinsic and extrinsic faculty motivation. Several reviews have demonstrated the strength of intrinsic motivators for faculty to adopt e-learning pedagogies (e.g., Birch & Sankey, 2008; Maguire, 2005). Intrinsic motivation to master and engage new technology may prompt faculty to explore tools like Phoebe and to experiment with new pedagogical techniques (Georgina & Olson, 2008; Panda & Mishra, 2007, as cited in Bolliger & Wasilik, 2009).

High self-efficacy perceptions related to information technology have been identified as one of the strongest factors in decisions to adopt learning technology (Zhen, Garthwaite, & Pratt, 2008), while low perceptions may hinder faculty adoption (Ertmer & Ottenbreit-Leftwich, 2010). Wozney, Venkatesh, and Abrami (2006) found the intersection of expectancy of success and perceived utility of the technology for teaching and learning to be the strongest influences on faculty technology use. If faculty experience poor student engagement or achievement with e-learning strategies, they may believe the technology has a low utility while the cause may be their individual TPACK. As was the case here, faculty may need to develop additional skills to provide good experiences with technology-enhanced learning (Bradley, 2009). A pedagogic planner such as Phoebe, and access to applied and theoretical research as provided in Phoebe's reference resources could direct faculty and administrators to best practices in line with identified student learning outcomes and individual faculty goals for developing TPACK and implementing e-learning strategies. However, not all motivation is intrinsic, and numerous external factors contribute to faculty decisions regarding learning technology.

Faculty may be motivated by institutional factors such as social support and peer-to-peer learning that can come of adoption and championing new technologies (Georgina & Olson, 2008). Peer support and institutional support can significantly influence faculty motivation to introduce e-learning pedagogies into their courses. When faculty members see the relevance of technology to student learning and their teaching, they are more likely to use the technology (Nicolle, 2005), reinforcing the idea that technology should not be adopted merely for its own sake. In this case study, social support was both local and distributed. The initial faculty support came from collaboration with the CIO and from collaboration with researchers in the United Kingdom.

On campus the CIO helped establish a community of "Moodlers" among the faculty who were pilot testing the LMS. Facilitated by new technology champions and faculty experienced with Moodle and other LMS platforms, the social group met to discuss initial adoption, questions about implementation and suggestions for best practices (Georgina & Olson, 2008); later in the roll out, faculty led peer training sessions on key features (Bonk, 2001). While these institutionally sponsored meetings promoted important collegial dialogue, faculty adoption of e-learning strategies may also be hindered by institutional barriers.

Supporting Faculty Adoption of E-Learning Pedagogy

A top barrier to faculty adoption is the lack of systemic planning for e-learning across an institution (Birch & Burnett, 2009). Developing a school-wide e-learning strategy requires building buy-in among community thought leaders and technology champions (Sharpe et al., 2006) as was presented in this case study. Institutions, faculty, and staff must be creative in supporting and engaging faculty as they develop TPACK and implement new technologies with their students. Introducing new technology or launching a newly blended course requires time and commitment, in addition to the technological skills necessary to complement the pedagogical content knowledge the faculty member already has (Georgina & Hosford, 2009). The resources in Phoebe provided numerous examples of the different technologies in use, including models and critiques of their integration into blended courses.

Assessing the new pedagogy and requisite levels or types of TPACK – along with student learning and engagement – requires time for implementation, analysis, and reflection, as is reinforced often on the Phoebe site and related literature (Masterman, 2008). Some faculty may feel time and effort expended to construct, implement, and assess e-learning environments takes them away from other more institutionally recognized and rewarded activities like disciplinary research and writing (Howell, Williams, & Lindsay, 2003). The lack of external institutional rewards for creating e-learning may discourage faculty from engaging technology (Birch & Burnett, 2009). To address the additional time and energies required for course development, academic administrators should consider making additional training resources available (Georgina & Olson, 2008; JISC, 2009). Rewards such as release time, curriculum development grants, and recognition in promotion and tenure decisions can be strong external motivators for faculty to adopt and develop e-learning tools in their courses (Birch & Burnett, 2009; Bonk, 2001; Cook, Ley, Crawford, & Warner, 2009).

A Model of Institutional Support

One successful and long-running model incorporating these recommendations and more is the Center for Research on Learning and Teaching (CRLT) at the University of Michigan, Ann Arbor. Acknowledged as the oldest teaching center set within a postsecondary institution (Cook, 2011), CRLT provides institutional support for faculty to develop e-learning pedagogies and their own TPACK in numerous key areas identified in this case study and analysis (Zhu, Kaplan, & Dershimer, 2011): showcasing faculty work with technology, grant funding for technology innovation, pedagogical and technological support, institutional white papers highlighting relevant issues and related research, and multiple training models such as one-to-one sessions with technologists and just in time training when faculty need it. The support to implement the innovations in this case study included some key elements for building a culture of e-learning and institutional support as demonstrated at the University of Michigan and in other settings and research:

- Grant funding for research and pedagogical innovation;
- CIO commitment to establish immediate and long-term strategic goals for e-learning adoption and curriculum development;
- Staff support in the office of Information Technology, including collaboration with academic technologists;
- Multiple training models and opportunities:
  - Staff-led training and knowledge sharing (Bonk, 2001);
  - e-learning thought leaders as guest speakers;
  - Webinars and podcasts of national conferences on e-learning research and practice;
  - One-on-one support from educational technologists (Zhu et al., 2011).

FUTURE DIRECTIONS

The trajectory from naïve application of discussion boards to more nuanced and sophisticated integration of online case simulations and in-class polling demonstrated the impact that small coordinated steps can have on faculty teaching and student learning and engagement. Important lessons of this case study include the contributions of current research and tools such as the Phoebe pedagogic planner and the value of broad-based collaboration to implement technological pedagogical changes as an institution develops a culture of e-learning.

The Phoebe pedagogic planner provided a solid foundation for multiple aspects of lesson planning and assessment. The most fruitful contributions from Phoebe, as noted earlier, were the reference tools of pedagogical practices linked to key learning outcomes and activities. Coupled with theoretical and practical research on the technologies under consideration, Phoebe helped us select appropriate technologies to begin to achieve our desired student learning outcomes and answer the driving research question "in what contexts and for what purposes are [learning technologies] best used?" (Cameron, 2008, p. 504).

Regarding the specific technologies, we learned discussion boards work best to extend thoughtful discussions when students are provided with purposeful scaffolding for their contributions. Future research should investigate the relationship between online discussions and classroom discussions to learn how each can best inform the other. Faculty development activities should be designed to guide professional staff on relevant models of prompting and scaffolding to help students gain the greatest depth from the discussions. The lessons of purpose and depth of preparation for discussion boards helped faculty introduce online psychological simulations with promising results, but future research is necessary to learn how much, if any, the simulations contribute to introductory psychology students' learning and engagement. Online simulations can afford a rich and safe environment for students to learn about sensitive practices. Faculty development should include best practices for their integration as both independent and collaborative exercises in authentic practice. We also learned that text-to-poll electronic voting systems can bring more student opinions or understandings into classroom discussions, but cell phone technology may not provide the most inclusive context when one considers socioeconomic disparities among participants. Future research and faculty development should address the participation rates of students using text-to-poll cell phone technology versus proprietary electronic voting systems to assure the digital divide is not innocently perpetuated in a rush to increase student engagement.

Bringing Phoebe and other e-learning planning tools into the higher education mainstream requires support for hosting, maintenance, updating, and dissemination to assure their timely relevance (Masterman, 2008). This is especially important to faculty and institutions that come to rely on such guidance and the windows into others' practices they can provide, windows which help to deepen an institution's own culture of e-learning. Phoebe's practitioner cases highlighted the value of colleagues sharing resources and experiences, and the numerous faculty and staff who populated Phoebe with cases and external links are as much a part of this case study as colleagues on campus and abroad. This extended network provided necessary social and intellectual capital, without which these projects would not have occurred.

ACKNOWLEDGMENT

This research was partially sponsored by a Summer Research Institute fellowship awarded to Dr. Mark J. Hager for study at Harris Manchester College, Oxford University.

REFERENCES

Adams, W. K., Reid, S., LeMaster, R., McKagan, S. B., Perkins, K. K., Dubson, M., & Wieman, C. E. (2008). A study of educational simulations. Part 1 – Engagement and learning. *Journal of Interactive Learning Research*, *19*(3), 397–419.

American Psychological Association. (2007). *APA guidelines for the undergraduate psychology major*. Washington, DC: Author. Retrieved from http://www.apa.org/ed/precollege/about/psymajor-guidelines.pdf

Baglione, S. L., & Nastanski, M. (2007). The superiority of online discussion: Faculty perceptions. *The Quarterly Review of Distance Education*, *8*(2), 139–150.

Birch, D., & Burnett, D. (2009). Bringing academics on board: Encouraging institution-wide diffusion of e-learning environments. *Australasian Journal of Educational Technology*, *25*(1), 117–134.

Birch, D., & Sankey, M. D. (2008). Drivers for and obstacles to the development of interactive multimodal technology-mediated distance higher education courses. *International Journal of Education and Development using ICT*, *4*(1). Retrieved from http://ijedict.dec.uwi.edu/

Blumenfeld, P. C., Soloway, E., Marx, R. W., Krajcik, J. S., Guzdial, M., & Palincsar, A. (1991). Motivating project-based learning: Sustaining the doing, supporting the learning. *Educational Psychologist*, *26*(3 & 4), 369–398.

Bolliger, D. U., & Wasilik, O. (2009). Factors influencing faculty satisfaction with online teaching and learning in higher education. *Distance Education*, *30*(1), 103–116.

Bonk, C. J. (2001). *Online teaching in an online world.* Bloomington, IN: CourseShare.com

Bradley, J. (2009). Promoting and supporting authentic online conversations – Which comes first, the tools or instructional design? *International Journal of Pedagogies and Learning*, *5*(3), 20–31.

Brown, C., & Czerniewicz, L. (2010). Debunking the 'digital native': Beyond digital apartheid, towards digital democracy. *Journal of Computer Assisted Learning*, *26*, 357–369. doi: 10.1111/j.1365-2729.2010.00369.x

Cameron, L. (2008a). Could pedagogical planners be a useful learning design tool for university lecturers? *Readings in Education and Technology: Proceedings of the ICICTE 2008*, 496–507.

Cameron, L. (2008b). Developing a pedagogical planner. In S. Walker, M. Ryan & R. Teed (Eds.), *Designing for learning, e-learning@greenwich/conference 2007: Post-Conference Reflections and Abstracts* (pp. 53–66).

Campbell, J., & Mayer, R. E. (2009). Questioning as an instructional method: Does it affect learning from lectures? *Applied Cognitive Psychology*, *23*(6), 747–759. doi: 10.1002/acp.1513

Champion, T., & Novicki, A. (2006). Instructional technology: A review of research and recommendations for use. In J. J. Mintzes & W. H. Leonard (Eds.), *Handbook of college science teaching* (pp. 233–250). Danvers, MA: NSTA Press.

Cook, C. E. (2011). CRLT and its role at the University of Michigan. In C. E. Cook & M. Kaplan (Eds.), *Advancing the culture of teaching on campus: How a teaching center can make a difference* (pp. 1–18). Sterling, VA: Stylus Publishing.

Cook, R. G., Ley, K., Crawford, C., & Warner, A. (2009). Motivators and inhibitors for university faculty in distance and e-learning. *British Journal of Educational Technology*, *40*, 149–163. doi: 10.1111/j.1467-8535.2008.00845.x

Covington, D., Petherbridge, D., & Warren, S. E. (2005). Best practices: A triangulated support approach in transitioning faculty to online teaching. *Online Journal of Distance Learning Administration*, *8*(1)Retrieved from. https://www.westga.edu/~distance/ojdla/spring81/covington81.htm

Crossgrove, K., & Curran, K. L. (2008). Using clickers in nonmajors- and majors-level biology courses: Student opinion, learning, and long-term retention of course material. *CBE Life Sciences Education*, *7*(1), 146–154. doi: 10.1187/cbe.07-08-0060

Dagger, D., Rogers, C., Wade, V.P., Gaffney, C., Armstrong, K., Fitzmaurice, B., …, Walsh, E. (2008). Adaptive simulations for communication skills training in healthcare. *Proceedings of the 2nd Workshop on Personalisation for e-Health, Corfu, 26th June 2007*, 21–27.

Davis, H. A., DiStefano, C., & Schutz, P. A. (2008). Identifying patterns of appraising tests in first-year college students: Implications for anxiety and emotion regulation during test taking. *Journal of Educational Psychology*, *100*(4), 942–960. doi: 10.1037/a0013096

Dennen, V. P. (2008). Pedagogical lurking: Student engagement in non-posting discussion behaviour. *Computers in Human Behavior*, *24*, 1624–1633.

Draper, S. W. (2002). *Electronically enhanced classroom interaction*. Retrieved from http://www.psy.gla.ac.uk/~steve/ilig/handsets.html

Draper, S. W. (2005). *Why use EVS? The short answer*. Retrieved from http://www.psy.gla.ac.uk/~steve/ilig/why.html

Draper, S. W., & Brown, M. I. (2004). Increasing interactivity in lectures using an electronic voting system. *Journal of Computer Assisted Learning*, *20*, 81–94.

Du, J., Zhang, K., Olinzock, A., & Adams, J. (2008). Graduate students' perspectives on the meaningful nature of online discussions. *Journal of Interactive Learning Research, 19*(1), 21–36. Retrieved from http://www.editlib.org/p/21871

ELI EDUCAUSE Learning Initiative. (2005). *7 things you should know about…clickers*. Retrieved from http://net.educause.edu/ir/library/pdf/ELI7002.pdf

Ertmer, P. A., & Ottenbreit-Leftwich, A. T. (2010). Teacher technology change: Confidence, beliefs and culture intersect. *Journal of Research on Technology Education, 42*(3), 255–284.

Finegold, A. R. D., & Cooke, L. (2006). Exploring the attitudes, experiences and dynamics of interaction in online groups. *Internet and Higher Education, 9*(3), 201–215. Retrieved from http://hdl.handle.net/2134/3279

Francis, R., & Raftery, J. (2005). Blended learning landscapes. *Brookes eJournal of Learning and Teaching, 1*(3), 1–5.

Gauci, S. A., Dantas, A. M., Williams, D. A., & Kemm, R. E. (2009). Promoting student-centered active learning in lectures with a personal response system. *Advances in Physiology Education, 33*, 60–71. doi: 10.1152/advan.00109.2007

Georgina, D. A., & Hosford, C. C. (2009). Higher education faculty perceptions on technology integration and training. *Teaching and Teacher Education, 25*, 690–696.

Georgina, D. A., & Olson, M. R. (2008). Integration of technology in higher education: A review of faculty self-perceptions. *Internet and Higher Education, 11*, 1–8. doi: 10.1016/j.iheduc.2007.11.002

Hager, M. J., & Clemmons, R. (2010). Faculty & IT: Conversations and collaboration. *EDUCAUSE Review, 45*(2), 58–59.

Heathcote, E. A. (2006). Learning design templates – A pedagogical just-in-time support tool. In G. Minshull & J. Mole (Eds.), *Designing for learning* (pp. 19–26). Dover, UK: JISC Development Group.

Howe, N., & Strauss, W. (2000). *Millennials rising: The next great generation*. New York, NY: Vintage Books Random House.

Howell, S. L., Williams, P. B., & Lindsay, N. K. (2003). Thirty-two trends affecting distance education: An informed foundation for strategic planning. *Online Journal of Distance Learning Administration, 6*(3).

Jeffries, A., Cubric, M., & Russell, M. B. (in press). Enhancing learning and teaching using electronic voting systems – The development of a framework for an institutional approach for their introduction. In C. Wankel and P. Blessinger (Eds.), *Cutting-edge technologies in higher education* (Vol. 5): *Increasing student engagement and retention using classroom technologies: Classroom response systems and mediated discourse technologies*. Bradford, UK: Emerald Publishing Group.

JISC. (2004). *Effective practice with e-Learning*. Bristol, UK: JISC Development Group.

JISC. (2008). *Effective practice with e-portfolios: Supporting 21st century learning*. Bristol, UK: JISC Innovation Group.

JISC. (2009). *Effective practice in a digital age*. Bristol, UK: JISC Innovation Group.

Jones, C., & Ramanau, R. (2009, June 8–13). Collaboration and the Net generation: The changing characteristics of first year university students. Paper presented at Computer Supported Collaborative Learning Practices, Rhodes, Greece.

Koehler, M. J., Mishra, P., & Yahya, K. (2007). Tracing the development of teacher knowledge in a design seminar: Integrating content, pedagogy and technology. *Computers & Education, 49*, 740–762.

Lave, J., & Wenger, E. (1991). *Situated learning: Legitimate peripheral participation*. Cambridge: Cambridge University Press.

Lim, D. H., & Morris, M. L. (2009). Learner and instructional factors influencing learning outcomes within a blended learning environment. *Educational Technology & Society, 12*(4), 282–293.

Lu, L. L., & Jeng, I. (2006/2007). Knowledge construction in inservice teacher online discourse: Impacts of instructor roles and facilitative strategies. *Journal of Research on Technology in Education, 39*(2), 183–202.

Mager, M. (2012, April 13–17). *Instructor and student participation in online discussion boards as predictors of student outcomes*. Paper presented at the Annual Meeting of the American Educational Research Association, Vancouver, B.C.

Manton, M. (2008). Phoebe: A pedagogic planner to promote innovative practice. In S. Walker, M. Ryan & R. Teed (Eds.), *Designing for learning, e-learning@greenwich/conference 2007: Post-Conference reflections and abstracts*. London, UK: University of Greenwich. Abstract retrieved from http://www.ceimh.bham.ac.uk/documents/designingforlearning.pdf#page=54

Masikunas, G., Panyiotis, A., & Burke, L. (2007). The use of electronic voting systems in lectures within business and marketing: A case study of their impact on student learning. *ALT-J, Research in Learning Technology, 15*(1), 3–20.

Masterman, L. (2008). *JISC Design for learning programme: PHOEBE pedagogy planner project evaluation report*. Bristol, UK: JISC.

Maurino, P. S. M. (2007). Online asynchronous threaded discussions: Good enough to advance students through the proximal zone of activity theory? *TechTrends, 51*(2), 46–49.

Mayer, R. E., Stull, A., DeLeeuw, K., Almeroth, K., Bimber, B., Chun, D, & Zhang, H. (2009). Clickers in college classrooms: Fostering learning with questioning methods in large lecture classes. *Contemporary Educational Psychology, 34*, 51–57.

Mishra, P., & Koehler, M. J. (2006). Technological pedagogical content knowledge: A framework for teacher knowledge. *Teachers College Record, 108*(6), 1017–1054.

Nicolle, P. S. (2005). *Technology adoption into teaching and learning by mainstream university faculty: A mixed methodology study revealing the "how, when, why, and why not."* Unpublished doctoral dissertation. Louisiana State University and Agricultural and Mechanical College, Baton Rouge, LA.

Poll Everywhere. (2011). *Text message (SMS) polls and voting: Audience response system*. Retrieved from http://www.polleverywhere.com

Prensky, M. (2001). Digital natives, digital immigrants. *On the Horizon, 9*(5), 1–6.

Price, L., & Kirkwood, A. (2011). *Enhancing professional learning and teaching through technology: A synthesis of evidence-based practice among teachers in higher education*. York, UK: The Institute of Educational Technology. The Open University. Higher Education Academy.

Raisinghani, M. S., & Vinaja, R. (2006). Teaching with online case studies: Implementation and evaluation issues. *Journal of Informatics Education Research, 8*(3), 1–36.

Ramli, R. (2010). Technology enhanced learning: Fostering cooperative learning through the integration of online communication as part of teaching and learning experience. *World Academy of Science, Engineering and Technology, 70*, 611–614.

Rathus, S. A. (2011). *Psychology concepts & connections: Brief version. Enhanced edition with PsykTrek 3.0*. Belmont, CA: Wadsworth.

Reeves, T. C., & Ho, E. (2007). Generational differences. In J. M. Spector, M. D. Merrill, J. van Merriënboer & M. P. Driscoll (Eds.), *Handbook of research on educational communications and technology* (3rd ed., pp. 295–304). New York, NY: Lawrence Erlbaum Associates; Taylor & Francis.

Roblyer, M. D., McDaniel, M., Webb, M., Herman, J., & Witty, J. V. (2010). Findings on Facebook in higher education: A comparison of college faculty and student uses and perceptions of social networking sites. *Internet and Higher Education, 13*, 134–140.

Seltz, J. (2010, December 2). School goal: Netbooks for students. *The Boston Globe*. Retrieved from http://www.boston.com/yourtown/dedham/articles/2010/12/02/dedham_considers_giving_netbooks_to_high_school_freshmen/

Shapiro, A. (2009). An empirical study of personal response technology for improving attendance and learning in a large class. *Journal of the Scholarship of Teaching and Learning, 9*(1), 13–26.

Sharpe, R., Benfield, G., & Francis, R. (2006). Implementing a university e-learning strategy: Levers for change within academic schools. *ALT-J, Research in Learning Technology, 14*(2), 135–151. doi: 10.1080/09687760600668503

Simpson, V., & Oliver, M. (2006). *Using electronic voting systems in lectures*. Retrieved from http://tlc.zmml.uni-bremen.de/resource_files/resources/384/ElectronicVotingSystems.pdf

Stark-Wroblewski, K., Kreiner, D. S., Boeding, C. M., Lopata, A. N., Ryan, J. J., & Church, T. M. (2008). Use of virtual reality technology to enhance undergraduate learning in abnormal psychology. *Teaching of Psychology, 35*(4), 343–348. doi: 10.1080/00986280802374526

Stowell, J. R., & Nelson, J. M. (2007). Benefits of electronic audience response systems on student participation, learning, and emotion. *Teaching of Psychology, 34*(4), 253–258.

Suler, J. (2004). In class and online: Using discussion boards in teaching. *CyberPsychology & Behavior, 7*(4), 395–401. doi: 10.1089/cpb.2004.7.395

Taylor, A., & McQuiggan, C. (2008). Faculty development programming: If we build it, will they come? *EDUCAUSE Quarterly, 31*(3), 28–37.

US Department of Education. (2009). *Evaluation of evidence-based practices in online learning: A meta-analysis and review of online learning studies*. Washington, DC: Office of Planning, Evaluation, and Policy Development.

Wang, S. (2011). Promoting student's online engagement with communication tools. *Journal of Educational Technology Development and Exchange, 4*(1), 81–90.

Wankel, C. (2009). Management education using social media. *Organization Management 6*, 251–262. doi: 10.1057/omj.2009.34

Wise, A. F., & Chiu, M. M. (2011). Analyzing temporal patterns of knowledge construction in a role-based online discussion. *International Journal of Computer Supported Collaborative learning, 6*(3), 445–470. doi: 10.1007/s11412-011-9120-1

Wise, A. F., Hsiao, Y. T., Marbouti, F., Speer, J., & Perera, N. (2012, April 13–17). *Building a taxonomy of "listening" behaviors in online discussions: Case studies of high- and low-activity students*. Paper presented at the Annual Meeting of the American Educational Research Association, Vancouver, B.C.

Worley, K. (2011). Educating college students of the Net generation. *Adult Learning, 22*(3), 31–39.

Wozney, L., Venkatesh, V., & Abrami, P. C. (2006). Implementing computer technologies: Teachers' perceptions and practices. *Journal of Technology and Teacher Education, 14*(1), 173–207.

Zhen, Y., Garthwaite, A., & Pratt, P. (2008). Factors affecting faculty members' decision to teach or not to teach online in higher education. *Online Journal of Distance Learning Administration, 11*(3), 1–18.

Zhu, E. (2007). *Teaching with clickers.* CRLT Occasional Papers, 22. Center for Research on Learning and Teaching. The University of Michigan: Ann Arbor, MI.

Zhu, E., Kaplan, M., & Dershimer, C. (2011). Engaging faculty in effective use of instructional technology. In C. E. Cook & M. Kaplan (Eds.), *Advancing the culture of teaching on campus: How a teaching center can make a difference* (pp. 151–166). Sterling, VA: Stylus Publishing.

WHERE TECHNOLOGIES COLLIDE: A TECHNOLOGY INTEGRATION MODEL

Christa L. Wilkin, Cristina Rubino, Deone Zell and Lois M. Shelton

ABSTRACT

Technology is transforming teaching in ways that break down classroom walls while improving course quality and capitalizing on educators' creativity. Rather than using technology in an ad hoc way, technology needs to fit the content and pedagogical style of the teacher.

Our chapter builds on the extant literature on the necessary knowledge to integrate content, pedagogy, and technology (TPACK) in the classroom. We propose a comprehensive model that outlines the factors that lead to the development of TPACK, the relationship between TPACK and the use of technology, and outcomes gleaned from technology-enhanced learning.

Our proposed model is an important first step to considering the precursors and outcomes of TPACK, which will need to be validated empirically. We extend the TPACK framework by identifying the predictors of TPACK such as teacher self-efficacy, experience with technology, and student factors. We argue that the extent to which educators develop their TPACK and use technology is bound by

Increasing Student Engagement and Retention using Classroom Technologies: Classroom Response Systems and Mediated Discourse Technologies
Cutting-edge Technologies in Higher Education, Volume 6E, 81–106

ISSN: 2044-9968/doi:10.1108/S2044-9968(2013)000006E006

contextual factors such as organizational culture, resources, and student characteristics. Without considering the extensions that are identified in the Technology Integration Model, the linkages between TPACK and desirable outcomes (e.g., student engagement) are unclear. As a result, our proposed model has implications for educators and institutions alike.

INTRODUCTION

Technology is transforming teaching in ways that break down classroom walls while improving course quality and capitalizing on educators' creativity (Rossy, Rubino, Wilkin, Shelton, & Zell, 2012). For example, a common context in higher education – large lecture classes – although widespread is not very conducive to student engagement (Cuseo, 2007). In this context, cutting-edge technologies can be beneficial to creating an engaging learning environment by incorporating alternative learning approaches such as "flipping" the classroom (i.e., online lectures and classroom discussion), student generated content (e.g., video, wikis), joint student/instructor-generated content, open content, lecture capture to "rewind the instructor," mobile learning, adaptive learning, "born digital" textbooks, and student portfolios. These technologies are beneficial in other contexts as well, as they have been demonstrated to lead to more engagement and learning (e.g., Laird & Kuh, 2005).

Technology itself is not inherently bad or good (Norman, 1993); it is how it is used that can lead to positive results. In other words, positive or negative results stem from how technology is used, not technology itself. The tendency of educators and scholars is to focus specifically on kinds of technology and ignore how technology is actually used or can be harnessed in the classroom (Mishra & Koehler, 2006). Much of the literature focuses on the outcomes of technologies on learning and teaching or on how to define technology (Sachau & Ku, 2012). Some scholars suggest that only emerging technologies ought to be recognized because well-established technologies are institutionalized in higher education (Cox & Graham, 2009), whereas other scholars suggest that technology includes both emerging and well-established technologies such as blackboards (Koehler & Mishra, 2009). Although these studies contribute to our understanding of technologies and their outcomes, they often fail to consider how pedagogy and curriculum can be harnessed to influence outcomes such as learning and engagement (Conole & Oliver, 1998; Harris, Mishra, & Koehler, 2009).

Rather than using technology in an ad hoc way, technology needs to fit the content and pedagogical style of the teacher (Harris et al., 2009). The knowledge necessary for educators to integrate technology, pedagogy, and content is known as TPACK (technological pedagogical content knowledge; Schmidt, Baran, Thompson, Mishra, Koehler, & Shin, 2009). TPACK (formerly TPCK) pertains to "the what" that teachers need to know about technology, pedagogy, and content to integrate technology into the classroom (Schmidt et al., 2009). In other words, TPACK is the extent to which an educator is knowledgeable about how to apply technology and use different pedagogical strategies to deliver course content. This knowledge varies by instructor, which suggests that there are individual characteristics that influence instructors' TPACK. Additionally, although educators may possess TPACK, this does not necessarily translate into the effective integration of technology in the classroom. Factors such as organizational and classroom context likely influence the extent that instructors use technology. For instance, organizational culture impacts technology use such that supportive cultures of technology will enable technology-savvy educators to flourish, whereas cultures that do not encourage technology will create obstacles for educators with high levels of TPACK to integrate technology in the classroom. These factors are a key motivation as to why we need to extend the current TPACK model because knowledge alone is insufficient. Although empirical results suggest that educators increase their know-how to integrate technology in their classrooms through professional development (e.g., Koh, & Frick, 2009; Wetzel, Foulger, & Williams, 2009), less is known about the factors that impact and result from TPACK.

We extend the TPACK framework by proposing a theoretical model (Fig. 1) that examines precursors to TPACK (e.g., educators' experience and attitudes) and educator, student, and school outcomes of using technology (e.g., educator satisfaction, student engagement and satisfaction, school resources). We also include several boundary conditions for these relationships in the proposed model. Specifically, we argue that developing TPACK and technology use is context-bound by environmental factors such as the classroom environment, the availability of technology, and students' needs and learning styles.

In this chapter, we aim to integrate the existing literature focusing on TPACK, as well as other areas of research that may shed light on the relationships between TPACK and its predictors, the context and resulting technology use. By synthesizing related research, our goal is to provide readers with a comprehensive model outlining the factors that impact technology integration within the classroom and its outcomes. As a result,

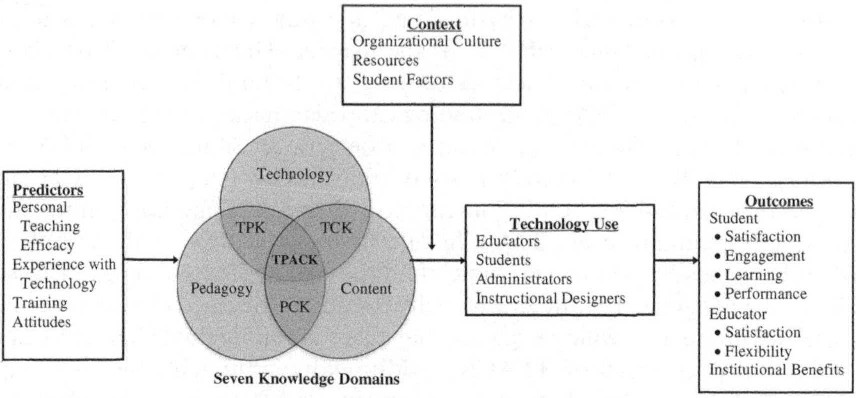

Fig. 1. Proposed Technology Integration Model.

the proposed model and supporting research will have implications for educators and institutions.

RELATED TECHNOLOGY MODELS

The TPACK model and our proposed extension of it differ substantially from a number of instructional technology adoption models that have been adapted for higher education (e.g., Diffusion of Innovation, Rogers, 1995; Model of Diffusion, Dooley, 1999; see Venkatesh, Morris, Davis, & Davis, 2003 for a review). These models were originally designed for different audiences such as public health, but have been used in the context of higher education. As such, the models may not be appropriate to describe how faculty use technology in higher education because they do not consider the nuances of higher education such as pedagogy and institutional structures. This perspective is consistent with the constructivist view of learning (Duffy & Jonassen, 1992), which calls for an increased sensitivity of context and adopting models for specific populations.

The Technology Acceptance Model (TAM) is a broad theoretical model that proposes that attitudes toward technology, such as perceived usefulness and ease of use, predict the adoption of computer-based technologies (Davis, Bagozzi, & Warshaw, 1989; Venkatesh & Davis, 2000). Our model considers another important factor, specifically the knowledge required to integrate technology, pedagogy, and content, which impacts the relationship between attitudes toward technology and the use of technology-enhanced learning.

Other technology models that have been specifically developed for a higher education context display further types of limitations. For example, Dong and Sun (2007) depicted a model where they identified how three key stakeholders (i.e., faculty, students, and instructional designers) interact to design and implement technology. The model suggests that faculty have content knowledge, whereas instructional designers are the technology experts. Although this model discusses different types of knowledge, it does not consider how important it is for faculty to also have knowledge of technology and pedagogy, as is the case with TPACK.

Scholars have also developed enhanced TPACK models by including assistive technology for students with disabilities (Marino, Sameshima, & Beecher, 2009), additional factors to enhance student-centered learning (e.g., information and communication technologies) and depicting students in the model (Angeli & Valanides, 2009), web knowledge (Lee & Tsai, 2010), the authentic learning approach for science teachers (Jimoyiannis, 2010), and a combined pedagogical knowledge factor that includes content-specific strategies such as subjects and topics (Cox & Graham, 2009). Although these models give us a broader perspective of TPACK, we still have limited knowledge of the predictors and outcomes of TPACK.

TECHNOLOGICAL PEDAGOGICAL CONTENT KNOWLEDGE

Educators need to be fluent in content, pedagogical, and technological knowledge domains so that they can increase student learning and engagement. The first type of knowledge, *content knowledge,* pertains to the subject matter to be taught and includes theories, concepts, ideas, methods of evidence, organizational frameworks, and established practices (Shulman, 1986). Educators who develop their content knowledge learn what to teach. Second, *pedagogical knowledge* requires an understanding of how students learn and acquire skills in different ways. This knowledge encompasses knowledge about teaching practices and assessment, educational purposes and strategies, and how theories of learning apply in classrooms (Koehler & Mishra, 2008). Educators who develop their pedagogical knowledge learn how to teach. Finally, *technological knowledge* requires that individuals have a deep understanding of how to apply information technology at work (Koehler & Mishra, 2009). It goes beyond simply being computer literate and suggests that this type of knowledge evolves by interacting with multiple technologies (Koehler & Mishra, 2005). Accordingly, educators who develop their knowledge of pedagogy, content, and technology should be able to better integrate technology in the classroom.

Because we cannot study these types of knowledge as mutually exclusive concepts, scholars suggest that we examine the intersections of these knowledge components, which form three more knowledge domains. Shulman (1986) had originally introduced the notion of *pedagogical content knowledge* (PCK) in which he suggested that we consider the relationship between the two concepts, rather than focus solely on pedagogy or subject matter. That is, PCK is the intersection between content and pedagogy in how we organize and adapt content for instruction (Mishra & Koehler, 2006). The interplay of knowledge between technology and content is termed *technological content knowledge* (TCK), which describes the knowledge required to understand how technology and content are mutually related (Harris, 2008). Knowing the subject matter is not enough; educators need to know how the application of technology can be used to help students learn (Mishra & Koehler, 2006). For example, science courses may be more amenable to lecture capture, while rapidly changing fields are not; English courses may be more amenable to extensive use of forums and student engagement than courses in statistics. *Technological pedagogical knowledge* (TPK) is composed of knowledge about how educators can use technology to instruct students and how technology can change the way in which subject matter is taught in the classroom (Koehler & Mishra, 2005). This knowledge includes an educator's understanding of how tools can be used for a given task and his or her ability to select tools that best fit with the delivery of the subject matter (Koehler & Mishra, 2009). For example, educators can use their TPK to maintain class records and encourage class participation through discussion boards and chat rooms.

It has been argued that our primary focus ought to be on the entire set of knowledge domains that teachers need to incorporate technology into their classrooms; this knowledge is known as "TPACK" or *technological pedagogical content knowledge* (Koehler & Mishra, 2008; Mishra & Koehler, 2006). TPACK is the intersection or "sweet spot" of technological, pedagogical, and content knowledge (see Fig. 1). This framework suggests that there is variation in disciplinary knowledge and pedagogical strategies, which needs to be considered when incorporating technology into the classroom (Harris et al., 2009).

A recent literature review found that scholars differ in how they conceptualize TPACK (Voogt, Fisser, Roblin, Tondeur, & van Braak, in press).

Some scholars understand TPACK as the interplay between the three knowledge domains, content, pedagogy, and technology, other scholars view it as a distinct knowledge domain, while other scholars suggest that TPACK is as an extension of pedagogical content knowledge (PCK). While debate exists on how to define TPACK (e.g., Cox & Graham 2009; Niess 2005), we adopt the first two conceptualizations and define TPACK as a distinct knowledge domain that stems from the interplay between technological, pedagogical, and content knowledge.

Although much of the literature has focused more on the professional development of K-12 educators, TPACK has been applied to various subject matters such as mathematics, science, and social studies from different levels of education from K-12 classrooms to post-secondary classes. Studies have mainly examined the use of technology in pre-service teaching from K-12 (e.g., Dexter & Riedel, 2003; Doering, Hughes & Huffman, 2003; Hughes, 2005), but some studies have focused on inservice teaching (e.g., Graham et al., 2009). Some studies have been conducted at the college level (e.g., Cox & Graham, 2009; Dong & Sun, 2007; Peruski, Mishra, & Koehler, 2007; Sachau & Ku, 2012; Sun & Deng, 2007), but for the most part, much of the emphasis remains on K-12 educators. Higher education differs from K-12 in terms of institutional characteristics and structure, student needs, and student capabilities; therefore, differences in how technology is used and how technology affects classroom outcomes may exist.

Moreover, most studies focus on how to train educators to increase their TPACK, without examining other predictors and outcomes of TPACK. We still do not know how educators acquire TPACK, or in other words, factors that lead to higher TPACK (Cox & Graham, 2009). Additionally, the role of specific technologies on outcomes has been examined, but we still do not know the benefits of TPACK. As such, we offer a comprehensive model that includes (a) factors that lead to TPACK such as educators' experience and attitudes, (b) outcomes of TPACK such as students' motivation and educators' satisfaction, and (c) boundary conditions such as the classroom environment, institutional expectations, and students' demographic characteristics. This theoretical model is in response to calls for research for a model to help faculty adopt technology and develop their TPACK (An & Reigeluth, 2011).

Although TPACK is an important concept to help us understand the knowledge required to incorporate technology into the classroom, there are issues with distinguishing between the different types of TPACK knowledge domains (Cox & Graham, 2009; Koehler & Mishra, 2008; Lee & Tsai, 2010). Researchers have encountered issues with empirically disintegrating each knowledge domain using factor analysis, which calls into question whether the domains are indeed separate (e.g., Archambault & Barnett, 2010; Koh, Chai, & Tsai, 2010; Yurdakul, Odabasia, Kilicera, Coklarb, Birinci, & Kurt, 2012). One difficulty is that there are a number of different surveys to assess TPACK, some that are more general and others that are contextualized for specific subject matter (e.g., science; Archambault & Barnett, 2010; Graham et al., 2009; Koehler & Mishra, 2005; Schmidt et al., 2009). Scholars have yet to create an instrument that clearly distinguishes each knowledge domain. Chai, Koh, and Tsai (2011) have recently adapted a new survey instrument based on other assessments (e.g., Chai, Koh, & Tsai 2010; Koh et al., 2010) with Singaporean primary and secondary level pre-service teachers. The results identify the seven knowledge domains (e.g., TPK, PCK) using factor analysis, which lends support to the TPACK framework.

PREDICTORS OF TPACK

This section identifies specific antecedents to TPACK and aims to answer questions surrounding the impact of educator characteristics on TPACK. Few studies examine factors that predict the intersection of technological, pedagogical, and content knowledge or the knowledge necessary to implement technology (TPACK). One study (Watson, 2006) that examined factors impacting Internet use in the classroom found that instructor characteristics, such as teaching experience, professional development related to technology, and teacher Internet self-efficacy, do influence technology use. Another study also found that teacher self-efficacy and professional development influenced the use of technology (Vannatta & Fordham, 2004). Based on their presence in the education literature and previous research examining predictors to technology use (e.g., Russell, Bebell, O'Dwyer, & O'Connor, 2003; Vannatta & Fordham, 2004; Watson, 2006), we focus on educators' personal teaching efficacy, experience with technology, training, and attitudes as predictors of TPACK.

Personal Teaching Efficacy

Self-efficacy is "the belief in one's capabilities to organize and execute the courses of action required to manage prospective situations" (Bandura, 1995, p. 2). While self-efficacy can apply to any context, personal teaching efficacy applies specifically to instructors. Personal teaching efficacy refers to educators' confidence in their ability to influence student learning (Burton, Bamberry, & Harris-Boundy, 2005). We suspect that self-efficacy impacts how willing instructors are to learn about and try different methods of teaching (pedagogy), new developments in field (content), and new ways to apply technology in the classroom (technology). Indeed, studies have found that teaching self-efficacy is related to attitudes toward implementing new instructional practices (Ghaith, & Yaghi, 1997; Guskey, 1988). Similarly, instructors who are confident in their abilities to influence students (i.e., high personal teaching efficacy) and are open to new practices are likely more keen to acquire new knowledge (e.g., TPACK) when compared to instructors who do not feel confident about their ability to influence learning (i.e., low personal teaching efficacy).

Proposition 1. Personal teaching self-efficacy will predict TPACK such that educators with higher levels of self-efficacy will acquire more TPACK.

Experience with Technology

Instructor experience can refer to different concepts such as experience as an educator, experience working in a specific context, and experience with technology. Experience as an educator may impact content and pedagogical knowledge, but it does not necessarily predict TPACK. An experienced instructor may be apprehensive to use technology in the classroom and, as a result, would not seek information or knowledge on how to best integrate technology in the classroom. Therefore, we focus on an educator's experience with technology. Teachers who have taken online courses or have been exposed to online teaching may be more apt to learn about ways to integrate technology. Also, the more experience educators have with technology, the more interested in and comfortable they may be with integrating technology. Indeed, some studies have found that teaching experience affects the extent to which instructors use technology (Mumtaz, 2000).

Proposition 2. Experience with technology will predict TPACK, such that instructors with a greater amount of experience using technology will be more likely to acquire TPACK.

Training

The extent to which educators are trained to use technology in their subject matter may also impact their TPACK. Traditional training tends to be technocentric, where the training is focused on learning how to use tools or develop skills, despite findings indicating that proficiency with technological tools does not influence educators' daily practices (Becker, 1994; Hadley & Sheingold, 1993; Schrum, 2005). Proficiency with technology is only one piece of the puzzle; educators often do not learn the skills in the context they need and may not perceive the usefulness of the tool in the classroom (McKenzie, 2000). While educators may be able to apply what they learn in one context to another, training needs to be content centric to show teachers how tools meet learning goals (Harris, 2008; Harris et al., 2009; Niess, 2005). Indeed, empirical studies have found that professional development programs generally increase educators' TPACK (e.g., Doering, Veletsianos, Scharber, & Miller, 2009; Graham et al., 2009; Guzey & Roehrig, 2009; Jimoyiannis, 2010; Richardson, 2009; Shin, Koehler, Mishra, Schmidt, Baran, & Thompson, 2009; Wilson & Wright, 2010).

Proposition 3. Training will predict TPACK such that educators who have been trained to use content-centric technology in their subject matter will acquire more TPACK.

Attitudes

Teachers' attitudes toward technology use (i.e., benefit of technology and effort associated with integrating technology) may impact the amount of TPACK that educators have acquired. First, educators who perceive that technology will positively impact student outcomes (e.g., learning, motivation) should be more likely to develop their TPACK. Cedillo and Kieran (2003) found that teachers who perceived little benefit of using technology for student learning were less likely to incorporate technology in the classroom. Studies have also found that instructors are more likely to use technology when they believe that it will increase students' motivation and enjoyment (Forgasz, 2006; Mumtaz, 2000). Second, educators who perceive that integrating technology is cumbersome will be less likely to develop their TPACK. A common perception exists that integrating technology requires more preparation time and in-class time (Coffland & Strickland, 2004). Instructors may not be inclined to develop their TPACK if it requires a substantial amount of additional work without the perception of added benefits. Using the technology with little effort is consistent with the "perceived ease of use" attitude in the TAM (Davis et al., 1989). Educators may also be unwilling to develop their TPACK due to their high anxiety toward technology or lack of interest (Duhaney, 2001).

Proposition 4. Attitudes will predict TPACK such that educators with more positive attitudes related to using technology will acquire more TPACK.

IMPACT OF TPACK ON TECHNOLOGY USE

We suggest that the outcomes of TPACK are mediated by the use of technology. Acquiring more TPACK or knowing how to use technology to deliver content using different pedagogical strategies directly affects the extent to which technology is used. Accordingly, increased technology use is positively associated with key educator and student outcomes. There are a number of different stakeholders in this process, and we identify the primary stakeholders as educators, students, administrators, and instructional designers. Although the chapter focuses specifically on teachers' TPACK, we propose that other stakeholders in higher education use technology and as a result need TPACK. We argue that higher levels of TPACK leads to greater technology use among these four critical groups for the following reasons. First, educators are more likely to integrate technology in the classroom when they have developed higher amounts of TPACK since they better understand how to harness the benefits of technology as a teaching tool. Conversely, when TPACK is low, educators are less likely to use technology or the level of technology use will be low due to the lack of knowledge necessary to implement technology. Similarly, students are more apt to use technology when educators' TPACK is high because they will be more likely to encounter technology-enhanced and/or technology-enabled assignments, projects, readings, and classroom activities. In a related vein, student teachers who are learning about technology need to develop their TPACK in order to use it appropriately in the future.

Instructional designers will utilize TPACK to help assist educators with setting up their courses. Instructional designers help educators first think about course objectives and how they align upward with higher level department or programmatic objectives, and downward with course modules. They then help instructors think through the proper balance of resources, activities and assessments, with an eye toward promoting engagement to achieve the benefits of constructivism. They may also introduce technology not as an end in itself but as a strategic lever to deliver content more effectively or engage students in the learning process.

Administrators also need some TPACK to use technology. Administrators must have basic awareness of usage patterns and effectiveness of instructional technology so that they can decide whether to invest resources in a time of limited budgets. They must also consider issues such as of information security, privacy, and the technology infrastructure (e.g., wireless access) to make technology use safe and possible. These decisions are especially critical in an era of cloud computing, mobile technology, and social media – all of which give the end user greater choices and flexibility in how they use technology in their daily lives. Today's students armed with laptops, tablets, and smartphones expect to be able to use their devices to access student records, surf the web anywhere, read textbooks, and even turn in assignments – meaning devices must be supported on campus and their learning management systems.

All of these examples illustrate how higher levels of TPACK foster greater use of technology use among these four key stakeholder groups. Active use of technology enables the potential inherent in TPACK to be realized in the classroom.

Proposition 5. The use of technology will mediate the relationship between TPACK and the outcomes of TPACK.

OUTCOMES OF TPACK

Once technology is integrated into the classroom, there are a number of potential positive outcomes for students, educators, and institutions. It is important to evaluate the extent to which TPACK and subsequent technology use influence valued outcomes including student learning and engagement, educator satisfaction and resources, and institutional benefits, especially in an era of accountability driven by scrutiny about the value of higher education in a budget-constrained economy.

Student Satisfaction and Engagement

We focus first on significant outcomes for students. Because students tend to live digitally, they expect that technology use in their academic lives parallels that of their personal lives with the integration of technology such as the Internet and social networking, but currently there is often a disconnect between the way that students live and the way in which they learn (Blackboard, 2008). However, when technology is integrated in students' academic lives, they may become more engaged with the material in such a way that they exhibit a greater willingness or motivation to learn, participate more in the learning process, and develop higher order skills such as critical thinking, as well as a more positive attitude toward learning. Increased student engagement may also be reflected by an increased desire from students to work hard and fully participate albeit online or in the classroom. Students may also experience increased satisfaction with learning the subject matter because technology is harnessed in new ways to deliver content using different methods of teaching. A meta-analysis found some indication that overall attitude outcomes that include satisfaction were slightly higher in traditional classrooms, although the effect size was small but significant (Bernard et al., 2004). Conversely, students may also experience an increased workload, reduced face-to-face time, and technology problems with technology-enhanced learning. In that case, they may be less satisfied with using technology in the classroom. Indeed, Haytko (2001) found that students were less satisfied with hybrid courses than those taught in a traditional manner.

Although there are some mixed reports of student satisfaction (e.g., Haytko, 2001; Sole & Lindquist, 2001), student satisfaction with technology-enhanced learning may depend primarily on the amount of TPACK that educators have acquired (Baldwin, Johnson, & Hill, 1994), as well as the extent to which students interact and communicate with educators (Sole & Lindquist, 2001). As a result, increased student engagement and satisfaction may result when instructors with the necessary knowledge integrate technology effectively in the classroom.

Proposition 6. Technology use will mediate the relationship between TPACK and student satisfaction and engagement; instructors with higher levels of TPACK will utilize technology in such way that students will be more motivated to perform and enjoy the class to a greater extent than in classrooms where technology is used by low TPACK instructors.

Student Learning and Performance

Technology use can also lead to increased student performance for a number of reasons. First, integrating technology into the classroom can tap into different learning styles. Students also go beyond rote memorization and foster new ways to apply the concepts that they learn. Technology has been found to improve student learning when it is aligned with the course objectives and fully integrated in the course (Turney, Robinson, Lee, & Soutar, 2009). Learning takes place anywhere and anytime especially when students use portable devices to read textbooks, turn in assignments, and access course content. Indeed, some studies show that students perceive that they learn more through technology-enhanced learning in the classroom but that technology is still not a substitute for good teaching (Draude & Brace, 1999). Using technology that involves a social aspect can help to develop important teamwork and collaboration learning (Kenny, 2002; Thiele, Allen, & Stucky, 1999). For example, new digital textbooks that allow for social sharing of notes can increase the enjoyment around studying and facilitate sharing of information and experiences. Students can also be inspired to be more creative, especially with student-generated content such as wikis. Using this and other technologies such as podcasting can empower students to creatively demonstrate their understanding and express themselves (Swan & Hofer, 2011). Notably, TPACK is required for effective and appropriate use of these technology tools. It is possible that without TPACK, greater technology use can lead to student frustration and resentment because technology does not fit the content or pedagogical style of the educator. Educators that use technology without having TPACK are more likely than their counterparts to use it in an effective manner because they do not grasp how to best integrate technology while taking into consideration pedagogy and content.

Proposition 7. Technology use will mediate the relationship between TPACK and student learning and performance such that at higher levels of TPACK, greater technology use leads to higher student learning and performance; at lower levels of TPACK, greater technology may lead to little or no improvement in student learning and performance.

Educator Satisfaction and Flexibility

While many educators cite positive outcomes for students (e.g., achievement) as a benefit to integrating technology into the classroom (Hadley & Sheingold, 1993), there may be several positive outcomes for educators as well. Most studies on educator satisfaction have focused on how satisfied educators are with professional development workshops that are designed to increase their TPACK (e.g., Pierson & Borthwick, 2010; Trautmann & MaKinster, 2010); studies from a related literature on technology-enhanced learning and educator satisfaction suggest that the introduction of technology in the classroom is positively related to educator morale and overall satisfaction (e.g., Baylor & Ritchie, 2002; Bloom & Hough, 2003).

Instructors can now incorporate their own research or other creative ideas into the classroom through digital textbooks they can create or modify themselves, or by creating their own instructional videos that provide personalized and tailored course content. The use of technology in the classroom can also free up valuable classroom time to focus on other activities. For example, educators can record their lectures using technology such as lecture capture and use classroom time to facilitate more interaction and hands-on learning with their students. Technology-enhanced learning may also enable more time for educators to heed attention to the needs of individual students. Instructors who adopt and use learner analytics, for example, can track student progress almost real-time and determine the immediate effectiveness of chosen activities and technologies, making it possible to tweak course design or intervene to assist students who are falling behind before it is too late.

Proposition 8. Technology use will mediate the TPACK–educator outcomes relationship such that instructors high in TPACK, compared to those low on TPACK, will be more likely to use technology in ways that will reach their student population more efficiently and effectively.

Institutional Benefits

Not to be overlooked are the benefits to institutions. Using technology such as hybrid or online learning can enable institutions to serve a great number of students, in part, because more physical resources (e.g., classrooms) are available. They can also reach additional numbers of students and help them to achieve their educational goals more effectively by enabling them to take hybrid or online classes that students would never be able to access in the traditional face-to-face manner, either because the classes are full or because of schedule constraints. Ultimately, becoming more student-oriented will increase institutional competitiveness. Institutional prestige can also increase when "star" faculty create open content or other teaching materials and make them available to the public, creating goodwill and an enhanced reputation.

Proposition 9. Technology use will mediate the TPACK–institutional benefits relationship such that instructors high in TPACK will use technology in ways that will enable institutions to serve a greater number of students.

BOUNDARY CONDITIONS OF THE TPACK–TECHNOLOGY USE RELATIONSHIP

Successful technological integration is also influenced by factors situated within an educational context. The environment needs to be conducive for the implementation of technology. Often assumptions are made that TPACK will influence technology use and classroom outcomes (e.g., greater student engagement), but environmental factors may influence the role of TPACK on technology use and classroom outcomes. Although educators may have the necessary knowledge and motivation needed to integrate classroom technology, if environmental constraints (e.g., lack of resources) exist, the integration of technology will not be successful. Some environmental factors found to impact technology use include lack of on-site support for teachers using technology, lack of technology availability, lack of time required to successfully integrate technology, and lack of financial support (Bauer & Kenton, 2005; Mumtaz, 2000; Watson, 2006). In the proposed model, we integrate this research and focus on the following environmental factors: (a) organizational culture, (b) organizational and personal resources, and (c) student factors.

Organizational Culture

The organizational culture will likely impact the extent to which instructors use technology in the classroom. Organizational cultures in part reflect the extent to which organizations, including other educators and management, value technology; we will refer to this as the technology culture. The technology culture can vary from one that values technology (i.e., encourages, supports, and creates norms around technology use) to one that does not value technology (i.e., does not support or facilitate technology use, discourages educators to use technology). The culture that surrounds educators to some extent drives their behavior. On one hand, teachers who have high levels of TPACK in an organizational culture that does not encourage, value, or reward technology will be unlikely to integrate technology within the classroom because it is frowned upon by their colleagues/supervisor (i.e., low technology culture). On the other hand, these technology-savvy educators will flourish in an environment that is supportive of technology use (i.e., high-technology culture). In line with this logic, studies have found that teachers are more likely to use technology when there is an expectation of technology use (Dexter & Riedel, 2003;

Kelly, 2008). Additionally, an environment with committed leaders that support faculty, lead by example, and use teacher evaluation instruments to extend technology use is likely to increase the relationship between TPACK and technology use (Byrom & Bingham, 2001; Duhaney 2001; Krueger, Hansen, & Smaldino, 2000; Wachira & Keengwe, 2011).

Proposition 10. Organizational culture will influence the relationship between TPACK and technology use such that TPACK will be less likely to result in technology use if the organizational culture is not supportive of it.

Organizational and Personal Resources

Another important environmental factor that will influence whether TPACK results in technology use is the availability of resources (e.g., technology, time, money). Without the needed resources, even motivated and high TPACK educators are unable to use technology. Resources needed to implement and use technology include equipment (e.g., availability of in-class technology, availability to students), time needed to integrate and implement technology, and the user-friendliness of technology. All these factors have been linked to use of technology within the classroom (e.g., Bauer & Kenton, 2005; Becker, 1994; Hadley & Sheingold, 1993; Zhao, Pugh, Sheldon, & Byers, 2002). For example, access to technical support and the number of Internet accessible computers in the classroom have been found to impact technology use (Watson, 2006). If a certain technology is not easily accessible to both students and instructors at the organizational level, then teachers will refrain from incorporating that technology in the classroom. Moreover, educators who lack personal resources such as time to learn how to use technology and incorporate it into their curriculum are less likely to adopt technology (Bauer & Kenton, 2005).

Proposition 11. Resources will influence the relationship between TPACK and technology use such that TPACK will be less likely to result in technology use if organizational resources needed to implement technology are not present.

Student Factors

Student characteristics are another external factor that may impact the TPACK–technology implementation relationship. Two important student factors that we discuss are student needs and learning styles, as well as demographic characteristics of the student body. An instructor high in TPACK will be able to discern whether the students will benefit from technology use. If an instructor perceives that students' needs and learning styles are not compatible with a particular classroom technology, a high-TPACK instructor will choose not to implement the technology. Students' needs and learning styles that instructors may consider include students' access to technology resources (e.g., mobile devices) and student comfort level with using technology (e.g., comfort studying from e-texts; Ahmedani, Harold, Fitton, & Gibson, 2011). Also, student demographics, such as age, may also play a role in whether technology is implemented. Although a high TPACK instructor may have found that a particular technology is effective in delivering the content, the age of the students may influence their openness to the technology. Some studies suggest that "digital natives," individuals born after 1982, are more familiar on average with using technology when compared to "digital immigrants," individuals born before 1982 who did not grow up surrounded by technology (Prensky, 2001). Although there is debate in the literature surrounding the terminology "digital natives" and "digital immigrants" and the assumptions that scholars make about these groups (e.g., Bennett, Maton, & Kervin, 2008; Jones & Shao, 2011), it remains a worthwhile endeavor to examine the potential impact of student demographics such as age on the TPACK–technology implementation relationship.

Proposition 12. Student factors will influence the relationship between TPACK and technology use such that TPACK will lead to lower technology use when it does not meet students' needs or demographic factors.

IMPLICATIONS

This chapter builds on the existing literature on the necessary knowledge to integrate content, pedagogy, and technology (TPACK) in the classroom. Our proposed theoretical model is an important first step to considering the precursors and outcomes of TPACK. We provide a comprehensive model that outlines the factors that lead to the development of TPACK, the relationship between TPACK and the use of technology, and outcomes gleaned from technology-enhanced learning. We extend the TPACK framework by identifying predictors of TPACK such as educators' attitudes and self-efficacy and outcomes for students, educators, and institutions such as satisfaction and engagement. We argue that the extent to which educators develop their TPACK and use technology is bound by contextual factors such as organizational culture, resources, and student characteristics. Without considering the extensions that we have identified in the Technology Integration Model, the linkages between TPACK and desirable outcomes are unclear. As a result, educators and institutions may not realize positive outcomes from investments in educational technology until all factors that can potentially explain variation in the outcome measures of choice can be documented and measured, and relationships between them determined.

There are several important contributions of our proposed model. First, prior research on TPACK has identified that contextual factors such as available resources are important, but has not clearly elaborated on how context impacts the development and use of TPACK. We outline various ways in which the environment influences the degree to which educators develop their TPACK and factors that enhance or diminish the opportunities for educators to use their TPACK and incorporate technology-enhanced learning in the classroom.

Second, most studies focus on the effectiveness of professional development of K-12 educators, or in other words, how to train educators to increase their TPACK, with a limited amount of research on other predictors and outcomes of TPACK. Our proposed model provides a more generalizable and comprehensive portrayal of how technology is integrated into the classroom and the outcomes of this technology-enhanced learning. Because we have integrated the existing literature on TPACK, as well as other areas of research, we shed light on the host of factors that can lead to the development and use of TPACK.

In addition to building on the nomological network of TPACK, our model has implications for educators, students, and institutions. While change is constant and organizations continue to evolve, the technologies now becoming available appear to be accelerating the pace of change in higher education through their "disruptive" potential. Educational technologies can now extend the classroom beyond traditional walls, reaching untapped scores of students and enabling them to access learning environments 24/7. Institutions that fail to adopt technology run the risk of losing market share and eventually becoming obsolete. However, this progress depends on successful implementation of TPACK, which as this analysis suggests also requires careful consideration of contextual variables to make sure they are favorable. Institutions considering initiatives aligned with TPACK may therefore wish to conduct contextual analyses before directing resources toward educational technologies to make sure they will have the chance to reach their potential.

Given the wide-ranging impact of TPACK on the technology-education nexus, as shown by the model presented here, the needs and potential contributions of each of the four key stakeholder groups identified here – educators, administrators, students, and instructional designers – should be addressed in initiatives to integrate technology in the classroom. Accordingly, administrators should be willing to view resources allocated to this purpose as long-range investments rather than short-term expenses. Instructors require appropriate resources (e.g., time, training, support) and training (e.g., self-efficacy, experience with technology) to use TPACK; these resources ideally should also include access to the expertise available from instructional designers. In creating an environment that is supportive of technology use (i.e., high technology culture), administrators might also develop systems of compensation and promotion that reward the successful implementation of technology in the classroom. Although the proportion of students who are digital natives is steadily increasing, students still require access to continuous and easily accessible technological support to ensure their seamless interfacing with innovative new pedagogical technologies. The comprehensive view provided by this model offers one pathway for moving away from ad hoc, piecemeal efforts by a few individuals in favor of systematic institution-wide adoptions.

FUTURE RESEARCH DIRECTIONS

This chapter has depicted the predictors and outcomes of TPACK, as well as boundary conditions that impact technology use in the classroom. We suggest several avenues for future research. It is useful to empirically test the proposed model in the context of higher education using the propositions that we have developed. Although the model was developed specifically for higher education, it may also be generalizable to other domains such as K-12 classrooms. Thus, it is important for future research to empirically test our proposed model in different contexts (e.g., organizations, curriculum). More research is also needed on the individual factors that lead to the development of TPACK. While we focused on four factors that, to some extent, have been studied in the literature, there is a wide range of individual predictors that may be instrumental in developing educators' TPACK. For instance, there may be certain personality characteristics (e.g., resistance to change, openness to experience) that may affect the extent to which educators acquire TPACK. We suggest that future research also consider how TPACK is developed and used among other key stakeholders such as students, instructional designers, and administrators. Although the chapter focused mainly on educators' TPACK, it stands to reason that TPACK is required among these other critical groups.

CONCLUSION

We can draw several important conclusions from this chapter. First, our proposed model is important in that it helps avoid a "silo" approach to implementing technology by providing a comprehensive approach to understanding TPACK. Second, organizations need to be adaptive in any evaluation because technology will keep changing. Organizations and researchers alike should continuously examine existing models to determine their relevancy given a specific technology and population. Finally, we also need to balance the risk of implementing TPACK without a complete understanding of contextual variables with the expectation that innovation requires failures before reaching success. As this balance can be tricky, it is useful to enlist the participation of those at the respected frontline – faculty.

REFERENCES

Ahmedani, B. K., Harold, R. D., Fitton, V. A., & Gibson, E. D. S. (2011). What adolescents can tell us: Technology and the future of social work education. *Social Work Education: The International Journal*, *30*(7), 830–846.

An, Y., & Reigeluth, C. (2011). Creating technology-enhanced, learner-centered classrooms: K-12 teachers' beliefs, perceptions, barriers, and support needs. *Journal of Digital Learning in Teacher Education*, *28*(2), 54–62.

Angeli, C., & Valanides, N. (2009). Epistemological and methodological issues for the conceptualization, development, and assessment of ICT–TPCK: Advances in technological pedagogical content knowledge (TPCK). *Computers & Education*, *52*(1), 154–168.

Archambault, L. M., & Barnett, J. H. (2010). Revisiting technological pedagogical content knowledge: Exploring the TPACK framework. *Computers & Education*, *55*(4), 1656–1662.

Baldwin, D., Johnson, J., & Hill, P. (1994). Student satisfaction with classroom use of computer-assisted instruction. *Nursing Outlook*, *42*(4), 188–192.

Bandura, A. (1995). *Multifaceted scale of mechanisms of moral disengagement*. Stanford, CA: Stanford University.

Bauer, J., & Kenton, J. (2005). Toward technology integration in the schools: Why it isn't happening. *Journal of Technology and Teacher Education*, *13*(4), 519–546.

Baylor, A. L., & Ritchie, D. (2002). What factors facilitate teacher skill, teacher morale, and perceived student learning in technology-using classrooms? *Computers & Education, 39*(4), 395–414.

Becker, H. J. (1994). How exemplary computer-using teachers differ from other teachers: Implications for realizing the potential of computers in schools. *Journal of Research on Computing in Education, 26*(3), 291–321.

Bennett, S., Maton, K., & Kervin, L. (2008). The 'digital natives' debate: A critical review of the evidence. *British Journal of Educational Technology, 39*(5), 775–786.

Bernard, R. M., Abrami, P. C., Lou, Y., Borokhovski, E., Wade, A., Wozney, L., ... Huang, B. (2004). How does distance education compare with classroom instruction? A meta-analysis of the empirical literature. *Review of Educational Research, 74*(3), 379–439.

Blackboard. (2008). *Teaching in the 21st century: A review of the issues and changing models in the teaching profession.* Washington, DC: Blackboard.

Bloom, K. C., & Hough, M. C. (2003). Student satisfaction with technology-enhanced learning. *CIN: Computers, Informatics, Nursing, 21*(5), 241–246.

Burton, J. P., Bamberry, N-J., & Harris-Boundy, J. (2005). Developing personal teaching efficacy in new teachers in university settings. *Academy of Management Learning & Education, 4*(2), 160–173.

Byrom, E., & Bingham, M. (2001). *Factors influencing the effective use of technology for teaching and learning: Lessons learned from the SEIR-TEC intensive site schools* (2nd ed.). Durham, NC: Communications and Publications Department at Serve.

Cedillo, T., & Kieran, C. (2003). Initiating students into algebra with symbol-manipulating calculators. In J. T. Fey, A. Cuoco, C. Kieran, L. McMullin & R. M. Zbiek (Eds.), *Computer algebra systems in secondary school mathematics education* (pp. 219–240). Reston: NCTM.

Chai, C. S., Koh, J. H. L., & Tsai, C. C. (2010). Facilitating preservice teachers' development of technological, pedagogical, and content knowledge (TPACK). *Educational Technology & Society, 13*(4), 63–73.

Chai, C. S., Koh, J. H. L., & Tsai, C-C. (2011). Exploring the factor structure of the constructs of technological, pedagogical, content knowledge (TPACK). *Asia-Pacific Education Researcher, 20*(3), 595–603.

Coffland, D., & Strickland, A. (2004). Factors related to teacher use of technology in secondary geometry instruction. *Journal of Computers in Mathematics and Science Teaching, 2*(4), 347–365.

Conole, G., & Oliver, M. (1998). A pedagogical framework for embedding C & IT into the curriculum. *Association for Learning Technology Journal, 6*(2), 4–16.

Cox, S., & Graham, C. R. (2009). Diagramming TPACK in practice: Using and elaborated model of the TPACK framework to analyze and depict teacher knowledge. *TechTrends, 53*(5), 60–69.

Cuseo, J. (2007). The empirical case against large class size: Adverse effects on the teaching, learning, and retention of first-year students. *Journal of Faculty Development, 21*(1), 5–21.

Davis, F. D., Bagozzi, R. P., & Warshaw, P. R. (1989). User acceptance of computer technology: A comparison of two theoretical models. *Management Science, 35*(8), 982–1003.

Dexter, S., & Riedel, E. (2003). Why improving preservice teacher educational technology preparation must go beyond the college walls. *Journal of Teacher Education, 54*(4), 334–346.

Doering, A., Hughes, J., & Huffman, D. (2003). Preservice teachers: Are we thinking with technology. *Journal of Research on Technology in Education*, *35*(3), 342–361.

Doering, A., Veletsianos, G., Scharber, C., & Miller, C. (2009). Using the technological, pedagogical, and content knowledge framework to design online learning environments and professional development. *Journal of Educational Computing Research*, *41*(3), 319–346.

Dong, C., & Sun, L. (2007). A model of faculty development for technology integration and its application in course design. In R. Carlsen, K. McFerrin, J. Price, R. Weber, & D. A. Willis (Eds.), *Proceedings of society for information technology and teacher education international conference 2007*, AACE, Chesapeake, VA.

Dooley, K. E. (1999). Towards a holistic model for the diffusion of educational technologies: An integrative review of educational innovation studies. *Educational Technology & Society*, *2*(4), 1–12.

Draude, B., & Brace, S. (1999). Assessing the impact of technology on teaching and learning: Student perspectives. In *Proceedings of the mid-south instructional technology conference*, March 28–30, Murfreesboro, TN.

Duffy, T. M., & Jonassen, D. H. (1992). *Constructivism and the technology of instruction*. Hillsdale, NJ: Lawrence Erlbaum Associates.

Duhaney, D. C. (2001). Teacher education: Preparing teachers to integrate technology. *International Journal of Instructional Media*, *28*(1), 23–30.

Forgasz, H. (2006). Factors that encourage or inhibit computer use for secondary mathematics teaching. *Journal of Computers in Mathematics and Science Teaching*, *25*(1), 77–93.

Ghaith, G. G., & Yaghi, H. H. (1997). Relationships among experience, teacher efficacy, and attitudes toward the implementation of instructional innovation. *Teaching and Teacher Education*, *13*(4), 451–458.

Graham, R. C., Burgoyne, N., Cantrell, P., Smith, L., St. Clair, L., & Harris, R. (2009). Measuring the TPCK confidence of inservice science teachers. *TechTrends*, *53*(5), 70–79.

Guskey, T. R. (1988). Teacher efficacy, self-concept, and attitudes toward the implementation of instructional innovation. *Teaching and Teacher Education*, *4*(1), 63–69.

Guzey, S. S., & Roehrig, G. H. (2009). Teaching science with technology: Case studies of science teachers' development of technology, pedagogy, and content knowledge. *Contemporary Issues in Technology and Teacher Education*, *9*(1), 25–45.

Hadley, M., & Sheingold, K. (1993). Commonalities and distinctive patterns in teachers' integration of computers. *American Journal of Education*, *101*(3), 261–315.

Harris, J. B. (2008). TPACK in inservice education: Assisting experienced teachers' planned improvisations. In AACTE Committee on Innovation & Technology (Ed.), *Handbook of technological pedagogical content knowledge for educators* (pp. 251–271). New York, NY: Routledge.

Harris, J., Mishra, P., & Koehler, M. (2009). Teachers' technological pedagogical content knowledge and learning activity types: Curriculum-based technology integration reframed. *Journal of Research on Technology in Education*, *41*(4), 393–416.

Haytko, D. I. (2001). Traditional versus hybrid course delivery systems: A case study of undergraduate marketing planning courses. *Marketing Education Review*, *11*(3), 27–39.

Hughes, J. (2005). The role of teacher knowledge and learning experiences in forming technology-integrated pedagogy. *Journal of Technology and Teacher Education*, *13*(2), 227–302.

Jimoyiannis, A. (2010). Designing and implementing an integrated technological pedagogical science knowledge framework for science teachers professional development. *Computers & Education*, *55*(3), 1259–1269.

Jones, C., & Shao, B. (2011). *The net generation and digital natives: Implications for higher education*. York, UK: Higher Education Academy.

Kelly, M. (2008). Incorporating context into TPCK-based instructional design. In K. McFerrin, R. Weber, R. Carlsen & D. A. Willis (Eds.), *Proceedings of society for information technology and teacher education international conference 2008*, AACE, Chesapeake, VA (pp. 5257–5262).

Kenny, A. (2002). Online learning: Enhancing nurse education? *Journal of Advanced Nursing*, *38*(2), 127–135.

Koehler, M. J., & Mishra, P. (2005). What happens when teachers design educational technology? The development of technological pedagogical content knowledge. *Journal of Educational Computing Research*, *32*(2), 131–152.

Koehler, M. J., & Mishra, P. (2008). Introducing TPCK. In AACTE Committee on Innovation and Technology (Ed.), *Handbook of technological pedagogical content knowledge (TPCK) for educators* (pp. 3–29). New York, NY: Routledge.

Koehler, M. J., & Mishra, P. (2009). What is technological pedagogical content knowledge? *Contemporary Issues in Technology and Teacher Education*, *9*(1), 60–70.

Koh, J. H. L., Chai, C. S., & Tsai, C. C. (2010). Examining the technological pedagogical content knowledge of Singapore preservice teachers with a large-scale survey. *Journal of Computer Assisted Learning*, *26*(6), 563–573.

Koh, J. L., & Frick, T. W. (2009). Instructor and student classroom interactions during technology skills instruction for facilitating preservice teachers' computer self-efficacy. *Journal of Educational Computing Research*, *40*(2), 211–228.

Krueger, K., Hansen, L., & Smaldino, S. E. (2000). Preservice teacher technology competencies. *TechTrends*, *44*(3), 47–50.

Laird, T. F. N., & Kuh, G. D. (2005). Student experiences with information technology and their relationship to other aspects of student engagement. *Research in Higher Education*, *46*(2), 211–233.

Lee, M. H., & Tsai, C-C. (2010). Exploring teachers' perceived self efficacy and technological pedagogical content knowledge with respect to educational use of the World Wide Web. *Instructional Science*, *38*(1), 1–21.

Marino, M. T., Sameshima, P., & Beecher, C. C. (2009). Enhancing TPACK with assistive technology: Promoting inclusive practices in preservice teacher education. *Contemporary Issues in Technology and Teacher Education*, *9*(2), 186–207.

McKenzie, J. (2000). *How teachers learn technology best*. Bellingham, WA: FNO Press.

Mishra, P., & Koehler, M. J. (2006). Technological pedagogical content knowledge: A framework for integrating technology in teachers' knowledge. *Teachers College Record*, *108*(6), 1017–1054.

Mumtaz, S. (2000). Factors affecting teachers' use of information and communications technology: A review of the literature. *Journal of Information Techology for Teacher Education*, *9*(3), 319–342.

Niess, M. L. (2005). Preparing teachers to teach science and mathematics with technology: Developing a technology pedagogical content knowledge. *Teaching and Teacher Education*, *21*(5), 509–523.

Norman, D. A. (1993). *Things that make us smart: Defending human attributes in the age of the machine*. Reading, MA: Addison-Wesley.

Peruski, L., Mishra, P., & Koehler, M. J. (2007). Developing technological pedagogical content knowledge (TPCK) through teaching online. In R. Carlsen, K. McFerrin, J. Price, R. Weber & D. A. Willis (Eds.), *Proceedings of society for information technology and teacher education international conference 2007*, AACE, Chesapeake, VA.

Pierson, M., & Borthwick, A. (2010). Framing the assessment of educational technology professional development in a culture of learning. *Journal of Digital Learning in Teacher Education, 26*(4), 126–131.

Prensky, M. (2001). Digital natives, digital immigrants. Part 1. *On the Horizon, 9*(5), 1–6.

Richardson, S. (2009). Mathematics teachers' development, exploration, and advancement of technological pedagogical content knowledge in the teaching and learning of algebra. *Contemporary Issues in Technology and Teacher Education, 9*(2), 117–130.

Rogers, E. M. (1995). *Diffusion of Innovations* (4th ed.). New York, NY: The Free Press.

Rossy, G. L., Rubino, C., Wilkin, C. L., Shelton, L. M., & Zell, D. (2012). *Achieving the best of all worlds through hybrid course design and open content textbooks*. Panelist for California State University, Northridge Faculty Retreat. Northridge, CA.

Russell, M., Bebell, D., O'Dwyer, L., & O'Connor, K. (2003). Examining teacher technology use: Implications for preservice and inservice teacher preparation. *Journal of Teacher Education, 54*(4), 297–310.

Sachau, L., & Ku, H. Y. (2012). Mathematics instructors' experiences stabilizing TPACK when using new technologies in a distance-based graduate program. In P. Resta (Ed.), *Proceedings of Society for Information Technology & Teacher Education international conference 2012* (pp. 841–843). Chesapeake, VA: AACE.

Schmidt, D. A., Baran, E., Thompson, A. D., Mishra, P., Koehler, M. J., & Shin, T. S. (2009). Technological pedagogical content knowledge (TPACK): The development and validation of an assessment instrument for preservice teachers. *Journal of Research on Technology in Education, 42*(2), 123–149.

Schrum, L. (2005). A proactive approach to a research agenda for educational technology. *Journal of Research on Technology in Education, 37*(3), 217–220.

Shin, T. S., Koehler, M. J., Mishra, P., Schmidt, D. A., Baran, E., & Thompson, A. D. (2009). Changing technological pedagogical content knowledge (TPACK) through course experiences. In I. Gibson, R. Weber, K. McFerrin, R. Carlsen & D. A. Willis (Eds.), *Society for Information Technology and Teacher Education international conference book 2009* (pp. 4152–4156). Chesapeake, VA: Association for the Advancement of Computing in Education (AACE).

Shulman, L. S. (1986). Those who understand: Knowledge growth in teaching. *Educational Researcher, 15*(2), 4–14.

Sole, M. L., & Lindquist, M. (2001). Enhancing traditional, televised, and videotaped courses with Web-based technologies: A comparison of student satisfaction. *Nursing Outlook, 49*(3), 132–137.

Sun, L., & Deng, L. (2007). Online community of practice for in-service faculty development of technological pedagogical content knowledge (TPCK). In R. Carlsen, K. McFerrin, J. Price, R. Weber & D. A. Willis (Eds.), *Proceedings of society for information technology and teacher education international conference 2007*, AACE, Chesapeake, VA.

Swan, K., & Hofer, M. (2011). In search of technological pedagogical content knowledge: Teachers' initial foray into podcasting in economics. *Journal of Research on Technology in Education, 44*(1), 75–98.

Thiele, J. E., Allen, C., & Stucky, M. (1999). Effects of web-based instruction on learning behaviors of undergraduate and graduate students. *Nursing and Health Care Perspectives, 20*(4), 199–203.

Trautmann, N. M., & MaKinster, J. G. (2010). Flexibly adaptive professional development in support of teaching science with geospatial technology. *Journal of Science Teacher Education, 21*(3), 351–370.

Turney, C. S. M., Robinson, D., Lee, M., & Soutar, A. (2009). Using technology to direct learning in higher education: The way forward? *Active Learning in Higher Education, 10*(1), 71–83.

Vannatta, R. A., & Fordham, N. (2004). Teacher dispositions as predictors of classroom technology use. *Journal of Research on Technology in Education, 36*(3), 253–271.

Venkatesh, V., & Davis, F. D. (2000). The theoretical extension of the technology acceptance model: Four longitudinal field studies. *Management Science, 46*(2), 186–204.

Venkatesh, V., Morris, M. G., Davis, G. B., & Davis, F. D. (2003). User acceptance of information technology: Toward a unified view. *MIS Quarterly, 27*(3), 425–478.

Voogt, J., Fisser, P., Roblin, N. P., Tondeur, J., & van Braak, J. (in press). Technological pedagogical content knowledge – A review of the literature. *Journal of Computer Assisted Learning*.

Wachira, P., & Keengwe, J. (2011). Technology integration barriers: Urban school mathematics teachers perspectives. *Journal of Science Education & Technology, 20*(1), 17–25.

Watson, G. (2006). Factors affecting teacher classroom internet use. In C. Crawford, R. Carlsen, K. McFerrin, J. Price, R. Weber & D. A. Willis (Eds.), *Proceedings of society for information technology and teacher education international conference 2006*, AACE, Chesapeake, VA (pp. 1870–1874).

Wetzel, K., Foulger, T. S., & Williams, M. (2009). The evolution of the required educational technology course. *Journal of Computing in Teacher Education, 25*(2), 67–71.

Wilson, E., & Wright, V. (2010). Images over time: The intersection of social studies through technology, content, and pedagogy. *Contemporary Issues in Technology and Teacher Education, 10*(2), 220–233.

Yurdakula, I. K., Odabasia, H. F., Kilicera, K., Coklarb, A. N., Birinci, G., & Kurt, A. A. (2012). The development, validity and reliability of TPACK-deep: A technological pedagogical content knowledge scale. *Computers & Education, 58*, 964–977.

Zhao, Y., Pugh, K., Sheldon, S., & Byers, J. (2002). Conditions for classroom technology innovations. *Teachers College Record, 104*(3), 482–515.

PART II
APPLICATION OF CLASSROOM RESPONSE SYSTEMS AND MEDIATED DISCOURSE TECHNOLOGIES

THE NETWORKED FACULTY AND STUDENT ENGAGEMENT: THE CASE OF MICROBLOGGING TO SUPPORT PARTICIPATION IN A HUMAN RESOURCES MANAGEMENT POSTGRADUATE COURSE

Antonella Esposito

ABSTRACT

This chapter stems from the need to focus on the inherent interplay of faculty and student engagement while studying the impact of social media in higher education teaching and learning. The discussion is specifically concerned with the role and affordances of microblogging in the rethinking of the teacher/student relationship and in blurring the boundaries of academic contexts. The chapter examines an early experimentation of Twitter use to foster and monitor participation by the master students enrolled in a Human Resources Management class in an Italian university.

Increasing Student Engagement and Retention using Classroom Technologies: Classroom Response Systems and Mediated Discourse Technologies
Cutting-edge Technologies in Higher Education, Volume 6E, 109–142

ISSN: 2044-9968/doi:10.1108/S2044-9968(2013)000006E007

The pilot is discussed referring to lessons learned from a range of accounted empirical cases and relevant studies on microblogging for teaching and learning in academia. A special focus addresses both a revised notion of academic scholarship and engagement, prompted by emergent profiles of networked faculty, and debates about the multiple ways of conceptualizing student engagement in the current academic cultures and contexts, being challenged by an increasingly complex digital landscape and by a varied typology of learners coming to university. As conclusion, issues related to the range of alignments to be taken into account when adopting social networking services in a higher education context are suggested as cues for an ongoing discussion.

INTRODUCTION

To what extent and under which conditions can social media be 'game changers' (Oblinger, 2012) in student engagement in higher education? How can we interpret student engagement without the danger of imposing a sort of 'tyranny of participation' (Gourlay, 2011) among increasingly differentiated cohorts of learners? The considered dilemmas are discussed with a particular focus on microblogging as an emerging tool in Web 2.0 learning ecologies (Conole, 2011) and taking cue from an early pilot of Twitter use in a postgraduate class in an Italian university. These initial questions are located in between the opportunity to harness the social web as enabling new modes of knowledge production and dissemination and employability skills (JISC/HEFCE, 2009), and the challenge to question a culturally 'coercive' approach (even if in a benign sense) to social media adoption by both students and teachers. In fact, the same techno-cultural pressures that prompt faculty to embrace new research practices in digital networks (Veletsianos & Kimmons, 2012) play a role in creating a mood for 'moral panic' (Bennett, Maton, & Kervin, 2008) in university teachers coping with new generations of students 'naturally engaged' with the so called 'open, social and participatory media' (Conole, 2011). Indeed, empirically grounded studies report nuanced accounts of faculty's (Brown, 2012; Pearce, 2010) and students' perceptions and uses of technologies (Sharpe, Beetham, & de Freitas, 2010). Moreover, critical approaches caution against the uncritical application of digitally mediated social behaviours and potentialities within educational contexts (Selwyn, 2010).

In this view, this chapter contends that teacher and student engagement should be designed and investigated at the same time in order to highlight the meaning-making practices that lead to the specific use of digital tools and prefigure future, more informed applications in a defined, situated context. To this purpose, this work embeds a notion of ICTs' (Information and Communication Technologies) affordances – rather than as inherent properties of a tool – as co-construction of cultural artefacts (Oliver, 2005) undertaken by participants in an (learning) experience situated in a specific social and historical setting.

Given this perspective, this chapter intends to discuss microblogging service as a potential change agent in teacher and student engagement in higher education, drawing on an empirical case of Twitter use in an Italian university. The examined case constitutes an instance of productive alignement among faculty's propensity towards practices as a 'digital scholar' (Weller, 2011), postgraduate students' motivation to enhance their professional skills, inherent needs of the subject matter and enabling factors provided by the microblogging service.

The propensity of the involved teacher to share his professional activities as a networked scholar with his students leads to interpreting this attitude as aligned with an emerging dimension of scholarship in the social media age. Such a dimension is being defined as 'co-creating learning' by Garnett and Ecclesfield (2011), and involves researchers, students and practitioners in the construction of a 'perpetual Beta' of knowledge.

In addition, considering a critical approach to the notion of 'student engagement' (Gourlay, 2011) suggests the necessity to distinguish meanings and forms of student engagement in increasingly multimodal higher education contexts (Kress, 2003; Kress & van Leeuwen, 2001). Such issues of student engagement are also referred to through the prevalent typology of 'online engagement' (White & Le Cornu, 2011) as a factor that significantly contributes to shape both faculty's and learners' behaviour while interacting in the social web.

The chapter starts presenting a brief overview of issues related to social media in higher education and their celebrated and proven impact on students and teachers and accounts for emerging profiles of networked, participatory faculty, drawn from recent debates. Then it explores the range of meanings that the notion of student engagement implies in higher education and highlights a framework to interpret online engagement. Hence, it examines basic characteristics and affordances of microblogging service as arising from relevant conceptualizations and case studies. Finally, an empirical case of Twitter use in a Human Resources Management class is sketched and discussed in the light of the previously articulated discourse on teacher and student engagement.

SOCIAL MEDIA IN HIGHER EDUCATION

New technologies are challenging 'academic cultures' (Elhers & Schnekenberg, 2010), which are the ways in which we learn, teach and research in universities. In the last decade the idea of the web as a product/environment provided by software developers to users/consumers has blurred towards a concept of the web as 'an artifact evolving according to shifting user engagement' (Brown, 2012, p. 50). While a line of continuity can be identified stemming from systems of computer-mediated communication and collaboration (CMC), social media are seen as changing 'the nature of social interaction, yielding a new pedagogical ecology embedding implications for academia and e-learning' (Dabbagh & Reo, 2010, p. 12). In fact, claims related to behaviours and models of a 'networked student' (Drexler, 2010) mirrors popular illustrations of the 'networked teacher' (Courosa, 2008; 2009), whereas both profiles are seen as sharing the social web environment, enabling 'powerful ideas' (Anderson, 2007) such as architecture of participation, user-generated content, openness and collaboration that as a whole constitute the 'Web 2.0 approach' or 'social web' (Boulos & Wheeler, 2007). This approach is variously seen as enabling the development of the twenty-first century skills (Jenkins, 2007), such as problem-solving, team-working, capacity to filter online information, creativity, leadership, technology proficiency (see also JISC/HEFCE, 2009) and as 'resembling academic world' (Haythornthwaithe, 2009) in its modes of knowledge production and dissemination. The hype on the potentialities of social media for education has been sharply criticized (Selwyn, 2010). One such criticism is that it has being acknowledged that the emphasis put on 'collaborative learning' enabled by social media has often overlooked the key role played by the networked individualism in the use of such tools in academia (Jones & Shao, 2011). From an organizational standpoint, issues have been raised about competing engagement between these emerging tools and well-established technological services provided by higher education institutions both to teaching staff and students.

But who are the actual users of social media in higher education? In the last decade, the popular assumption that new generations coming to university are 'naturally' digitally literate because they have been growing up in a technology-mediated environment has been variously contested and empirically proven to be wrong (see Bullen, 2009–2012). On the contrary, empirical studies have given evidence that the socio-economic, cultural conditions and the family context play a more important role as drivers or inhibitors in adoption of digital tools by young learners (Hargittai, 2010). Moreover, the persistence of the digital divide among university students belonging to a same cohort is widely reported (e.g. Ferri, Cavalli, Mangiatordi, & Scenini, 2010; Fitzgerald et al., 2009, p. 43; Franklin & van Harmelen, 2007, pp. 25, 26; Jones & Cross, 2009; Kennedy et al., 2008; Minocha, 2009). Large-scale studies (LLIDA (Learning Literacies for the Digital Age), 2009) have started to give ample evidence of the variety of spaces, modes and motivations of digital practices undertaken by higher education students across different university contexts. Commenting on the empirical findings of the LLIDA project, Sharpe et al. (2010) stress the importance, against the generational arguments, to locate such diverse kinds of engagement within a developmental framework of digital literacies. The lowest level of this framework is represented by the 'functional access' to technology (featured by the construction of the related 'skills'). The intermediate level is related to 'practices' (featured by the increasing awareness of the tools to be selected for specific learning needs). Finally, the top level is assigned a sense of 'creative appropriation' of technologies in which learners build on the previously acquired skills and practices to develop their own digitally mediated learning environments. In this view, prospective digitally literate students are seen as learners being situated in discipline-grounded knowledge, in which they strive to build conceptual approaches, in combination with tools and tecniques that fit academic practice and professional development (Sharpe et al., 2010). At the same time they need to become well acquainted with the current complex digital landscape and to develop critical thinking about the potentialities and challenges of such evolving ecologies of tools and practices.

Focusing on faculty, the hypothetical gap between teachers and students in their perceptions and uses of ICTs does not appear as a key finding from recent empirical investigations (Jones & Shao, 2011; Waycott, Bennet, Kennedy, Dalgarno, & Gray, 2010). Indeed, the current lack of field research focusing on academic's perception of social media for teaching and learning (Brown, 2012) constitutes a hindrance to overcoming the limitations of the body of knowledge characterized by an 'essentialist' view of social media in education, that is 'a view concerned more with notions of universal best practice than with practice oriented to specificities of context' (2012, p. 51).

Moreover, Crook notices that the integration of social media significantly depends on 'considerable creative involvement from teachers' (2008, p. 35) and that adoption of these technologies may be more related to a propensity of these pioneer-faculty to embrace the 'Web 2.0 approach' rather than to a disposition to experiment with new tools. Within this view, it is worth considering the twofold nature of faculty's work as researchers and teachers and how social media are affecting scholarly practices towards more participatory approaches. Such approaches are likely to create new ties between research and teaching, between teachers and students, and to expand the role and number of the involved stakeholders in the teaching and learning process.

THE NETWORKED FACULTY: 'CO-CREATING' AS A NEW SCHOLARSHIP DIMENSION

In recent years, some discussions about what counts as 'scholarship' for academics in the digital age have been informed by reflections on the disruptive impact of the Web 2.0 approach and related tools on the traditional asset of the scholarly communication practices. Perspectives such as those of the 'open scholar' (Burton, 2009), 'participatory scholar' (Veletsianos, 2010) and a 'digital scholar' as 'digital, networked and open' academic (Weller, 2011) are being proposed both as a consequence of epoch-making environmental transitions and as an intentional project towards a more radical culture of sharing in academia. In these views the underlying assumptions of 'open scholarship' (Anderson, 2009) refer to the abundance of resources and data to be analysed in enquiry work and to complexity of problems to be faced. Both of these issues would require innovative approaches on the part of researchers, such as adopting collaborative forms of research conduct and communication, finding new rules for peer reviewing, data sharing, and modes of academic discourse and reputation and involving new subjects – for example students and non-specialist communities – in the research process.

On the other hand, Garnett and Ecclesfield (2011) focus on the epistemological transition being enabled by the current social media age, which fosters a blurring distinction between knowledge production and knowledge transmission in higher education. They work on a significant conceptual rethinking of Boyer's (1990) popular model of scholarship, articulated in the dimensions of 'discovery' (creation of new knowledge in a specific area), 'integration' (position of the individual discoveries in a wider context), 'application' (engagement with the world beyond university) and 'teaching' (management of all the needed procedures supporting teaching and learning). Garnett and Ecclesfield add the dimension of 'co-creating', which refers to the participation process of both teachers and students (and practitioners) to the 'permanent Beta' (2011, p. 13) of knowledge, to be pursued through a collaborative creation of learning. Indeed, such a new dimension becomes constitutive and informs all the four dimensions in Boyer's model of scholarship: for instance the dimension of 'discovery' – especially focused on enquiry work in the closest meaning – is being reformulated as 'co-creation of research agendas' (2011, p. 14), which in an original way updates the traditional role of the individual researcher and goes beyond Boyer's institution-centric approach to research activities. This position is explicitly inspired by the Open Scholarship movement (Anderson, 2009) and is linked to arguments endorsing a close relationship between 'e-research' (here being used as an alternative term for 'digital scholarship') and 'e-learning' (Borgman, 2006; Haythornwaythe, 2009).

However, these authors acknowledge that such an evolution in scholarship is still 'emergent' and can be better understood within an ecological framework of a 'digital scholarship resilience matrix' (Weller, 2011) in which both conservative motifs and drivers of innovation should be identified at governmental, institutional, disciplinary and individual levels. On the other hand, it can be said that while Boyer (1990) aimed to value teaching in his rethinking of academics' categories of activities, Garnett and Ecclesfield (2011) redesign the conceptualization of scholarship focusing on a value-laden, open and democraticized engagement required of faculty. So, it is apparent that such a revisited form of scholarship aims to a more inclusive research/teaching approach that, when occurring, enables the active involvement of higher education students as co-creators of knowledge.

THE ENTANGLED MEANINGS OF 'STUDENT ENGAGEMENT'

How should we think of student engagement in the digital age? Setting the scene to answer this question implies a close attention to the web of meanings related to the notion of 'student engagement' in higher education. Issues related to student engagement keep on drawing attention in conventional university learning settings, in online learning research (Young & Bruce,

2011) as well as in emergent forms of open education (Downes, 2011). This popular term can be referred either to the time and endeavours devoted by learners to achieve the expected outcomes (Kuh, 2009) such as retention, completion and employability (Zepke & Leach, 2010) or to the strategies planned by higher education institutions in order to attract and retain students. Sometimes the attention is especially drawn to students' cognitive investement and active participation in and emotional commitment to their learning (Chapman, 2003). Otherwise the focus is on 'students' involvement with activities and conditions likely to generate high quality learning' (ACER, 2008, p. vi). In fact, the concept of 'student engagement' is often attributed a benign sense, either as a key factor in enabling a successful academic performance (Hu & Kuh, 2001; Krause & Coates, 2008) or as underlying a democratic open disposition by higher education institutions aiming to develop a student-centred educational policy (ACER, 2008; JISC/HEFCE, 2009; Kuh, 2009). This notion can be traced to two broad long-standing traditions (Trowler, 2010): one developed in North America and Australasia, and properly adopting the term 'student engagement' as a manifold opportunity for student involvement; the second one being elaborated in the United Kingdom and mainly focusing on student feedback, representation and student approaches to learning. Student engagement is an integral part of the ethos of a university when active participation is promoted as well as a sense of legitimacy, belonging and a supportive learning environment being provided. On the other hand, student engagement is grounded in the teacher-learner relation and entails forms of active, collaborative and transformative learning and a role of teacher and students as co-producers of knowledge (O'Sullivan & Cleary, 2011). Among the range of factors influencing student engagement, Kuh (2009) emphasizes two major aspects equally important for student success and of key interest in a social media age: in-class (academic) engagement and out-class engagement, in which learners develop co-curricular activities. However, positive, neutral (non-engagement) and negative dimensions of engagement can be identified at behavioural, emotional and cognitive levels (Trowler, 2010, p. 6), providing a basis for a heuristic of student engagement. Building on an extensive literature review on the term, Trowler merges individual and institutional levels of its meaning and defines student engagement as 'concerned with the interaction between the time, effort and other relevant resources invested by both students and their institutions intended to optimize the student experience and enhance the learning outcomes and development of students and the performance, and reputation of the institution' (2010, p. 3).

It is worth noting that often the term 'student engagement' is being used without sharing a conceptual background (HEA, 2010) and, more importantly, the nature of its cultural construct and of ideologically bounded stance usually is not made explicit (Gourlay, 2011). Gourlay argues for 'a "constructively critical" stance towards the concept of student engagement, to allow us to gain genuine insights into the many and varied forms of student engagement' (2011). She highlights the current tensions between the 'student experience' and 'student engagement' notions, whereas the former mostly underlies a conceptualization of student as 'consumer' and is often merely grounded in quantitative surveys. There is an incumbent risk to overlook the interplay of different actors at work in the 'student engagement' construct and to produce a reductively unified view of what the student experience really is. As a consequence, an impoverished meaning of student engagement is accounted, as built on an idealized model of 'student'.

Gourlay holds that the current understanding of student expectations relies on a 'pre-massification age of full funding' and to 'a pre-networked age'; they do not take properly into account either the varied demographics of the current student population enrolled in university classes or the display of concurrent places and meaning-making practices occurring in the digital university (Beetham, 2010). In this line, Zepke and Leach (2010) propose to overcome an operational view of student engagement with a more inclusive vision, which entails the multiple actors (students, teachers, administrators) and resources (locations, structures, cultures, technologies, equipment) involved in the situated context:

> What is needed is a democratic–critical conception of engagement that goes beyond strategies, techniques or behaviours, a conception in which engagement is participatory, dialogic and leads not only to academic achievement but to success as an active citizen (2010, p. 173).

These critical stances also lead to the consideration – for the purpose of this chapter – of the extent to which digitally mediated practices constitute a key issue in better understanding current typologies of teacher and student engagement. While considering stances referring to the Net generation's expectations of technology-enhanced environments and learning practices is worthwhile to some degree (Junco & Timm, 2009), it is simplistic to state that new generations coming to university are to be viewed by default tech-savvy (Bullen & Morgan, 2011; Jones, 2011), or to assume that such stances instigate teachers to adopt Web 2.0 tools (Brown, 2012, p. 56; Jones & Shao, 2011, p. 2). However, it is also true that potentially there are 'invisible' digitally mediated practices undertaken by students that merit acknowledgement (White, 2012) as a basis for rethinking student engagement along with student experience, conceived as the interplay of situated practices within and beyond institutional borders. Undertaking such investigative efforts implies opportunities for rethinking assessment approaches towards more open-ended forms by involving students and 'authentic audiences' (Collis, 2012) and evaluating new kinds of peer support crossing formal and informal boundaries (Timmis, 2012).

VISITORS/RESIDENTS: A CONTINUUM OF ONLINE ENGAGEMENT

Student and teacher engagement in higher education is also being conceptualized focusing on the nature of the 'social web' (Boulos & Wheleer, 2007), intended as an ecology of tools evolving along with their users. In fact, the emergent digital landscape, beyond the traditional issues related to an actual access to technologies and to the capacity to adopt them in their functionalities, suggests to consider different types of online engagement that individual teachers and students are likely to undertake with respect to 'old' and 'new' web-based technologies be considered. Some recent reflections (White, 2012; White & Le Cornu, 2011) help to overcome the discourse of the 'generation factor' in the adoption of new web-based tools and identify diverse orientations in the online engagement being enabled by the social web. These reflections indicate that new kinds of computing applications that are better explained with the metaphor of 'place', that is of a sense of being present with others' (White & Le Cornu, 2011) rather than with the term 'tool', as 'a means to an end'. The authors argue for a shift in the paradigm from a type of online engagement by individuals as 'Visitors', who use the web as a shed from which selecting the appropriate tool if needed for a specific purpose, to a view of users as 'Residents', who interpret the web as 'a place to express opinions, a place in which relationships can be formed and extended' (2011), and where content and persona (or digital identity) overlap. The Visitors/Residents typology is considered by White and Le Cornu (2011) as a continuum in which individual's digital behaviour can be located. One might assume a prevailing 'Visitor' approach when working in a digitally resilient context, but orientate oneself towards a 'Resident' approach in social extra-work activities. The propensity towards the former or the latter can also be examined within a frame of digital literacies (Belshaw, 2011), that refer to the whole set of digitally mediated situated behaviours required by the specific context and by the subject area in which the individuals (teachers/students) are used to carry out their research, teaching and learning activities. The prevailing approach is not dependent on technology proficiency. Tech-savvy individuals may be reluctant to disclose and build their own digital identity. Moreover, a digital literacies approach can vary according to different kinds of social media. For example some users could feel comfortable in a social networking site such as Facebook, but find Twitter unuseful and distressing. It also shifts the inter-generational contrast, implied in the dyad of digital natives/digital immigrants, towards more profound and subtle intra-generational differences in the social web use, specifically towards a range of changing attitudes among Visitors and Residents. Given this contrast, we can interpret social web behaviour along new lines. For instance, faculty aiming for more research impact by using social web and intersecting activities of 'networking' and 'celebrity' (personal branding) in their set of academic commitments are likely to be more successful by adopting a Resident approach rather than a Visitor one; but it is also plausible that faculty endorsing a Resident approach are likely to be more open to include 'teaching' activity in their own experimentation with digitally mediated practices. On the other hand, students that are able to manage and develop their own digital identity in their social life might be reluctant to expand a Resident approach to a formal education context, unless the motivation to undertake this shift emerges from a real education interaction with the teacher and/or the institution.

This perspective of a continuum of online engagement in the social media age provides a useful frame within which the scholarship dimension of co-creating knowledge (Garnett & Ecclesfield, 2011) can be pondered and unfolded. Moreover, the debates above which summarized about the notion of student engagement and focused on online engagement as modelized in the social web era suggest to consider that at a microlevel of a single class 'student engagement' could be properly defined as 'the process of renegotiating the relationship between tutor and student to bring about a situation where each recognises and values the other's expertise and capability and works together to capitalise on it' (JISC/HEFCE, 2009, p. 9). However, such a process is not straightforward, as some teachers are experiencing. In fact 'moving students from a Visitor to a more Resident mode online is often a painful process' (White, 2012), distressing both for students and teachers.

The Nature of Microblogging

The microblogging services refer to 'the practice of posting small pieces of digital content – which could be text, pictures, links, short videos, or other media – on the Internet' (EDUCAUSE, 2009). The most popular microblogging application is undoubtedly Twitter (Common Craft, 2007), which was launched in 2006 and rapidly became a mainstream phenomenon: in the timespan of 4 years it counted 40 million users, as many the radio broadcasting had reached after 40 years. It deals with a free, open platform in which a user can (publicly or privately) publish posts (called 'tweets') with a maximum of 140 characters, including shortened links to websites or to self-authored multimedia files. A microblogging service can be primarily intended as a quick means to write concise and timely blog posts, but it also enables instant messaging and can be used with any device connected to the Net. Like many social media, Twitter draws its own strength from being an instrument for social networking activity (Ramsden, 2009a), characterized by the logic of 'following' users sharing a similar interest (for instance in educational technology) and being followed by others interested in what we usually publish in our micro-posts. The inherent value of microblogging just relies on the network of contacts that we build over time and within which we can exchange information, thoughts and ideas (Grosseck & Holotescu, 2008). The apparent, even banal simplicity of the basic functions of microblogging constrasts the efforts undertaken by newcomers to effectively come to terms with its key convention of 'retweeting' (re-posting of others' tweets), where 'authorship, attribution, and communicative fidelity are negotiated in diverse ways' (Boyd, Scott & Gilad, 2010). However, unlike other social networking platforms, Twitter allows for asymmetric relations, that is it is possible to follow an account (individual or organization) without being followed by it. In this sense, even if other microblogging platforms (e.g. Yammer) are adopted in business or educational contexts, due to their option to allow institution-bounded communication, they substantially differ from Twitter, which allows interaction and information search in an open network, similar to a search engine (Bernstein, Kairam, Suh, Hong, & Chi, 2010). The progressive construction of a Personal Learning Network (PLN) – a web of digital relations with experts and peers sharing a learning journey or a field of interest – plays a central role in the utilization of Twitter as a source of information and means for the dissemination of one's own contributions, under the form of links, comments or original articles (Belshaw, 2007).

The Affordances of Microblogging for Student Engagement

The role of Twitter for teaching and learning activities was investigated in various ways, for instance considering its add-on value in social learning activities (Dunlap & Lowenthal, 2009), its role in a likely transmission of tacit knowledge (Hansen, Ronne, & Jensen, 2008) and its relation with opportunities for serendipitous learning (Buchem, 2011). However, the impact of microblogging on student engagement and learning outcomes is to date underesearched. On the other hand, early experimental trials (Junco, 2010; Junco, Elavsky & Heiberger, 2012; Junco, Heiberger & Loken, 2011) give some evidence that 'using Twitter in educationally relevant ways can increase student engagement and improve grades' (Junco, Heiberger, & Loken, 2011, p. 130) and create a communication channel between teachers and learners aligned with their digital lifestyles. The researchers argue that microblogging can be important for students' academic and psychosocial development and can increase their sense of connection to faculty and institution, which is one aspect of engagement. Elsewhere, it is highlighted that the style of engagement evolves over time and opens up to unexpected outcomes: 'as the students became more comfortable with the technology and its format in relation to class applications, their related skills and acumen increased, positioning as a stronger supplemental asset in developing the course discourse in novel ways that extended it beyond traditional limitations' (Elavsky, Mislan, & Elavsky, 2011, pp. 223, 224).

Student engagement can be fostered by an informal rapport teacher/student characterized by mutual trust. In this sense, Twitter use can also help to reinforce students' perception of a teacher's credibility. In a recent study, Johnson (2011) demonstrates that faculty 'tweeting' about their social and professional activities, beyond more conventional academic communication, can increase their perceived credibility in terms of competence, trustworthiness and caring. Johnson builds on research investigating an instructor's credibility which can affect learning outcomes and learner motivation. Considering the probed impact of the teacher's self-disclosure on the perceived teacher's credibility, Johnson provides some evidence that this kind of impact can be extended to the adoption of a social networking tool like Twitter, given that the dimension of 'caring' seems to be even more important than 'competence' in determining teacher's credibility in microblogging interaction (2010, p. 32). This statement resonates with other empirical findings reporting that 'students are looking for traditional approaches, notably personal contact, in a modern setting' (JISC/HEFCE, 2009, p. 7) that are also in a digitally mediated environment. Finally, in

Johnson's study a positive student attitude towards Twitter is shown to be a key predictor of more highly perceived teacher credibility.

In the field of online learning, Dunlap and Lowenthal (2009) make a case for microblogging to enhance social presence among distance learners and between them and tutors, which is at the heart of student engagement in e-learning settings. They hold that Twitter is good for 'sharing, collaboration, brainstorming, problem solving, and creating within the context of our moment-to-moment experiences' (Dunlap & Lowenthal, 2009b). Dwelling on their field research, they also reflect on unexpected Twitter affordances related to a 'cognitive' and 'teaching' presence which enabled former students interacting with tutors, peers and practitioners to 'construct(ed) meaning through sustained communication' (2009b, p.132) and helped faculty to 'attend to instructional management issues and students' knowledge building' (2009b, p. 133).

On the other hand, Buchem (2011) focuses on microblogging affordances as an open network for unplanned discoveries of resources and unexpected encounters on the part of individual users. She argues that 'provided a certain degree of intellectual readiness and a set of exploratory skills, microblogging can become a serendipitous learning space'. In fact, the opportunity to increase the number of accounts to be followed, far from circles and groups that are familiar to the individual, raises the possibility to stumbling upon hints and personal contacts that may produce unexpected results, in terms of new research ideas, references, peer critiquing and prospective collaboration. In the literature (e.g. Riley, 2007), these unexpected discoveries are seen as engaging and motivating, since they overcome the constraints of the designed instruction. Such a Twitter use, due to 'size and diversity' and volume of information (Buchem, 2011), provides university students with opportunities similar to those of their professors to acquire and keep contacts with professional and/or academic communities of practices that may be useful for their study, research and work.

HOW MICROBLOGGING IS SPREADING IN ACADEMIA

Large-scale surveys recently carried out in US universities (Faculty Focus, 2009; 2010; Moran, Seaman, & Tinti-Kane, 2011) demonstrate that Twitter has started to be utilized in higher education by a minority of 'early adopter' faculty, although the percentage of adopters dramatically varies according to different studies. In Moran's et al. (2011), the percentage of Twitter adopters in universities is not higher than 13% both for professional (non-class) use or for teaching use; for the other studies there would have been an increase in adoption from 30.7% (Faculty Focus, 2009, p. 4) to 35% in 2010 (Faculty Focus, 2010, p. 5), noting that among Twitter users 'to share information with peers' and to utilize the service 'as a real time news source' were reported as the most popular activities. On the other hand, the recent dissemination of practical guides addressing faculty and exclusively devoted to Twitter uses in research, teaching and learning (LSE Public Policy Group, 2011) demonstrates the growing reputation gained by this social networking service in academia, despite the ephemeral nature of its communicational affordance, outwardly contrasting the rigour and complexity of academic discourse.

Furthemore, an increasing collection of empirical studies gives some evidence that Twitter is being adopted both for piloting new ways to disseminate research and building networks (Grosseck & Holotescu, 2011; Lalonde, 2011; Letierce, Passant, Breslin, & Decker, 2010; Veletsianos, 2011) and to support teaching activities in the classroom, in online settings and in work-based learning (Dunlap & Lowenthal, 2009a; Grosseck & Holotescu, 2008; Torrance, Mistry, Higginson, & Jones, 2010). Currently, Twitter is an object of study as a powerful means to create backchannels in scholarly conferences (Costa, Beham, Rheinardt, & Sillaots, 2008; Ebner & Reinhardt, 2009; McNeill, 2010a; Ross, Terras, Warwick, & Welsh, 2011) as well as an instrument to enhance 'social presence' in online courses (Dunlap & Lowenthal, 2009b; 2009c), a tool to make traditional lectures more interactive (Ebner, 2009; Ranking, 2009; Young, 2009) or as an efficient communication channel to inform students about availability of technical and administrative services (Hodges, 2010). To date, microblogging affordances have sparked a range of teaching and learning pilots by individual faculty belonging to a variety of disciplinary contexts: from foreign languages teaching (Antenos-Conforti, 2009) to history (Jensen, Caswell, Ball, Duffin, & Barton, 2010) and English literature (McNeill, 2010b); from engineering (Minocha, 2009) and economics (Ramsden, 2009) to medicine (Torrance et al., 2010).

Lessons Learned from Case Studies of Twitter Use in Academia

The pilots so far undertaken have returned a range of Twitter uses in academia at very different levels of complexity: from the basic 'broadcasting' model, in which the teacher is particularly engaged in conveying to her students logistic information about the course or pointing out links and references related to the topic being studied (Ramsden, 2009), to the most sophisticated and tailored model, in which the teacher re-designs her own teaching through technology mediation, in order to improve quality in the instructional process (Dunlap & Lowenthal, 2009a).

In the 'Twitter experiment' carried out at the University of Texas-Dallas microblogging was adopted in a large class, for the purpose of increasing comments and reflections during and after the lectures. The interviewed students stated that the pilot helped them to express their own opinions in a large theatre hall, where they usually feel shy and rarely raise their hands to pose questions. Despite the apparent limitations of interacting in 140 characters, the teacher also highlights the opportunity for students to listen to multiple threads while posting their own contributions. This capability is recognized as a key issue by Grosseck and Holotescu (2008) to prompt full engagement in the student body. Likewise, in a 250-enrolled learners engineering class at the Purdue University it was asserted that the setting up of a Twitter channel 'alters power dynamics of the class and points out to students that they have the power' (Young, 2009). The teachers involved recognized that microblogging forced them to change attitude towards their students by requiring a continuing interaction that it is likely to be extended beyond the traditional 'office hours'. However, they also underline that this implicit 'non-stop availability' may not fit most faculty, since it makes time management between teaching and research somewhat unpredictable.

In an engineering course delivered at the University of Glamorgan, in the United Kingdom (Minocha, 2009, pp. 119–121), Twitter was adopted in combination with a wiki in order to supervise and support individual projects that students were required to develop and complete in the timespan of 4–5 months. Whereas the wiki played a 'formal' role, enabling the posting of the respective works in progress and the subsequent feedback by the teacher, Twitter worked more informally, allowing students to share technical and methodological issues and enabling the teacher to provide timely help and support. The experiment was introduced by a face-to-face session focusing on practical suggestions of possible Twitter uses within the course context. The pilot resulted in successful in student engagement, since the Twitter stream even triggered the cancellation of the two weekly classroom sessions, usually planned to discuss the ongoing projects. On the one hand, the teacher recognized the potentiality of microblogging for enhancing the sense of community and above all in gaining understanding about ways in which own students work. On the other hand, the service was sometimes unavailable, and issues such as data protection and privacy on some types of messages (e.g. informal assessment of an individual student's work) precipitated the teacher reflecting on what steps were necessary and seeking advice from the institution. The microblogging use in a Business English class led the teacher to state that Twitter 'may contribute to such important things as reducing fears of participation, offering experience in negotiating different points of view, offering opportunities to enquire of others as well as support them, never mind offering an audience for thoughts in general' (Spear, 2009).

At the University of Glamorgan (Torrance et al., 2010) a pilot involving medical students aimed to explore new modes for developing a stronger tie between theory and clinical practice, planning activities that could spur autonomous learning, the capacity to rapidly recall and summarize knowledge and critical thinking. The experiment was highly structured, since it was supported by a JISC-funded initiative endevouring to gain insights on any productive uses of microblogging in health education. Four different clinical scenarios were outlined by the teachers. They progressively disclosed the scenario to students through tweeting them chunks of information about the patient's conditions and waiting for their questions and directions related to possible medical treatments. Among the positive results, teachers acknowledged that Twitter use induced self-reflection on the clinical practice as ever observed before. On the other hand, students appreciated the ability to pose questions out of the classroom context and to receive real-time feedback from their tutors.

However, there are also accounts of students reluctant to adopt microblogging in instructional activities. McNeill (2010b) reports that his English literature class students to a degree were reticent about using Twitter to discuss academic assignments. In this case students were not used to texting through Twitter in their social life and seemed to prefer Facebook, which let them exchange opinions with like-minded people. Nonetheless a small group of students involved in the pilot used the microblogging service with a growing capacity over the course of the semester to undertake a critical discussion. Despite that fact, McNeill foresees that educational pilots using Twitter are at risk of being marginalized, because this tool neither belongs to the institutional sphere of ICTs nor is popular among younger generations.

These lessons learned well account for issues of teacher and student engagement that need to be considered in order for microblogging, as well as for any social media, to be appraised in educational contexts. A social networking service should be familiar to and be accepted by the teacher (for personal or professional purposes) before starting an experiment. The actual adoption of a specific communication tool by students cannot be taken for granted and differs in diverse group of learners. Reasons why a new communication tool is added to an educational process should be clarified and made explicit to the class as well as the expectations of participation. Finally, the use of an additional tool should be balanced within the ensemble of the planned learning activities and clearly valued in the assessment process.

Dunlap and Lowenthal summarize the recommended engagement of social media, which is appropriate to teachers and students: 'With Twitter, as with all social-networking tools, the value of the experience hinges on three things: (1) who you are connected to and with; (2) how frequently you participate; and (3) how conscientious you are about contributing value to the community' (Dunlap & Lowenthal, 2009c).

The Empirical Case: Microblogging to Monitor Ongoing Project Works

The empirical case being examined deals with a 'Twitter experiment' carried out at the University of Milan in 2010, in the timespan of about four months during a semester. The aim of the experiment was to use microblogging to support communication activities among 25 postgraduate students enrolled in an Organization and Human Resources Development face-to-face class, run by Professor Luca Solari within a master's degree program in Diritto del Lavoro e Relazioni Industriali (Labour Law and Industrial Relations). This pilot constituted a pioneering experience in the Italian higher education, and for this reason the most important national financial newspaper (*IlSole24Ore*) hosted a series of diaries blogged by the professor and some students (Santonocito 2010a, 2010b, 2010c, 2010d).

It is worth noting that the researcher was aware of the Twitter experiment when it had just started. However, she was at least able, agreed with the teacher, to collect tweets for a subsequent study. The present account, undertaken 2 years after the pilot, has therefore mainly the form and the value of a vignette, aiming to reconstruct the case through written texts and informal conversations with the teacher and to highlight aspects of the experience that are relevant for the discourse of teacher and student engagement.

The teacher based his instructional approach (as in the master degree program as a whole) on experiential learning and planned a mix of lecture-based sessions, group work and simulations of real-life cases, aiming to discuss critically presented theoretical stances. On this ground the teacher designed a learning ecology encompassing a combination of Twitter, Facebook, a Ning website and the institutional VLE (Virtual Learning Environment). The latter had the functions of a repository of materials, space for the communication of the assessments and detailed feedback by the teacher. According to the teacher, Twitter, being used by the 30% of students at the beginning of the course, was explicitly adopted to 'enhance participation also by shy students' (Santonocito, 2010a). Students were asked to create a Twitter account and were made aware both of the relevance of microblogging use in the organization of the course as well as of the expectations related to their participation. In fact, the teacher considered the qualitative aspects of interaction occurring in Twitter as a holistic component of the assessment process. He initiated and channelled communication via microblogging through the hashtag #lucalearning. The editor of the section Job24 of the *IlSole24Ore Online* played the role of an observer and 'spread the word': she systematically re-tweeted the individual posts, occasionally adding its own hashtag #24job in order to reach a wider audience, especially among the usual readership of the newspaper. However, sometimes students added the hashtag #24job to their own posts. The researcher created an archive of tweets (about 300) labelled with such hashtag, using the service Twapperkeeper starting on March 6, 2010, in order to draw a Twitter stream to be analysed. It is worth noting that whereas the Italian language was commonly adopted in the interaction, some tweets in the English language emerged, both by the teacher and some students. If the English version of the reported tweet was the original one, the researcher indicated it with (*sic*) in italics and between brackets.

Referring to ethical decision-making, the researcher considered the peculiarity of the participants' experience, which developed beyond the boundaries of the password-protected institutional learning platform. Moreover, the students were fully aware of being part of an experiment to be carried out on the open web and shared posts in the capacity of apprentice professionals. Given that, the researcher also took into account that publishing posts in an open social network can be to a degree considered as an 'aspiration to publicity' (Vieweg, 2010). Finally, from a practical standpoint, asking for the informed consent to former students was almost impossible. However, in order to reduce the overexposure of the authors of the reported tweets and to guarantee privacy and confidentiality, the researcher preferred not to disclose students' real accounts being examined and indicated them with the convention @S1, @S2 etc. Moreover, when needed, personal details were omitted in the reported tweets.

The section 'The University Context' intends to briefly present the university context in which the pilot was carried out and the participants involved in the experimentation. A selection of tweets are reported in order to highlight typologies of posts and signs of engagement on part of the teacher and students. Moreover, excerpts from diaries blogged by the teacher and students (and published in the section Job24 of the *IlSole24Ore*) are utilized to draw expectations and feelings of teacher's and learners' engagement as occurring in this instance of microblogging use.

The University Context

The University of Milan is one of the largest research-intensive universities in Italy: it counts about 2,600 faculty, 2,400 non-teaching staff and more than 60,000 students. The most recent data related to perceptions and instructional uses of web-based technologies by faculty dates back to 2007, when an extensive online survey was organized (Esposito & Scaccia, 2008, p. 8). Referring to emerging tools in didactics, only 23 teachers (out of 800 respondents) stated that they were using podcasting and 12 managed a wiki for collaborative knowledge production (neither blogging or microblogging were listed among the options). It is very likely that these numbers have been increased since then and that a range of new tools have been added in the 'learning ecology' of diverse classes. However, there is some evidence from a recent small-scale qualitative study at the same university (Esposito, 2011) that also the uptake of social media for enquiry purposes is also fairly low, due to a variety of reasons, but among which exists a diverse ICT appropriation in the different broad research areas (Fry, 2006; Fry & Talja, 2007).

The Networked Teacher: Suggestions for Engagement

The profile of the teacher promoting the pilot can be soundly ascribed to the Resident type of online engagement in which the propensity for experimenting with new tools comes along with his interest in building an academic digital identity. In fact he took part in a recent interview study in which these characteristics as a 'digital researcher' clearly emerged (Esposito, 2011). He sees his research ideas as 'strongly affected and continuously fed with all that is being shared on the web, through digital mechanisms' (Esposito, 2011, p. 53). The teacher is an internationally acknowledged expert of Human Resources Management who is used to adopting a range of tools and environments, for personal, professional and academic purposes, and for a variety of motives, including networking, project management, scheduling of meetings, annoting reflections and bookmarking resources. Specifically, he utilizes Twitter both as a 'knowledge feeder', drawn from an international network of peers and professionals, and to create readership for his blog posts. Moreover, he considers Facebook as a reserved circle within which it is possible to continue discussing emerging themes, with peers and students, beyond the temporal boundaries of the course.

During the Twitter experiment, the teacher showed a variety of behaviours, which are synthesized in Table 1.

The Networked Students: 'The Resource Is Us'

Following the hashtag #lucalearning were about 10 different accounts revealing significant contributions to the Twitter stream, with 3 accounts that can be classified as 'super-users', having more than 10 posts per

Table 1. A Selection of Tweets Posted by the Teacher.

Motivation	Examples of Tweets
Suggestions on management of digital identity	@T: No lie! Your Facebook Profile is the Real You (*sic*) via @sharethis #lucalearning http://www.wired.com/wiredscience/2010/02/no-lie-your-facebook-profile-is-the-real-you/ [Saturday, 27 February 2010] @T: The network is a resource 4 problem solving (*sic*) #lucalearning #richardcollin
Providing encouragement	@T: It's time to take a deep breath and open up reflexion on what we are entitled to manage; in relation to people (*sic*) #lucalearning #job24 [Saturday, 27 February 2010]
Communicating assignments and assessment	@T: #lucalearning assignment for next Monday: 1 slide on strategy, 1 on actual facts, 1 on results and 1 on what u learnt @T Groups' assessment published on Ariel as well as directions to the last group activity #lucalearning [Tuesday, 9 March 2010]
Live commenting on the presentations of the project works	@T: Rushing up at the end ruins presentations. Time is key! (*sic*) #lucalearning
Sharing his extra-academia activities	@T Had a wonderful day at ESA HQ talking about actions to improve women's careers in science (sic) #lucalearning #24job
Sharing self-reflection on his own commitment	@T: Group had great presentations, it will be hard to grade them differently, I know that's my role. a wonderful experience (*sic*) #lucalearning #24job

account. The manifold challenges provided by this course are apparent in one of the diaries.

'A course planned beyond the classroom can indeed frighten us if we are not well acquainted with technologies, if we have not enough relational skills to be applied in group working, if our pre-defined expectation was to complete the course with a traditional written exam' (Santonocito, 2010d). As a student blogged at the beginning of the course, 'the atmosphere we are breathing seems to be collaborative and challenging at the same time' (Santonocito, 2010b). Indeed, the belief of being explorers of 'unknown territories' constituted for some a key motivational driver, as a student commented, 'I think that the secret consists in being willing to experiment and learn to enter the proposed new dimensions without fear of asking, sharing and integrate' (Santonocito, 2010d). The enthusiasm to cope with

Table 2. A Selection of Tweets Posted by Students.

Motivation	Examples of Tweets
Suggestions on management of digital identity	@T: No lie! Your Facebook Profile is the Real You (*sic*) via @sharethis #lucalearning http://www.wired.com/wiredscience/2010/02/no-lie-your-facebook-profile-is-the-real-you/ [Saturday, 27 February 2010]
	@T: The network is a resource 4 problem solving (*sic*) #lucalearning #richardcollin
Providing encouragement	@T: It's time to take a deep breath and open up reflexion on what we are entitled to manage; in relation to people (*sic*) #lucalearning #job24 [Saturday, 27 February 2010]
Communicating assignments and assessment	@T: #lucalearning assignment for next Monday: 1 slide on strategy, 1 on actual facts, 1 on results and 1 on what u learnt
	@T Groups' assessment published on Ariel as well as directions to the last group activity #lucalearning [Tuesday, 9 March 2010]
Live commenting on the presentations of the project works	@T: Rushing up at the end ruins presentations. Time is key! (*sic*) #lucalearning
Sharing his extra-academia activities	@T Had a wonderful day at ESA HQ talking about actions to improve women's careers in science (sic) #lucalearning #24job
Sharing self-reflection on his own commitment	@T: Group had great presentations, it will be hard to grade them differently, I know that's my role. a wonderful experience (*sic*) #lucalearning #24job

real-life cases was enhanced by the opportunity to make their efforts publicly visible through Twitter. 'The idea of a virtual space in which the teacher and students are enabled to keep in contact is surely innovative: we can exchange points of view and first impressions also beyond lesson hours' (Santonocito, 2010c).

The students' tweets included a range of typologies, from the comments on lectures that points to self-empowerement, to the numerous state-of-the-art posts of the project works, to the attempts to summarize key concepts in a few characters. Interactions among students, probably intense in face-to-face group work, through Twitter are instead often limited to the use of 'retweeting', even if there are some isolated attempts to start a conversation or raise further discussion or polemics.

The Table 2 provides a selection of tweets showing the most frequent typologies.

DISCUSSION

The narrative of the empirical case above presented has evident limitations, since it merely relies on the recorded tweets and cannot provide the account of an in-depth case study. However, the provided account reports one of the earliest experiments with social media in the Italian higher education settings and can add to the knowledge of empirical cases of Twitter uses in different subject domains. Above all, this narrative provides some starting points from which interpreting suggestions coming from literature and envisioning future research.

The typologies and content of the communication that occurred in this microblogging pilot highlight features of social and cognitive presence characterizing a 'community of enquiry' (Garrison, Anderson, & Archer, 2000). Above all, students make sense of what they are learning and applying in their project works, facing real problems with real companies, 'through sustained communication' (p. 89). It can be said that microblogging worked as a monitoring tool of the social presence as occurring in the course as a whole. In fact the main interaction was developed in face-to-face contexts, being distributed among lectures, workshops and group work.

Moreover, the organization and approach of the outlined course as a whole, as evidenced by teacher's and students' comments in the diaries and by the microblogging use, is consistent with many of the 'good practice' principles of student engagement as recommended by Chickering and

Gamson (1987, as mentioned by Dunlap & Lowenthal, 2009c). It encourages student-faculty contact, cooperation among students, and active learning, gives prompt feedback, emphasizes time on task, communicates high expectations and respects diverse talents and ways of learning.

Focusing on the interactions that actually occurred in Twitter, diverse alignments seem to emerge as products of effective engagement with social media for teaching and learning purposes:

- Faculty endorsing an approach both as a networked researcher *and* teacher.
- The topic studied is compliant with the rhetoric of microblogging: the subject of organizational studies is likely to take advantage of the social web because this is the place in which experimentations and observations of what counts as 'enterprise 2.0' occur.
- The teaching method is strongly characterized by active and collaborative learning: so, resulting participation in a social networking activity is coherent in an educational context demanding capacities such as continuing interaction with others, leadership, team building, creativity and problem solving.
- Master level students, aiming to bridge between academic and professional knowledge, and opportunities provided by an open social network such as Twitter to expand contacts and to expose participants to professional communities.

It can be said that in this short but focused experience, the implicit commitment of the networked teacher was that to foster the move of students from a 'Visitors' to a 'Residents' approach. He played the role of a 'gatekeeper' to the social web as a space in which knowledge building of the organizational change could be expanded. For instance, choosing the hashtag #lucalearning the teacher confirms that he is the first participant to put himself at stake in the experiment. Moreover, his posts encouraging students and his recurrent recalls to target the planned instructional goals help to recursively establish relevance for students and confirm expectations of their participation. Furthemore the active contribution of a minority of students, mainly the group leaders, to microblogging reveals an unexpected outcome with respect to the teacher's initial aim (to prompt a wider participation). In fact the Twitter stream worked as an informal monitoring service of the project works, arising from the voices of students being elicited as leaders within the groups. This also suggests future research on microblogging focusing on leadership in collaborative learning. On the one hand, this minority participation might have implied an indirect benefit also to 'lurkers', through the access to the Twitter stream. As already noticed, 'contribution of a single student might prompt further student participation' (Brown, 2012, p. 56). On the other hand, this suggests the opportunity to diversify spaces and modes of participation in order to address diverse styles of engagement. However, the diversification of spaces and modes makes the instructional relationship more complex. Alternative spaces such as the Ning website were not equally 'colonized' because the scope of using such spaces was not clear to the class, and certainly they were not assigned an equal attention by the teacher and the external observer (the financial newspaper).

In this small experiment, a fundamental tension produced by social media is at work: that of the 'walled garden' versus open arena (Crook et al., 2008), wherein the individual student and the group of learners (together with the teacher) are engaged in an ongoing discussion potentially being open to all the web users, rather than in the password-protected space of an institutional learning management system. This implies a shift in communication style and personal responsibility: students become aware of 'writing to an audience' (Dunlap & Lowenthal, 2009b, p. 131) while providing commentaries in real time about successful or failed activities or hazarding tentative explanations of key concepts. In addition the teacher makes his teaching presence visible and maintains continuity between one lecture and the next one.

The pilot also seems to be aligned with the 'environmental factors' (JISC/HEFCE, 2009, p. 8) pointed out among the ongoing drivers to change in the digital university: instructional materials are digitized; the audience of students is receptive and motivated to explore how to link social practices with learning and professional practices; teaching staff are interested in experimenting new approaches to research *and* teaching and learning enabled by social networking tools.

Finally, it can be argued that the engagement and digital literacy of the individual faculty to activate an experiment are necessary but not sufficient condition to activate effective and lasting uses of social networking tools (Fitzgerald et al., 2009). The institutional support (e.g. through social media policy, consultancy on instructional uses and enquiries and monitoring services) constitutes a key issue in addressing the quality of student engagement, for instance taking care to avoid a disorienting and redundant plenty of adopted tools without clear aims and system of reward or even incompatible with respect to the institutional software platforms. For instance, in this specific case, appropriate advice might have been provided to students to enhance a topic-focused social presence in the social networking tool by curating a space aggregating selected resources or to foster discussion by urging timely comments to prompting questions.

Some suggestions for further research come to mind on the topic of microblogging (and other social media) for educational purposes and student engagement, starting from this early experiment. For instance, one possible research development focuses on the role of microblogging for student engagement in the learning ecologies of higher education students, belonging to diverse subject areas. In addition, a thread could investigate the relationship between emerging Web 2.0 ecologies and the design of hybrid (formal and informal) learning ecologies, aiming to identify a sustainable and shared interpretation of student engagement in an increasingly digitally rich environment.

CONCLUSIONS

The chapter outlined issues of teacher and student engagement in higher education in the social media age. In particular, microblogging was examined in its affordances for teaching and learning as drawn from relevant research and lessons learned from real cases. The report of a small-scale case of Twitter use aimed to show the interplay of the underlying conditions that led us to considering this pilot as an early success for the quality of student participation and teacher involvement. Referring to the latter, his prevailing behaviour as a Resident (White & Le Cornu, 2011) in the social web is at work and affects his choice to add the extra challenge of microblogging to group working engagement and to involve an external observer in a conventional classroom-bounded activity. In fact, the ecology of the social web tools implies a further shift for faculty engagement, because it affects their (digital) identity as researchers and as teachers: it can be argued that the engagement as a networked researcher is likely to lead at least to a tentative engagement as a networked teacher and so to blur the traditional tension between the teacher's and researcher's role. In turn, this twofold and correlated online engagement opens up to peer-to-peer forms of academic scholarship, whereas the dimension of 'co-creating learning' (Garnett & Ecclesfield, 2011) involves at the same time professors and students and potentially expands their knowledge exchange beyond the boundaries of the university. However, disciplinary culture matters. In this case, organizational studies as a taught subject are compliant with the use of an open social network such as Twitter and enable teacher and students to start productive conversations. Teachers and researchers are in fact called to interpret the 'distributing potential' (Brown, 2012) of social media in their own university and course settings.

Moreover, in an ever changing digital landscape, it becomes practically impossible (and useless) to become familiar with every tools and environments. On the contrary 'the approach needs to shift to harnessing the networked aspects of new technologies, so that individuals foster their own set of meaningful connections to support their practice' (Conole, 2011, p. 12). In this scenario, it is therefore less important that the totality of students learn to adopt, for instance, microblogging, than that they grasp, also vicariously, how networking activity works and what kinds of advantages can be drawn by a personal engagement. As a consequence, the networked teacher/researcher is likely to play the role of a 'gatekeeper' to social networking for research/learning purposes and to cope with complex, diverse and evolving forms of digital participation by students, which need to be acknowledged and valued in the situated educational context.

In conclusion, student engagement being intended as a partnership between faculty and students (JISC/HEFCE, 2009) appears to be the unique, challenging path to build informed, situated and productive ways of digitally mediated modes of knowledge production and distribution in the social media era.

REFERENCES

ACER. (2008). *Attracting, engaging and retaining: New conversations about learning. Australasian student engagement report.* Camberwell, Victoria: Australian Council for Educational Research. Retrieved from http://dtl.unimelb.edu.au/R/2MHQQ421JRMRRR3Y81P46IB2NR1EX6LPQ29HDIBHF47S4PJ8D7-01857?func=dbin-jump-full&object_id=264257&local_base=GEN01&pds_handle=GUEST

Anderson, P. (2007). *What is Web 2.0? Ideas, technologies and implications for education.* JISC Report. Retrieved from http://www.jisc.ac.uk/whatwedo/services/techwatch/reports/horizonscanning/hs0701.aspx

Anderson, T. (2009). *The open access scholar.* Paper presented at the Open Access Week 2009, Athabasca University. Pdf and audio recording retrieved from http://hdl.handle.net/2149/2320

Antenos-Conforti, E. (2009). Microblogging on Twitter: Social networking in intermediate Italian classes. In L. Lomicka & G. Lord (Eds), *The next generation: Social networking and online collaboration in foreign language learning* (pp. 59–90). Calico Monograph Series, No. 9. Retrieved from http://chss.montclair.edu/~antenose/mytwitter.pdf

Beetham, H. (2010). *Digital literacies development framework* [PowerPoint slides]. Retrieved from http://www.slideshare.net/hbeetham/literacies-development-framework-v1

Belshaw, D. (2007, September 27). *3 scenarios for using Twitter with your students*. [Blog post]. Retrieved from http://teaching.mrbelshaw.co.uk/index.php/2007/09/27/3-scenarios-for-using-twitter-with-your-students/

Belshaw, D. (2011). *What is 'digital literacy'? A pragmatic investigation*. Unpublished doctoral dissertation. Durham University. Retrieved from http://neverendingthesis.com/index.php?title=Main_Page. Acccessed on January 5, 2012.

Bennett, S., Maton, K., & Kervin, L. (2008). The 'digital natives' debate: A critical review of the evidence. *British Journal of Educational Technology*, *39*(5), 775–786.

Bernstein, M., Kairam, S., Suh, B., Hong, L., & Chi E. H. (2010). *A torrent of tweets: Managing information overload in online social streams*. Paper presented at CHI 2010 Workshop on Microblogging, ACM. Atlanta, GA. Retrieved from http://www.parc.com/content/attachments/torrent-of-tweets.pdf

Borgman, C. (2006). What can studies of e-learning teach us about collaboration in e-research? Some findings from digital library studies. *Computer Supported Cooperative Work*, *15*(4), 359–383.

Boulos, M., & Wheeler, S. (2007). The emerging Web 2.0 social software: An enabling suite of sociable technologies in health and health care education. *Health Information and Libraries Journal*, *24*(1), 2–23.

Boyd, D., Scott G., & Gilad, L. (2010). Tweet, tweet, retweet: Conversational aspects of retweeting on Twitter. *HICSS-43*. IEEE, Kauai, HI, January 6. Retrieved from http://research.microsoft.com/apps/pubs/default.aspx?id=135165

Boyer, E. (1990). Scholarship reconsidered. Priorities of the Professoriate. Retrieved from https://depts.washington.edu/gs630/Spring/Boyer.pdf. Accessed on October 23, 2010.

Brown, S. A. (2012). Seeing Web 2.0 in context: A study of academic perceptions. *Internet and Higher Education*, *15*, 50–57.

Buchem, I. (2011). Serendipitous learning: Recognizing and fostering the potential of microblogging. *Form@re* [online], 74 (February/March, Special Issue). Retrieved from http://formare.erickson.it/wordpress/it/2011/serendipitous-learning-recognizing-and-fostering-the-potential-of-microblogging/

Bullen, M. (2009–2012). *Net gen skeptic blog*. Retrieved from http://www.netgenskeptic.com/

Bullen, M., & Morgan, T. (2011). Digital learners not digital natives. *La Cuestion Universitaria*, *7*, 60–68. Retrieved from http://www.lacuestionuniversitaria.upm.es/web/articulo.php?id_articulo=84. Accessed on January 25, 2012.

Burton, G. (2009, November 8). *The open scholar*. Retrieved from http://www.academicevolution.com/2009/08/the-open-scholar.html

Chapman, E. (2003). Alternative approaches to assessing student engagement rates. *Practical Assessment, Research & Evaluation*, *8*(13). Retrieved from http://PAREonline.net/getvn.asp?v=8&n=13

Chickering, A. W., & Gamson, Z. F. (1987). Seven principles for good practice in undergraduate education. *AAHE Bulletin*, *40*, 3–7.

Collis, B. (2012). *Digital learners: Will they surprise us?* Key note talk presented at TIES 2012 – III European Conference on Technology in Education and Society: A Critical Insight, Barcelona, Spain, January 1–3, 2012. Recording retrieved from http://ties2012.eu/en/pg-ponents.html#ponent-collis

Common Craft (2007). T*witter in plain English* [Video clip]. Retrieved from http://www.commoncraft.com/twitter

Conole, G. (2011). Open, social and participatory media. In G. Conole (2012). *Designing for learning in an open world*. New York, NY: Springer. Draft chapter retrieved from http://cloudworks.ac.uk/cloud/view/5408

Costa, C., Beham, G., Rheinardt, W., & Sillaots, M. (2008). *Microblogging in technology enhanced learning: A use-case inspection of PPE summer school 2008*. Paper presented at ECTEL SIRTEL 2008. Retrieved from https://togather.eu/handle/123456789/365

Courosa, A. (2008, October 7). *Networked teacher diagram* [Flickr image]. Retrieved from http://www.flickr.com/photos/courosa/2922421696/

Courosa, A. (2009). *How a 21st century teacher can help networked students*. Presentation for the 2009 Virtual School Society of BC conference, April 21–23, 2009. PowerPoint retrieved from http://www.slideshare.net/tuchodi/how-does-the-21st-century-teacher-help-the-networked-student-learn

Crook, C., Cummings, J., Fisher, T., Graber, R., Harrison, C., Lewin, C., … Oliver, M. (2008). Web 2.0 technologies for learning: the current landscape – Opportunities, challenges and tensions. Report Becta. Retrieved from http://partners.becta.org.uk/uploaddir/downloads/page_documents/research/web2_technologies_learning.pdf. Accessed on May 25, 2012.

Dabbagh, N., & Reo, R. (2010). Back to the future. Tracing the roots and learning affordances of social software. In M. Lee & C. McLoughlin (Eds.), *Web 2.0-based e-learning: Applying social informatics for tertiary teaching* (pp. 1–20). Herschey, PA: Idea Group.

Downes, S. (2011, November 22). Engagement and motivation in MOOCs. Retrieved from http://halanhour.blogspot.it/2011/11/engagement-and-motivation-in-moocs.html

Drexler, W. (2010). The networked student model for construction of personal learning environments: Balancing teacher control and student autonomy. *Australasian Journal of Educational Technology*, *26*(3), 369–385. Retrieved from http://www.ascilite.org.au/ajet/ajet26/drexler.html

Dunlap, J. C., & Lowenthal, P. R. (2009a). Instructional uses of Twitter. In P. R. Lowenthal, D. Thomas, A. Thai & B. Yuhnke (Eds.), *The CU online handbook – Teach differently: Create and collaborate* (pp. 45–50). Raleigh, NC: Lulu Enterprises. Retrieved from http://www.cudenver.edu/Academics/CUOnline/FacultyResources/Handbook/Documents/2009/Chapter_8.pdf

Dunlap, J. C., & Lowenthal, P. R. (2009b). Tweeting the night away: Using Twitter to enhance social presence. *Journal of Information Systems Education*, *20*(2), 129–136.

Dunlap, J. C., & Lowenthal, P. R. (2009c). Horton hears a tweet. *EDUCAUSE Quarterly*, *32*(4). Retrieved from http://www.educause.edu/EDUCAUSE+Quarterly/EDUCAUSEQuarterlyMagazineVolum/HortonHearsaTweet/192955

Ebner, M. (2009). Interactive lecturing by integrating mobile devices and microblogging in higher education. *Journal of Computing and Information Technology*, *17*, 371–381.

Ebner, M., & Reinhardt, W. (2009). Social networking in scientific conferences. Twitter as a tool to strengthen a scientific community. *Workshop Science 2.0 for TEL, ECTEL 2009*. Retrieved from http://oa.stellarnet.eu/open-archive/browse?resource=2197_v1.

EDUCAUSE. (2009). *7 things you should know about microblogging*. Retrieved from http://www.educause.edu/Resources/7ThingsYouShouldKnowAboutMicro/174629#comment-960

Elavsky, C. M., Mislan, C., & Elavsky, S. (2011). When talking less is more: Exploring outcomes of Twitter usage in the large lecture hall. *Learning, Media and Technology*, *36*(3), 215–233.

Elhers, U., & Schnekenberg, D. (Eds.). (2010). *Changing cultures in higher education.* Heidelberg: Springer.

Esposito, A. (2011). *Research practices in transition: investigating the relationship between emerging digital scholarship and open scholarship in higher education settings.* Unpublished thesis, Master of Research in Educational and Social Research. Institute of Education, University of London. Retrieved from http://independent.academia.edu/AntonellaEsposito/Papers/1300803/Research_practices_in_transition_investigating_the_relationship_between_emerging_digital_scholarship_and_open_scholarship_in_higher_education_settings

Esposito, A., & Scaccia, D. (2008). *Questionario e-learning. Analisi preliminare dei dati raccolti.* Unpublished report. Ctu – Università degli Studi di Milano. Retrieved from http://www.ctu.unimi.it/pdf/indagineEL/Indagine%20eL%20-%20Report%20analisi%20-quantitativa%20preliminare.pdf

Faculty Focus. (2009). *Twitter in higher education 2009: Usage habits and trends of today's college faculty.* Magna Publications Special Report. Retrieved from http://www.facultyfocus.com/free-report/twitter-in-higher-education-usage-habits-and-trends-of-todays-college-faculty/

Faculty Focus. (2010). *Twitter in higher education 2010: Usage habits and trends of today's college faculty.* Magna Publications Special Report. Retrieved from http://www.facultyfocus.com/free-reports/twitter-in-higher-education-2010-usage-habits-and-trends-of-todays-college-faculty/

Ferri, P., Cavalli, N., Mangiatordi, A., & Scenini, F. (2010). *Digital learning. La dieta mediale degli studenti universitari italiani.* Milano: Ledizioni Editore.

Fitzgerald, R., Barrass, S., Campbell, J., Hinton, S., Ryan, Y., Whitelaw, M. ... McGinness, N. (2009). Digital learning communities (DLC): Investigating the application of social software to support networked learning (CG6-36). Retrieved from http://eprints.qut.edu.au/18476/

Franklin, T. & van Harmelen, M. (2007). *Web 2.0 for content for learning and teaching in higher education* JISC Report. Retrieved from http://www.jisc.ac.uk/media/documents/programmes/digitalrepositories/web2-content-learning-and-teaching.pdf

Fry, J. (2006). Scholarly research and information practices: A domain analytic approach. *Information Processing and Management, 42*, 299–316.

Fry, J., & Talja, S. (2007). The intellectual and social organization of academic fields and the shaping of digital resources. *Journal of Information Science, 33*, 115–133.

Garnett, F., & Ecclesfield, N. (2011). A framework for co-creating open scholarship. *ALT-C 2011 Proceedings papers. Thriving in a colder and more challenging climate*, 5–17. Retrieved from http://repository.alt.ac.uk/2177/

Garrison, D. R., Anderson, T., & Archer, W. (2000). Critical inquiry in a text-based environment: Computer conferencing in higher education. *Internet and Higher Education, 2*(2–3), 87–105.

Gourlay, L. (2011). *The tyranny of participation? Critically exploring notions of student engagement* [Video recording]. Key note talk at the NAIRTL Annual Conference & Galway Symposium on Higher Education. National University of Ireland, Galway, 9–10 June 2011. Recording retrieved from http://blip.tv/iainmacl/the-tyranny-of-participation-critically-exploring-notions-of-student-engagement-lesley-gourlay-5595298.

Grosseck, G., & Holotescu, C. (2008). *Can we use Twitter for educational activities?* Paper presented at the 4th International Scientific Conference eLSE eLearning and Software for Education, Bucarest, 17-18 April 2008. Retrieved from http://adl.unap.ro/else

Grosseck, G., & Holotescu, C. (2011). Academic research in 140 characters. Paper presented at the 7th international scientific conference eLSE "eLearning and Software for Education", Bucharest, April 28–29. Retrieved from http://www.scribd.com/doc/54084667/Academic-research-in-140-characters-or-less. Accessed on December 12, 2011.

Hansen, K. S., Ronne, K., & Jensen, M. (2008). *Microblogging: Facilitating tacit knowledge?* Unpublished dissertation. Copenhagen Business School. Retrieved from http://www.scribd.com/doc/3460679/Microblogging-as-a-Facilitator-for-Tacit-Knowledge

Hargittai, E. (2010). Digital na(t)ives? Variation in Internet skills and uses among members of the net generation. *Sociological Inquiry*, *80*, 92–113.

Haythornthwaite, C. (2009). Learning in the age of web 2.0. Public lectures on the theme of learning networks, London Knowledge Lab, London, UK, December 1. Retrieved from https://docs.google.com/Doc?docid=0AU3Sqf774fhGZGNmOGNtN3ZfMjY0enM3cjJ2ZzM&hl=en. Accessed on October 30, 2011.

HEA – Higher Education Academy. (2010). *Framework for action: Enhancing student engagement at the institutional level*. York, UK: Higher education Academy. Retrieved from http://www.heacademy.ac.uk/resources/detail/studentengagement/Frameworks_for_action_index

Hodges, C. B. (2010, June 24). If you Twitter, will they come? *EDUCAUSE Quarterly, 33*(2). Retrieved from http://www.educause.edu/EDUCAUSE+Quarterly/EDUCAUSEQuarterlyMagazineVolum/IfYouTwitterWillTheyCome/206544. Accessed on 20 August 2010.

Hu, S., & Kuh, G. D. (2001). *Being (dis)engaged in educationally purposeful activities: The influences of student and institutional characteristics*. Paper presented at the American Educational Research Association Annual Conference. Seattle, WA, 10–14 April.

Jenkins, H. (2007). *Confronting the challenges of participatory culture: Media education for the 21st century*. Report from the project Building the Field of Digital Media and Learning, MacArthur Foundation. Retrieved from http://digitallearning.macfound.org/atf/cf/%7B7E45C7E0-A3E0-4B89-AC9C-E807E1B0AE4E%7D/JENKINS_WHITE_PAPER.PDF

Jensen, M., Caswell, T., Ball, J., Duffin, J., & Barton, J. (2010). TwHistory: Sharing history using Twitter. *Proceedings Open Ed 2010, Barcelona. UOC*, 227–229. Retrieved from http://open-ed-2010-proceedings-book.pdf

JISC/HEFCE. (2009). *Higher education in a web 2.0 world*. Committee of inquiry into the changing learner experience, UK. Retrieved from http://www.jisc.ac.uk/publications/documents/heweb2.aspx

Johnson, K. A. (2011). The effect of Twitter posts on students' perceptions of instructor credibility. *Learning, Media and Technology*, *36*(1), 21–38.

Jones, C. (2011). Students, the Net Generation and digital natives: Accounting for educational change. In M. Thomas (Ed.), *Deconstructing digital natives: Young people, technology, and the new literacies* (pp. 30–48). Abingdon, UK: Routledge.

Jones, C., & Cross, S. (2009). Is there a Net generation coming to university? *ALT-C 2009 Proceedings "In dreams begins responsibility" – choice, evidence and change*. 8–10 September 2009, Manchester. Retrieved from http://repository.alt.ac.uk/645/

Jones, C. & Shao, B. (2011). *The net generation and digital natives: Implications for higher education*. York, UK: Higher Education Academy. Retrieved from http://oro.open.ac.uk/30014/

Junco, R. (2010, November 1). Academic excellence in 140 characters [Video clip]. Retrieved from http://www.youtube.com/watch?v=SVOY2x81_bg

Junco, R., Elavsky, C. M., & Heiberger, G. (2012). Putting twitter to the test: Assessing outcomes for student collaboration, engagement and success. *British Journal of Educational Technology*. doi: 10.1111/j.1467-8535.2012.01284.x[Online first].

Junco, R., Heiberger, G., & Loken, E. (2011). The effect of twitter on college student engagement and grades. *Journal of Computer Assisted Learning*, *27*(2), 119–132.

Junco, R., & Timm, D. (2009). *Using emerging technologies to enhance student engagement: New directions for student services*. San Francisco, CA: Jossey-Bass.

Kennedy, G., Dalgarno, B., Bennet, S., Gray, K., Waycott, J., Judd, T., & Chang, R. (2008). Immigrants and natives: investigating differences between staff and students' use of technology. *Proceedings ASCILIITE Melbourne 2008*, 482–492.

Krause, K., & Coates, H. (2008). Students' engagement in first-year university. *Assessment and Evaluation in Higher Education*, *33*(5), 493–505.

Kress, G., & van Leeuwen, T. (2001). *Multimodal discourses: The modes and media of contemporary communication*. London: Hodder Landon.

Kress, G. R. (2003). *Literacy in the new media age*. London: Routledge Falmer.

Kuh, G. D. (2009). What student affairs professionals need to know about student engagement. *Journal of College Student Development*, *50*(6), 683–706.

Lalonde, C. (2011). *The Twitter experience: the role of Twitter in the formation and maintenance of personal learning networks*. Unpublished master's thesis. Royal Roads University, Colwood, British Columbia. Retrieved from http://dspace.royalroads.ca/docs/handle/10170/451

Letierce, J., Passant, A., Breslin, J., & Decker, S. (2010). Understanding how Twitter is used to spread scientific messages. In *Proceedings of the WebSci10: Extending the Frontiers of Society On-Line*, April 26–27, 2010, Raleigh, NC. Retrieved from http://journal.webscience.org/314/

LLIDA (Learning Literacies for the Digital Age). (2009). *Framework of frameworks*. Retrieved from http://caledonianacademy.net/spaces/LLiDA/index.php?n = Main.FrameworkOf-Frameworks

LSE Public Policy Group. (2011). *Maximising the impacts of your research: An handbook for social scientists*. Retrieved from http://blogs.lse.ac.uk/impactofsocialsciences/2011/04/14/maximizing-the-impacts-of-your-research-a-handbook-for-social-scientists-now-available-to-download-as-a-pdf/. Accessed on July 7, 2011.

McNeill, T. (2010a). *More than just passing notes in class? Reflections on the Twitter-enabled backchannel* [Draft paper]. Retrieved from http://www.scribd.com/doc/16287533/More-than-just-passing-notes-in-class-The-Twitterenabled-backchannel

McNeill, T. (2010b). *Twitter, elearning and digital culture*. Unpublished master's dissertation. University of Edinburgh. Retrieved from http://www.scribd.com/doc/24731566/Twitter-Elearning-Digital-Cultures

Minocha, S. (2009). *A study of the effective use of social software by further and higher education in the UK to support student learning and engagement*. JISC Report. Retrieved from http://www.jisc.ac.uk/whatwedo/projects/socialsoftware08.aspx#downloads

Moran, M., Seaman, J., & Tinti-Kane, H. (2011). *Teaching, learning, and sharing: How today's higher education faculty use social media*. Pearson Learning Solutions. Retrieved from http://www.pearsonlearningsolutions.com/blog/2011/05/09/teaching-learning-and-sharing-how-todays-higher-education-facutly-use-social-media/

Oblinger, D. G. (2012). IT as game changer. In D. G. Oblinger (Ed.), *Game changers. Education and information technology* (pp. 37–51). Washington, DC: EDUCAUSE. Retrieved from http://www.educause.edu/game-changers

Oliver, M. (2005). The problem with affordances. *E-Learning and Digital Media*, *2*(4), 402–413.

O'Sullivan, I., & Cleary, L. (2011). *Peer-tutoring in academic writing. The infectious nature of engagement.* Paper presented at the NAIRTL Annual Conference & Galway Symposium on Higher Education. National University of Ireland, Galway, 9–10 June 2011.

Pearce, N. (2010). Digital Scholarship Audit Report, Open University, Milton Keynes. Retrieved from http://oro.open.ac.uk/23143/2/pearce(1).pdf. Accessed on October 18, 2010.

Ramsden, A. (2009). *Using Microblogging (Twitter), in your teaching and learning. An inroductory guide.* Discussion paper. University of Bath.

Ranking, M. (2009). *Some general comments on the "Twitter Experiment."* University of Texas at Dallas. Retrieved from http://www.utdallas.edu/~mrankin/usweb/twitterconclusions.htm

Riley E. (2007). *The effects of a Cuban musical exchange tripon the musical journeys of students from a sydney high school.* Bachelor of music's thesis. University of Sydney. Retrieved from http://ses.library.usyd.edu.au/bitstream/2123/2177/1/Riley%202007.pdf

Ross, C., Terras, M., Warwick, C., & Welsh, A. (2011). Enabled backchannel: Conference Twitter use by digital humanists. *Journal of Documentation*, *67*(2), 214–237. Retrieved from http://www.ucl.ac.uk/infostudies/claire-ross/Digitally_Enabled_Backchannel.pdf

Santonocito, R. (2010a, January 18). *Alla Statale di Milano al via il primo corso con Twitter in aula.* In *Job24* [Il Sole24Ore online]. Retrieved from http://job24.ilsole24ore.com/news/Articoli/2010/01/twitteruniversity-apre-18012010.php?uuid = ac7475a0-0506-11df-9833-731e880466d4&type = Libero

Santonocito, R. (2010b, February 7). *Diari/L'università su Twitter: ecco il primo diario dalla Statale di Milano.* In *Job24* [Il Sole24Ore online]. Retrieved from http://jobtalk.blog.ilsole24ore.com/jobtalk/2010/02/diari-luniversita-su-twitter-ecco-il-primo-dario.html

Santonocito, R. (2010c, April 8). *Diari/L'università su Twitter, il 2° diario dalla Statale di Milano. Da Giulia.* In *Job24* [Il Sole24Ore online]. Retrieved from http://jobtalk.blog.ilsole24ore.com/jobtalk/2010/03/diari luniversita-su-twitter-ecco-il-secondo-diario-dalla-statale-di-milano-da-giulia.html

Santonocito, R. (2010d, April 8). *Diari/L'università su Twitter, il 4° diario dalla Statale di Milano. Emma: "La risorsa siamo noi!".* In *Job24* [Il Sole24Ore online]. Retrieved from http://jobtalk.blog.ilsole24ore.com/jobtalk/2010/04/diari-luniversita-su-twitter-il-4o-diario-dalla-statale-di-milano-emma-la-risorsa-siamo-noi.html

Selwyn, N. (2010). The educational significance of social media: A critical perspective. Key note talk at the *ED-MEDIA 2010 conference*, Toronto. Retrieved from http://www.scribd.com/doc/33693537/The-educational-significance-of-social-media-a-critical-perspective

Sharpe, R., Beetham, H., & de Freitas, M. (2010). *Rethinking learning for a digital age: How learners are shaping their own experiences.* London: Routledge.

Spear, B. (2009, January 22). How we Twitter. [Blog post]. Retrieved from http://englishforpros.wordpress.com/2009/01/22/how-twitter/. Accessed on 8 July, 2010.

Timmis, S. (2012). Constant companions: Instant messaging conversations as sustainable supportive study structures amongst undergraduate peers. *Computers & Education*, *59*(1), 3–18. (August 2012).

Torrance, C., Mistry, V., Higginson, R., Jones, B. (2010). *Scaffolding learning (ScaLe) with Twitter*. JISC Final Report. Pontypridd, University of Glamorgan. Retrieved from http://www.jisc.ac.uk/media/documents/programmes/elearning/ltig/ScaLeFinalReport1.docx

Trowler, V. (2010). *Student engagement literature review*. York, UK: The Higher Education Academy.

Veletsianos, G. (2010). *Participatory scholars and 21st century scholarship*. Paper presented at the ITForum, April 12–16, 2010. Draft paper [online], in George Veletsianos's blog. Retrieved from http://www.veletsianos.com/2010/04/06/participatory-scholars-scholarshi/

Veletsianos, G. (2011). Higher education scholars' participation and practices on Twitter. *Journal of Computer Assisted Learning, 28*(4), 336–349. doi: 10.1111/j.1365-2729.2011.00449.x

Veletsianos, G., & Kimmons, R. (2012). Networked participatory scholarship: Emergent techno-cultural pressures toward open and digital scholarship in online networks. *Computers & Education, 58*(2), 766–774. Retrieved from http://www.veletsianos.com/wp-content/uploads/2011/11/NPS_final_published.pdf

Vieweg, S. (2010). *The ethics of Twitter research*. Paper presented at the workshop Revisiting Research Ethics in the Facebook Era: Challenges in Emerging CSCW Research, The ACM Conference, Savannah, GA. Retrievedfrom http://www.cc.gatech.edu/~yardi/ethics-cscw2010_files/AcceptedPapers.htm

Waycott, J., Bennet, S., Kennedy, G., Dalgarno, B., & Gray, K. (2010). Digital divides? Student and staff perceptions of information and communication technologies. *Computers & education, 54*, 1202–1211.

Weller, M. (2011). *The digital scholar. How technology is transforming academic practice*. Bloomsbury Academic, London [Open access version]. Retrieved from http://www.bloomsburyacademic.com/view/DigitalScholar_9781849666275/book-ba-9781849666275.xml

White, D. (2012, April 24). Education should move us. [Blog post]. *TALL blog – Online education with University of Oxford*. Retrieved from http://tallblog.conted.ox.ac.uk/index.php/category/presentations/

White, D., & Le Cornu, A. (2011, September 5). Visitors and residents: A new typology for online engagement. *First Monday* [online], *16*(9). Retrieved from http://firstmonday.org/htbin/cgiwrap/bin/ojs/index.php/fm/article/view/3171/3049

Young, J. R. (2009, November 22). Teaching with Twitter: Not for the faint of heart. *Chronicle of Higher Education*. Retrieved from http://chronicle.com/article/Teaching-With-Twitter-Not-for/49230/?sid=wc&utm_source=wc&utm_medium=en

Young, S., & Bruce, M. A. (2011, June). Classroom community and student engagement in online courses. *MERLOT Journal of Online Learning and Teaching, 7*(2). Retrieved from http://jolt.merlot.org/vol7no2/young_0611.htm

Zepke, N., & Leach, L. (2010). Improving student engagement: Ten proposals for action. *Active Learning in Higher Education, 11*, 167–177.

ENHANCED *CLASS REPLAY*: WILL THIS TURN INTO BETTER LEARNING?

Ferdinando Pennarola and Leonardo Caporarello

ABSTRACT

The purpose of this chapter is to illustrate and discuss an exploratory research about an educational innovation project to be introduced in a higher education institution. The background of the initiative belongs to the rolling upgrades of information and communication technology infrastructures and services on modern university campuses. The chapter discusses the benefits of the decoupling Classroom Replay *system, i.e., a classroom technology that records lectures and makes them available on dedicated online channels as video files or audio podcast. The chapter argues that learners will benefit from the service if a social tagging system is offered, such that users can quickly browse the files and create their own learning path through the recorded material.*

INTRODUCTION

Educational institutions compete by offering (a) up-to-date content, (b) advanced educational methods, and (c) better services to their learning

Increasing Student Engagement and Retention using Classroom Technologies: Classroom Response Systems and Mediated Discourse Technologies
Cutting-edge Technologies in Higher Education, Volume 6E, 143–162

ISSN: 2044-9968/doi:10.1108/S2044-9968(2013)000006E008

community. This chapter focuses on the latter and explores its implications on the second, thus highlighting to what degree this form of competition enhances the attractiveness of the institution to the wider market. The globalization of content transforms the contest on educational methods and services as the main battlefield to fascinate talented students. The enrichment of educational methods and the improvement of services both require the cooperation of the faculty, who are the indispensable mediating factor in the delivery of the educational initiative. The project described in this chapter is the result of a fruitful collaboration between faculty and support staff within a leading university in Italy: it designates the traits of an important research initiative, the findings of which can be of future interest to other educational institutions. The technological solutions adopted are described, allowing other interested parties to replicate them and design a similar study. The research described is at its initial stages, thus in this chapter we describe its unfolding, the literature review supporting our research goal, the research assumptions and propositions, and some expected outcomes.

Project Background

The case of the OpenCourseWare (OCW) at Massachusetts Institute of Technology (MIT) deserves attention and brings to some reflections: it is a remarkable story of innovation in higher education, successfully adopted by the vast majority of MIT faculty – over 90% as their website states. The full potential of the OCW project is still unknown and its impact on global education needs to be evaluated. Nonetheless, MIT has a clear vision that knowledge can work as a public good for the benefit of all, and the thousands of feedbacks received seem to confirm that OCW is improving education and bringing new opportunities to people everywhere. The spirit of open sharing has contaminated many institutions: unsurprisingly, MIT states on its website (ocw.mit.edu): "we also encourage you to share your scholarship with others, as hundreds of other universities are already doing through their own OCWs."

Despite the pioneering efforts of the MIT's OCW experience, and despite clear improvements of students' services, which provides the possibility to rewatch missed classes and/or access to a growing knowledge databank, little has been done to explain the expected outcomes of these investments in terms of learning impact and the overall quality of the learning processes.

Since 2002, Bocconi University, a leading Italian university with a growing international reputation, started following, with some differences, the MIT experience. In particular, over the last 8 years, part of the technology budget was spent in video recording the lectures of the best teachers. Video files were made available to students through an e-learning web portal at the end of each lecture: the number of recorded classes per course ranged from 24 to 36, according to a two to three times per week schedule, depending on course credit impact. Class feedback provided by the attendees was significantly better compared to similar course evaluations. Students said that they appreciate the feature and the possibility of rewatching class lectures in preparation of their exams. The video files were made available together with other learning material provided by the instructor through the university e-learning web portal services: material ranged from class notes to slides projected in class, cases and exercises and other published articles quoted during lectures. A number of other additional features originated from the initiative, including the possibility to download the content to personal mobile devices.

Despite a strong support from the university leadership, a significant limitation to the initiative was dictated by serious budget constraints, allowing only a limited number of professional staff to record the lectures. This has led to fewer and fewer lectures being recorded per academic term. During the 2010/2011 academic year a new project was launched to bypass the above constraints, by cutting the cost of the video recording and concurrently expanding the best lectures series to a wider number of courses. The project named "Class Replay" originates as a solution to avoid the limitations of the original idea.

The Decoupling of the Video Recording Systems: The "Class Replay" Project

This project, named *Class Replay*, is part of a major review of the teaching technology infrastructure, currently undergoing at Bocconi University. A committee, formed by support staff and representative academics involved in teaching innovation through technology, examined the situation, designed and tested a number of solutions. The authors of the present essay were part of the committee and proposed the research initiative described below.

The *Class Replay* project takes the lead from the mentioned issues, and aims at spreading – university wide – a hassle free system that will be adopted by a larger faculty body. The objective of the project is to continue providing a set of post-class services, among which the class recording is the most relevant. The *Class Replays* will be made available via the university e-learning portal. Even though the project aims at providing more learning resources to attending students only, it will not inhibit non-attending students to browse through the recorded files and access the same resources. Enrolled, but non-attending students will not be able to use only the *Class Replays* to pass the corresponding exam and gain credits, since the evaluations are made of a variety of tasks – including group work assignments – addressed only to the attending. The *Class Replays* will be particularly helpful to those students who will occasionally miss a class; at the same time, the service works as an additional learning resource to review all the material, and rewatch the lecturing and the discussions had in class.

An experimental laboratory classroom was identified and equipped with new and updated teaching technologies, among which we quote two: (a) powered Wi-Fi coverage that allows all accommodating people to simultaneously connect to the Internet, (b) an automated, voice activated, 360 degrees high definition camera, placed on the ceiling of the classroom, able to record the class scene from any desirable perspective. The software provided to control the camera allowed multiple recording settings, and is able to fit with infinite combination of needs. For example, one of the tested settings was to follow the instructor, identified by wearing a wireless microphone, by monitoring his/her movements around the classroom; another programmed situation assumed "*n*" classroom scenes (i.e., the computer desk, the teacher writing on the blackboard, the instructor interacting with students in the middle of the amphitheater-like room) and the camera was able to recognize the situation and switch to the appropriate framing shot. The study of the possible shooting angles and classroom teaching scenes required the full collaboration between the faculty representatives within the committee, the outside technicians, and the support staff, with the aim of incorporating a variety of teaching styles and needs of the wider faculty body of the institution.

The heart of the project is based on the recording technology provided in the laboratory: it decouples the sources into two separate but interlaced streams: (a) a video server that stores all the recordings on separate audio and video tracks, which we will call the "class stream" and (b) a visual and audio recording of all the material shown in class by the teacher through the classroom networked PC (i.e., slides, websites, video and audio files, documents in various formats, any application software available on the campus network) which we will call the "PC stream." Should the teaching faculty adopt a tablet technology and use it to write with a digital pen, all the writing will be recorded too, being a substitute of what appears on the traditional blackboard, and it will be channeled as a PC stream.

The video camera is voice activated and can also point to students that want to jump into the class debate with the instructor, and participate with their views. Thanks to the full Wi-Fi coverage, designed to load the highest number of simultaneous access to the campus network (equal to the number of classroom seats, in our case the lab classroom accommodates 90), the instructor can activate a desktop sharing feature from any of the students' devices to the classroom screen. This unleashes a whole new set of teaching possibilities, among which leveraging the contribution from attendees, by producing and showing in real time what they have found on their own networked devices (either laptop or tablet) to the instructor and the rest of the class, and channel it into the PC stream. For example, one possible teaching/learning setting may require students to search for information and/or examples by browsing web resources: the instructor could ask a volunteer to share what he/she found with the rest of the class and make it appear on the classroom screen. All of this learning environment will be properly recorded according to the two separated streams of data: class and PC stream.

The *Class Replay* project assumes that the recorded material will not require further post-production (beyond putting a title page at the top and the end of its segments) and it is made available to students via the campus e-learning web portal at the end of the day. The teacher in class will only be required to wear and activate a radio microphone and start lecturing, by pressing the start recording button. One advanced version of the project will give to the teacher an extra remote button that, when pressed, will leave a time mark on the recorded channels. The assumption is that the teacher can magnify some key learning of his/her lecture, thus allowing users to skip to the time mark and hyper-navigate any of the recorded material.

The students' interface is rather straightforward. They will receive the option of a full, high definition, *Class Replay* by watching the full streamed class video (class stream) and/or combining it with the dedicated information flow recorded from the classroom PC (PC stream). This solution is expected to have a much greater learning impact: traditional class video recording, with one camera only, was not appropriate when filming the projected slides, or worse, a video in the class. The quality of the shooting was unsatisfactory. Decoupling the two streams of recorded material allows the user to follow both of them on separate windows of the same interface.

As a consequence, the pre-existing service budget, needed to outsource the video recording to professional staff, has been brought to zero and a significant improvement in the quality of the recording has been achieved. The project went through a wide communication and training initiative throughout the university, and it is being evaluated the possibility of making this solution a standard feature of every classroom over the next 5 years.

Lessons Learned from the Relevant Literature

The *Class Replay* project is part of a wider movement of literature that considers the opportunities brought by information technology and networked devices in the learning environment, and it also matches the requirements of well-established methodologies that account for the importance of learning in a blended way. Engaging students to actively participate to class discussions, rather than passively listening to their instructors, is a long established evidence of how to enhance the learning process.

For more than a decade, authoritative critics such as Derek Bok (1986) have been calling for a revolution in higher education, with new curricula that put less emphasis on transmittal of information to passive students and more emphasis on teaching methods that enable the students to actively build their own knowledge and skills (Mundell & Pennarola, 1999; Pennarola & Mundell, 2001; Venkatesh & Davis, 2000). What we know today is that learning is such a fascinating phenomenon that does not take place only in traditional classroom settings: teaching methodologies that allow students to interact beyond class appointments have been investigated.

In fact, the learning paradigm has shifted from a teacher-centric approach to a learner-centric one characterized by the following elements: (1) content will shift from limited to rich, (2) process will move from traditional to experiential, (3) expected outcomes will move from knowledge acquisition to knowledge creation and integration, (4) location will be more by the course participant, and (5) tools will shift from traditional to blended (Brown, 2003).

The *Class Replay* project aims at being a non-obstructive technology that allows the teacher to augment the effectiveness of the overall learning environment, either during traditional class hours or after calendared appointments with students. Within this context, technology – when properly designed and adopted – provides a positive support in terms of accelerating traditional learning processes and enabling new ones. As a matter of fact, technology for education has made great advances in the last two decades. The technology integration in learning processes allows participants to extend learning outside the class, promote learners' critical thinking approach, enhance interaction among participants, and their problem-solving and collaboration skills (Crocco, 2001; Jonassen, Pfeiffer, & Wilson, 1998; Pope, Hare, & Howard, 2005; Wenglinsky, 2005). Thus, technology integration in learning processes is no longer a "to-be" situation for academics, but it is already a way to widen learning opportunities and a method of making education (Bauer & Kenton, 2005).

The use of technology for learning offers a variety of opportunities, for both teachers and students, including instant global communication, real-time access to limitless information, access to environments that can be inaccessible or too expensive in a classroom setting, living a simulated experience otherwise costly and time consuming, allowing them to repeat the experience as many times as necessary (Buckenmeyer, 2010).

In a Ph.D. dissertation given at Fielding Graduate University in 2005, Barry J. Vroeginday showed the existence of "significant differences in final exam and overall course scores between the traditional and online learners taking nearly identical introductory environmental science courses with the same instructor" (Vroeginday, 2005). Aziz, Khan, and Singh (2010) found out that using computers promotes students' learning engagement and increases students' interactions "with fellow students and/or instructors."

Nowadays, teachers take advantage of multiple technology-based learning tools and lecture-enriching tools, and methodologies. Among the first group (technological tools and lecture-enriching tools), projectors, Wi-Fi, laptop computer, PowerPoint presentations, web pages, electronic bulletin boards, video conferencing systems are commonly in place (ECAR, 2011; Wright & Wilson, 2009). Among the technology-based learning methodologies, management simulations and business games are very much used now. Computer simulations are a method often used for learning purposes, as such simulations allow to live an experience that provides useful insights and concepts that are, or will be, discussed during the course (Peluchette & Rust, 2005). Business games support the development of different abilities just like the ability to process information very quickly and in parallel, the tendency to access information at first instance through imagery, the embodied empathy for a complex system, and fluency with a cross-functional affiliation (operating in a team to achieve a common goal). Business games differ from simulations because of the lack of game dynamics in simulations (like the "win state"). Nevertheless, simulations and business games have many benefits in common.

Although it is easy to figure out the advantages and opportunities offered by technology integration in learning processes, such integration process might be very difficult. The real challenge is not just getting some technology into classrooms, but understanding how to use the appropriate technology for learning purposes (Buckenmeyer, 2010). Indeed, some researches have highlighted the lag of soft skills needed to successfully integrate technology in learning processes (Becker, 1994; Ertmer, Addison, Lane, Ross, & Woods, 1999; Firek, 2003). This is coherent with a previous research suggesting that the availability of technology in classroom is not significantly related to the use of technology (Buckenmeyer, 2010).

To fully exploit the potential of technology for education, three relevant driving factors have to be taken into consideration. The first driving factor refers to the teacher's level of confidence with the technology itself (Dusick, 1998; Mitchell, 1997; Spotts, 1999), and its method of use for learning purposes. So, time spent on such familiarizing process represents a key factor (Dockstader, 1999; Liu et al., 2004). According to Mellon (1999), effective implementation of technology for education requires teachers to be aware of different learning styles and always have "alternative approaches to the use of technology" considering the fact that some students might prefer learning individually while others in group. Learners, instead, might own several technological tools, but this doesn't mean they are "tech-friendly" as expected. In fact, a recent study shows that there is no significant relationship between owning a lot of high-tech tools (e.g., smartphones, laptops) and being a technology expert (Caporarello & Sarchioni, 2010). Consequently, students may need to be educated on how to get the most out of the technological tools they might already have and/or use.

The second driving factor is about the teachers' ability of shape the technology to meet participants' needs (Craig, Goold, Coldwell, & Mustard, 2008; Sheingold & Hadley, 1990). According to Mandell, Sorge, and Russell (2002), teachers are the most important success factor when using and integrating technology in learning processes. In other words, whatever is the change in the learning process, it should not begin with the technology, but with the teacher, who is central to the creation of a technology-integrated environment that is learner-centered (Beckett, Marquez-Chisholm, & Wetzel, 2003).

The third driving factor relates to the pivotal role played by the institutional support for integrating technology in learning processes (Boose, 2001; Spotts, 1999). Spending too much time in managing the technology (i.e., technological equipment set-up, slow equipment delivery) can foster barriers to use technology for learning (Papo, 2001).

In addition to the above considerations, further research (Alavi & Gallupe, 2003) showed that culture – and not cost factors – does represent a big impediment to effective technology-for-education implementation in schools. The fact that some initiatives do not work as expected can be the result of a refractory culture rather than the inefficacy of the technology itself.

Technology integration in a learning process requires an intertwined relation between technology, pedagogy, and content (Mishra & Koehler, 2006). From here, using a pedagogical lens of analysis, when the process of technology integration in a learning process is successfully implemented, at least four pedagogical principles emerge: active learning, mediation, collaboration, interactivity (Jaffee, 1997).

Active learning refers to the students' interaction with the content that allows knowledge creation (Bonwell & Eison, 1991). It is demonstrated that technology for active learning helps to keep students focused, engaged, and motivated (Barak, Lipson, & Lerman, 2006). Mediation refers to the interaction between teachers and students in order to discuss topics and content related to the course, solve problems, and respond to questions. The objective of using technology for mediation is twofold: increasing the frequency and amount of human-to-human interaction between teachers and students while meeting the needs of the students' changing learning styles (Schroeder, 1993).

Collaboration refers to the interaction among students through discussions, questions, and information sharing. Technology supported the learning paradigm shift into a learner-centric rather than teacher-centric one (Caporarello, 2011). Consequently, students' role changed from listeners to collaborators (Jurist, 1999). Also, the teacher's role changed from lecturer to collaborator and facilitator.

Finally, interactivity has the greatest pedagogical potential for technology-mediated learning processes. Interactivity refers to the process of building the understanding and knowledge through interaction with other students, teachers, and resources. The use of technology facilitates that process, and also allows customizing content to meet individual needs and learning style (Pantazis, 2002; Papo, 2001; Sherer & Shea, 2002).

According to a recent study (ECAR, 2011), almost 60% of learners stated they learn more on a blended learning environment.

Extending the Learning Experience: The Innovative Social Tagging Feature

The *Class Replay* key feature relies mainly on its recording system. The service of providing to students the integral recording on multimedia files has some limitations, primarily because of the length of the recording (most of the class sections will be of 90 minutes). Rewatching the recording could be perceived as arduous and by someone not very useful either unless the system will be powered with quick and easy tools to find information in big 90 minutes high definition files.

This is the reason why a further enhancement of the system is under design, evaluation, and testing. The possibility of marking/tagging the video files will increase significantly the usefulness of the recording by giving students the opportunity to jump over sections of the recorded material that are less relevant for the user. The system will allow using tags in either the video recording of the class experience (first stream), or the PC stream.

A social tagging system will be made available to students re-viewing the files online. The tagging system will allow users to drop a marker in the preferred position of the file, after naming the marker and choosing a title, and then leaving a comment. Name of the tagging person (only people with registered credentials will be allowed to tag the files), name of the tag and its description will be made available, transparently, to anyone browsing the file.

We expect to formally keep the tagging feature open to anyone who is browsing the lecture files. Nonetheless, since the service is mainly addressed to the attending students, we would suggest that each instructor using the system encourage his/her learners to work on the tags during the time window of the course, before the end of the class term. The reason for this is to contribute to the improvement of the browsing of the 90 minutes long files, in preparation for the evaluation of the learning at the end of the class term.

Together with the markers left by the instructor, which will remain as an optional feature during the recording of the lecture, we would expect that each class section, deposited into the *Class Replay* feature, will appear as a much richer database of insights regarding the class experience. Tags provided by the learners and tags eventually left by the instructor will feed an entirely new post-class learning experience that goes much beyond the traditional video recording of any university lecture. It is noteworthy to say that the system being tested is by itself of high interest for non-learning contexts also.

Why Contribute to the Tagging System? Conceptual Foundations of Online Collaboration and Research Propositions

One key aspect of the *Class Replay* system is the contribution of those that will take part to the social tagging feature. In such a way, teachers create a learning context, which facilitates students' engagement in and active contribution to learning activities. This is coherent with the social constructivism theory (Vygotsky, 1962). According to this theory, learning is first constructed in a social context and then at the individual level (Eggen & Kauchak, 2006).

We assume that, based on the very successful past experiences of the previous *Class Replay* services, attending students will like the new one, as well: nonetheless, the question is how many, and why, will contribute to deposit their tags on the recorded material. This is a fundamental issue of online collaboration and learning, and it needs further exploration.

The debate on the impact of information technology use on learning processes is ample and it produced many controversies. IT applications can be designed to support individual or team-based learning (Basaglia, Caporarello, Magni, & Pennarola, 2010), but a fundamental difference needs to be underlined: learning-from-computers is substantially different from learning-with-computers. Learning-from-computers occurs when the computer is the medium of instruction (e.g., computer-based training). Research comparing the effectiveness of individual learning-from-computers to standard methods of instruction has provided inconclusive results in both education (Kovalchick & Dawson, 2004) and information systems (IS) literature (Gupta & Bostrom, 2009). Though initial results in team-based learning-from-computer treatments are positive (Kovalchick & Dawson, 2004), there have been few such studies in both IS and education. Learning-with-computers occurs when information technology is used as a tool to support learning (e.g., use of a website by instructor or use of collaborative technology). An educational meta-analysis at the individual level showed that learning-with-computers had a positive impact (Kulik, 1994). However, an educational meta-analysis of team-based learning-with-computers shows inconclusive results (Strijbos, Martens, & Jochems, 2004). Within the IS field, research results of learning-with-computers studies have been inconclusive at both individual and team levels. For example, at the individual level, Zhang, Zhao, Zhou, and Nunamaker, (2004) found a positive impact, whereas Piccoli, Ahmad, and Ives (2001) did not, except for an increase in self-efficacy. At the team level, Leidner and Fuller (1997) found a positive impact of the use of collaborative technology, but Hiltz, Coppola, Rotter, Turoff, and Benbunan-Fich (2001) and Alavi (1994) did not.

The *Class Replay* system will turn value to users if it will be used as a collaborative team-based learning tool to enhance learning. This leads to our first research proposition:

RP 1. Over the 90 minutes long media files, users will navigate better if they will get value from other peers contributing to the social tagging feature.

Collaboration will come from peers that substantially participate to the identical learning environment (the traditional class schedule) being the system primarily offered to the attending students.

Even though its origins date far back in time, the modern concept of online collaboration is quite recent. Starting from the 1980s, people working together began using machines instead of meeting face-to-face in order to save time and travel costs. Only a few years later, the idea of physical presence was considered old fashioned, with remote connections linking almost every corner of the world, drastically reducing distances, and facilitating collaboration. Internet boom, which in some cases generated skepticism among users, has been characterized by wild and deregulated uploading: the apparent goal was to move online everything from the real world, in search for a perfect natural-virtual correspondence.

Thus, the issue of online collaboration can be analyzed under two perspectives: (1) amplified collaboration in case of a student-centered learning approach and (2) collaboration as a result of a mass effect of network externalities constructs and related findings.

Mundell and Pennarola (1999) found that collaboration can be amplified if the learning environment is designed to emphasize the group-based, student-centered learning approach. People need trust more than reality, and the new technologies are consistent with users' expectancies. Communication and collaboration do not express the same concept, even if the two often overlap in the common language. While the former is an exchange of information without any long-term goal, the latter is a more structured dialogue with some kind of interaction expected among the parties. To make the difference clear, we can consider the term collaboration as collaborative value creation, which not only implies communication, but also coordination, cooperation, and a common objective, regardless of its voluntariness nature (Mundell & Pennarola, 1997, 1999).

The *Class Replay* system needs all of this, since it helps rewinding the class learning context and highlighting its most important steps. A student-centered approach is characterized by "an almost complete role reversal between teachers and students, putting the latter in the driver's seat and requiring teams of students to teach each other based on their particular talents and experience" (Mundell & Pennarola, 1999). Mundell and Pennarola (1999) found that the findings for both structural and attitudinal variables confirm that participants in the course played an active role in their own learning at both the individual and group level. "Individuals are more motivated and learn more when they work in groups, thereby explaining the synergy that is often created by groups. Giving to groups a greater delegation of autonomy and responsibility creates opportunities for teaching and learning among groups of students. In integrating the work of the separate subgroups into a coherent response to a complex assignment, the students are forced to negotiate to convince the other subgroups to adopt their proposed solutions" (Mundell & Pennarola, 1999). These findings lead to the second research proposition:

RP2. The social tagging system will produce higher results if students:

2(a). will be assigned to groups in class and their group composition will be transparent in the system.

2(b). will be challenged – as a team – to accomplish a learning task by using the Class Replay system.

Collaborative action and complex interdependencies play a major role (Basaglia, Caporarello, Magni, & Pennarola, 2009; Rheingold, 2008). Open Sourcing is a relevant example of the changing times, in a period where patent portfolios are distributed to the commons and suppliers are treated as a network instead of third parties along the value chain: they are trained to produce better, even if the improved quality will benefit competitors as well (Dyer & Nobeoka, 2000). These behaviors, driven by personal interests rather than altruism, stress the idea supported by Conlon and Giovagnoli (1998), who argued that "No organization – no matter how big or how smart – knows as much as two organizations (or as much as an alliance network)". Working together along the production line or across distinctive sectors is beneficial and economically convenient. There are, however, some constituting elements typically characterizing the interaction (Spekman, Kamauff, & Myhr, 1998):

- a voluntary agreement between otherwise independent parties;
- the pursuit of collaborative objectives, basically the pooling, transfer and development of resources; and
- a substantial degree of individual based collaboration.

Collaborative value creation, hence, is based on complementary and strategic resources, regarded as technical instruments, commercial goods, and social capital, pivotal in the analysis. People, in fact, generate further collaboration, being a value-creation asset themselves. These other quoted findings will lead us to the third research proposition:

RP3. Collaborative value creation, enhanced by the Class Replay system, will be higher if students will be free to form their teams, and group their resources according to their preferences.

Finally, the so-called "network externalities effect," namely the influence that one consumer of a product or a service has on the other users (Cowan & Jonard, 2004), must be taken into account. In this very case, the utility of a single platform not only depends on its actual functionality, but also, and mainly, on the number of individuals that already use the same technology. The "value" or "power" of a network, hence, increases in proportion to the square of the number of nodes on the network. The phenomenon, known as Metcalfe's Law (Nielsen, 1999), is typical of the telecommunication environment, the Internet, and the social networks. The result is an exponential progression that is clearly steeper than the geometrical return offered by collaboration deployment, suggesting a mitigation of the network effect by external factors and structural limitations. We believe that the *Class Replay* system will turn into a success to the extent to which it will be widely adopted by a large community of users. As a consequence, this leads to our final fourth research proposition:

> **RP4.** Being the social tagging feature open to anyone that will have access to the system, regardless of the class attendance requirement, groups of attending students will be more motivated to contribute to the tagging feature if the number of the overall users of the system will increase rapidly short after the publication of the media files.

As a consequence, we plan to heavily advertise the new *Class Replay* system by using a number of strategies that will allow the university to spread out the results of the system and encourage more users to practice the new services.

The Research Project Design and Implementation

The research project consists in closely monitoring how students will use the *Class Replay* feature to review material for their learning. Furthermore, we expect that the magnifying feature used by the teacher will allow to underline some key aspect of the lecture and/or to emphasize definitions and important notions.

We decided to follow a pre-defined path to build this research project and answer to the above four research questions. The literature we have been consulting suggested us the design of a technology-mediated learning experience (TML) that is in the mainstream of research and findings on this topic. That is why we want to recall the TML general framework

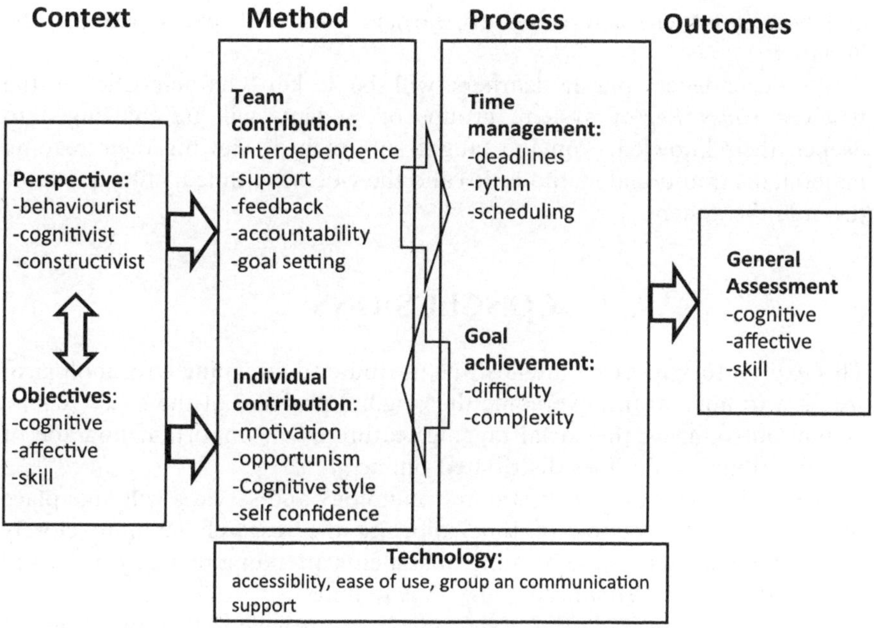

Fig. 1. Measuring the Learning Outcomes of the Class Replay System. Adapted from Gupta and Bostrom (2009).

model designed by Gupta and Bostrom (2009) as a departing platform to describe:

1. how the research will be conducted?
2. what are the key elements of the research design that will lead to our expected outcomes?

The model is replicated in Fig. 1.

The research outcomes will be linked to the four research propositions. Attending students that will use the *Class Replay* services and system will be strictly monitored in terms of their learning and take away, not only from a content perspective but also from an effective point of view, in particular linked to their group-based experience. Data about students' behavior and performances will be collected and analyzed.

The research project will also, consistent with the Gupta and Bostrom (2009) findings, provide a wide platform of individual and group appropriation data: we expect to collect a detailed data set on group demographics and individual characteristics of learners that will participate to the initiative.

Interdependence among learners will be a key characteristic of the renewed *Class Replay* system: groups of students will be challenged to deepen their knowledge on the taught subject by reviewing their reading material (as traditional methods do) and the video/multimedia files available through the system.

CONCLUSIONS

This exploratory research intends to contribute to designing a technological solution to answer and overcome the original problem of the *Class Replay* system, introducing the social tagging feature as an important upgrade of the traditional media files distributed online.

The deployment of this classroom technology and services will take place over an extended period of time allowing the research team to closely monitor the impact on the learning of students attending regular classes and those attending the enhanced *Class Replay* only.

Although still in its initial design phase, we believe that implications of this project are many. First, it will open a chapter on the impact on learning of technology-based services that are wide spreading today in many universities. Administrators and faculty can collect data on the real learning impact and can measure the returns of their investment. Second, it will allow learners to hyper-navigate course resources instead of sequentially reading/viewing/listening to the whole recorded material, replicating a somewhat well-known experience of hypertext reading on web pages. Third, the system will contribute to the wider field of knowledge construction through long and complex media files, designed to be sequentially viewed, turning them into more fruitful resources. If successful, the consequences of this solution can be extraordinarily important: readers may refer to the huge amount of video streams available on the web, not only provided by the You Tube platform – these streams can become a gigantic podium for knowledge building according to personalized needs. We hypothesize that this will initiate a new perspective in teaching and learning through technology-mediated infrastructures. We hope that readers have increased their appreciation of the importance of integrating twenty-first-century technology into the classroom in a way that goes beyond the gee-whiz aspects. We hope to stimulate educators to deeply rethink the value that can be added by teachers in our fields.

This essay is not to be intended as a definitive statement on the role that technology can play in shifting from a pedagogical to an andragogical paradigm. By sharing one particularly exciting and rich experience, we open a dialogue with management educators about the opportunities for and limits to integrating information technology into the core technology of learning. We hope that our 1-year design journey can inspire others to embark on similar adventures.

REFERENCES

Alavi, M. (1994). Computer-mediated collaborative learning: An empirical evaluation. *MIS Quarterly*, *18*(2), 150–174.

Alavi, M., & Gallupe, R. B. (2003). Using information technology in learning: Case studies in business and management education programs. *Academy of Management Learning Education*, *2*(2), 139–153.

Aziz, T., Khan, M. B., & Singh, R. (2010). Effects of information technology usage on student learning: An empirical study in the United States. *International Journal of Management*, *27*(2), 205–217.

Barak, M., Lipson, A., & Lerman, S. (2006). Wireless laptops as means for promoting active learning in large lecture halls. *Journal of Research on Technology in Education*, *38*(3), 245–263.

Basaglia, S., Caporarello, L., Magni, M., & Pennarola, F. (2009). Individual adoption of convergent mobile technologies in Italy. *Review of Managerial Science*, *3*(1), 1–18.

Basaglia, S., Caporarello, L., Magni, M., & Pennarola, F. (2010). IT knowledge integration capability and team performance: The role of team climate. *International Journal of Information Management*, *30*(6), 542–551.

Bauer, J., & Kenton, J. (2005). Toward technology integration in the schools: Why it isn't happening. *Journal of Technology and Teacher Education*, *13*(4), 519–546.

Becker, H. J. (1994). How exemplary computer-using teachers differ from other teachers: Implications for realizing the potential of computers in schools. *Journal of Research on Computing in Education*, *26*, 291–321.

Beckett, E. C., Marquez-Chisholm, I., & Wetzel, K. (2003). Preparing technology-competent teachers: A strategy for multicultural schools. *T.H.E. Journal*, *30*(11), 14–24.

Bok, D. (1986). *Higher learning*. Cambridge, MA: Harvard University Press.

Bonwell, C. C., & Eison, J. A. (1991). *Active learning: Creating excitement in the classroom (Higher Education Report No. 1)*. Washington, DC: ASHE-ERIC.

Boose, M. A. (2001). Web-based instruction: Successful preparation for course transformation. *Journal of Applied Business Research*, *17*(4), 69–80.

Brown, K. L. (2003). From teacher-centered to learner-centered curriculum: Improving learning in diverse classrooms. *Education*, *124*(1).

Buckenmeyer, J. A. (2010). Beyond computers in the classroom: Factors related to technology adoption to enhance teaching and learning. *Contemporary Issues in Education Research*, *3*(4), 27–36.

Caporarello, L. (2011). *The paradigm of managerial education: Role of management simulation.* White Paper, SDA Bocconi Learning Lab. Retrieved from http://www.sdabocconi.it/en/learning-lab

Caporarello, L., & Sarchioni, G. (2010, March 11). *Web 2.0 and gen Y: The hidden truth.* Milan, IT, Bocconi University. Translated by Alex Foti. Retrieved from http://www.viasarfatti25.unibocconi.eu/notizia.php?idArt=6466

Conlon, J. K., & Giovagnoli, M. K. (1998). *The power of two: How companies of all sizes can build alliance networks that generate business opportunities.* San Francisco, CA: Jossey-Bass.

Cowan, R., & Jonard, N. (2004). Network structure and the diffusion of knowledge. *Journal of Economic Dynamics and Control, 28*(8), 1557–1575.

Craig, A., Goold, A., Coldwell, J., & Mustard, J. (2008). Perceptions of roles and responsibilities in online learning: A case study. *Interdisciplinary Journal of Knowledge & Learning Objects, 4*, 205–223.

Crocco, M. S. (2001). Leveraging constructivist learning in the social studies classroom: A response to Mason, Berson, Diem, Hicks, Lee, and Dralle. *Contemporary Issues in Technology and Teacher Education, 1*(3), 386–394.

Dockstader, J. (1999). Teachers of the 21st century know the what, why, and how of technology integration. *T.H.E. Journal, 26*(6), 73–74.

Dusick, D. M. (1998). What social cognitive factors influence faculty members' use of computers for teaching? A literature review. *Journal of Research on Computing in Education, 31*(2), 123–140.

Dyer, J. H., & Nobeoka, K. (2000). Creating and managing a high-performance knowledge-sharing network: The Toyota case. *Strategic Management Journal, 21*(1), 345–367.

ECAR. (2011). National Study of Undergraduate Students and Information Technology. Retrieved from http://net.educause.edu/ir/library/pdf/ERS1103/ERS1103W.pdf

Eggen, P., & Kauchak, D. (2006). *Educational psychology: Windows on classrooms* (7th ed.). Upper Saddle River, NJ: Prentice Hall.

Ertmer, P. A., Addison, P., Lane, M., Ross, E., & Woods, D. (1999). Examining teachers' beliefs about the role of technology in the elementary classroom. *Journal of Research on Computing in Education, 32*, 54–72.

Firek, H. (2003). One order of ed tech coming up … You want fries with that? *Phi Delta Kaplan, 84*(8), 596–597.

Gupta, S., & Bostrom, R. P. (2009). Technology-mediated learning: A comprehensive theoretical model. *Journal of the Association of Information Systems, 10*(9), 686–714.

Hiltz, S. R., Coppola, N., Rotter, N., Turoff, M., & Benbunan-Fich, R. (2001). Measuring the importance of collaborative learning for the effectiveness of ALN: A multi-measure, multi-method approach. *ALN Journal, 4*, 103–125.

Jaffee, D. (1997). Asynchronous learning: Technology and pedagogical strategy in a distance learning course. *Teaching Sociology, 25*(4), 262–277.

Jonassen, D. H., Pfeiffer, W. S., & Wilson, B. G. (1998). *Learning with technology: A constructivist perspective.* Upper Saddle River, NJ: Prentice Hall.

Jurist, R. (1999). The promise of technology. Implications for business teacher education. In P. A. Gallo Villee & M. G. Curran (Eds.), *The 21st century: Meeting the challenges to business education (1999 NBEA Yearbook, No. 37).* Reston, VA: National Business Education Association.

Kovalchick, A., & Dawson, K. (Eds.). (2004). *Education and technology: An encyclopedia*. Santa Barbara, CA: ABC-CLIO.

Kulik, J. A. (1994). Meta-analytic studies of findings on computer-based instruction. In E. L. Baker & H. F. O'Neil, Jr. (Eds.), *Technology assessment in education and training* (pp. 9–34). Hillsdale, NJ: Lawrence Erlbaum.

Leidner, D. E., & Fuller, M. (1997). Improving student learning of conceptual in formation: GSS supported collaborative learning vs. individual constructive learning. *Decision Support Systems*, *20*(2), 149–163.

Liu, P., Ku, H., Falvo, D., Charsky, D., Cheng, Y., Yeh, H., & Van Buskirk, E. (2004). The current state of attitude toward computer use for pre-service teachers. In R. Ferdig, C. Crawford, R. Carlsen, N. Davis, J. Price, R. Weber & D. A. Willis (Eds.), *Proceedings of Society for Information Technology and Teacher Education international conference* (pp. 3469–3471). Chesapeake, VA: AACE.

Mandell, S., Sorge, D. H., & Russell, J. D. (2002). TIPS for technology integration. *TechTrends for Leaders in Education and Training*, *46*(5), 39–43.

Mellon, C. A. (1999). Technology and the great pendulum of education. *Journal of Research on Computing in Education*, *32*(1), 28–35.

Mishra, P., & Koehler, M. J. (2006). Technological pedagogical content knowledge: A new framework for teacher knowledge. *Teachers College Record*, *108*(6), 1017–1054.

Mitchell, R. (1997, October). *Building a learning society [Interview of Mitchel Resnick]*. Wired, 5, 136, 137.

Mundell, B., & Pennarola, F. (1997, January). *From instructor-centered to student-centered learning: Designing virtual interactive business environments*. Paper presented at International Organizational Behavior Teaching Conference, Hong Kong.

Mundell, B., & Pennarola, F. (1999). Shifting paradigms in management education: What happens when we take groups seriously. *Journal of Management Education*, *23*(6), 663–683.

Nielsen, J. (1999). Metcalfe's law in reverse. Retrieved from http://www.useit.com/alertbox/990725.html. Accessed August 2012.

Pantazis, C. (2002). Maximizing e-learning to train the 21st century workforce. *Public Personnel Management*, *32*(1), 21–26.

Papo, W. (2001). Integration of educational media in higher education large classes. *Educational Media International*, *38*(2/3), 95–99.

Peluchette, J. V., & Rust, K. (2005). Technology use in the classroom: Preferences of management faculty members. *Journal of Education for Business*, *80*(4), 200–205.

Pennarola, F., & Mundell, B. (2001). The functioning of student hybrid virtual teams. In *Conference material – Learning challenges in the new millennium*, NYU-Stern and ISBM.

Piccoli, G., Ahmad, R., & Ives, B. (2001). Web-based virtual learning environments: A research framework and a preliminary assessment of effectiveness in basic IT skills training. *MIS Quarterly*, *25*(4), 401–426.

Pope, M., Hare, R. D., & Howard, E. (2005). Enhancing technology use in student teaching: A case study. *Journal of Technology and Teacher Education*, *13*(4), 573–617.

Rheingold, H. (2008, February). *Howard Rheingold: The new power of collaboration* [Video file]. Retrieved from http://www.ted.com/index.php/talks/howard_rheingold_on_collaboration.html

Schroeder, C. (1993). New students-new learning styles. *Change*, *25*(5), 21–26.

Sheingold, K., & Hadley, M. (1990). *Accomplished teachers: Integrating computers into classroom practice*. New York, NY: Bank Street College of Education.

Sherer, P., & Shea, T. (2002). Designing courses outside the classroom. *College Teaching*, *50*(1), 15–20.

Spekman, R. E., Kamauff, J. W., & Myhr, N. (1998). An empirical investigation into supply chain management: A perspective on partnerships. *Supply Chain Management*, *3*(2), 53–67.

Spotts, T. H. (1999). Discriminating factors in faculty use of instructional technology in higher education. *Educational Technology and Society*, *2*(4), 92–99.

Strijbos, J. W., Martens, R. L., & Jochems, W. M. G. (2004). Designing for interaction: Six steps to designing computer-supported group-based learning. *Computers and Education*, *42*, 403–424.

Venkatesh, V., & Davis, F. D. (2000). A theoretical extension of the technology acceptance model: Four longitudinal field studies. *Management of Science*, *46*(2), 186–204.

Vroeginday, B. J. (2005). *Traditional vs. online education: A comparative analysis of learner outcomes*. Doctoral dissertation, Fielding Graduate University, 2005. *Dissertation Abstracts International*, *66*, 10A

Vygotsky, L. S. (1962). *Thought and language*. Cambridge: MIT Press.

Wenglinsky, H. (2005). *Using technology wisely: The keys to success in schools*. New York, NY: Teachers College Press.

Wright, V. H., & Wilson, E. K. (2009). Using technology in the social studies classroom: The journey of two teachers. *Journal of Social Studies Research*, *33*(2), 133–154.

Zhang, D., Zhao, J. L., Zhou, L., & Nunamaker, J. (2004). Can e-learning replace traditional classroom learning-evidence and implication of the evolving e-learning technology. *Communication of the ACM*, *47*, 75–79.

BRINGING THE WORLD INTO OUR CLASSROOMS: THE BENEFITS OF ENGAGING STUDENTS IN AN INTERNATIONAL BUSINESS SIMULATION

Tine Köhler, Iris Fischlmayr, Timo Lainema and Eeli Saarinen

ABSTRACT

VIBu – Virtual Teams in International Business – is the name of a training concept, which is aimed at familiarizing participants with collaborating in a virtual environment. Based on the online business simulation RealGame™, participants are assigned to multicultural virtual teams that represent different companies. These companies are either competing with or depending on each other in typical business processes of an internationally operating manufacturing company. Interaction and negotiation are required throughout the whole simulation. All communication takes place via information and communication technology, mainly Skype and Skype chat. The main challenge in the environment is that participants are located in different countries and time zones all over

Increasing Student Engagement and Retention using Classroom Technologies:
Classroom Response Systems and Mediated Discourse Technologies
Cutting-edge Technologies in Higher Education, Volume 6E, 163–198

ISSN: 2044-9968/doi:10.1108/S2044-9968(2013)000006E009

the world. The book chapter first outlines some of the challenges of global teamwork that organizations face. We argue that students need to learn how to navigate in global teams before they leave university as they are bound to become involved in organizational global teamwork sooner rather than later. We draw on frameworks for experiential learning (e.g., Kolb's learning model, Kolb, 1984) and the constructivist learning paradigm (Lainema, 2009) to outline the learning experiences that students need to gather in order to become effective global team members. In addition, we highlight the potential for learner engagement that this approach offers. The chapter concludes by highlighting the key learning and teaching outcomes from incorporating this cutting-edge simulation technology. Furthermore, we direct the reader's attention to ways in which the simulation can be used for research purposes, international inter-university collaborations, and multidisciplinary research on teaching practices and engaged learning.

In recent years, global teams – teams that are both geographically distributed and culturally diverse – have been increasingly used to collaborate on projects involving innovation and complex team processes. It is not uncommon that teams are quickly put together and have to perform in an ad hoc fashion on a project-type task. Especially when team members have not worked together before, they have to establish their teamwork processes and invent their collaboration quickly. They further have to be adaptive to an ever-changing context. Success in this kind of environment comes with experience.

Many business schools are trying to prepare their students for the challenges accompanying this kind of teamwork. There are an increasing number of classes on virtual work, on social media and online communications, on change and adaptability, and on similar topics. However, without concrete experiences it is difficult to form the kind of skills and awareness necessary to navigate in a virtual business world and to manage the complexities of projects in which many events happen simultaneously in an interconnected web of intricate relationships between the different aspects of the project.

In the current chapter, we are introducing an online training concept for virtual teamwork that utilizes an online business simulation. This simulation is aimed at providing students with exposure to complex virtual team tasks similar to what might await them after graduation. It further strives to help students obtain the necessary skills to manage and thrive in this environment. The student teams are made up of team members from around the world, who have never met each other before and who have to perform together during the simulation almost instantly without prior training or preparations to facilitate their teamwork. This forces team members to create rudimentary team processes and rules for engagement quickly and to shape them during the collaboration to adapt to the quickly changing context of the business simulation. Students have to be innovative and flexible, while learning how to build norms and accountability into their teamwork practices.

The purpose of the current chapter is to introduce the simulation and to demonstrate its utility for supporting student learning. Our chapter will start with a description of the specific challenges of global teamwork and the training that we believe is necessary to help students learn about global teamwork. We then highlight the advantages of using simulation games as a learning environment. We will specify the learning opportunities of such games and will then link these opportunities more specifically to theories of experiential learning and exposure. Our theoretical argumentation builds on Kolb's (1984) framework for experiential learning and on the constructivist learning paradigm (CLP) (Duffy & Cunningham, 1996; Lainema, 2009). We will then describe in detail the online business simulation VIBu (Virtual Teams in International Business) we used as a learning environment. In particular, we will describe how each of the participating instructors used the same simulation and training slightly differently in their respective classes to demonstrate the flexibility of this learning approach and the adaptability to different learning contexts. Based on data from a large international student collaboration that was organized in 2011, we will highlight the utility of this approach for student learning. We will pay particular attention to the students' learning of teamwork skills and their awareness of the complexities and interdependencies of project-based work. Finally, we will conclude the chapter with the highlights and implications of our study for virtual and international business education.

GLOBAL TEAMWORK: NEW CHALLENGES FOR BUSINESS EDUCATION

Team-based projects, innovation, or task forces are common-place in many companies. Generally, teams have the advantage to be flexible, dynamic and can easily undergo change processes. More and more, they are also temporal, i.e., they are set up for specific tasks or projects and dissolved afterwards. Team members might be part of different teams simultaneously and team membership can often fluctuate (Maznevski, 2008).

With ongoing globalization, diversification in team composition has become inevitable. Today's 'global teams' are multicultural, i.e., they have team members coming from different cultural backgrounds. Evidently, this brings along certain challenges for the team, its members, and its leaders. Different approaches toward teamwork, hierarchy, and team membership, diverging patterns in communication and collaboration, different decision-making styles, and expectations are well-known challenges presented by cultural diversity (e.g., Bachmann, 2006; Cseh, 2003; DiStefano & Maznevski, 2000; Powell, Piccoli, & Ives 2004). On the other hand, the same cultural diversity generates a high potential for innovation and creativity, through different mindsets, socialization processes, and values. Overall, whether multicultural teams can outperform monocultural teams strongly depends on the management of those teams (DiStefano & Maznevski, 2000). Consequently, leading a multicultural team and being an efficient team member require specific skills and abilities such as cultural sensitivity, basic knowledge of cultural differences and different communication patterns, openness, and tolerance.

Frequently, global teams are not only multicultural, but also geographically distributed across different locations and time zones. Hand in hand with the advancement in information and communication technology (ICT), global teams have become more virtual, meaning that they bridge their geographical distances with the support of electronic media. Research on virtual teams has enjoyed great popularity in the last decade and so have trainings on skills for virtual team collaboration (Blackburn, Furst, & Rosen, 2003; Bryant, Albring, & Murthy, 2009; Hertel, 2005; Rosen, Furst, & Blackburn, 2006; Rusman, Bruggen, Sloep, & Koper, 2010).

These developments are not only observable in the business world but also in higher education. At universities projects and tasks are increasingly conducted on a team basis, which might be seen as an "integral part of the instructional process" (Watson, Johnson, & Zgourides, 2002, p. 1). But teamwork at universities faces similar challenges as in the business world. In 2011, more than 3 million students studied in places different from their home country (Rienties, Beausaert, Grohnert, Niemantsverdriet, & Kommers, 2011). This increasing student mobility makes classrooms increasingly international and multicultural. Thus, sensitizing students to the inherent potential in diversity, has become a main challenge for teachers in higher education.

Additionally, ICT brings along a second challenge to teaching. Fruchter (2004) calls the "synergy of sociotechnical pedagogical objectives, powerful computers, good software, and the Internet" (p. 265) the biggest challenge in pedagogy "since the introduction of the chalkboard in the 19th century" (p. 265). She questions the way we teach, the relationship between students and their teachers, the structure of curricula and classes, and the relevance of universities and businesses in modern learning environments.

One of the things we see is that universities increasingly use multicultural, virtual settings to prepare students for their future jobs, in which they will be confronted with similar settings. In their jobs, graduates will have to exchange business information via e-mail, negotiate over Skype, or lead a virtual meeting with the support of a web conferencing tool. Due to the ongoing and increasing globalization of all types of business, they will most probably be members in different global teams and will have to collaborate with people from different cultures and time zones. But rarely will they have been provided special training for acquiring these skills. For many, working in global teams might therefore enhance stress, passiveness, distraction, and, as a consequence, weaken performance. Therefore, business educators need to implement skill building into their curricula that familiarize students with collaboration in global teams.

Training for Global Teamwork

In this chapter we present a training tool that has been created to allow students to acquire skills needed in virtual, multicultural teamwork and would like to stress its usefulness as a modern teaching method. The aims of our training are fourfold: First of all, students are exposed to a holistic picture of an internationally operating company. Second, being confronted with challenges such as cultural diversity of team members, geographical dispersion, and time zone differences, participants build sensitivity and skills for communication, collaboration, and coordination in multicultural, virtual settings. Third, technical skills are strengthened by using electronic media as communication and collaboration tools during the training. Last but not the least, students gain a general awareness of the challenges of global teamwork.

The core aspect of our training is that it is experience based. Experiential learning theory (ELT) is one of the most influential theories of management learning. ELT points to the significance of learning through direct experience as opposed to learning through "instruction." According to ELT, the most powerful learning comes from direct experience – through taking action and observing the consequences. Learning is said to occur through the resolution of conflicts regarding different ways of dealing with the world. It suggests a holistic, integrative perspective on learning that combines experience, perception, cognition, and behavior (Kolb, 1984). Experiential learning applies specifically to the development of adults (Cheetham & Chivers, 2001). There are several different models of experiential learning which all share the belief in direct experience and reflection on it.

Kolb's (1984) experiential learning approach emphasizes the role of concrete experiences for in-depth learning, in conjunction with reflection and application of the learned material to real problems. Learning is conceived as a four-stage iterative cycle which begins with a relevant experience followed by the collection of data and observations about that experience. The data are then analyzed, and conclusions from this analysis are used to modify subsequent behavior and to choose new experiences. The four-stage cycle of experiential learning is very similar to the organizational structure of typical simulation games (Herz & Merz, 1998). Kolb (1984, pp. 26–38) bases his approach on the following prerequisites for learning:

1. Learning is a process, not a result: students must be involved in a process which accelerates their learning.
2. Learning is re-learning: a topic that has been taught once is reflected upon, tested, repeated, etc.
3. Learning is a holistic process for a better adaptation to the world: thinking, feeling, perceiving, and behaving.
4. Learning needs conflicts, difficulties, and differences.
5. Learning is a result of transactions between persons and their environment.
6. Learning is gaining knowledge with acquiring social knowledge as a side-product. It is not the transfer of stable ideas.

Following from these prerequisites, learning happens through the process of transforming experiences into knowledge.

Kolb's model has been the target of much criticism because of its potential theoretical limitations. According to this criticism, Kolb's model provides only a limited account of the many factors that influence learning. One of the criticisms, for example, posits that individual experience comes at the expense of social and institutional aspects of learning (Kayes, 2002). Cheetham and Chivers (2001) note that the proposition that learning through experience takes the form of a neat cycle is also questionable. Learning seems likely to be a more complicated and multifaceted process.

Thus, learning is more fragmented and often more chaotic than Kolb's model suggests.

Kayes (2002) suggests that an alternative approach should preserve the dialectic nature of experience and account for its social aspect more fully. Kolb's model looks at learning primarily from the individual's point of view, which does not sufficiently explain learning within a team context. However, while the formulaic way in which Kolb has been interpreted may not represent reality accurately, his theory provides those who wish to be more learner-centered with a starting point for thinking about their practice (Marsick & Watkins, 1990).

Going beyond Kolb's framework of experiential learning, the current chapter would like to refer to the Constructivist Learning Paradigm. Constructivism suggests that we need to assess the meaning that learners have co-constructed from their interactions with the world. The CLP is widely used and acknowledged in educational studies. However, in the teaching and learning literature in management and business, this paradigm has largely remained unexplored. We believe that this is a shortcoming of the literature in management and business and would like to demonstrate in this chapter the utility of this approach for understanding and assessing student learning from concrete experiences.

Duffy and Cunningham (1996) note that the term constructivism has come to serve as an umbrella for a wide diversity of views. However, they find two similarities among them: (1) learning is an active process of constructing rather than acquiring knowledge and (2) instruction is a process of supporting that construction, rather than communicating knowledge. The principles of constructivism support the use of microworlds like simulation games (Jonassen, Peck, & Wilson 1999). Constructivist learning environments are typically technology-based environments in which students explore, experiment, construct, converse, and reflect on what they are doing, so that they learn from their experiences. Learners are presented with a complex and relevant experience that they accept or reject as a challenge. Then the environment provides them with the tools and resources that they need to understand the problem and to solve it (or attempt to solve it).

In this chapter we refer to the constructivist view of learning – instead of the experiential theory – because of its evident ability to describe how social interaction and collaboration in a learning environment support participants' learning. This does not mean that we do not believe in the basic message of the ELT – that learning arises from experience – quite on the contrary.

In the next section, we will discuss the particular learning environment that simulation games offer. We will then describe our online simulation and training approach before we discuss in detail how our simulation and training applies the principles of the CLP. In this latter section, we will provide concrete evidence from a recent international student collaboration for how the students constructed their learning about global teamwork.

SIMULATION GAMES AS LEARNING ENVIRONMENTS

In computerized business (simulation) games, players receive a description of an imaginary business and environment and make decisions (on price, advertising, production targets, etc.) about how their company should be run. Keys and Wolfe (1990) define a management game as a simplified simulated experiential environment that contains enough verisimilitude, or illusion of reality, to include real-world-like responses by those participating in the exercise.

According to Senge and Lannon (1997), in business games managers are free to experiment with policies and strategies without fear of jeopardizing the company. Thus, Senge and Lannon argue, participants learn about the long-term, systemic consequences of their actions. Such "virtual worlds" are particularly important in team learning. Participants can learn to think systemically if they can uncover the subtle interpersonal interactions that thwart their efforts. This process includes the kind of reflection and inquiry for which there is no time in the hectic everyday world.

The traditional business gaming setting and process have changed very little since the introduction of the first computerized business games in the late 1950s. Thus, the description by Naylor (1971) gives quite an accurate view on the contents, structure, and operating of a typical business game: Business games are built around a hypothetical oligopolistic industry consisting of firms whose decision-makers or managers are the participants in the game. Each firm or team is allocated a specific amount of resources in the form of cash, inventories, raw materials, plant and equipment, and so forth. Before each operating period the players make decisions. Naylor mentions that these decisions can concern, among other things, price, output, advertising, marketing, raw material acquisition, changes in plant capacity, and wage rate. This information is read into a computer that has been programmed on the basis of a set of mathematical models that provide a link between the operating results and operating decisions of the individual firms, and the external environment (the market). On the basis of (a) a set of behavioral equations, such as demand and cost functions, and a set of accounting formulas that have been programmed into the computer, and (b) the individual decisions of each firm, operating results are generated by the computer in the form of printed reports at the end of each operating period.

The Internet has changed the possibilities of how simulation games can be run and played, but also provides opportunities for collaborative learning processes. The Internet integration of business simulations provides four significant advantages (Henriksen & Löfvall, 2012). First, the simulations can be played in a web browser (*distribution*). Second, *feedback* between the simulation and participants' actions may be reviewed online (in real time) by the administrator, without delay. Third, simulation content can be downloaded from a server and changed in real time (*updates*). Fourth, *collaboration* in the simulation may allow the participants to communicate among each other, thereby breaking with physical boundaries and making business gaming purely an online experience.

The case simulation described in this chapter includes all the above characteristics. Furthermore, the simulation game used in our teaching sessions differs from traditional business games in that it creates a time-urgent decision-making environment in which the game's internal clock runs independently, hour-by-hour, at a gradually increasing pace. The continuous and clock-driven nature of the game makes the simulation business processes transparent and incorporates complexity in the experience.

This chapter also adds to the research on teaching virtual collaboration. Tutty and Klein (2008) claim that there is little empirical evidence to indicate if the positive effects of collaborative learning transfer to environments where communication is mediated by computers. Further, despite technological and theoretical advances, many existing virtual learning environments have been designed to support well-defined, teacher-led activities in instructional settings rather than new organizational practices like virtual team work (Ballesteros, 2006). This chapter sheds light on the possibilities of using technology in collaborative learning and virtual team work.

The case simulation game and the learning environment built upon it is called *Virtual Teams in International Business* (VIBu). In VIBu, the teams are dispersed over global time zones and communicate about running their company using tools of virtual collaboration. We will describe this training in detail in the next section.

THE DESIGN OF AN INTERNATIONAL, VIRTUAL BUSINESS SIMULATION

VIBu is based on an existing online, clock-driven business simulation game called RealGame™ (Lainema, 2003). RealGame™ represents typical business processes (e.g., the order-delivery process) of a production company. The participants are able to follow their company's operations and material flow in real time, providing a dynamic and transparent view of cause-and-effect relationships found in business organizations. The decision-making process in the simulation game demands participants' attention and their focus on several decision-making tasks on multiple levels (operational and strategic) at the same time. In addition to managing the operational tasks in their simulation companies, participants need to plan their strategies and decide which markets to enter, which products to manufacture and sell, or whether to start the product development process for a new product. Decision-making success is measured with several performance indicators, such as cash flow, profitability, production costs, inventory levels, and market shares.

VIBu was designed by researchers from the Turku School of Economics (TSE) in Finland, Johannes Kepler University (JKU) in Austria, and the University of Melbourne (UoM) in Australia. In VIBu the traditional on-site RealGame™ simulation game setting has been changed into a virtual and dispersed one over the years. This facilitates the learning of novel topics not present in local simulation game installations, such as virtual communication, coordinating with team members without meeting them face-to-face, or negotiating via electronic media (such as Skype or e-mail). VIBu is conducted across different time zones, allowing the inclusion of up to 200 participants. A typical session runs for 12–18 hours, and the full experience includes two of these full-day sessions with one week in between the sessions. A minimum of six students form a team, and each team represents a company.

In the simulation, there are two different types of companies: sub-producers, who manufacture electrical components, and bio-analysis instrument manufacturers, who manufacture analysis instruments from the sub-producers' end products. Companies of both types have a similar user interface (see Fig. 1). Typical for the case simulation is that it is clock-driven and the processes in the simulation companies are transparent, showing how the internal processes (like the manufacturing process) evolve on an hourly basis (see the simulation internal clock on the right-hand upper corner in Fig. 1).

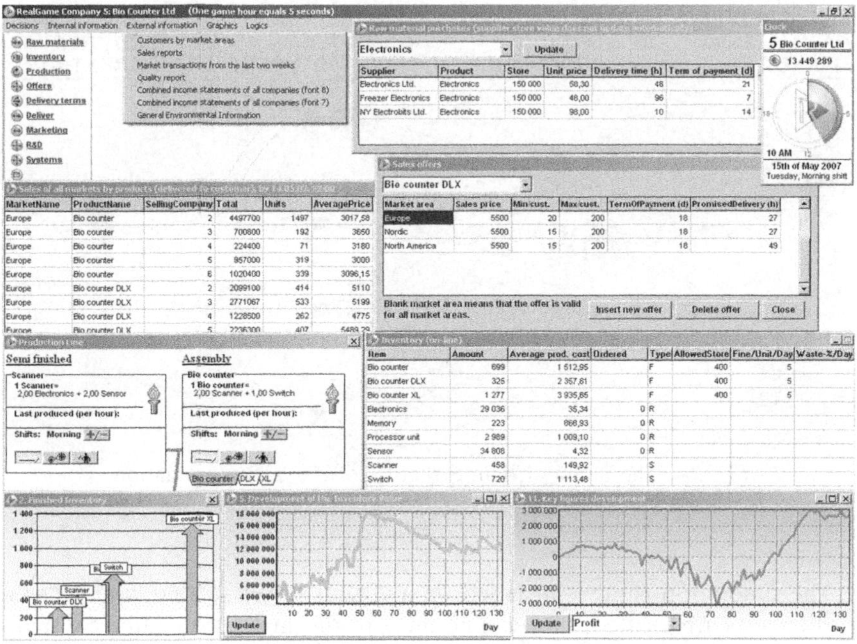

Fig. 1. The Case Simulation Game User Interface (Manufacturer Company).

Sub-producers compete against each other when selling components to the instrument manufacturers. Instrument manufacturers compete with each other for the cheapest components to produce their instruments and then to sell the instruments in a simulated marketplace. Sub-producers and instrument manufacturers depend on each other, while they both have to compete for the best deals (Fig. 2).

During the collaboration, team members have to make decisions continuously and on a real-time basis. The simulation provides them with the opportunity to learn more about the complexity of managing a company that is part of a long supply chain. Along with gaining a holistic view of their company's operations and dependence on the other players along the supply chain, the participants face challenges arising from the virtual, multicultural context of the collaboration. Participants across locations need to manage the coordination of shift work over different time this and Skype chat). For many of the students it is the first time that they participate in a virtual team, let alone a team consisting of students distributed around the world.

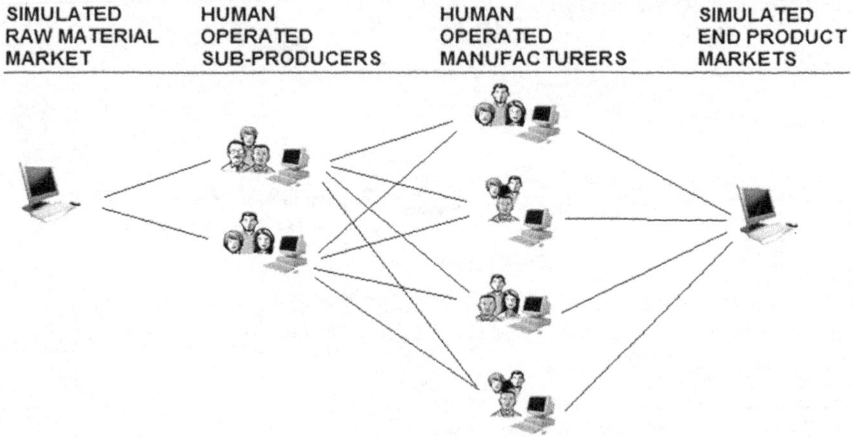

Fig. 2. The Supply Chain Structure of the VIBu Simulation.

The simulation game is installed on a virtual server so that wherever the participants are located, they can connect to the simulation game company as if it was locally installed. Thus, on their local computers the students start a remote connection program which takes over a virtual computer in the remote virtual server. The simulation game interface is presented on the students' computer screens. As the students form dispersed teams, each member of a particular team connects to the same virtual computer and so the team members have exactly the same real-time view and user interface of their common company. This kind of structure allows the dispersion of the teams and companies as illustrated in Fig. 3.

The constellation described above requires that only one member at a time is responsible for interacting with the user interface as a decision-maker. Thus, there is a natural call for the role of responsible decision-maker, who is collaborating in real-time with the other team members. This requires some organizing and agreement (e.g., roles, task distribution, etc.) in the participating team. To facilitate the virtual communication, we have used Voice over Internet Protocol (Skype) for the communication between the team members (and teams). Communication also takes place using email and real-time chat. There are two advantages of this architecture. First, the simulation game environment provides a time-driven environment, where time runs independently of the participants. The simulation companies need to be managed in a continuous and synchronous manner, requiring

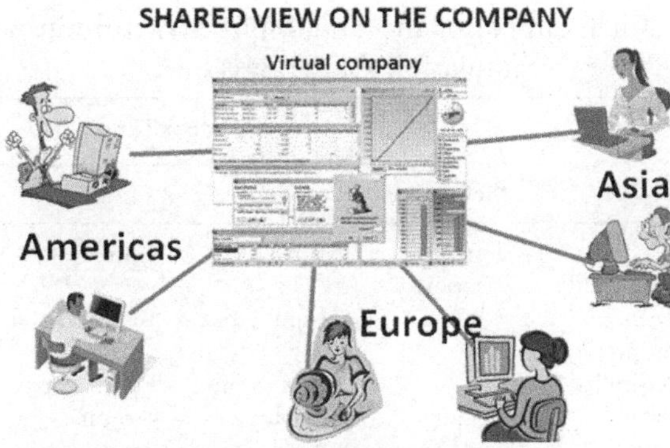

Fig. 3. The Dispersed Team Members Have a Shared View of Their Simulation Game Company.

uninterrupted virtual communication, collaboration, monitoring, and decision-making within the groups. We think this is one of the major difference compared to many similar international student collaboration courses, where communication is asynchronous. The second advantage in our setting is globalization. As the participants may be located all over the globe, the different team members come from different time zones and reside in different country contexts, as shown in Table 1.

The time-shift brings along an additional requirement. The teams must agree on virtual shifts and shift plans within their group, when each participant will be responsible for making decisions in the company. This agreement requires working towards a joint target and trust between the team members.

VIBu as a Business Process Learning Tool

The basic online simulation behind VIBu was originally developed to illustrate business processes unfolding in steps of one hour, revealing the different phases in business processes. Thus, the simulation game's internal processes are transparent to the participants. In this aspect the simulation game differs from traditional business games in which the internal structure of the simulation generating the results is not known to the participants (Machuca, 2000). This clock-driven and process-based operation of the simulation is also present in the VIBu concept. Although the emphasis of VIBu is on the dispersed, virtual nature of the simulation setting, it should

Table 1. An Example of the Time-Shift Structure in a Global Simulation Game Session.

VIBu Sessions, October 7 and 14, 2010	Local Time			
	Melbourne	Turku	Linz	New York
Start of the session	2 pm	6 am	5 am	11 pm
Australia, main responsibility	2–8 pm			
Common time between Australia and Europe	7–9 pm	11 am–1 pm	10 am–Noon	4–6 am
Europe, main responsibility		Noon–6 pm	11 am–5 pm	
Common time between Europe and America	1–3 am	5–7 pm	4–6 pm	10 am–Noon
America, main responsibility				11 am–4 pm
End of the session	7 am	11 pm	10 pm	4 pm

be clear that the participants also learn to manage the business processes in the simulation game and learn to understand how the processes affect cash flow and profitability.

Prior studies have shown that the RealGame™ reveals the complexity and procedural nature of business operations, uncovers causal dependencies between decisions and their outcomes (Lainema & Makkonen, 2003), presents authentic tasks rather than abstract instructions, increases the realism and enjoyability of the gaming experience (Lainema, 2004), inspires intense interaction and collaboration between the team members (Lainema & Nurmi, 2006), and provides a holistic view of a business and the interrelatedness of separate business functions (Lainema & Lainema, 2007). Moreover, VIBu can be used in several different ways. In the following, we present how VIBu has supported the aims and goals of three different courses taught by the authors of the current chapter at their respective institutions. These, of course, are just examples. The simulation could also be used to support other class topics such as classes on economics, negotiation, strategy, or globalization.

VIBu as a Learning Tool for Leadership and Teamwork in Virtual Context

One instructor uses VIBu for a course titled Leadership and Teamwork in Virtual Organizations, a part of a curriculum for advanced level studies in Management and Organizations. The purpose of the course is to develop a continuous interplay between the theory and practice of virtual organizations. Lectures focus on this new form of work and how it impacts organizations and leadership. Taking a multidisciplinary approach, the lectures highlight the special characteristics of virtual organizations in comparison to traditional organizations. The aim is to discuss current leadership and organization theories and then proceed to the latest theoretical developments and their practical implications. The counterpart to this discussion is then based on an experiential learning exercise, i.e., the VIBu business simulation. During VIBu, participants practice decision-making in a global virtual setting and analyze the results from their decisions. The aim is that students experience firsthand the challenges of virtual organizing and learn the basics of managing a business in a global, dynamic business environment.

It has proven to be quite fruitful for the students to be confronted with the real-life-like challenges and give them the possibility to evaluate and examine different theoretical approaches in realistic organizational contexts. As a student from one of the earlier VIBu sessions put it: "I learned a great deal of this exercise, I basically had the chance of experimenting with learned leadership theories [...] and I really saw how they worked." The course instructor tries to make these connections more evident by facilitating further discussion from that perspective and indicating links between student experiences and different theoretical approaches.

In the final part of the course, after participating in a series of conversational lectures, taking part in two simulation day sessions, finishing a team assignment, and writing two session-based immediate reflections, students are finally asked to pull everything together in a longer theoretical discussion paper. Compared to the instructor's experience with similar courses without the virtual team exercise, the students have clearly been able to give more meaning to the discussed topics and form a more comprehensive understanding of the subject. In many cases, they have also started to build skills based on the acquired knowledge (implying ways of utilizing gained knowledge in practice).

VIBu as a Learning Tool for Virtual, Multicultural Collaboration

The second instructor teaches a class on "virtual multicultural collaboration" which is part of a curriculum for International Management and Global Strategy in a master's program on general management. After discussing different challenges inherent in virtual multicultural teamwork, students experience them themselves in VIBu. Afterwards, they reflect in-depth on their experience and learning and use their acquired skills in a different virtual setting, namely in a seminar taught via a web-conferencing tool.

Thus, before the simulation game the students get to know the basics of virtual collaboration, the role of technology, the differences and difficulties inherent in virtual communication, and different behavioral aspects influencing virtual multicultural teamwork (such as isolation, neglect, power and leadership, or trust). With this input they are better prepared and aware of the different challenges that might occur in the simulation.

Furthermore, a few days prior to the first game session, the students get a basic introduction to the simulation. This is done by explaining the setting, the main idea behind it, the structure of the whole training, and the tasks related to VIBu. Although they do not get specific information on frequently occurring pitfalls (such as difficulties with knowledge transfer between the shifts), they are introduced to some general challenges that might take place (e.g., technical problems, non-responding or even non-appearing members).

After the two simulation sessions, the students have a face-to-face class session where they engage in an intensive reflection. They talk about their experiences, challenges, and learning. Furthermore, the previous theoretical learning is compared to their practical experience. Due to conflicting schedules with other participating international universities, the simulation is sometimes scheduled at the very beginning of the semester. In this case, students are thrown into the cold water. They gain their individual experiences and are provided with the theoretical underpinning afterwards. This allows enriching the theoretical aspects using their own VIBu examples. All in all, the students report to that they gain more insights and understanding on the topics compared to other courses or team tasks by being confronted with the challenges and by being somehow forced to solve these issues themselves.

VIBu as a Learning Tool for Multicultural Teamwork

One of the instructors uses VIBu to support student learning in her class on cross-cultural management and multicultural teamwork. After focusing on theories of cross-cultural differences and management in the first half of her class, she uses VIBu in the latter half of the class to provide the students with an opportunity to experience the effects of cultural differences and geographic dispersion on teamwork.

Before the students engage in the collaboration, they talk about topics such as cross-cultural communication, differences in leadership preferences and behavior, differences in teamwork expectations, and differences in cultural values. The students are asked to pay particular attention to these topics while they engage in the simulation. In addition, the course instructor asks the students to spend an additional hour in the game, during which they do not play the game but observe the other players in the team as well as their negotiation partners. The students are asked to write down what they observed and what they found especially noteworthy with regards to differences in the approach taken.

In between the two game days, the students have a regular class session during which the instructor debriefs the simulation experiences with them and asks the students to share some of their experiences and simulations. In discussion, the students then analyze the experience using the cultural theories and concepts introduced earlier in the class. The students and instructor also talk about what things the students might still struggle to understand. The instructor then offers advice and, together with the students, develops a list of things the students might want to pay attention to in their next simulation game.

Of course, the VIBu training could also be used at the beginning of the semester as a basic experience that introduces students to multicultural teamwork. The instructor would then use this experience during the remainder of the semester to link theoretical concepts to the students' practical experience.

THE CURRENT INTERNATIONAL COLLABORATION

In the following, we would like to provide a concrete example of an international student collaboration that used the VIBu training. We will first briefly describe the sample and setting of the international collaboration. We will then explore how VIBu helps the students to create learning experiences and construct their own learning. Along these lines, we will demonstrate how VIBu aligns with constructivist learning principles and provide evidence for student learning from the international collaboration. We want to note here that it is not the aim of the current chapter to present a comprehensive analysis of the data available from the international collaboration. Such a comprehensive analysis goes beyond the scope of this chapter. Rather, we would like to present some exemplary data from one of the more recent installments of the VIBu game to highlight the particular learning experiences of the students involved in the simulation.

Sample

In October 2011, we conducted the largest ever online VIBu training with 131 student participants from eight different universities in six different time zones, including Australia, Indonesia, Austria, Finland, Sweden, Denmark, and the United States. The majority of the students were master's level business students who came from more than 25 different national backgrounds. All participating classes were highly diverse (see Fig. 4).

Procedure

Students played the simulation game on two different days in October that were one week apart. On the second game day, the simulation continued to run from the end situation of the first game day. About two days before the first game day, the students were informed of their simulation teams and provided with contact information for their team members and with login information for their assigned simulation companies. The students were also provided with a set of instructions about their specific company and task.

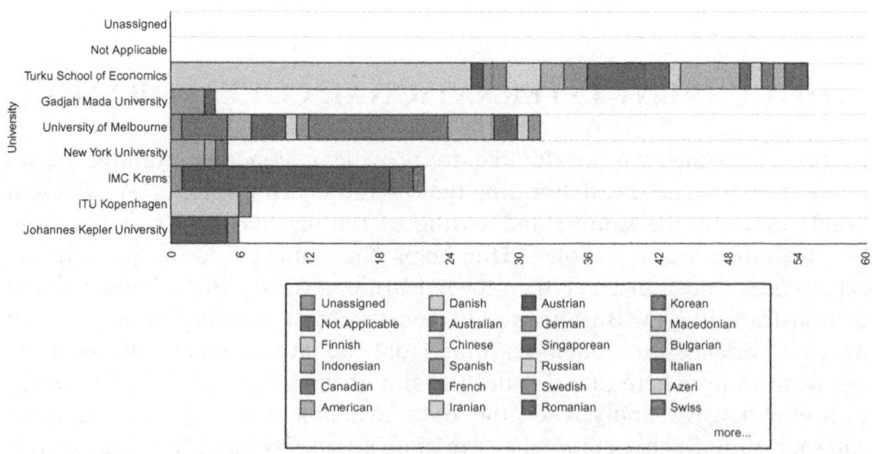

Fig. 4. Distribution of Student Nationalities Across Participating Universities.

During the two days before the game, the students could engage in a practice session to familiarize themselves with the simulation. In addition, the students had to communicate with their team members to determine during which "shifts" they were going to work. Given that the simulation ran for 18 hours, the students had to ensure as a team that the company was always running and producing something. This meant that they had to coordinate their efforts and come up with a shift plan during which certain team members would be responsible for running the simulation company. These shift plans needed to be submitted to the organizers of the simulation in Finland.

On the day of the simulation, the students who took the first shift were briefly introduced to the simulation and the simulation organizers (tutors) gave a few last minute instructions. The game was then started and the students started playing. At certain intervals, the tutors stopped the game clock and provided feedback about the companies' performance. They met with the students in Adobe ProConnect (a video conferencing tool) and provided the students with the performance spreadsheets the simulation automatically generated. The simulation itself generates some 50 different financial key figures in the format of developmental trends over time. This data is automatically consolidated into spreadsheets and can be disseminated to the students to be used for teaching purposes and developmental feedback. The organizers of the simulation talked the students through the performance of the different companies and how the teams had to interpret their performance up until this point. After these feedback sessions, the students returned to playing the game and the simulation clock was started again.

During the game, students had to organize their shift changes as well. When a student left and a new student logged into the game to continue the simulation for the team, the students had to ensure that they introduced the next shift of students to the current context of the game, the previous performance, and what they had learned and experienced about the game so far. Some only became aware of "all of a sudden" at the end of the first shift, and started to think about different ways to meet that challenge. Others thought about the shift change in advance. However, different teams chose different strategies to accomplish this. For example, some teams created a data repository (such as a shared document) in which they captured the results of their negotiations (e.g., on prices and delivering conditions), their main insights and suggestions for the next shift. Other teams ensured that the students of the next shift came online earlier than the start of their shift to observe for a while before taking over or to receive an instruction by one of the team members during the overlap. In other teams, some of the team members from an earlier shift came online again at a later time (i.e., during somebody else's shift) to see if they could provide additional information.

Student Assignments

In order to support student learning, several approaches and sources of data were used in addition to the performance sheets. In the week between the two game sessions, the students had two tasks. First, each team had to reflect on their company's performance and on their teamwork. The students were asked to write a SWOT analysis on their experience and on their performance based on the feedback and company results. As part of this assignment, they had to come up with a strategy for the next round of the game. They needed to think about how they want to improve their performance and teamwork.

Second, students were asked to write individual reflective papers of roughly three to five pages in length, covering critical incidents, conflicts, and their biggest learning experiences. They also needed to think about what they found particularly surprising and insightful. Often, instructors for each course pay specific attention to the kinds of topics they introduced in their respective classes. So, an instructor who teaches a cross-cultural management class might ask the students in particular to reflect on their experiences with cultural differences, while an instructor teaching a class on virtual teamwork might ask the students to focus in particular on issues with technology or virtual communication. Similarly, an instructor who teaches economics might ask the students to focus on their learning experiences regarding the company's performance and balancing the financials.

At the end of the collaboration, the students also write long reflective essays in some of the classes. These reflect more generally on the concepts learned in the classes and how they relate to the simulation experience.

Data Presented in the Current Paper

For the current paper, we coded data from the short reflective essays. Each team was analyzed as a case, using the dimensions of the CLP as a broad framework for analysis. One coder was used to code all the data. In intermittent intervals throughout the coding process, the coder met with the first author of this chapter to discuss the coding scheme, the preliminary findings, and possible alterations to the coding approach. In the following section, we will provide some examples for student learning from the coded data to show how the students constructed their learning through the business simulation. The findings are summarized under the dimensions of the CLP. As noted earlier, the coding does not include all available data at this point and it is not meant to be comprehensive. It merely provides anecdotal evidence highlighting the utility of the introduced approach.

THE CONSTRUCTION OF STUDENT LEARNING THROUGH VIBU

The CLP sees learning to occur when the individual's expectations are not met and the discrepancy between what was expected and what was actually encountered must be resolved. The socio-cultural approach of constructivism emphasizes the socially and culturally situated context of cognition. Duffy and Cunningham (1996) present their version of constructivism – which very well supports learning environments like business simulation games – as follows (the headings in italics directly quote the characteristics of a constructivist learning environment as presented by Duffy and Cunningham, 1996, pp. 178–182).

"All Learning is a Process of Construction"

Duffy and Cunningham (1996) view learning as a "matter of changes in one's relation to the culture to which one is connected." In VIBu the students are actively dealing with dissonances which they see between what they know and what is observed. They will actively seek to make sense of things. Resolving dissonance ensures ownership of the ideas (Jonassen et al., 1999). What is learned becomes more relevant, important, and meaningful. In the simulation, this is the learner's responsibility, not the teacher's. The teacher does not teach students what they should do/know and when they should do/know it. Rather, the environment supports the students in developing their critical thinking skills, self-directed learning skills, and content knowledge in relation to the realistic challenges in the environment.

The following example highlights these learning experiences. A student in Finland noted that one of the biggest learning experiences came from not knowing people initially and from learning how to overcome this challenge. The student said:

> "This communication and not knowing people beforehand were also for us the biggest challenges but I think we made it very well. Also very fruitful was when our company had a big loss of money and we all tried to make everything to get it positive. That kind of showed how some bad times may bring the group, also virtual group, together more." (Finnish student 1)

A foreign exchange student in Australia highlighted that one of her team's biggest challenges was effective communication early on. The challenges she experienced made her question her own approaches to communication, other team members' willingness to listen, but also the team's ability to cope with the situation.

> "[…] in the beginning I felt people were not listening to each other. As I was connected in the first hours of the game I tried to initiate a strategy (task division and keeping a specific level of supply in inventory based on previous calculation made from another group member). I repeated several time the urgent need of having an objective to follow, and even wrote it down on Skype chat so that everyone could hear my idea out but it seem to have fail. I am still trying to understand if this communication issue was due to me not being assertive enough, having team members not appreciating to be given direction or if the chaotic environment of the game was to blame. Only after our company situation became critical would people start realizing a clear strategy was needed, although this was a bit late, once we all agreed, things started moving pretty fast and smoothly." (Foreign exchange student in Australia 1)

"Many Worldviews Can Be Constructed, Hence There Will Be Multiple Perspectives"

Duffy and Cunningham (1996) write that the "engagement with others […] creates the awareness of multiple perspectives." In VIBu, the participants need to agree on common decisions. This requires discussion on, negotiation about, and an understanding of the views of the other students acting in the same team. Without common agreements and decisions none of the teams would be able to succeed in the complex and demanding environment. Sharing insights and perspectives makes the teams more dynamic and functional. This certainly makes the different world views of the team members visible. Furthermore, as the teams are multicultural, the students are exposed to perspectives arising from cultural differences.

In the following example, a Finnish student explains their experience with cross-cultural communication differences. The student says:

> "Especially cross-cultural communication becomes hard, when people from different cultures have different ideas about "what is good communication." In some cultures it is really important to just small-talk all the time, others stay silent and wait for questions." (Finnish student 2).

Along similar lines, a foreign exchange student in Australia observed:

> "I learned a lot about cross-cultural negotiations. Different cultures have different processes and customs when it comes to negotiating, and they have to be taken into account when communicating. Some people were more aggressive and non-yielding in the negotiations, while others were friendly and helpful. Adapting to different negotiation styles was an important part of the simulation." (Foreign exchange student in Australia 2).

Another Finnish student explains how the multicultural background of the group presented challenges in the beginning of the collaboration. But this student also explains, how their group managed to overcome the challenges. This student says:

> "One challenge we faced was the multiculturality of the group. There were people from Australia, U.S., Singapore, Austria ... all over the world. So it could have been hard to work together, especially with such a momentary group, with no real ties combining us. But actually we turned this challenge into a strength. We discussed our cultural backgrounds openly and even joked about some typical culture-related habits. [...] It was also interesting to talk to people from different corners of the globe, which was also one thing that contributed to the learning experience." (Finnish student 3)

"Knowledge is Context Dependent, So Learning Should Occur in Contexts to Which it is Relevant"

As Duffy and Cunningham (1996) state "the physical character of the environment is relevant only to the extent that it impacts on the character of "thinking" and skill requirements." The aim of VIBu is to illustrate the challenges of virtual and multicultural communication in the dispersed and global real-world environment. The learning in VIBu takes place exactly in this kind of context, where the students are dispersed and working on different time zones, using virtual collaboration and communication artifacts. The content of the actual simulation company run by the participants is a simulated one, but its content and logic are equivalent to the logic and dynamic of a real-world business organization. VIBu generates challenges that elevate the relevant concepts and principles to the real-world domain.

An American student noted that

> "I've always heard that large part of a business decision is based on human expectation and estimation, and it was wonderful to actually experience this" (American student 1).

A foreign exchange student in Finland perceived the reality of the exercise in the same way and added that the real character of the game motivated them to really engage in the game. This student says:

> "To sum up, this game was the most interesting exercise for me ever. I felt like in a real market, responsible for conducting company. The spirit in my team gave me opportunity to behave motivated as one should be when he/she works in a real firm. This experience gave me higher belief in myself, because I proved to myself that I can conduct my knowledge in practice, that I can communicate with people from different cultures and that I can do that perfectly in a language which is not my native." (Foreign exchange student in Finland 1).

In addition to the motivational aspects of the real-life context, the students also felt that they gained valuable insights into working in virtual business teams. An Austrian student commented:

> "I learned that you cannot align everything beforehand. It is good to have an overall strategy which everybody is aware of. But if real life is different you can only win if you are flexible and can adapt to new situations within short time and without any kind of disagreement, discussion or conflict." (Austrian student 2)

"Learning is Mediated by Tools and Signs"

According to Duffy and Cunningham (1996), "all distinctly human instances of learning are constructions situated within a context that employs some form of mediational means, tools, and/or signs." In VIBu, the whole environment functions as a tool which relates the characteristics of the real-world business environment to the participating students. In addition, challenges of the environment contribute to the learning in VIBu. Given that the virtual context is predominantly shaped by the use of technology for communication and interaction, it is important that students derive learning from experiencing the tools that shape that context. In VIBu, students experience the pitfalls and benefits of online communication. As a foreign exchange student in Finland put it:

> "[...] even with the best preparation and communication you are not free of unforeseen events like the sudden dropout of a team member or technical problems" (Foreign exchange student in Finland 2).

Similarly, a foreign exchange student experienced challenges with regard to the use of the available technology and described how this affected team member interaction and participation:

> "Another issue arose when some of our teammates could not use voice Skype. Typing everything is quite tedious and time consuming so voice Skype was really ideal. We had to both speak and type the important parts. The person probably felt a little left out. Once again, it was complicated to type, speak and keep up with roles." (Foreign exchange student in Australia 2)

"Learning is an Inherently Social-Dialogical Activity"

Duffy and Cunningham (1996) write "knowledge and thereby learning, is a social, communicative, and discursive process, inexorably grounded in talk. [...] The way in which a student comes to manifest the effective behavior of a community [...] is to speak with the voice of that community [...]." In VIBu, it is very clear that the participants are immersed in the roles of decision-makers and managers of their virtual companies. Sense-making in the environment results from conversation and dialogue between the different parties in the simulation environment, forming a community where people share their interests and experiences.

As an example of this social-dialogical activity, a Finnish student describes the following situation from the international collaboration:

> "I entered the game in the middle of a briefing session and was quite lost with everything. However, after the briefing my team mate explained me all the basics about our prices, products and so on. She had been doing marketing so she told me about selling our products, making deliveries, ordering new raw material and so on. Then another member came back from a break and also showed me some things. All this was a bit messy as we didn't have any check list for what to tell the inexperienced participants. I somehow took over marketing and selling our products to other teams as well as buying recycled silicon from them. [...] All in all it worked quite well that there were some people with more time and consequently more knowledge that they then spread among us others. I have experienced also in a physical context that it's often good to have leaders in a team to delegate and to take the main responsibility." (Finnish student 4)

This example illustrates how the students experience the need to work together, to hand off to new team members during shift changes, and how they negotiate the complexities of the experience. This involves that they are not instructed about how to manage this process prior to playing the game. The students have to figure it out themselves and derive meaning from this process. Along similar lines, an Austrian student highlights how this decision-making process and the acquired knowledge shape power relationships in the team and how that affected the team's negotiation experiences.

> "The guy who has the responsibility for the production and purchasing has the highest power in the team. Afterwards the pricing guy has also high power because of the decision power he had. It was organized in that way, because we had experienced that we need fast decision making, and it would not be possible to negotiate for each and every decision. It is better to make a fast decision than no decision." (Austrian student 1)

"Learners are Distributed, Multidimensional Participants in a Socio-cultural Process"

Duffy and Cunningham (1996) state that "a distributed concept of self shifts the activity of learning to the connections one has with communities, to the patterns of participation, and away from efficient internalization of knowledge." Here Duffy and Cunningham (1996) refer to Lave and Wenger (1991) and state that "learning is not the lonely act of an individual", but "a matter of being initiated into the practices of a community, of moving from legitimate peripheral participation to centripetal participation in the actions of a learning community." VIBu requires extremely active communication within the small groups of participants, but also communication between the groups. VIBu is most of all an environment where there is absolutely no possibility of acting alone; rather, every team's success depends on the team members' ability to communicate with others. During this process, the students grow from novices trying to grasp the rules of the decision-making environment into experts managing their own companies and collaborating with other teams along the supply chain. This growth is very visible in the student reflections. The students learn to think critically in the simulation domain to collaborate with peers and use them to test ideas about issues.

The following student experiences highlight this distributed learning context. A foreign exchange student in Finland observed:

> "The Indonesian guy and me didn't know really what to do so we discussed a lot and asked each other if we were not sure what we should do. But during the game I got a clue what to do and how to do it, but the first 2 hours were really hard." (Foreign exchange student in Finland 3)

A different foreign exchange student in Finland added to this by underlining how important constant discussions were to share responsibility among team members. This student said:

> "From my point of view, managing the inventory in the beginning is a suitable way to learn and to understand how the simulation works. For this, most of the responsibility

> and decision making power was hold by the experienced person. But we discussed every decision and action, so that I got used to why we make certain moves very quickly. Later, responsibility was automatically shared very equal among both of us. I started more and more to make decisions when I felt sure and confident about the situation and the right action. But we still hung on to explain every move we made, so that the other person was informed in every point of time and could intervene in cases of doubt." (Foreign exchange student in Finland 4)

An Australian student summarized that the commitment and collaboration in his team helped the team to manage the interdependent nature of the task:

> "Thankfully, although the team was inexperienced and lacked understanding, each member was keen to try and understand and were more than willing to work together. This provided me with a sense of confidence in my team. After an initial rough patch whilst trying to understand the game, due to the teams level of commitment and strong collaborative efforts the members that were present were able to understand the process of the game." (Australian student 1)

As these examples highlight, the interdependent nature of the game that requires students to distribute the task responsibilities lets them experience and learn about real teamwork and collaboration.

"Knowing How We Know is the Ultimate Human Accomplishment"

According to Duffy and Cunningham (1996), "we are generally unaware of the beliefs we have adopted or created to live and teach by, but raising them to awareness can have salutary effects." In VIBu, the reflective essays written by the students make the learning from experience visible to the students. Thus, the students are forced to reflect on their experiences and learning and have to articulate what they have learned; they think about what they did and then try to find explanations what it meant.

A Finnish student observed about the learning approach:

> "I think, that the tutors want to show us just how big mayhem international team work can be if not organized properly." (Finnish student 5)

An Austrian student described her learning experiences as follows:

> "I learned that the biggest challenge is to integrate yourself in a team and find out what you can do best and how you can help your group. I had a completely different role compared to the role I have normally in team work: I had to make decisions for the whole team and take control over a project. Still, the most important lesson I have learned is that learning by doing is not just any phrase." (Austrian student 4)

An exchange student in Finland highlighted in particular the practical aspect of the game and how it helped them increase their knowledge about production, marketing, and teamwork. This student says:

> "All in all, I acquired lot of practical experience about how things that I had studied theoretically are unfolded in real situation. I was especially satisfied to see how each part of one company is working. In the past I was more familiar with marketing field and I had some insufficient knowledge about production, purchasing and accounting. So, during the game I had a chance to practically utilize my marketing abilities and at the same time increase knowledge about production process. Furthermore, I experienced business team working atmosphere and found out that when members are interested in collaboration and contribution to the firm, distance and cultural differences aren't problem. Therefore, I understood that working in a team which has high cohesion and collaboration level is very important for company success." (Foreign exchange student in Finland 5).

Duffy and Cunningham (1996) suggest that the technology should be seen as an integral component of the cognitive activity. The focus is not on the individual but on the activity in the environment. The task of the learner is no longer seen as static – the computer as applied to the task – but rather it is dynamic. The computer opens new opportunities and makes available new learning activities (Duffy & Cunningham, 1996, p. 188): "Success [of learning] will increasingly depend on exploring interrelationships in an information-rich environment rather than on accepting the point of view of one author who pursued one set of relationships and presents conclusions reflecting his or her implicit biases." With our data and the analysis from it we hope to have shown how this has succeeded in the VIBu experiments.

Key Learning and Teaching Outcomes

So how can we know when students have learned? Jonassen et al. (1999) suggest that assessing learning should take place while learning is occurring. This assessment is process-oriented. When assessing learning, the questions we are interested in are as follows: does it make sense; is it well founded, well presented; can it be applied; is it consistent with the standards? These are the questions we are trying to answer with the data from the VIBu sessions and related activities.

The conflicts, challenges, and critical incidents that occur during the virtual collaboration lead to increased emotional involvement and thus allow the students to gain both social and factual knowledge. The students' embeddedness in the complex, stressful, and unknown environment forces them to gather experiences related to intercultural communication, coordination over time zones, different cultural backgrounds, trust building, and sometimes erosion of relationships in a purely virtual surrounding. These experiences create an awareness and understanding of issues common in global virtual collaboration. Besides acquiring this social knowledge, they develop strategies to overcome these challenges and acquire technical abilities for working in a dispersed context.

But how could we assess whether and exactly which skills the students acquired through the simulations? Analyzing the individual reflections gave us a first idea about the participants' self-assessment and evaluation. It provided insight on how the single members of a team observed and analyzed a certain situation, how they estimated their own learning, and how they tried to implement that learning afterwards. Also the level of depth the reflection took place gave hints on how critical incidents were taken and how deep understanding was happening. Second, the group tasks provided a further insight into how the different situations were analyzed, on which points students focused, or which level of analysis was used by the group.

After the second simulation day the individual essays, teacher observation, and Skype protocols gave us a better idea about how development happened at the group and individual level. This could be seen, for example, in the teams' strategic plans, their communication, their awareness of needing a role distribution, or their patterns in coordination. Our interpretation is that the ongoing reflection at different levels and from different perspectives (e.g., essay, SWOT, group discussion, strategy making) enhanced these developments. One of the statements reflected that clearly:

> "In the beginning I was a bit skeptical about it but it was really fun and a nice and fruitful experience. Compared to other "normal" courses at university I would say that one benefits the most for the real business life from such simulations. Of course I would have been happier if we could have been able to reach a better result, but as the tutors told us and we all know, it is not really about the result but about the experience everyone gains from this."

Furthermore, the key business figures of each team (e.g., cash flow, return on investment, costs for inventory) imply that the groups have engaged in efficient communication and decision-making. Thus, they rose to the challenge and even improved their group performance.

DISCUSSION

We would like to conclude the current chapter with a discussion that highlights the utility of the current approach for teaching, research, and managers in organizations. We will also discuss the limitations of this approach.

Utility for Teaching

As we described in our detailed analysis above, we believe that the benefits of using business simulations such as VIBu as a teaching method are manifold. First, students are embedded in a real-life-like context, in which they have to make decisions and collaborate as an interdependent team in an uncertain context and under stress. The simulation requires them to act fast, to distribute responsibilities, and to continuously assess and evaluate the effectiveness of their chosen strategies. In that way, the students learn by experience and exposure, but also by analyzing and reflecting on their own interactions and behaviors. In this way, we find that students learn a lot about the actual task but also about themselves as a learner.

Second, the game exposes students to a teamwork context that has become increasingly common in organizations, but that is still not very common in many universities. The game allows students to engage in a task in an environment in which all of the communication happens with the support of technology and in which students need to interact with counterparts from many different cultures, negotiate time zone differences, have different access to technology, and also cultural preferences for communication and teamwork. This context provides students with a unique learning opportunity that has high relevance for their future business lives and is typically not part of university curricula.

Third, the game is fun and self-motivating. Students become strongly engaged in the game and most students are highly committed to their team and to the task at hand. This was also shown in the additional hours many participants spent in the game, even when their shifts had already ended. In that way, students are working in an environment in which their learning becomes meaningful and their interactions matter. Many students commented on how much they felt that the game really drew them in. A lot of them enthusiastically reported that it was the best learning experience they had in their student life. Creating an environment in which engagement and learning become self-reinforcing is invaluable for teachers.

Finally, students become responsible for their own learning. Students learn that what they get out of the experience is highly dependent on how much they become involved and on how much they reflect upon their experiences to draw their own conclusions. While the course instructors engage the students in debrief sessions during the class time, the instructors do not in fact teach the students about what they should be doing or how they should interact differently. It is the students' responsibility to distill knowledge about effective team functioning while playing the game and writing the reflective essays. This important aspect of the learning experience moves responsibility for student learning away from the instructor teaching the students to the students learning from their experiences and from each other. They can use the instructor as a source of information or as a coach, but they become responsible for their own learning, which ultimately creates the strongest form of student engagement.

Utility for Research Purposes

We believe that there are several specific strengths and benefits for teaching and research that go beyond the benefits for learning described above. In particular, we believe that the simulation and online training can be successfully used for research purposes, international inter-university collaborations, and multidisciplinary research on teaching practices and engaged learning. The current group of researchers has successfully used data collections from the simulation game sessions in writing and publishing papers on topics such as "virtual" leadership styles (Lähteenmäki, Saarinen, & Fischlmayr, 2007; Saarinen, Lähteenmäki, & Fischlmayr, 2011), trust building in virtual teams (Fischlmayr & Auer-Rizzi, 2007), social influence (Fischlmayr, Lähteenmäki, Saarinen, & Lainema, 2008), virtual organizations (Lähteenmäki, Saarinen, Fischlmayr, & Lainema, 2009), and culture and virtual teams (Fischlmayr, 2006, 2012).

Our belief is that this kind of "university laboratory" of virtual, global work using real-world communication tools also provides a relevant research laboratory on virtual work. The environment surely is not the same as a network of real-world business organizations, but when discussing multicultural, team-based, and temporal virtual work that requires innovative solutions, we think VIBu represents the real-world challenges very authentically. In this sense, VIBu also offers a valuable research laboratory in which to study virtual work.

Finally, we also believe that this approach lends itself well to research teaching and learning experiences. The students in VIBu experience a unique setting. They also experience a contrived learning situation that can be modulated to highlight and emphasize particular experiences and learning situations. These situations could be highly useful to create controlled learning experiences that help researchers better understand how students learn from practical experiences.

Utility for Managers in Organizations

The benefits described above are not only applicable to students but serve business organizations as well. VIBu is an appropriate tool for training employees who are involved in virtual, dispersed collaboration and face challenges from managing business processes over time zones. VIBu has already been used in in-house training sessions of Finnish business organizations. The feedback is very promising. So far, our experience with the training has told us several things: (a) employees in organizations are often still not aware of the challenges arising from cultural differences and time zone differences, (b) they are also not familiar enough with the kind of tools to be used in virtual communication, and (c) they do not know how each respective communication tool should best be applied. Thus, benefits from participating in VIBu entail: (a) understanding cultural differences, (b) the nature of virtual and international collaboration over different time zones, (c) the use of virtual collaboration tools, and (d) the challenge of managing international supply chains. Put together, VIBu forms a unique learning environment that is engaging and highly relevant to companies in today's globalized work context.

Limitations

Business simulations are just one way to engage students in learning. The utility of this approach naturally depends on how it is incorporated into the overall course structure and embedded into the theoretical concepts covered in class as well as on the quality of the debrie. With this chapter, we do not want to propagate business simulations as the solution to all our teaching problems. Rather, we would like to offer them as one way to generate real learning experiences in an online environment. Educating students on global issues is not an easy task, and instructors have to become creative in order to provide students with real international experiences in their classrooms. International business simulations can offer that.

One of the limitations, of course, lies in the technology itself. Things do not always work as they are supposed or arranged to. However, this represents the reality of global work in which technology fails from time to time and in which team members have to cope with uncertainty and unreliability. The simulation underlies the same challenges as any other global collaboration and provides the students with a real environment.

Finally, simulations such as the one described here are not easy to create. Most course instructors who want to engage in a simulation join an existing simulation, rather than creating their own. This can become problematic when the simulation they join was not designed to support the learning goals of their class. Hence, we recommend that instructors who are interested in joining business simulations with their students pay particular attention to the aims of the simulation. They should pay particular attention to how the simulation will support the students' construction of learning.

CONCLUSION

In conclusion, we believe that business simulations are a valuable contribution to our teaching toolbox. Our chapter has highlighted in particular how business simulations support students' construction of learning as proposed by the CLP. It is important to understand how students benefit from concrete experiences in their classes, so that these experiences can be used more strategically and in a more targeted fashion to support learning. We have offered our experiences with the VIBu training as a concrete example for the types of learning experiences students might get from participating in a business simulation. We believe that simulations provide a great example for the use of cutting-edge technology to support the preparation of our students for a complex, globalized business world.

REFERENCES

Bachmann, A. S. (2006). Melting pot or tossed salad? Implications for designing effective multicultural workgroups. *Management International Review*, *46*(6), 721–747.

Ballesteros, I. L. (2006). *New collaborative working environments 2020. Report on industry-led FP7 consultations and 3rd report of the experts group on Collaboration@Work*. Brussels: European Commission. Retrieved from http://www.ami-communities.eu/www.amiat

work.com/europa.eu.int/information_society/activities/atwork/hot_news/publications/documents/new_collab_environments_2020.pdf

Blackburn, R., Furst, S., & Rosen, B. (2003). Building a winning virtual team. In C. B. Gibson & S. G. Cohen (Eds.), *Virtual teams that work* (pp. 95–120). San Francisco, CA: Jossey-Bass.

Bryant, S. M., Albring, S. M., & Murthy, U. (2009). The effects of reward structure, media richness and gender on virtual teams. *International Journal of Accounting Management Systems*, *10*, 190–213.

Cheetham, G., & Chivers, G. (2001). How professionals learn in practice: An investigation of informal learning amongst people working in professions. *Journal of European Industrial Training*, *25*(5), 248–292.

Cseh, M. (2003). Facilitating learning in multicultural teams. *Advances in Developing Human Resources*, *5*(1), 26–40.

DiStefano, J. J., & Maznevski, M. L. (2000). Creating value with diverse teams in global management. *Organizational Dynamics*, *29*(1), 45–63.

Duffy, T. M., & Cunningham, D. J. (1996). Constructivism: Implications for the design and delivery of instruction. In D. H. Jonassen (Ed.), *Handbook of research for educational communications and technology* (pp. 170–198). New York, NY: Macmillan Library Reference.

Fischlmayr, I. C. (2006). The influence of culture on multicultural virtual teams – The example of Finns and Austrians. In A. Paalumäki (Ed.) Reflections on the relationship between academic business knowledge and society (pp. 212–235). Series C-1:20069. Turku: Turku School of Economics.

Fischlmayr, I. C. (2012). *Bridging cultures via an online business simulation over different time zones*. Paper presented at the 4th ACM International Conference on Intercultural Collaboration (ICIC), 2012, Bengaluru, India.

Fischlmayr, I., & Auer-Rizzi, W. (2007). Trust in virtual multicultural teams. In L. Brennan & V. Johnson (Eds.), *Computer-mediated relationships and trust: Managerial and organizational effects* (pp. 100–116). Hershey, PA: Information Science Reference.

Fischlmayr, I., Lähteenmäki, S., Saarinen, E., & Lainema, T. (2008). In *Proceedings of the IAREP/SABE Conference, Italy. Factors of social influence in virtual multicultural teams*. Rome: Luiss University Press.

Fruchter, R. (2004). Global teamwork: Cross-disciplinary, collborative, geographically distributed e-learning environment. In J. Bento, J. P. Duarte, M. V. Heitor & W. J. Mitchell (Eds.), *Collaborative design and learning: Competence building for innovation* (pp. 265–297). Westport, CT: Praeger.

Henriksen, T. D., & Löfvall, S. (2012). Current and past experiences with games at business schools. In *Transforming university teaching into learning via games, simulations and roleplays*. Faringdon: Libri Publishing.

Hertel, D. A. (2005). Managing virtual teams: A review of current empirical research. *Human Resource Management Review*, *15*, 69–95.

Herz, B., & Merz, W. (1998). Experiential learning and the effectiveness of economic simulation games. *Simulation & Gaming*, *29*(2), 238–250.

Jonassen, D. H., Peck, K. L., & Wilson, B. G. (1999). *Learning with technology: A constructivist perspective*. Columbus, OH: Prentice Hall.

Kayes, D. C. (2002). Experiential learning and its critics: Preserving the role of experience in management learning and education. *Academy of Management Learning and Education*, *1*(2), 137–149.

Keys, B., & Wolfe, J. (1990). The role of management games and simulations in education and research. *Journal of Management, 16*(2), 307–336.

Kolb, D. (1984). *Experiential learning: Experience the source of learning and development.* Englewood Cliffs, NJ: Prentice Hall.

Lähteenmäki, S., Saarinen, E., & Fischlmayr, I. C. (2007). Embracing the new leadership paradigm—Gateway to building trust and commitment in virtual multicultural teams. In *Proceedings of the eBRF 2007 conference.* Finland.

Lähteenmäki, S., Saarinen, E., Fischlmayr, I. C., & Lainema, T. (2009). Virtual organizations. In H. Bidgoli (Ed.), *The handbook of technology management* (pp. 189–206). Oxford, UK: Wiley.

Lainema, T. (2003). *Enhancing organizational business process perception – Experiences from constructing and applying a dynamic business simulation game.* Turku School of Economics, Series A-5:2003. Retrieved from http://info.tse.fi/julkaisut/vk/Ae5_2003.pdf

Lainema, T. (2004). Redesigning the traditional business gaming process – Aiming to capture business process authenticity. *Journal of Information Technology Education, 3*, 35–52.

Lainema, T. (2009). Perspective making – Constructivism as a meaning structure for simulation gaming. *Simulation & Gaming: An Interdisciplinary Journal of Theory, Practice and Research, 40*(1), 48–67.

Lainema, T., & Lainema, K. (2007). Advancing acquisition of business know-how: Critical learning elements. *Journal of Research on Technology in Education, 40*(2), 183–198.

Lainema, T., & Makkonen, P. (2003). Applying constructivist approach to educational business games: Case REALGAME. *Simulation & Gaming: An Interdisciplinary Journal of Theory, Practice and Research, 34*(1), 131–149.

Lainema, T., & Nurmi, S. (2006). Applying an authentic, dynamic learning environment in real world business. *Computers and Education, 47*(1), 94–115.

Lave, J., & Wenger, E. (1991). *Situated learning. Legitimate peripheral participation.* Cambridge, UK: Cambridge University Press.

Machuca, J. A.-D. (2000). Transparent-box business simulators: An aid to manage the complexity of organizations. *Simulation & Gaming, 31*(2), 230–239.

Marsick, V. J., & Watkins, K. E. (1990). *Informal and incidental learning in the workplace.* London, UK: Routledge.

Maznevski, M. L. (2008). Leading global teams. In M. E. Mendenhall, J. S. Osland, A. Bird, G. B. Oddou & M. L. Maznevski (Eds.), *Global leadership* (pp. 94–113). Abingdon, Oxfordshire: Routledge.

Naylor, T. H. (1971). *Computer simulation experiments with models of economic systems.* New York, NY: Wiley.

Powell, A., Piccoli, G., & Ives, B. (2004). Virtual teams: A review of current literature and directions for future research. *The Database for Advances in Information Systems, 35*(1), 6–36.

Rienties, B., Beausaert, S., Grohnert, T., Niemantsverdriet, S., & Kommers, P. (2011). Understanding academic performance of international students: The role of ethnicity, academic and social integration. *Higher Education, 63*(6), 685–700. doi:10.1007/s10734-011-9468-1.

Rosen, B., Furst, S., & Blackburn, R. (2006). Training for virtual teams: An investigation of current practices and future needs. *Human Resource Management, 45*(2), 229–247.

Rusman, E., Bruggen, J., Sloep, P., & Koper, R. (2010). Fostering trust in virtual project teams: Towards a design framework grounded in a TrustWorthinessANtecedents (TWAN) schema. *International Journal of Human-Computer Studies, 68*, 834–850.

Saarinen, E., Lähteenmäki, S., & Fischlmayr I. (2011). *Waiting for the leader to take action? – Leadership in virtual collaboration context*. Paper presented at 15th European Congress of Work and Organizational Psychology, 2011. Maastricht, The Netherlands.

Senge, P. M., & Lannon, C. (1997). Managerial microworlds. *Technology Review*, *93*(5), 62–68.

Tutty, J. I., & Klein, J. D. (2008). Computer-mediated instruction: A comparison of online and face-to-face collaboration. *Educational Technology Research and Development*, *56*(2), 101–124.

Watson, W. E., Johnson, L., & Zgourides, G. D. (2002). The influence of ethnic diversity on leadership, group processes, and performance: An examination of learning teams. *International Journal of Intercultural Relations*, *26*, 1–16.

MEDIATED DISCOURSE IN HIGHER ED CLASSROOMS USING TEXT MESSAGING

Binod Sundararajan, Lorn Sheehan and Sarah Gilbert

ABSTRACT

Mediated communication can be thought of as a mediated discourse, involving the knowledge of language, symbols, metaphors, and shared meaning. We describe here a funded study where we investigate the effectiveness of text messaging as a learning tool for higher level courses and provide insight into the use of texting as a supplemental, yet critical learning tool in the teaching and learning process. The design, based on the Vygotskian constructivist paradigm, where learning can happen in social and collaborative interactions, assesses three types of communication within student groups, (1) face-to-face (FTF), (2) using only Instant Messenger (IM), and (3) using only cell phone texting. For analyzing the IM and text exchanges we follow the recommendations of Thurlow (2003) using thematic referential coding schemes. Using the concept of Grice (1975), we detect the presence of conversational maxims and implicature and also the presence of adjacency pairs (Sacks, Schegloff, Jefferson, 1974), indicating turn-taking in IM and texting conversations. Results from content and conversational analyses indicate that while there is an

Increasing Student Engagement and Retention using Classroom Technologies: Classroom Response Systems and Mediated Discourse Technologies
Cutting-edge Technologies in Higher Education, Volume 6E, 199–232

ISSN: 2044-9968/doi:10.1108/S2044-9968(2013)000006E010

innate preference for FTF discussions among participants, participants felt that IM and texting would be useful if used intermittently and as a supplementary learning tool in classrooms to mediate discussions. Participants also felt that IM and texting focused them on tasks and despite any frustrations with the technology they did gain a shared understanding of the subject matter and gained new and conceptual knowledge. The findings from this research can be used to explore the use of an additional dimension of learning in school and university classrooms.

INTRODUCTION

In many modern university classrooms and technologically driven organizations, computer-mediated communication (CMC) tools, consisting of highly interactive technologies, including email, electronic bulletin boards, asynchronous multimedia notebooks, remote screen-sharing, desktop video teleconferencing, and more recently cell phone and PDA-based texting (Carpenter, Froese, & Barnes, 2010; Sheneman, 2008; Sundararajan, 2009, 2010) are used to facilitate collaborative interaction among students and co-workers. Thus, CMC can enable individuals or groups to work together, even when they cannot be temporally or spatially co-located. This study looks at the social dynamic (Respect, Influence, Teamwork – Sundararajan, 2009, Sundararajan & Hübscher-Younger, 2006) and communication factors (use of face-to-face (FTF), Instant Messenger (IM), and Short Messaging Service (SMS) – texting) that are critical for successful collaboration in a technologically mediated group deliberation exercise and how this mediated deliberation process aids in the individual and group learning outcomes for abstract material from English Literature, Management, and Business and the social sciences. We also look at whether these learning outcomes are supported or hindered by communication technology.

In recent years, text messaging (texting) has emerged as the preferred means of person-to-person communication of a wide range of people for a variety of activities. While it was popularized by the "thumb tribes" of Japanese and Scandinavian youth (Rheingold, 2002), it is no longer the exclusive domain of the younger generation, with older people adopting the technology due to the relative ease of use and the convenience of communicating with others quickly. Recently an 86-year-old Japanese woman authored an entire novel using a cell phone in order to reach out to a new audience (MSNBC, 2008) and popular YA (Young Adult) horror author R. L. Stine has published a short story via Twitter (Goosebumps Twitter Story). Sheneman (2008) reports on the appearance of "text-message-speak" in tests and other learning situations and suggests that it can provide an environment for non-native speakers of the language to foster good English. Researchers like Jones and Schieffelin (2009) have discussed the use of text messaging in main stream media TV ads, while others like Thurlow (2005) and Grinter and Eldridge (2003) have reported on the prevalence of texting among the youth and how it affects their communication and social interactions, the role of new technologies in the lives of young people, and the blurred boundary between computer-mediated and FTF communication. Brett (2011), summarizing previous studies on SMS-texting use in learning environments, concludes that there is a strong student preference for the use of SMS for administrative purposes and for personal tutor contacts; that interactive SMS is of value to language learners; and that it can increase classroom interactivity – students also felt that the phone was a personal device and that class information pushed into these personal devices would be considered an intrusion.

The purpose of this study is to investigate the effectiveness of text messaging to be a discussion medium in class groups for higher level courses in literature, business, management, and the social sciences and hence be a supplementary classroom learning tool. The research design has three groups of students: the first discussed the lecture material FTF, the second used only IM and the third used only cell phone text messaging (texting or SMS – SMS and texting are used interchangeably in the paper). During the study, all participants (after a pre-test to establish baseline subject matter knowledge, experience with the technologies, and perceptions) were given instruction in a FTF classroom on the subject matter. This was followed by deliberation and discussion of lecture-specific probing questions with their respective teams using their assigned technologies. The data collected allow for both quantitative and qualitative analyses, network analysis, and a total mixed methods approach. Thus, study differs from recent efforts at investigating the effectiveness of texting in learning environments (Brett, 2011; Cheung, 2004; Kennedy & Levy, 2008; Markett, Sanchez, Weber, & Tangney, 2006).

In this research, we focus on the text exchanges of student and work group members (in comparison to other mediated environments) to see where in the decision-making and deliberation process knowledge creation (learning) takes place. The findings from this study provide insight into the use of texting as a critical communication tool to disseminate and create knowledge across diverse populations and for the use of texting as an additional teaching and learning tool, which can be used as a standalone teaching device or integrated with all other technologies prevalent in classrooms today. Additionally, we foresee that this can be used to reach people who otherwise do not have access to regular classrooms or more elaborate teaching environments (Virtual classrooms like Blackboard, Wimba, etc.). We also foresee its use among learners whose first language may not be the language of instruction (in this case English) and also foresee this as an inclusive technology to allow those with speech and hearing impairments to be included in classroom discussions.

TECHNOLOGICALLY MEDIATED COMMUNICATION

It was recognized early on that a new communication theory was needed for our rapidly developing technologically mediated environment. This new communication theory needed to encompass all the aspects of CMC including email, IM, teleconferencing, videoconferencing, presentation media (electronic whiteboards), and electronic discussion boards. Such a theory has been founded on a constructivist theory of knowledge: with knowledge no longer viewed as a body of facts that teachers package as explicit messages for reception by students, but more as a subtle developmental process in which students construct new understanding based on their current conceptualizations (Papert, 1980). Furthermore, following the principles of Vygotsky (1978), knowledge is seen to be constructed socially in interactions between people before it is internalized as individual knowing. This social aspect has been further developed into activity theory, emphasizing that individual cognition is mediated by physical and symbolic artifacts and that it centrally involves sociocultural aspects. From here we derive our first research question.

RQ1. Did participants find the technology (IM or texting) useful in discussing the subject matter and whether the technology improved their ability to understand the subject material as compared to the FTF group?

Students in general and participants in this study are expected to work in classroom groups. Instructors provide seed questions for discussion and deliberation based on subject matter concepts and students discuss the possible answers to these questions based on the new concepts presented to them and by way of argument (claim, background, evidence, rebuttal, grounds, warrant, backing, and qualifiers – Toulmin, 1969) arrive at an understanding of the subject matter concepts and possibly reach consensus. This leads to the possible creation of new and conceptual knowledge.

Whereas in a FTF setting, turn-taking allows for the various levels of argument to flow among the discussants (group members in this case), our aim is to see if deliberating in a mediated environment (IM or texting) provides discussants with the same levels of opportunities to reach a shared understanding and create knowledge, thereby finding the medium useful for the purpose of discussing subject matter concepts.

Mediated communication (technologically or otherwise) can be thought of as a mediated discourse, involving the knowledge of the language, symbols, metaphors, and shared meaning. It is the purpose of this study to investigate how this mediated discourse lends itself to individual and group knowledge creation using the relatively new medium of cell phone or PDA texting. With the advent of texting among not just young people but also people in work roles in organizations, it becomes critical that we study this technology and its impact on individual and institutional knowledge creation in both academic and work settings. While texting involves the use of a unique language of its own, it is definitely a medium of choice for students and business people because of the convenience, relative ease of use, level of informality, relatively short turnaround times for responses, and that it almost synchronously mimics FTF or IM conversations. Grinter and Eldridge (2003) mention that the cost of sending text messages is so low now that it offers very low barriers for adoption. We therefore focus on the text exchanges of students in class groups (in comparison to other mediated environments, particularly IM conversations) to see where in the deliberation process knowledge creation takes place. This then gives rise to the second research question.

> **RQ2.** Did participants learn new and conceptual knowledge during the process of deliberation using the medium (FTF, IM, texting) of communication? (Sundararajan, 2009)

Finally, in order to assess learning gains in a more formal manner, we administered pre- and post-subject matter content tests (pretest for benchmarking). While results from such tests may indicate learning gains, we can never be sure that any specific treatment or intervention was the direct cause of a learning gain, but when seen along with other aspects of the learning process (active participation in class and in discussions, requesting and receiving normative and summative feedback, individual self-efficacy and motivation among other things), results can suggest that learning took place and knowledge was created. When we further match these with specific survey questions (that ask participants whether they learnt new and conceptual knowledge, whether they were satisfied with their performance, whether they will get an A and whether they felt that discussing the subject matter with their group mates helped in the learning process), we can usually surmise whether the social interaction in the mediated environment lead to learning gains and knowledge creation. This then gives rise to our third research question.

RQ3. Did participants' post-test results match their perception of having learnt new and conceptual knowledge? (Sundararajan, 2009)

To help us answer these research questions, we have collected content test data, survey data and network data (quantitative), recorded conversations (audio, video, text, and chat logs – quantitative and qualitative), observed group interactions (qualitative), and debriefed participants in a focus group (qualitative and quantitative). We now look at the methodology and data collection procedures. However, for this chapter we will only focus on the content analysis of the IM and text exchanges, the focus group responses that address these questions, and the subject matter pre- and post-test results to answer the research questions.

CONVERSATION ANALYSIS

For analyzing the IM and text (SMS) exchanges (conversations), we followed the recommendations of Thurlow (2003, 2005) to create thematic referential message categories. Thurlow's (2003) coding scheme (Fig. 1) refers to general text interactions among friends and family. We adapted Thurlow's codes (a priori) to fit the context of texting in a learning environment, and added new codes as needed to describe the content and

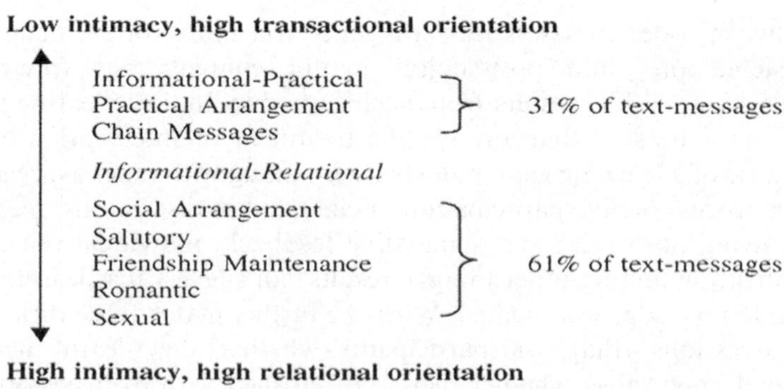

Fig. 1. Referential Thematic-Functional Categories Model (Thurlow, 2003).

conversations noted in our data. These new codes are presented in Fig. 2 and will be discussed shortly.

Thurlow (2003) presents a coding scheme to categorize text messages and outlines nine broad categories reflective of the functional orientation of each message (Fig. 1). While this is a fairly broad set, we noted that these categories related more to general text messages say between friends and family and occasionally among co-workers. We created a few new categories to indicate when participants were discussing the specific aspects of the assigned topic. Based on Toulmin's (1969) levels of argument, often an initial claim is made (for a particular context) and this claim is supported by some evidence. This initial claim with the supporting evidence can be accepted by others unchallenged, but often listeners would proffer a different opinion or a qualifier for the initial claim. The initial speaker then has to provide a rebuttal with supporting evidence or warrant. This continues iteratively until speakers and listeners reach a consensus. To capture these aspects of argumentation,

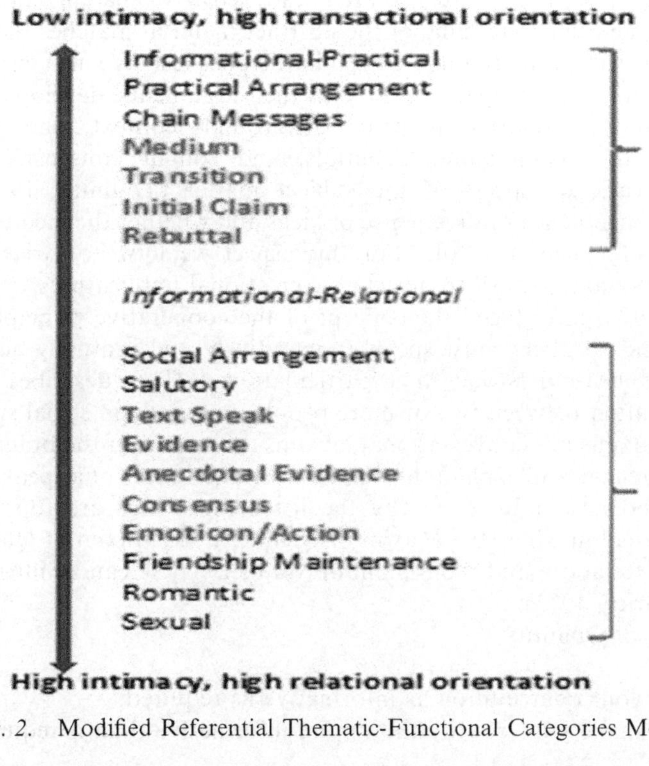

Fig. 2. Modified Referential Thematic-Functional Categories Model.

we created thematic categories for Initial Claim, Evidence, Rebuttal, and Anecdotal Evidence. We also created a category called "Consensus" to see if words or phrases like agree, yeah (variants), good point, etc. clustered around conceptual ideas during the discussions, a category called "Medium" to classify exchanges that had to do with the communication medium, and one called "Emoticon/Action" to indicate the presence of commonly used texting/IM emoticons. We also had a category called "Transition" where participants indicated that they needed to move on to another topic or another point. To capture specific instances of "text lingo" in both IM and text exchanges, we created a category called "Text Speak." We thus modified Thurlow's referential thematic-functional categories model to include applicable codes developed by Thurlow, Toulmin's (1969) levels of argument, and our own ad hoc codes. We present the modified referential thematic-functional categories model in Fig. 2; Table 1 outlines the various code categories, their definitions, and their origin.

The aim of this content analysis was to see whether the participants' perception of having created shared knowledge or having gained new knowledge and understanding of the abstract material matches their actual grasp of the subject matter as assessed in the post-test. We also examine the process by which participants conducted their arguments, developed a claim or hypothesis, supported it with background, context, and evidence, responded to qualifiers and rebuttals, and sought consensus as they discussed various aspects of the subject matter (Toulmin, 1969). This indicates convergence or divergence of ideas and whether the medium (FTF, IM, or TXT) plays any role. For this aspect we look to Grice's (1975) "conversational maxims" to detect conversational implicatures.

Grice (1975) introduced the concept of the cooperative principle, where listeners and speakers must speak cooperatively and mutually accept one another to be understood in a particular way. This describes effective communication between two or more people, especially in social situations. Gricean maxims are conversational maxims derived from the pragmatics of natural language and explain the link between utterances of a speaker(s) and what is understood by them (by the listeners). There are four Gricean conversational maxims, the Maxim of Quantity, the Maxim of Quality, the Maxim of Relation, and the Maxim of Manner. These can be illustrated as follows (Grice, 1975):

Maxims of Quantity

1. "Make your contribution as informative as required."
2. "Don't make your contribution more informative than is required."

Table 1. Outline of Codes and their Origin.

Code Origin	Code	Definition
Adapted from Thurlow (2003)	Salutary orientation	Messages sent to participants to indicate greeting or departure (e.g., "hello," "good bye," "see you tomorrow," etc.)
	Sexual orientation	Messages with sexual overtones relating to instincts, physiology, and activities connected with physical attraction
	Informational-relational	Messages with the intent to relate information to other participants (e.g., responses to direct requests for information/clarification or statements of unrelated or off-topic information)
	Informational-practical orientation	Requests for information, such as clarifications or definitions. Primarily formatted as questions
	Friendship maintenance	Casual, friendly messages between participants. Includes compliments, jokes, expressions of thanks, and sharing personal information
Adapted from Toulmin (1969)	Transition	Used to indicate a change in topics of conversation
	Initial claim	First statement of opinion (task-related)
	Evidence	Statement supporting a claim (using objective and fact-based evidence)
	Anecdotal evidence	Statement supporting a claim (using personal evidence)
	Rebuttal	A statement which refutes a claim using indicators such as "yes, but …" and "however"
	Consensus	Final agreement
Ad hoc	Medium	Messages in which participants discuss the medium they are using
	Corrections	Messages in which the sole purpose is to correct and error or typo from a previous message
	Text Speak	Used to describe words that have been abbreviated to speed up communication, excluding common contractions. Examples include "btw" (by the way), "@participant name" (indicating a response to a particular participant's statement), and "gov't" (government)
	Emoticon/Action	Textual representations of feelings, emotions, or sounds (e.g., "?," "lol," and "whoa"); IMs had features imbedded in the program which allowed them to express actions such clapping, agreement, etc. Use of these are included as emoticon/action
	Repeat	Used for all texts but the original sent message (i.e., used to indicate received messages)
	Unknown	Used when the intent of the message is incompressible (often occurred when participants were learning to use the phone)

Maxims of Quality: Be truthful

1. "Don't say what you believe to be false."
2. "Don't say what you lack adequate evidence for."

Maxim of Relation

1. "Be relevant."

Maxims of Manner: "Be perspicuous."

1. "Avoid obscurity of expression."
2. "Avoid ambiguity."
3. "Be brief (avoid unnecessary prolixity)."
4. "Be orderly."

According to Grice, when these maxims are violated we are forced to make inference as to meaning. Grice further asserted that different ways of violating the maxims gives rise to different types of implicatures. For example, if a friend asks you your salary, you have the option of either telling them the amount you make or not. If you say what your salary is, you do not violate any maxim, especially the maxim of quality, because you were truthful. However, if you make X and you say 1.5X, then it is a lie and a violation of the maxim of quality. Another option, because you may want to maintain the conversation (and possibly the friendship), is to decline by saying something like, "I am sorry, that is confidential information." This is an interesting, yet face-saving overt opting-out-of-a-maxim technique, which allows you to maintain the conversation (and probably the friendship), but since this information is overtly expressed, there is no need to either violate the maxim of quantity (provide only as much information as required) or add implicature. In another example, if your friend wants to know the whereabouts of another mutual friend you again have a choice of either giving the exact whereabouts of this mutual friend or you can say, "Oh! John is out and about today." So rather than lying (which would violate the maxim of quality), you give general information that violates the maxim of quantity (giving less information than required) and the maxim of manner (by being ambiguous).

In addition to looking for conversational implicatures in the IM and texting exchanges, we will also look for the presence of turn-taking (seen typically in FTF conversations), where each speaker awaits their turn to offer a comment or opinion. One way to detect turn-taking in conversations is to look for adjacency pairs (Sacks et al., 1974), i.e., where pockets of conversation pieces cluster around a particular topic or ideas and speakers (IMs or texters) converge their contributions to deliberate this topic using claims, evidence, etc. Thus, the content analysis of these IM and text exchanges proceeds by first categorizing conversations by adapting Thurlow's (2003) coding scheme and incorporating Toulmin's (1969) levels of argument into code categories, followed by actual analysis of comparable IM and text exchanges (on the same topic for ease of comparison) to detect conversational implicature and turn-taking.

METHODOLOGY

The Research Facility

The research is being conducted in a Groupwork Behaviour Lab in our University. The lab is specifically designed to facilitate this type of research and accommodates 16 people in a configurable space with 4 video cameras, 6 microphones, 10 laptop/tablet computers with network connections, and a 52 inch monitor. An observation room, with a one-way mirrored window, and recording capabilities, enables remote observation of the activities.

Data Collection

We divided the study into two phases. Each phase has four rounds (with between 15 and 18 participants per round) of data collection. Data presented and discussed in this chapter was collected during phase 1 of the study. Students recruited to participate in the study for monetary compensation signed an informed consent form indicating that participation was voluntary and that they were being video and audio recorded. They had the option to withdraw at any time during or after the 5-day period. At the commencement of the study, all participants were given a pre-test on the lecture material (In rounds one and two the subject matter was Leisure and Tourism Management and in rounds three and four the subject matter was Corporate Communication) and also complete a survey of their experience using the technologies under study, i.e., IM and texting (SMS). For five days of each round, the 15 or so students meet at the Groupwork lab to listen to a lecture on the subject matter. Members of the IM group were given laptops to log into a course space created in the Online Web Learning (OWL) Management system, which also ran the Wimba™ Classroom for chat discussions. Members of the TXT group were given a variation of the latest Blackberry Curve smartphone.

After the lecture, each group of five or so students were asked to get together with their assigned group and discuss questions posed by the instructor using one of the methods of communication, i.e., FTF only, IM only, or texting only. At the end of the 5-day period, participants were given a post-test on the subject matter (identical to the pre-test) to determine knowledge gained and a post-survey to assess their experiences and perceptions with the medium of communication, and their levels of satisfaction with the way their interactions and learning progressed. They were also asked if they faced any group dynamics issues, whether they were able to form working relationships with their group members, and whether these factors impacted their motivation to learn and create knowledge. We also collected demographic information (Table 2). At the end of the 5-day period, participants are interviewed in a focus group session. These focus group interviews add a qualitative understanding of the group dynamics during the deliberation process, which augment audio and video data, survey data, pre- and post-test data, and actual recorded group conversations (FTF, IM, and text). The aim was to see if the medium of communication for discussions affected motivation to learn, participation, and interaction, as well as where learning gains occurred. Such rich data help triangulate results over time, across different lecture materials and different teaching styles, and allow us to evaluate these mediums (specifically IM and texting) as supplementary learning tools. Here we report the results from phase 1 involving 58 participants.

Table 2. Demographic Information of Participants.

Age	Year of Study	English as First Language	Own a Phone	Model	Texts Per Day
18–20: 19	1st: 10	Yes: 45	Yes: 54	Blackberry: 17	>10: 13
21–23: 19	2nd: 7	No: 11	No: 4	iPhone: 12	10–30: 21
24–26: 9	3rd: 13	Bilingual: 2		Other: 12	30–60: 7
27–29: 3	4th: 14				60–100: 9
30+: 8	Grad: 13				100+: 7
	N/A: 1				N/A: 1
		$N = 58$; $F = 37$; $M = 21$			

RESULTS

The results are organized as follows:

1. The demographic information of the participants
2. Content and conversation analysis of the IM and text messages using:
   a. Thurlow's (2005) coding schemes and Toulmin's (1969) levels of argument
   b. Grice's (1975) conversational maxims
   c. Adjacency pairs (Sacks et al., 1974)
3. Revisiting the research questions using excerpts from the focus group debriefing sessions
4. Performance on subject matter pre- and post-tests

We illustrate the content analysis with both excerpts of IM and text conversations and code category network diagrams (sociograms) to see if consensus, task-related discussions, and other code categories cluster together to indicate convergence in these discussions.

Demographics

The demographic makeup of the participants in four rounds can be seen in Table 2. We had students from different majors, different age groups, and from different years. There were 37 female and 21 male participants, 2 were bilingual (French and English) and 11 whose first language was not English. Except for four participants, all of them owned cell phones, and the models and brands that they owned varied. We also note the number of text messages sent by these participants on a normal day using their own phones.

Content Analysis of IM and Text Message Conversations

2a: Content Analysis Using Thurlow's (2003) Coding Scheme and Toulmin's (1969) Levels of Argument

To perform content analysis on the IM and text conversations, we used QDAMiner™ and WordStat™ from Provalis Research, by using our modified referential thematic-functional code categories. We present below some category dendrogram clusters, proximity plots, and code network plots of IM and text conversations. We started with the IM conversations first so that we could create benchmarks and then performed the content analysis on the text messages. We also performed an inter-rater agreement test on the presence or absence of the code in the cases for both the IM and text exchanges (all days, all four rounds). In the absence of knowledge of the risks of drawing false conclusions from unreliable data, social scientists commonly rely on data with reliabilities $\alpha \geq .800$, consider data with $0.800 > \alpha \geq 0.667$ only to draw tentative conclusions, and discard data whose agreement measures $\alpha < 0.667$ (Krippendorff, 2004). Initially, the alpha was less than .800, and so the coders returned to the codes, clarified definitions, and discussed disagreements to reach 100% agreement.

We now present the coding frequency tables for both the IM and TXT conversations for all days of the four rounds of the study. Tables 3 and 4 provide the frequency distribution for the thematic code categories for IM and TXT messages. We note from Tables 3 and 4 that the thematic code distribution for the IM and TXT conversations are fairly reflective of the Thurlow model. We will discuss this when we present the updated or modified thematic referential category model.

We present the cluster dendrograms and plots for both the IM and texting group side-by-side making it easier to compare the results. The clustering was done using Jaccard's coefficient for occurrence which measures the

Table 3. Coding Frequency for IM Conversations.

Code	Count	%Codes
Evidence	465	22.5
Friendship maintenance	300	14.4
Consensus	262	12.7
Informational-relational	217	10.5
Initial claim	156	7.5
Emoticon/Action	133	6.4
Information practical orientation	120	5.8
Rebuttal	100	4.8
Transition	68	3.3
Anecdotal evidence	64	3.1
Text Speak	54	2.6
Salutory orientation	51	2.5
Medium	40	1.9
Corrections	32	1.5
Sexual orientation	9	0.4
Unknown	0	0

Table 4. Coding Frequency for Text Messages.

Code	Count	%Codes
Evidence	692	28.6
Consensus	355	14.7
Informational-practical orientation	243	10
Rebuttal	232	9.6
Initial claim	196	8.1
Emoticon/Action	156	6.4
Informational-relational	135	5.6
Friendship maintenance	114	4.7
Text Speak	74	3.1
Anecdotal evidence	69	2.8
Medium	53	2.2
Unknown	31	1.3
Corrections	27	1.1
Salutory orientation	24	1
Transition	22	0.9
Sexual orientation	0	0

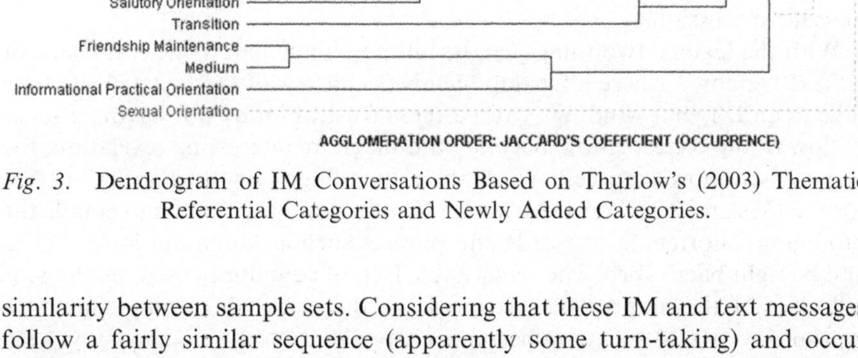

Fig. 3. Dendrogram of IM Conversations Based on Thurlow's (2003) Thematic Referential Categories and Newly Added Categories.

similarity between sample sets. Considering that these IM and text messages follow a fairly similar sequence (apparently some turn-taking) and occur within the same context (learning situation), the Jaccard coefficient is suitable for such a comparison. The cluster dendrograms of both the IM and TXT group conversations (Figs. 3 and 4, respectively) reveal fairly similar

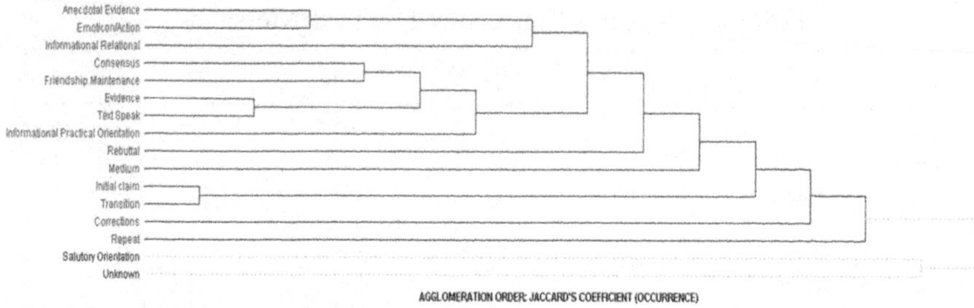

Fig. 4. Dendrogram of Text Message Conversations Based on Thurlow's (2003) Thematic Referential Categories and Newly Added Categories.

patterns. The clustering is consistent around the Consensus category for both mediums, specifically with respect to the Evidence category. In both IM and TXT messages, the Evidence category clusters close to (or with) the Consensus category, indicating the proximity of these types of conversations to one another. Whether this indicates agreement or not can only be determined by looking at the actual conversation which we do shortly when we revisit the research questions.

The "Repeat" category in the Text Message Dendrogram is where duplicate messages were placed. Duplicates were present because texters could send a message to the entire group, but the recipients could only reply to the sender. In order for them to send to the entire group they had to create an entirely new message. This was one of the causes of frustration and ensuing complaints of "no flow" and "not organic" with respect to the text message discussions.

With the texters, two things can be inferred immediately. One, the lack of a "text window" where all group members can see all the texts all the time (like in an IM chat window), caused them frustration by not having a sense of flow of the conversation. Second, and the more interesting revelation, the texters used more complete words than "text lingo" or "text speak" (2.6% for the IMs and 3.1% for the texters – Tables 3 and 4). Text lingo entails the prodigious shortening of words and phrases such as laugh out loud – LOL and be right back – brb. The remarkable lack of commonly used text lingo is reflective of the number of text messages this particular group sent on a typical day (10–30 – determined from a pre-study technology survey – see Fig. 1). The texters were typing in complete words and phrases, taking longer to compose their messages and replies, missing out on the flow of information, and getting frustrated with the process.

This is indeed relevant, and points to what needs to be done: (1) with the form factor of the texting device – though that is entirely up to the manufacturer; (2) with the course design where texting is adopted as one of the learning tools (albeit a supplementary one); and (3) allowing the use of acceptable text lingo and maybe even running a couple of lecture classes to inform students about the possibilities of using text lingo to save time during discussions. The danger of this can be the percolation of text lingo into other forms of class work (reports, presentations, etc.) as reported by Sheneman (2008) – the appearance of "text-message-speak" on tests and other learning assessments. Interestingly, Kyobe and Shongwe (2011), while studying the use of text messages for discussing group projects (with engineering students), report that teams with weak social ties found text messaging to be useful for sharing tacit knowledge and frequent users could also use texting to share explicit knowledge. However, Kyobe and Shongwe found that "most students do not utilize the affordances of mobile phones for sharing tacit knowledge" and advocate that students be encouraged to use their mobile phones for sharing tacit and explicit knowledge and become aware of the use of mobile phones for knowledge transfer.

To confirm that these categories (Consensus, Evidence, and others) indeed cluster around one another, we look at the proximity plots of Consensus, Informational-Practical Orientation, and Informational-Relational Code Categories vs. the rest of the code categories. These are shown in Fig. 5 (IM conversations) and Fig. 6 (TXT conversations). We note that in both

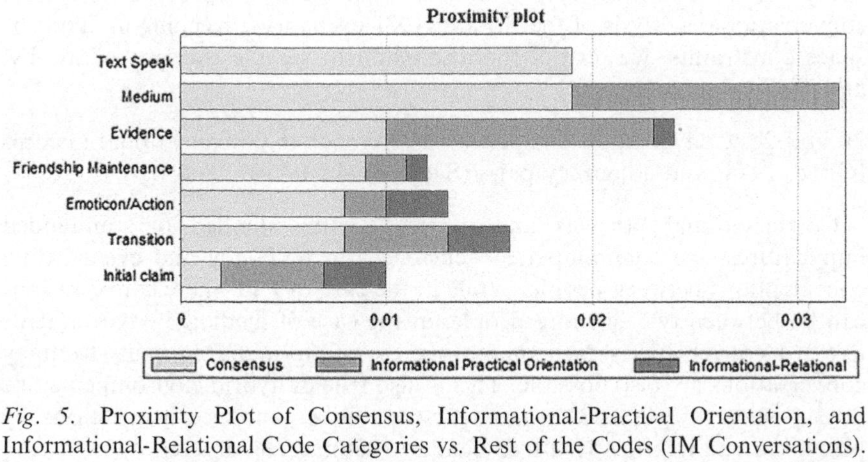

Fig. 5. Proximity Plot of Consensus, Informational-Practical Orientation, and Informational-Relational Code Categories vs. Rest of the Codes (IM Conversations).

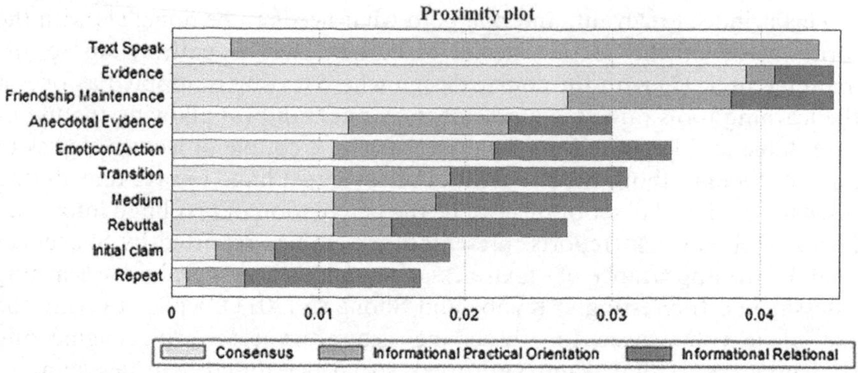

Fig. 6. Proximity Plot of Consensus, Informational-Practical Orientation, and Informational-Relational Code Categories vs. Rest of the Codes (Text Message Conversations).

cases (IM and TXT) the Evidence, Anecdotal Evidence, Friendship Maintenance, and Emoticon/Action categories all have close proximity to the Consensus, Informational-Practical Orientation, and Informational-Relational code categories. This proximity is indicative of both IM and TXT conversations mimicking FTF conversations where discussions and deliberations following general rules of argumentation (claim, evidence, rebuttal, warrant, etc.) often leads to consensus and a shared understanding.

Having thus detected the proximity of evidence-based argumentation to consensus in IM and TXT conversations, we now proceed to actual conversational analysis of the IM and TXT exchanges. Keeping in mind the space constraints, we restrict the discussion to sample excerpts of the IM and TXT conversations.

2b and 2c: Conversation analysis with reference to conversational maxims (Grice, 1975) and adjacency pairs (Sacks et al., 1974)

Conversational "thrusts and parries," with intended or unintended implicatures, are commonplace occurrences in FTF, IM and even texting conversations between people. While in the case of FTF these conversations can be between two or more people, in the case of mediated environments like IM conversations such one-to-one or one-to-many or many-to-many conversations are also possible. This is also true of hybrid environments like Skype where video, audio, and text capabilities enhance interactions by providing cue richness (Daft & Lengel, 1986), videoconferences, and to a certain extent telephone calls. However, text messaging appears to work best in one-to-one situations. Looking at the content of these IM and text exchanges according to the modified Thurlow's scheme (as seen in the previous discussion), there actually appears to have been some discussion, many-to-many conversations (even in the texting exchanges), a fair amount of consensus and agreement on the points discussed.

We present below some IM and text exchanges from day 1 of round 2 because on day 1 the group members are only getting to know one another and there usually is a sense of formality, professionalism, and politeness during initial interactions, with minimal disagreement. Usually by day 4, there is much camaraderie and possible friendships that occur in such group activities and the sense that if they do disagree, it is not a personal affront. Rather, a level of comfort has been established that allows for collaborative work despite disagreement. Our analysis of the last day of each round indicated higher levels of agreement, and much informality among group members and most had gotten used to or worked out any issues with the technologies. However, the pattern of argumentation and conversation was not very different to those on day 1 of each round. Also, space restrictions prevent us from presenting more information.

Day 1 IM Round 2 – Partial Conversation Segment (*sic*)

R2IMP04 says, "hey" _
R2IMP04 says, "which question are we on" _
R2IMP01 says, "yeah, I like the idea that you don't necessarily have to be spending time doing something that betters you. Sometimes I just wanna lay and do nothing"
R2IMP03 says, "first one"
R2IMP01 says, "but I suppose that relaxes and destresses me so that is bettering in a way ... "
R2IMP04 says, "lesiure is something you are not paid to do"
R2IMP04 says, "but that did not include obligations"
R2IMP04 says, "the second one was leasire and not obligations"
R2IMP01 says, "the issue I have with that is that maybe in your leisure time you write novels and get paid to do so, something like that?"
R2IMP04 says, "but that did not encompass tihngs like sleeping"
R2IMP02 says, "yeah that's true"
R2IMP02 says, "and like the sports players he suggested"
R2IMP03 says, "well if you are writting then it could be classified as 'paid work' as educaiton can be"
R2IMP02 says, "they may find leisure in playing the sport however are paid to do so"
R2IMP04 says, "what would you say this research project would be to you"
R2IMP01 says, "but if you have anoter job and writing is something you do in your spare time, an activity that betters you does that mean it's no longer leisure?"
R2IMP04 says, "could that be classifed as a hobby"

R2IMP01 says, "hahaha this research project is not leisure time"
R2IMP04 says, "beer is a great pass time"
R2IMP01 says, "agreed"
R2IMP04 says, "IM is tough to read" _
R2IMP02 says, "I need size 20" __

We extract from above the following excerpts:

R2IMP04 says, "which question are we on" _QUERY
R2IMP01 says, "yeah, I like the idea that you do'nt necessarily have to be spending time doing something that betters you. Sometimes I just wanna lay and do nothing" – POINT/CLAIM/OPINION
R2IMP03 says, "first one" ANSWER TO QUERY
R2IMP01 says, "but I suppose that relaxes and destresses me so that is bettering in a way…" POINT/CLAIM/OPINION Continued
R2IMP04 says, "lesiure is something you are not paid to do" – COUNTERPOINT
R2IMP04 says, "but that did not include obligations" FOLLOWED BY ELABORATION/QUALIFICATION
R2IMP01 says, "the issue I have with that is that maybe in your leisure time you write novels and get paid to do so, something like that?" DIFFERING OPINION

From this IM conversation excerpt we see two conversations, a short one between participants R2IMP04 and R2IMP03 (a query followed by a response to that query) and a longer one between participants R2IMP01 and R2IMP04. In the short conversation, we see no violations of any of the Gricean maxims and the overt answer satisfies participant R2IMP04, who then proceeds to view participant R2IMP01's response to a discussion topic. Here begins the second mini-conversation between participants R2IMP01 and R2IMP04. Participant R2IMP01 professes an opinion on the topic to which participant R2IMP04 responds with a counterpoint that is supported by an elaboration or a qualification. Participant R2IMP01 now replies with an opinion that differs from participant R2IMP04 and the conversation continues till they appear to have reached consensus and proceed with discussing other things. While there appear to be no violations, this could be considered partial flouting of the maxim of relation (as to the direct relevance of the point or counterpoint to the main discussion topic). But, such is the nature of conversations everywhere and this bit of analysis indicates that conversational implicatures exist in mediated discourses like IM conversations.

The IM conversations on other days follow similar patterns of development of argument/debate, where a claim is first proposed (an opinion with relevance to the context and background), supported by evidence, which is soon followed by a counter claim or a qualifier and the participant making the counter claim provides relevant evidence and rebuttals to the initial claim and the process continues iteratively till some consensus is reached (as seen in earlier figures where Evidence clusters with Consensus). Also, the fairly adjacent positioning of these conversational dyads/triads points to the turn taking nature of such conversations, indicating the presence of adjacency pairs (Sacks et al., 1974), a further indication of IM conversations mimicking FTF conversations in nature and outcome.

A network sociogram (Fig. 7) of round 2 IM conversations for all days reveals that as a code category network node, Consensus is aligned fairly closely with many of the other code categories, specifically, Evidence, Informational-Relational, Friendship Maintenance, Text Speak, and Emoticon/Actions (an indication of the usefulness of emotional cues – happy, clapping, etc. that this medium offers adding to the richness of the interactions – Daft & Lengel, 1986).

2b and 2c: Day 1 Round 2 TXT – Partial Conversation Segment (*sic*)

We look at exchanges on the same topic between the participants in the texting group.

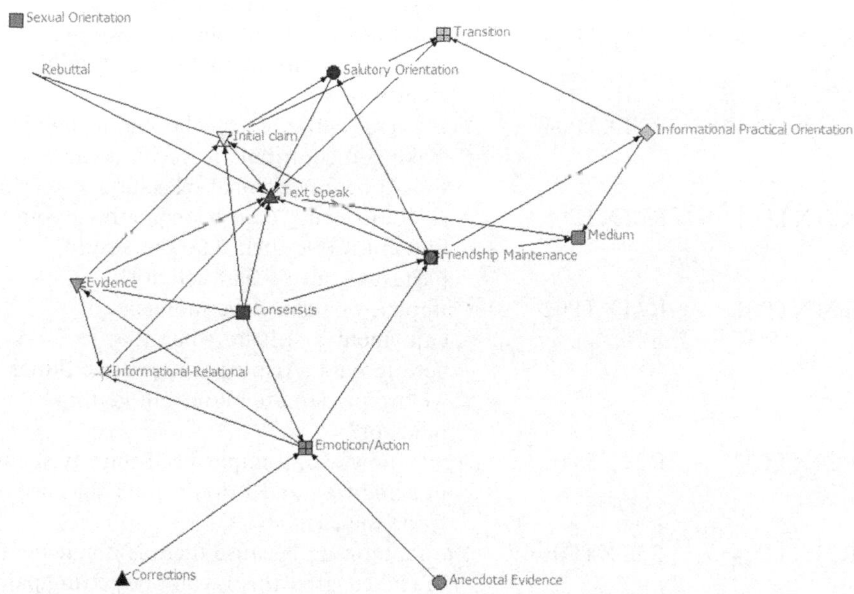

Fig. 7. Code Category Network Sociogram – IM Conversations.

Sender	Receiver	Message [sic]
R2TXTP04	R2TXTP05	What do you think is a pro to experience leisure
R2TXTP01	R2TXTP04	I think it has to have a component of pleasurenn
R2TXTP04	R2TXTP06	What do you think is a con to time-based leisure?
R2TXTP04	R2TXTP02	Yea it kindof incorperates all the other defs as well
R2TXTP04	R2TXTP06	Its too limited and dichotomous
R2TXTP04	R2TXTP05	I'm not sure what a pro would be but maybe a con is that it put a lot of pressure on having a life changing experience every time you have free time…?
R2TXTP04	R2TXTP01	What are cons of defining leisure as an activity for which you are not paid? Is it a limiting def?
R2TXTP05	R2TXTP02	The only issue I have with it is that it seems pretty goal oriented … What do you hope to gain "is on that first slid"
R2TXTP06	R2TXTP02	I would agree. I think the first two are necessary components but not totally inclusive
R2TXTP04	R2TXTP06	Yea I agree with the girl who said it shoudlnt make you contribute to socity because it should be for personal relaxation
R2TXTP01	R2TXTP05	And does getting paid for something you find enjoyable then take the leisure/pleaasure out of that activity?
R2TXTP01	R2TXTP02	I suppose one can have moments of enjoyment or leisure when they're getting paid. Also does it exclude things we are passionate about but getting paid for?
R2TXTP02	R2TXTP01	Agree; however, it implied self-improvement in some way and I don't think that needs to be the case
R2TXTP04	R2TXTP01	Yes its limiting because there is no element of choice, after this I won't be getting paid but I won't be in leisure time

R2TXTP01	R2TXTP06	I believe so. Like his pro sports ex things you are paid for can feel like leisure
R2TXTP05	R2TXTP02	Yeah even self-actualization is goal oriented
R2TXTP02	R2TXTP01	Definetly not. Seems to be in all of these definitions and I think it veers away from the point
R2TXTP05	R2TXTP01	I think you must think about time when you think about leisure because you can't carry out an activity if you don't have free time
R2TXTP04	R2TXTP05	Yea that's true I was thinking leisure time should allow you relaxation not pressure to become a better person

Straightaway, you can notice that these conversations do not follow a specific structure. However, participants' conversations are definitely following the principles of argument (claims, opinions, evidence, counter-claims, qualifiers, and rebuttals) much like one would do so in normal unmediated conversations. There are even clear disagreements and eventually agreement and consensus. It appears that the Gricean maxims are rarely violated. Arguably, one exception to that and that is presented in the following conversation excerpt between participants R2TXTP01 and R2TXTP02 of the texting group.

	Sender	Receiver	Message
POINT/OPINION	R2TXTP01	R2TXTP02	I suppose one can have moments of enjoyment or leisure when they're getting paid. Also does it exclude things we are passionate about but getting paid for?
RESPONSE WITH QUALIFIER	R2TXTP02	R2TXTP01	Agree; however, it implied self improvement in some way and I don't think that needs to be the case
COUNTERPOINT – DIFFERING OPINION	R2TXTP01	R2TXTP02	Definetly not. Seems to be in all of these definitions and I think it veers away from the point

The first opinion is received by participant R2TXTP02, to which she/he responds by agreeing partly, but also professes another counterpoint, and then adds a further qualifier to stress his counterpoint. While participant R2TXTP01 is adhering to the maxim of relation (being relevant to the discussion topic), she/he is emphatically indicating that either the definition or part of the opinion professed by participant R2TXTP02 appears to not be relevant "and veers away from the point." We are thus able to detect the presence of conversational implicature in texting exchanges by way of the presence of conversational maxims and even occasional violations of these maxims. There are other such occurrences in the text exchanges across all days and in all the rounds.

According to Clifton and Ferreira, (1989), "Conversational implicatures are not tied to linguistic form. To make a conversational implicature, a listener must have already parsed the sentence, assigned it its literal interpretation, realised that additional inferences must be added to make it conform to the Gricean maxim, and determined what these inferences are. Such activity could not reasonably affect the initial steps of parsing." Investigation of the text exchanges appears to lead us to the conclusion that if conversational implicatures are not tied to linguistic form, can they then also be independent of the medium and any affordances (or lack of) in the medium, such as in the case of texting – the small form factor, the inefficient keyboard, etc.? The form factor is specifically the geometry of a product and in the case of a mobile phone it is the fundamental design of the phone, its screen, the keys, and the ability of users to access the various functions of the device and determines the usability of the product. And if the phone's form factor were modified accordingly, can this device then be appropriate for use as a supplementary learning tool in classrooms? To complete the cycle, we look at the network sociogram of the code categories in the text exchanges (Fig. 8).

From Fig. 8. we see that the Consensus code category is more closely connected to the Evidence, Emoticon/Action, Text Speak, Initial Claim, and Friendship Maintenance code categories, as opposed to the other categories. This appears to provide additional support to the participants' own admission that the texting forces them to stay on task (also evident in the analysis of focus group responses below). While turn taking appears to be an issue when there are more than two participants, they appear to overcome this by putting all of their thoughts in one message and then waiting for responses. Considering that texting is an asynchronous medium, this should be expected. Since people are constantly texting and messages keep popping up constantly, there is an illusion that this is a synchronous exchange like IM or FTF. So part of the frustration for the texters is that the expectation of an instant response is not met.

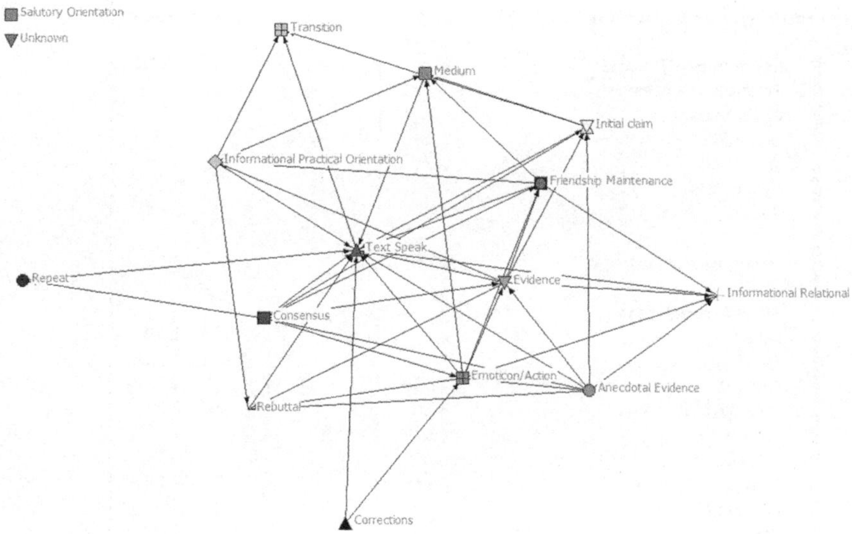

Fig. 8. Code Category Network Sociogram – Text Conversations.

Based on the results of the content analysis and the code category frequency distribution presented in Tables 3 and 4, we now present the modified thematic-functional referential code model for analyzing IM and texting conversations with the percentages for each code category. This model is shown in Fig. 9.

While not identical to Thurlow's model (Fig. 1), our updated model is not very different either. The distribution of codes across the spectrum is about the same and appears equivalently proportional. These percentages are obtained from Tables 3 and 4. In both models, the original and the updated one, Informational-Practical, Informational-Relational, Evidence, Consensus, Rebuttal and Friendship Maintenance have a proportionally similar share (percentage) of the overall messages, indicating alignment of the two models. The data from further research will help us standardize this modified thematic referential model.

Revisiting the Research Questions

Now that we have had a chance to look at the IM and TXT exchanges of participants in this study, we can revisit the results with the research questions in mind. Research Question 1 *(RQ1) asked if participants found*

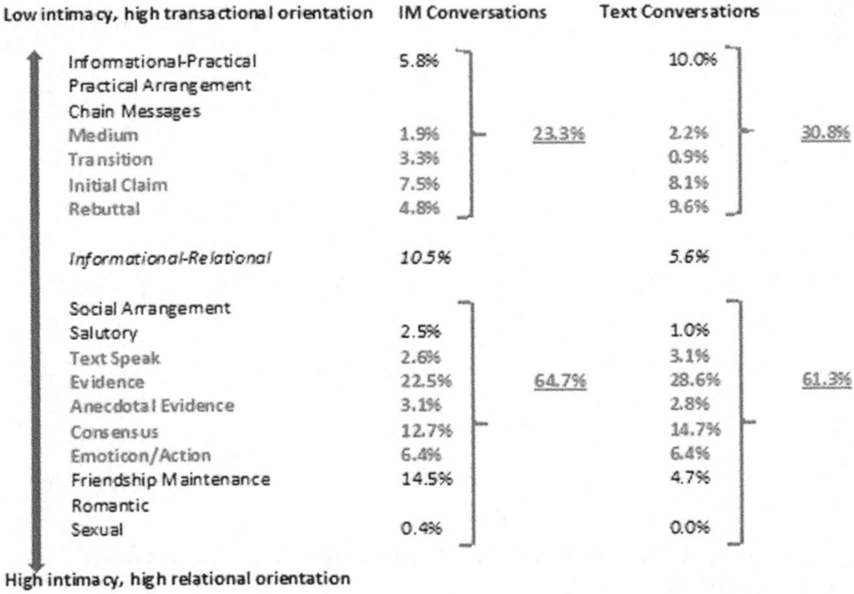

Fig. 9. Modified Referential Thematic-Functional Categories Model with Percentages.

the technology (IM or texting) useful in discussing the subject matter and whether the technology improved their ability to understand the subject material as compared to the FTF group. To address this, we asked participants about their overall experience in the study, whether they learnt anything, and whether the group discussions were productive. We also asked them if they preferred any particular medium over another.

Most of the FTF group members were happy with their groups, said that they learnt new concepts and new knowledge and preferred FTF over other mediated environments. One participant in the IM group said, "the conversation moved so fast that by the time I responded, my response was no longer relevant and so I would delete it." Another participant from the texting group remarked: "Texting not the best for facilitating discussion; disconnected from the people around you; do discussion; required a lot of effort to debate [using texting]."

While another participant, also from the texting group, said, "texting not useful, tough to track 4 conversations at one time; conversations were always one-on-one, no flow"; "tiny keys/sent many incomplete messages." Another texter had a more positive experience and he said, "I am an expert user so everyone else seemed too slow – would have liked FTF, Barriers like language can be overcome with IM; learned a lot."

Most, if not all, of the participants felt that the group discussions did go well and while there were technological issues (especially with the texting group), in general, they were able to "keep focused on topic" (especially the IM and TXT groups), "got solid points out" and IM and texting kept things structured and they had to respond and "move on quickly." However, all of the participants did feel that they were able to create a shared understanding (despite the difficulties with the texting and the speed of the IM conversations) of the topics discussed.

Also, most of the participants were unanimous in their preference for FTF as the primary discussion medium, but given a choice, they would opt for IM as it was synchronous and the group chat feature allowed everyone to see all the responses and allowed the participants to frame and phrase their own responses accordingly. While the texters advocated IM or FTF, one of the texters mentioned the following, "I loved it but I am a Blackberry guy, I used to have a Blackberry with bigger buttons." Many said that they would choose an iPhone over the Blackberry as the iPhone was easier to use. The consensus was that while it was a great idea to use texting as a discussion tool, it would probably be more effective if it were used in short bursts, "text students before class to stimulate them to think about concepts, and use texting as a supplementary tool for learning, not as a primary discussion tool."

Other comments relating to the usefulness and issues related to the IM and texting technologies are given below and indicate a general preference for FTF over IM and texting, and given a choice, a preference for IM over texting.

"productive/quick discussion/team";
"Good experience, but texting was hard for learning";
"Did find IM helpful, would prefer FTF";
"FTF more efficient/easier to disseminate ideas";
"Found the messages would be more effective with BBM" – Blackberry Messenger;
"IM provides anonymity"; share ideas quicker and faster, but "ideas weren't followed to the end of an idea";

We infer that while learning probably occurred during the deliberation process (regardless of the medium as can be seen from the content analysis of the IM and TXT conversations), participants did not particularly like texting using the phones. The apparent frustration of the participants in the texting group is related more to the affordances of the Blackberry device. The standard QWERTY keyboard on the device is rather small (leading to

"Blackberry Thumb"), and the frequent appearance (and expectation of appearance) of text messages gives participants an illusion of synchronous communication in a medium that is essentially asynchronous. Once participants realized the asynchronous nature of the texting medium, they were able to better craft their queries and responses and as a result eventually "got used" to the affordances of the device. Thus, despite their frustration, they were able to deliberate using the texting medium and arrive at some shared understanding of the subject matter being discussed.

Research question 2 *(RQ2) asked if participants learned new and conceptual knowledge during the process of deliberation using the medium (FTF, IM, texting) of communication. (Sundararajan, 2009)*

To answer RQ2 we refer again to some of the focus group responses where participants felt that the discussions were productive. Many of their responses indicate that they learned a lot and gained new and conceptual knowledge.

> "message styles useful, Learned a lot about method and technique" – (SUBJECT MATTER CONCEPT and NEW KNOWLEDGE);
> "helpful online, looked across at others responses" – (SHARED MEANING);
> "interesting to see open-ended teaching style and case method" – (CONCEPT);
> "I still got to know people in my group" – (FRIENDSHIP MAINTENANCE);
> "IM was useful but the problem was waiting to get responses to your comment – lag time, Good for people that are sick or far away" – (SUGGESTION);
> "Anonymous: some people won't ask questions (nervous or shy) good way for people to get their questions out there that they wouldn't have otherwise" – (SUGGESTION);

While these are just a few of the responses, most reflect similar sentiments, ideas, and opinions. We again see that while participants had some issues with the technology, they did have a good learning experience, got to know people in their groups (collaborative and friendship aspects of social learning according to the constructivist paradigm), and many even suggested that IM and texting would be good for those who were nervous, shy, poor communicators, or were unwell and were learning from a distance.

Performance on Subject Matter Pre- and Post-Tests

Finally to answer RQ3 (Did participants' post-test results match their perception of having learnt new and conceptual knowledge? (Sundararajan, 2009)I, we analyzed participants' performance on the subject matter pre- and post-tests. We conducted a benchmark subject matter pre-test prior to the start of the lectures. The pre and post subject matter content

Table 5. Group-Wise Means Comparison of Content Pre- and Post-Test Scores.

Round	Group	Stats	Pre-Test	Post-Test	Difference
Round 1 – Tourism and Leisure	FTF; $N=4$	mean	7.75	14.75	7.00
		stdev	1.50	3.86	2.36
$N = 13$	IM; $N=4$	mean	9.50	14.75	5.25
		stdev	3.79	2.50	−1.29
	TXT; $N=5$	mean	10.80	16.20	5.40
		stdev	3.03	2.17	−0.87
Round 2 – Tourism & Leisure	FTF; $N=5$	mean	13.80	18.00	4.20
$N = 17$		stdev	4.44	4.42	−0.02
	IM; $N=6$	mean	12.33	19.00	6.67
		stdev	3.44	2.68	−0.76
	TXT; $N=6$	mean	12.17	16.50	4.33
		stdev	4.36	4.46	0.11
Round 3 – Corporate Communication	FTF; $N=4$	mean	24.00	27.25	3.25
		stdev	2.16	0.96	−1.20
$N = 12$	IM; $N=4$	mean	16.00	20.25	4.25
		stdev	2.83	2.63	−0.20
	TXT; $N=4$	mean	20.50	21.75	1.25
		stdev	1.91	2.50	0.59
Round 4 – Corporate Communication	FTF; $N=5$	mean	18.20	25.80	7.60
		stdev	1.92	2.05	0.13
$N = 16$	IM; $N=5$	mean	18.40	24.80	6.40
		stdev	3.21	3.35	0.14
	TXT; $N=6$	mean	18.67	22.33	3.67
		stdev	4.46	4.46	0.00

tests both had 34 questions, 32 of which were multiple-choice, while the last two were open-ended. We present in Table 5 the group wise means comparison of content pre- and post-test scores for all four rounds. As we can see from Table 5, there appears to have been dramatic improvement in the scores for most participants, except in the cases of participants in round 3 where the improvements are not as dramatic, from the pre-test to the post-test. The low scores on the pre-tests are indicative of the relative unfamiliarity with the subject matter and this is understandable.

While the means are different, we see that the standard deviations are roughly the same, indicating a somewhat uniform increase in the level of knowledge (or at least recognizing the relevant answers to test questions to be able to perform better). Whether this constitutes knowledge is debatable. The improvements in scores are likely due to some or all of the following factors: the ability of the instructors to clearly present the information, the ability of the participants to focus during the lecture period (motivated by money for the most part) and maybe in part due to any discussions they had during the 5-day study period. There is no information available (nor was any collected) to indicate whether they met offline or socially to discuss the subject matter. However, despite this being an experimental setup and participants were compensated monetarily and they faced some issues with the technology, we conclude that knowledge was imparted, knowledge was gained, collaboration did occur, and at several points the discussions did lead to consensus. Much of this is supported from participants' admission of having learned a lot from these lectures and that the discussions were useful (focus group debriefing).

DISCUSSION AND CONCLUSION

An overview of this rich data generates a few immediate inferences. FTF, offering the highest media cue richness (Daft & Lengel, 1986), is often the most preferred form of communication for discussions of any sort. IM communication, a synchronous mediated form of communication, is a more mature technology; it has been around for more than a decade and people are comfortable using this form of communication for a multitude of purposes including socializing, setting up appointments, and having detailed discussions on various topics. This is evidenced by several studies in the computer-mediated communication (CMC, computer-supported collaborative learning (CSCL), and computer-supported cooperative work (CSCW) literature. The use of emoticons (also present in texting devices) has allowed IM conversations to be more acceptable for these purposes. On the other hand, texting is an asynchronous medium that has been around probably for a decade now and is mainly seen as a socializing technology and for keeping in touch with friends and family (and by business people with clients and co-workers). The possible use of texting as a learning technology, as currently explored in this study, is not embraced and can be viewed with legitimate caution (by users) as often happens with new technologies or new uses for existing technologies.

According to the participants' responses, it is evident that they did not like using texting for discussion purposes mainly because there was no flow in the text conversations, typing in the tiny keyboards was difficult, there was no structure, and they could not see all of the responses. While the form factor of the device was one issue (the miniature QWERTY keyboard and unfamiliarity with the Blackberry device), the fact that they could only send texts to the group, but not reply to all the group members at the same time, made the flow appear to be disorganized and erratic. This appears to have caused a lot of frustration. Interestingly, several participants suggested the use of Blackberry Messenger (BBM). We considered this as it could provide the option to send and reply to the group. However, we decided not to use BBM as it only mimicked IM conversations on the cell phone. Furthermore, BBM is a proprietary technology not available on other phones. Finally, since we already had an IM group, using BBM would not have served the purpose of testing the efficacy of texting, even with all its attendant difficulties.

Participants also preferred to send small texts to friends and family, but trying to type large chunks of text (discussion points) appeared to be an onerous task and led to frustration. Almost all of the participants felt that the classroom atmosphere was realistic and that using such technologies was not a bad idea as long as relative improvements were made and appropriate incentives were given for participation and performance. While a few would have preferred to use their own cell phones (familiarity), they would not like to have work interfere in their personal space (which is their phone), similar to the findings of Brett (2011). This is an interesting paradox. One thing that did come out in these focus group discussions is that while the FTF group members do complete tasks, they tend to go off on tangents. However, IM or texting appears to keep the students focused on the task at hand. With IM the presence of some structure and flow appears to ease any frustration associated with the speed of the "conversation flow," and being a relatively more mature technology (with respect to social and business uses), there might be more acceptance of IM as a supplementary technology in classrooms (not only distance classrooms but also the FTF ones).

In the case of texting, while an apparent lack of structure and flow was causing frustration, it still kept them focused on the task at hand. This is interesting and if used intermittently in the classroom, texting could get the students to focus on specific tasks and probably even draw out the lurkers and the shirkers to interact and participate (Sundararajan, 2010) in class discussions or activities. Going forward, we only expect increased presence of cell phone and tablet use in classrooms and we believe, if form factor is improved and texting was used appropriately in short bursts, this might actually prove to be a useful tool.

Despite technological difficulties, participants apparently did converge on ideas, and appeared to arrive at consensus indicating a shared understanding of concepts. Participants did establish working relationships, collaborated, earned, and gave respect to their group members, generally felt good about their experience, felt that they had gained conceptual and new knowledge, and felt that the environment was similar enough to a real classroom learning situation. Also, since only 11 of the 58 participants reported that English was not their native language, all of the participants indicated that using IM or texting in the classroom would help them overcome their natural shyness and also any language barriers. It also appears that the participants apparently did a better job with texting and IM than they themselves perceived and the analysis of multiple datasets have helped guide our interpretations and overcome some of the issues with perceptions and self-reporting. Being an experimental design, it can be fraught with validity issues, social desirability bias, self-efficacy issues, and the Hawthorne effect. While we did not specifically test or control for any of these, these biases and issues of this nature were not evident.

In our effort to seek better ways to engage with students in the classrooms, especially where subject matter can be varied, at times interesting and at times tedious, we felt that reaching out to the students through the technological devices of their choice would be a good way to get them interested, engaged, involved, and increase their participation and interaction in the classroom. The findings from this study lend support to the possible inclusion of texting as a supplementary communication tool to disseminate and create knowledge across diverse populations. With an increase in enrollment of international students in North American schools, many of whom struggle with the language or the cultural changes they experience in North American classrooms, having a medium that will draw them into classroom discussions will only boost their confidence and motivate them to interact and participate more. Texting can also be seen as an inclusive technology for people with speech and hearing impairments and we expect to collect data from this population in phase 2 of the study. We additionally hope to standardize the modified "referential thematic-functional" categories to augment Thurlow's (2003) list and also advocate such a mixed methods approach for similar studies. While the scope of this study allows for several research questions, in this chapter we restricted ourselves to the three research questions presented above. We have also collected pre- and post-study survey data on technology use, knowledge gained, experience with the study, collaborative behavior, and learning outcomes, and analyses of these surveys indicate support to many of the findings presented here. The results from these analyses have helped answer other research questions and we will be reporting these other results elsewhere.

ACKNOWLEDGMENTS

We wish to thank the Social Sciences and Humanities Research Council of Canada, Insights Development Grant for funding this 2-year research project. This funding has made it possible for us to recruit really talented, able, and willing Research Assistants and pay honoraria to study participants. We wish to thank Brett McDonald, the undergraduate Research Assistant, who has not only shown great initiative in offering his time, talents, and efforts to set up the Blackberry phones, research, identify, and procure the software that extracts the text data from the phones and also coded the surveys along with Sarah, but both he and Sarah have shown an amazing attitude toward, and a natural aptitude for, research and learning. We also wish to thank the Faculty of Management at Dalhousie University for making available to us a state-of-the-art Usability and Behavioral Lab/Classroom, which has made this study possible.

REFERENCES

Brett, P. (2011). Students' experiences and engagement with SMS for learning in higher education. *Innovations in Education and Teaching International*, *48*(2), 137–147. doi: 10.1080/14703297.2011.56400.

Carpenter, C. N., Froese, A., & Barnes, R. B. (2010). College students' texting habits and expectations of effects on learning. In *Southwestern Psychological Association, 56th Convention*, Seguin, Texas Lutheran University, April 8–10, 2010.

Cheung, S. L. (2004). Fun and games with mobile phones: SMS messaging in microeconomics experiments. In R. Atkinson, C. McBeath, D. Jonas-Dwyer, & R. Phillips (Eds), *Beyond the comfort zone: Proceedings of the 21st ASCILITE conference* (pp. 180–183). Perth, December 5–8, 2004. Retrieved from http://www.ascilite.org.au/conferences/perth04/procs/cheung.html

Daft, R. L., & Lengel, R. H. (1986). Organizational information requirements, media richness and structural design. *Management Science*, *32*(5), 554–571.

Goosebumps Twitter Story. http://www.geekosystem.com/r-l-stine-goosebumps-twitter-story/

Grice, H. P. (1975). Logic and conversation. In P. Cole & J. L. Morgan (Eds.), *Speech acts* (pp. 41–58). New York, NY: Academic Press.

Grice's Conversational Maxims. http://www.cog.brown.edu/courses/cg45/.../Gricean%20Maxims.pdf

Grinter, R., & Eldridge, M. (2003). *Wan2tlk?: Everyday text messaging*. Paper presented at the Conference on Human Factors in Computing Systems archive. Ft. Lauderdale, FL, USA, pp. 441–448.

Jones, G. M., & Schieffelin, B. B. (2009). Talking text and talking back: "My BFF Jill" from boob tube to YouTube. *Journal of Computer Mediated Communication*, *14*(4), 1050–1079. doi: 10.1111/j.1083-6101.2009.01481.x

Kennedy, C., & Levy, M. (2008). L'italiano al telefonino: Using SMS to support beginners' language learning. *ReCALL*, *20*, 315–330.

Krippendorff, K. (2004). Standards for data reliability. In K. Krippendorff (Ed.), *Content analysis: An introduction to its methodology* (pp. 241–243). Beverly Hills, CA: Sage.

Kyobe, M., & Shongwe, M. (2011). Investigating the extent to which mobile phones reduce knowledge transfer barriers in student project teams. *SA Journal Of Information Management*, 13. doi: 10.4102/sajim.v13i1.424.

Markett, C., Sanchez, I. A., Weber, S., & Tangney, B. (2006). Using short message service to encourage interactivity in the classroom. *Computers & Education*, *46*(3), 280–293.

MSNBC. (2008). *OMG! Buddhist nun is texting a mobile novel: At the age of 86, Jakucho Setouchi has tapped into a publishing revolution.* Retrieved from http://www.msnbc.msn.com/id/26901218/

Papert, S. (1980). *Mindstorms: Children, computers and powerful ideas.* New York, NY: Basic Books.

Rheingold, H. (2002). *Smart mobs: The next social revolution.* Cambridge, MA: Perseus.

Sacks, H., Schegloff, E. A., & Jefferson, G. (1974). A simplest systematics for the organization of turn-taking for conversation. *Language*, *50*, 696–735.

Sheneman, K. (2008). Teaching through text message: Cell phones emerge as a learning tool. *The Rebel Yell.* Las Vegas, University of Nevada. Retrieved from http://www.unlvrebelyell.com/article.php?ID = 10765

Sundararajan, B. (2009). Impact of communication patterns, network positions and social dynamics factors on learning among students in a CSCL environment. *Electronic Journal of eLearning*, *7*(1), 71–84.

Sundararajan, B. (2010). Emergence of the most knowledgeable other (MKO): Social network analysis of chat and bulletin board Conversations in a CSCL system. *Electronic Journal of e-Learning*, *8*(2), 191–208.

Sundararajan, B., & Hübscher-Younger, T. (2006). *Social factors and collaborative learning communities.* Paper presented at the Conference on College Composition and Communication, March 22–25, 2006, Chicago, IL, USA.

Thurlow, C. (2003). Generation Txt? The sociolinguistics of young people's text-messaging. *Discourse Analysis Online*, *1*(1), 1–27.

Thurlow, C. (2005). Deconstructing adolescent communication. In A. Williams & C. Thurlow (Eds.), *Talking adolescence: Perspectives on communication in the teenage years* (pp. 1–20). New York, NY: Peter Lang.

Toulmin, S. (1969). *The uses of argument.* Cambridge, UK: Cambridge University Press.

Vygotsky, L. (1978). *Mind in society.* Cambridge, MA: Harvard University Press.

CATALYZING LEARNER ENGAGEMENT USING CUTTING-EDGE CLASSROOM RESPONSE SYSTEMS IN HIGHER EDUCATION

Julie Schell, Brian Lukoff and Eric Mazur

ABSTRACT

In this chapter, we introduce a new technology for facilitating and measuring learner engagement. The system creates a learning experience for students based on frequent feedback, which is critical to learning. We open by problematizing traditional approaches to learner engagement that do not maximize the potential of feedback and offer a research-based solution in a new classroom response system (CRS) two of the authors developed at Harvard University – Learning Catalytics. The chapter includes an overview of cognitive science principles linked to student learning and how those principles are tied to Learning Catalytics. We then provide an overview of the limitations of existing CRSs and describe how Learning Catalytics addresses those limitations. Finally, we describe how we used Learning Catalytics to facilitate and measure learner engagement

Increasing Student Engagement and Retention using Classroom Technologies: Classroom Response Systems and Mediated Discourse Technologies
Cutting-edge Technologies in Higher Education, Volume 6E, 233–261

ISSN: 2044-9968/doi:10.1108/S2044-9968(2013)000006E011

in novel ways, through a pilot implementation in an undergraduate physics classroom at Harvard University. This pilot was guided by two questions: How can we use Learning Catalytics to help students engage with subject matter in ways that will help them learn? And how can we measure student engagement in new ways using the analytics built into the system? The objective of this chapter is to introduce Learning Catalytics as a new instructional tool and respond to these questions.

INTRODUCTION

"Any questions? *Anybody*?"

Throughout the globe, in every institutional type and across the disciplines, instructors use this line of interrogation as a universal attempt at eliciting learner engagement. The phrase represents a well-meaning attempt by faculty to address the shortcomings of the lecture method, which has dominated higher education for more than 500 years. Indeed, lecture remains the pedagogy of choice among faculty despite consensus that interactive approaches are more effective at maximizing student learning (see Hake, 1998).

Most of the time, faculty pleas for student engagement echo unanswered throughout lecture halls. Other times, only the bravest, most confident students respond. The danger in either situation is the potential for faculty to misinterpret lack of student responses to the ubiquitous "any questions" query as understanding or learning. Armed with this false sense of teaching effectiveness, faculty may journey on, continuing to deliver material unaware of the depth of student misunderstanding left in their lectures' wake. Worse, students usually receive little to no feedback on their misunderstandings before their first exam or assessment, leaving them without the critical insights they need to learn effectively (Ambrose et al., 2010; Bransford, Brown, & Cocking, 2000).

Education does not have to be this way. In the new millennium, instructors have at their disposal a large array of technologically-advanced resources for both facilitating meaningful learner engagement and providing frequent and useful feedback. In this chapter, we examine a new technology that offers the ability to enact and measure learner engagement in novel ways. This system, Learning Catalytics, is a new classroom response system (CRS).

According to Derek Bruff (2009), "classroom response systems are instructional technologies that allow instructors to rapidly collect and analyze student responses to questions posed during class" (p. 1). Clickers, or small, handheld devices that students use to submit responses to multiple-choice questions, are examples of the most popular implementation of CRSs in education. Studies across disciplines have demonstrated that using clickers in the classroom has a number of positive benefits for learner engagement, including student attendance and participation in class (Bruff, 2009). Clickers also provide instructors and students with a low-threshold system for soliciting and delivering frequent feedback on student learning.

Learning Catalytics is a CRS that addresses many of the limitations of clickers. Instead of being restricted to multiple-choice questions, instructors can create and pose a variety of closed- and open-ended questions (e.g., enter free text, sketch a graph, highlight a passage) to students who can then use any web-enabled device (laptop, smartphone, tablet, portable media player, etc.) to respond and review immediate feedback from instructors on their personal device (Fig. 1.). Learning Catalytics can also automatically and intelligently group students for discussions of their responses.

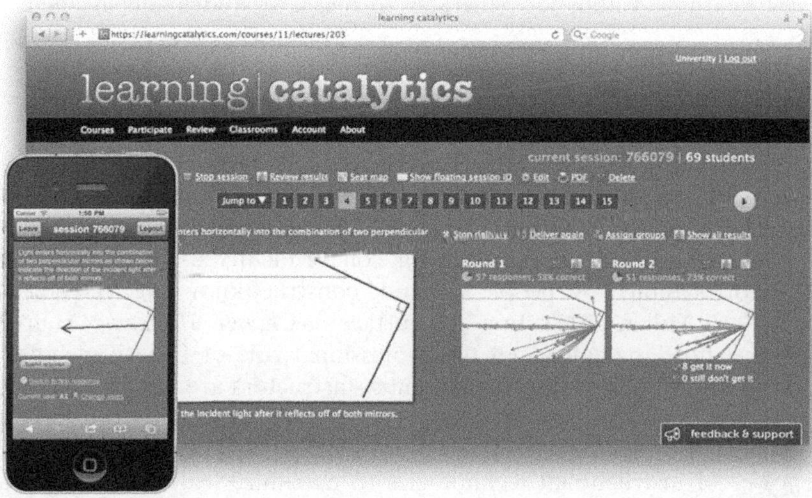

Fig. 1. Learning Catalytics, Both from the Instructor Perspective (Large Window) and Student Perspective (iPhone Display). The Student is Responding to an Open-Ended Graphical Question by Using a Finger on the Screen to Indicate the Direction of a Vector. The Instructor Sees All Student Responses Aggregated into a Single View, and Can See How Student Responses Change from Before ("Round 1") to After ("Round 2") Discussion.

In this chapter, we explore Learning Catalytics and present pilot research we conducted in one course to suggest a model for effective technology-enabled learner engagement in higher education. The pilot collected data from 90 students in an introductory physics course at Harvard University in the spring of 2011. With the exception of the first class, we used Learning Catalytics between three and ten times during every class meeting. All students in the pilot course had access to web-enabled devices, every class period – most students used their own devices, and we purchased a small number of used iPod Touches for students that did not own a device or did not bring it to class.

We begin with a brief review of the literature on effective learning and respond to our first research question by explaining how the system can promote intellectual growth using established principles in the cognitive and learning sciences. We also respond to the second research question by offering three examples of ways faculty can gain insights into learner engagement using Learning Catalytics. After reading this chapter, faculty will be able to understand how Learning Catalytics can be used to 1) get students engaged, 2) provide them useful feedback, and 3) how to use the metrics Learning Catalytics generates to measure student engagement in novel ways.

EFFECTIVE LEARNING

How can we use Learning Catalytics to help students engage with subject matter in ways that will help them learn? For at least a decade, cognitive scientists have argued for the need for college faculty to be familiar with basic theories about how people learn and construct knowledge (Halpern & Hakel, 2003; Miller, 2011). In a 2003 article in *Change Magazine,* Halpern and Hakel note that although the professional role of faculty includes a responsibility to help students learn, most instructors are not familiar with theories that explain how learning works and/or the cognitive strategies that are associated with effective learning. In order for faculty to truly harness the power of instructional technologies to maximize learning and learner engagement, it is essential for them to have familiarity with a few key cognitive science principles.

Piaget's (1985, 1971) explanations of cognitive development persist as a dominant framework for defining learning, despite his and others' acknowledgement of limitations in his theory and method (see Bruner, 1974; Posner, Strike, Hewson, & Gertzog, 1982; Vygotsky, 1998 cited in

Rieber, 1998). Piaget offered a clear definition of learning as represented by *cognitive growth*. We define effective learning as learning that best facilitates and maximizes cognitive growth. Bjork and Bjork (2011) define learning as "the more or less permanent change in knowledge or understanding that is the target of instruction" (p. 57) but emphasize "that it is something we must try to infer" (p. 57).

What promotes effective learning? One of the most enduring Piagetian concepts for explaining the mechanisms of cognitive growth is that it occurs when there is a conflict between prior or existing knowledge and new knowledge, or *disequilibrium*. Bjork and Bjork (2011) further suggest that learning is enhanced when learners are presented with "desirable difficulties," or specific learning tasks that are not too hard but not too easy. Cognitive scientists have identified specific cognitive activities, such as *metacognition* and the related tasks of *self-monitoring* and *self-regulation*, that catalyze disequilibrium and in turn promote cognitive growth (Ambrose et al., 2010; Bransford et al., 2000; Flavell, 1979). When these cognitive activities involve desirable difficulties, they may be particularly beneficial for long-term retention of the knowledge learned (see Bjork & Bjork, 2011).

Metacognition, Self-Monitoring, and Self-Regulation

Educators commonly use the phrase "thinking about one's own thinking" to define the concept of metacognition. Flavell (1979) introduced metacognition as "knowledge and cognition about cognitive phenomena" (p. 906), with knowing and understanding being examples of such phenomena. Individuals with high levels of metacognition monitor their own learning, are able to recognize gaps in their existing knowledge and understanding, and are able to accurately predict their abilities to perform knowledge tasks (self-monitoring) (see Ambrose et al., 2010). Feedback plays an important role in metacognition – students must have cues to alert them to their understandings and misunderstandings (Ambrose et al., 2010; Bransford et al., 2000). In addition metacognitively-adept individuals purposefully direct their learning in ways that will help them maximize their knowledge strengths and fill gaps, a process known as self-regulation (Ambrose et al., 2010; Bransford et al., 2000; Flavell, 1979; Schoenfeld, 1987, 2010).

Extensive research on metacognition indicates that when students engage in instructor-guided metacognitive practices, learning outcomes increase (Ambrose et al., 2010; Bransford et al., 2000; Palinscar & Brown, 1984;

Schoenfeld, 1987, 2010). But despite metacognition's fundamental relationship with effective cognitive growth, learning experts suggest that instruction often neglects to build students' metacognitive capacities (Ambrose et al., 2010).

A growing area of cognitive science research suggests that when students are asked to retrieve information, such as through testing, such action "is a powerful memory modifier" (Bjork, 1975 as cited in Bjork & Bjork, 2011). This research suggests that despite its powerful effects, retrieval-based testing is also underutilized as an instructional tool; typically, teachers use testing solely as a grading, versus a teaching or learning, instrument (Bjork & Bjork, 2011).

The effects of retrieval may be even more powerful when students are asked to "generate" an answer (Bjork & Bjork, 2011), rather than recognize it as correct (as they do when responding to multiple-choice questions) (Duchastel, 1981; Glover, 1989; Kang, McDermott, & Roediger, 2007; McDaniel, Derbish, & Morrisette, 2007). When students are asked questions that require them to retrieve and produce information, rather than simply retrieve and recognize it, they are engaging in *effortful retrieval*, a different and deeper exercise of self-monitoring (Duchastel, 1981). Before they can produce the information a question prompt elicits, they must ask themselves, "do I know this? Or not?" As they "generate" (Bjork & Bjork, 2011) rather than select a choice they believe is right, they may be further cued as to areas of their existing knowledge that are weak or strong. Once they finish their response to the prompt, students' awareness of their ability to answer those questions gives them immediate feedback as to what areas they might target for further practice. In addition, when students respond to questions using CRSs and faculty provide feedback on the right answer, they are further made aware of the strengths and limitations of their understanding. In this way, giving students opportunities to retrieve and produce responses may build their metacognitive skills.

Learning Catalytics and Metacognition

Learning Catalytics, when used with question-based teaching methods, allows instructors to engage students in hundreds of metacognitive activities throughout a course by getting students to generate responses to a mini-test or question and then, following an intense discussion with one or more peers, reevaluate their original response in the context of the discussion and consider whether their own thoughts have changed. The wide array of constructed-response (non-multiple-choice) question types available in Learning Catalytics allows students to engage in the deeper metacognitive tasks associated with effortful retrieval, rather than recognition (although the system can easily deliver multiple-choice questions as well). In addition, the system also provides another way for students to engage in self-monitoring: students can select an option on their devices to report to instructors right away, in class, "I get it now" or "I still don't get it" after a round of voting and discussion. If students "still don't get it" – or if they have a question they simply do not want to raise in front of the whole class – they can also self-direct in class by sending a question to the instructor, without waiting for their instructor's "any questions" query *and* without having to raise their hands or say the question out loud in front of their peers.

Using this new CRS, faculty have multiple lines of evidence to determine whether their students are understanding or not: if they have data suggesting most students responded correctly, and they receive no "I still don't get it" responses and no questions through the system, instructors can proceed with more confidence than is possible by simply soliciting "out loud" questions from the class.

Effective Learning Indicators

Actual cognitive growth occurs within many levels of the human brain, represented by subtle changes in brain structure (Zull, 2006). In particular, cognitive growth is evidenced by developments in the neocortex, the outer layer of the brain responsible for sensory perception (Zull, 2006). Of course, measuring effective learning by measuring changes to students' brain structures poses a challenge for anyone who is not a neuroscientist. So what indicators of effective learning are more realistic to measure in educational settings? In this chapter, we discuss two: conceptual change and knowledge transfer.

Conceptual Change

Philosophers of science have suggested that conceptual change is an important indicator of learning (Posner et al., 1982). Conceptual change occurs when students, often aided by specific instructional strategies (Heron, Shaffer, & McDermott, n.d.), resolve conflicts between their preexisting conceptions and the concepts they are taught, and when these new conceptions are sustained (Posner et al., 1982). When students possess rigid preexisting conceptual frameworks – a particularly pervasive phenomenon in the science disciplines – it is not enough to simply resolve their misunderstanding by offering an alternative framework (Posner et al., 1982), or by telling them the correct answer. Indeed, if simply telling students were enough to evoke conceptual change and cognitive growth more generally, empirical evidence would support the use of lecture as a more effective teaching method than current research suggests (see Hake, 1998; Mazur, 2009).

One research-based strategy for creating conceptual change is the *elicit, confront, and resolve* process developed by the McDermott Group at the University of Washington (Heron et al., n.d.). In this approach

> the first step is to *elicit* a known difficulty by contriving a situation in which students are likely to make an error that exposes that particular difficulty. If the difficulty is sufficiently serious and not addressed, it may remain latent and arise in other contexts. It is therefore the responsibility of the instructor to insist that students *confront* and *resolve* underlying difficulties. (pp. 2, 3)

Although conceptual change is just one of many indicators of effective learning, it is an important one to consider because student conceptions are often powerfully resistant to change (Posner et al., 1982).

Knowledge Transfer

Wiggins and McTighe (2005) discuss another indicator of effective learning: knowledge transfer, or the ability to successfully navigate novel contexts using existing knowledge. For example, a student who uses her prior knowledge to solve new, foreign problems she has never seen before is exhibiting knowledge transfer. The ability to transfer knowledge may also be an indicator of conceptual change: presumably, a student who has experienced a permanent conceptual change would be better able to solve novel problems that require the use of new conceptual frameworks than a student who is still working from an old and "incorrect" framework (Posner et al., 1982). Bransford et al. (2000) cite an extensive research literature that suggests that the metacognitive practices of self-monitoring and self-regulation "have been shown to increase the degree to which students transfer their learning to new settings and events" (p. 12).

Learning Catalytics and Conceptual Change and Knowledge Transfer

Learning Catalytics offers numerous facilities for instructors to promote conceptual change and knowledge transfer. For example, instructors can use the system to construct numerous question types that elicit students' misunderstanding; facilitate student activities, such as intelligently paired student discussion (where students are assigned to discuss their responses in non-arbitrary groups that the instructor believes are most likely to benefit from a discussion with each other) that promote the confrontation of those misconceptions; and provide students with resolution of misconceptions, including explanations and the reasoning underlying correct answers.

In addition, instructors can use this CRS to provide students with opportunities to practice knowledge transfer during every class period, by posing specific questions that require them to apply what they know in new contexts. Finally, Learning Catalytics provides a robust feedback mechanism that immediately and frequently alerts students *and* instructors of student progress.

Feedback

While students can and do learn through passive engagement (Bonwell & Elison, 1991), it is no secret that they learn more when they are actively engaged. Bonwell and Elison (1991) posit that active learning occurs when students are involved in activities beyond passive listening and note taking, including reading, discussing, and writing, and when students receive "immediate feedback" from their instructor. And when it facilitates self-monitoring and self-regulation, feedback promotes student engagement; in other words, feedback helps engage students when it pulls them into activities that allow them to both self-assess their knowledge and consider what they need to do to improve their current learning state (Ambrose et al., 2010; Bransford et al., 2000). According to Ambrose et al. (2010), feedback is most effective when it signals to students the specific knowledge and skills they are expected to learn; is given to students at times and frequencies that are aligned with when they are most likely to need and use it; and provides additional and specific opportunities for students to practice.

Learning Catalytics and Feedback

Learning Catalytics is, at its core, a feedback engine. When instructors use the CRS to pose conceptually-based questions, they signal to students several levels of expectation: the general topic of importance (which also occurs in traditional lecture); the deeper conceptual understanding the instructor expects students to build; and what students should be able to do with that understanding. Second, in traditional educational settings, instructors only periodically check in on students' understanding through formal quizzes and exams. In those settings, students usually do not engage in an "elicit, confront, resolve" process or receive corrective feedback on their responses in a timely manner. Timely, immediate feedback is important in order to convert student misunderstandings into learning (Epstein et al., 2002). Learning Catalytics allows instructors to give students immediate feedback on their performance on conceptual tests and collects performance data in a student dashboard for later review. Students can review such feedback for later directed practice and self-study.

Peer instruction

Learning Catalytics is designed around the approach of Peer Instruction (Mazur, 1997). The next section discusses the Learning Catalytics technology in more detail, but first we present an overview of Peer Instruction and some of the research results that have led thousands of instructors around the world to adopt this pedagogy in their own classrooms. Peer Instruction emphasizes teaching by questioning. Instructors pose questions to students in class; for each question, students commit to an initial answer, and then students are tasked with discussing their responses with a neighbor and trying to convince that neighbor that their response is correct. After the discussion, students are prompted to respond to the question again. Typically, second round (post-discussion) responses are correct at a much higher rate than first round (pre-discussion) responses, suggesting that discussions are a productive way for students to learn (Lasry, Charles, Whittaker, & Lautman, 2009; Smith et al., 2009).

Different types of groups can be effective at promoting learning. If a question has a correct answer (which is not true of all questions, especially outside of STEM disciplines), we consider a group effective when its members answer correctly in the second round, especially after answering incorrectly in the first round. Surprisingly, there is evidence (see Smith et al., 2009) that groups where all students initially give incorrect responses can be effective. Even in groups where one student has initially responded correctly, none of the group members are given right/wrong feedback about their responses prior to their discussions. As a result, students usually must argue based on the merits of their responses and reasoning; since group members do not know who gave the correct response (if anyone did), a student cannot simply blindly copy another student's response.

Peer Instruction as it is described above is one of the most popular of a class of so-called "interactive teaching" or "interactive engagement" methods (see Henderson & Dancy, 2009); in a meta-analysis of about 6000 students, Hake (1998) identified a large number of classes that administered conceptual inventories both at the beginning and end of the course and found that interactive engagement methods produce student conceptual gains that are on average about double those for traditional teaching methods. Work on Peer Instruction specifically has shown substantial and stark differences in conceptual gains over time for two courses that switched between traditional lectures and Peer Instruction (Crouch & Mazur, 2001). Research also demonstrates that Peer Instruction contributes to increased student retention in STEM majors (Watkins, 2010).

Limitations of Existing Classroom Response Systems

The effectiveness of Peer Instruction at both the micro (individual question response pattern) and macro (conceptual gain) levels suggests that Peer Instruction provides a solid pedagogical foundation for building an interactive teaching technology. Traditionally, students respond to questions in Peer Instruction by using clickers, by using flashcards (by holding up one of four or five flashcards either labeled A through E or differently colored), or by placing a number of fingers in front of one's chest so that they are visible by the instructor but by no one else. The latter two methods have logistical disadvantages. For example, using flashcards or raised hands does not allow the instructor to collect, save, or accurately analyze responses – instructors can only take a visual survey. Clickers, on the other hand, quickly and automatically collect student response data and, when used well, can promote student engagement in retrieval practice (see Bjork & Bjork, 2011). When it comes to conceptual gain, however, according to one study, clickers do not seem to have any appreciable impact when compared to flashcards (Lasry, 2008).

However, both clickers and non-technology CRS methods like flashcards share a number of limitations. First, they are usually limited to multiple-choice questions. Constructed-response questions – questions where students must generate a response from scratch, rather than simply recognize one of the given response options as correct – can push students to engage in different cognitive processes than multiple-choice questions, although this depends on the ways in which the question author makes use of a particular question format (Martinez, 1999). Perhaps even more importantly, question content and format make a statement to students about what is important, and few instructors are likely to agree with the notion that the goal of their course is to teach students how to answer multiple-choice questions correctly, no matter how cleverly constructed. In addition, multiple-choice questions are particularly difficult to write, because they require the instructor to develop appropriate distractors (Haladyna, 2004). Most instructors are not professional question writers and as a result the writing of good multiple-choice questions is particularly challenging.

A second limitation of clickers is that while they provide a mechanism for collecting response data, they do not guide the instructor to create an effective interactive teaching environment. For example, the traditional approach to Peer Instruction – telling students to simply "turn to your neighbor" – frequently results in the formation of groups that are created out of convenience: students often turn to their friends, or they simply turn to the same neighbor each time, and as a result often miss out on a potentially more pedagogically beneficial discussion that they might have with a different group.

In addition, the use of clickers or any non-technological CRS method requires that instructors closely monitor the timing of questioning so that the class moves at a good pace while also monitoring the incoming responses to plan the next phase of instruction. Two common approaches are to either wait for the last few students to respond, making the majority of the class bored and fidgety, or to use a timer (e.g., 30 seconds per question), which generally will not match the actual time needed on a broad variety of questions.

Finally, some of the existing CRS technology makes it challenging for instructors to make the most of the formative assessment data collected. Non-technology CRS methods do not save any information about student responses, of course: the instructor can only make a mental note of the approximate percentages of students holding up each kind of flashcard. But it can even be challenging to make use of the data collected using some kinds of existing response technologies: the most useful data is often the longitudinal data of student performance between class sessions, and this data is not always presented in pedagogically useful ways.

Learning Catalytics

Learning Catalytics' CRS features are designed to help instructors create more authentic and engaging interactions with students in the classroom, regardless of class size. Learning Catalytics is web-based and hosted in the cloud; all data is stored centrally and securely. Instructors control the delivery of course material using a computer or iPad, and students participate in class using any modern web-enabled device:

- Laptop computers
- Smartphones, including iPhone, Android, and Blackberry phones

- Tablets, including iPad
- E-readers, including Amazon Kindle
- Any other modern web-enabled device (e.g., iPod Touch).

Both students and instructor access Learning Catalytics through their device's web browser, so there is no software to install or configure. Because these devices provide the opportunity for complex two-way interactions, they provide a medium for Learning Catalytics to overcome the limitations described in the previous section and create a flexible platform for formative assessment, Peer Instruction, and other interactive teaching pedagogies.

Learning Catalytics was first piloted in a medium-sized physics class (about 90 students) taught at Harvard University in Spring 2011. During the 2011–2012 academic year, Learning Catalytics was used by a number of instructors in both secondary and higher education across different disciplines and in both small and large classes.

Instructor Workflow

In typical use, the instructor uses the laptop computer used to display slides by connecting the laptop to the classroom projector and placing the laptop into dual monitor mode. The instructor is provided with an instructor "control panel" – updated in real time with information about student responses – as well as a "student window" that displays the current question without prematurely revealing information about student responses before the instructor is ready to make that data available to students. The instructor configures the display so that the control panel displays on the laptop monitor and the student window displays on the classroom projector.

Typically, instructors prepare the questions that will be posed to students in advance of class. During class, instructors can deliver questions to students in any order. When ready to pose a question, the instructor clicks a "Deliver" button and the question is posted in the student window and simultaneously pushed out to student devices. As students respond, the control panel updates in real time with a visual representation of student responses. (The format of the visual representation depends on the format of the question; for a simple multiple-choice question a histogram of student responses is shown, but for constructed-response questions the visual representation will be some sort of appropriate aggregation of student responses.) While students are responding, the instructor may also call up a seating chart showing the arrangement of seats in the classroom, with seats colored red, yellow, or green to indicate which students have responded to the question correctly, partially correctly, or incorrectly.

An instructor wishing to engage students in Peer Instruction discussions can click a button to automatically assign groups based on a grouping policy; for example, the instructor may want to pair students so that at least one student in the pair responded to the question correctly. (At this point, students have *not* been given any feedback about the correctness of their responses, so even if students know the grouping policy they do not know whether it is they or their partner that responded correctly.) Learning Catalytics uses the geographical location of students within the classroom when assigning students to groups, and issues personalized messages on the students' devices indicating who they should turn to for discussion of their responses. Students are then given a second opportunity to respond to the same question.

Finally, when ready to "wrap up" the discussion of a question, the instructor can push the visual representation of student responses to each student's device. This is the same visual representation that previously was visible only to the instructor. Based on this visual display, the instructor can engage the entire class in a discussion of the question and the responses received. The most common use of this display is to explain to students what the right answer is and why; for constructed-response questions, student responses provide a window into the specific misconceptions that students brought to the question, and instructors can use this data to address those misconceptions in their explanation. For questions where there is no right answer, the visual representation of student responses might be used to generate debate about the question; since students have all responded to the question individually prior to the debate, they already have a "stake" in the debate, energizing the discussion.

For constructed-response questions, another use of this visual representation of student responses is to highlight a particular response given by one or more students, and to engage the class in a discussion of that response. For example, when each student has sketched a graph in response to a question prompt, one possible visual representation is a set of "thumbnails" of each student graph. The instructor can select one particular graph, enlarge it, and publicly analyze its features; since the students do not know the identity of the author of the graph, the focus is on the response itself and not on the student that constructed it. In this way, students can feel more comfortable about actively participating in class.

Student Workflow

From the student's perspective, Learning Catalytics is used in a manner similar to a traditional clicker. This simple design was intentional, as it allows students to be up and running using the system with no help from the instructor – essential in a large class where it is simply impractical to work with students individually to help them configure their devices. When students enter the classroom, they point their devices to lcatalytics.com and they are prompted to log in and enter the number of the class session to join. After logging in, they are prompted to indicate where in the classroom they are sitting (Fig. 2.) – this information is used both to group students for discussion and to aid the instructor in managing and

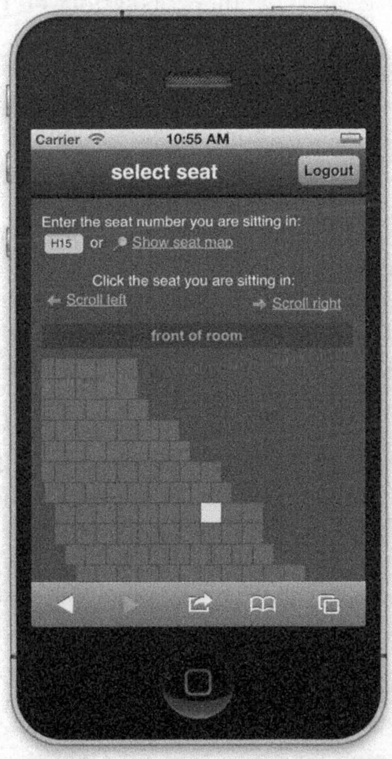

Fig. 2. A Student Selecting a Seat When Logging into Learning Catalytics.

monitoring the class. Once a student selects a seat, the student's device indicates that they should wait for a question to be presented. When the instructor is ready to pose a question to the class, it is "pushed" to student devices automatically and the question appears immediately on each student's device.

When the instructor is ready to wrap up the discussion surrounding a particular question, the class results are pushed to student devices, so that students can inspect the results on their own screens. While the instructor is engaging in a wrap-up activity for a question – typically a whole-class discussion of the different answers – students also have the opportunity to press buttons labeled "I get it now" and "I still don't get it" to provide asynchronous feedback to the instructor. Tallies of the numbers of students pressing each of these buttons are made available to the instructor in real time, so the instructor can calibrate the post-question activity properly: if the instructor has just finished an explanation of the correct reasoning behind a question and is ready to move on, a plurality of students indicating "I still don't get it" can prompt the instructor to circle back and perhaps spend more time on the concepts underlying that particular question; conversely, if the instructor is about to start a long discussion of a concept because of poor student performance, a chorus of students indicating "I get it now" may suggest that a shorter activity is warranted.

Students also have the ability to provide asynchronous feedback in another way. At all times during the class, students have access to a button labeled "Send a message to the instructor." This allows the student to asynchronously send a question or comment that shows up in an unobtrusive way on the instructor's screen. This encourages students who are reluctant to raise their hand in class – or students that have a comment or question that may not be appropriate to raise directly – to communicate with the instructor, and the asynchronous nature of the communication means that the instructor can respond to the question as they see fit: in the moment, later in the class period, or even by email to the student after the lecture ends.

After class, students can log back into the system to review what happened in class: for each question, they can see the question itself and their response(s) to that question. Instructors can optionally write an explanation of the correct answer to accompany each question, and students will see this explanation when reviewing questions only after class. This makes the active learning activities that take place in the classroom more permanent, as the tool becomes a study aid for students to use when working on homework or preparing for exams.

Overcoming the Limitations of Existing Technologies

Going Beyond Multiple-Choice Questions

Learning Catalytics permits instructors to ask questions in a wide variety of constructed-response formats, incorporating question formats that are adaptable to many different disciplines and questioning styles. The goal in designing Learning Catalytics is not to provide different question formats simply for variety's sake, but to provide question formats that will facilitate higher-order cognitive activities and make asking certain kinds of questions as natural as possible.

Many of the different question formats in Learning Catalytics were developed as we piloted the system; we analyzed existing multiple-choice questions that the instructor planned to use in class and developed formats to make those questions as open as possible. We did this by creating an environment where we asked students to construct a response rather than selecting from among several given choices. For example, one multiple-choice question asked students which direction an electric field is pointing in, and provided response options such as "the positive *x*-axis," "the negative *x*-axis," "the positive *y*-axis," etc. By converting this question to a constructed-response question where students simply click (or tap their screen) to indicate a direction, we can shift the focus from selecting an answer (which can involve a cognitive process adapted from standardized test-taking strategy) to the problem itself. By providing this more authentic environment for responding to the question, we were able to elicit misconceptions that were not possible in the multiple-choice format (i.e., from students whose response did not match one of the original response options), and this can improve the in-class interactions when this question is used in class.

Fig. 3 shows four different examples of constructed-response questions: the larger images show the instructor control panel display – which updates with responses in real time – and the smaller iPhone images show what a student sees.

- *Direction* questions (upper left), where students indicate the direction of an arrow or vector. This question, based on an existing activity (TERC, n.d.), asks students to study a satellite image and determine in which direction the winds blow. Examining the results show that there are clusters of responses, which, a priori, may not have been clear to a question author.
- *Sketch* questions (upper right), where students sketch a graph or diagram. In the implementation shown here, instructors can see thumbnails of

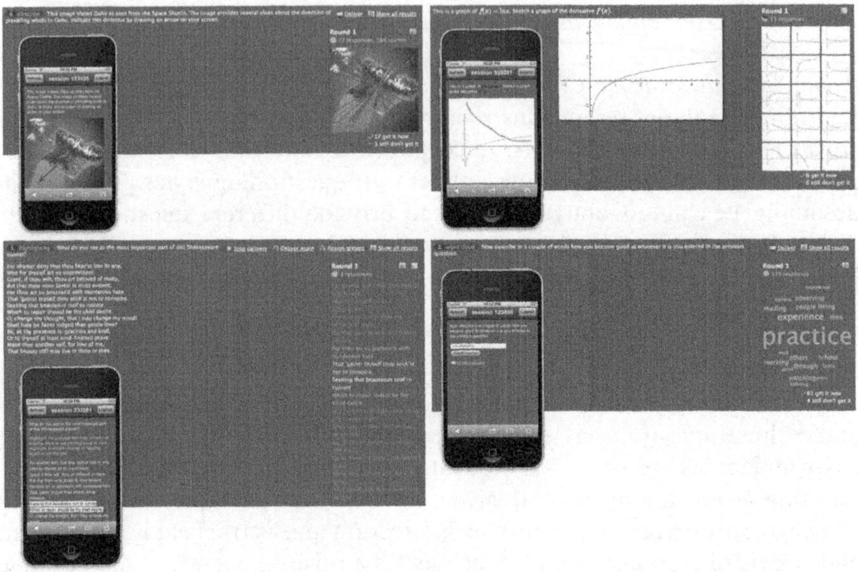

Fig. 3. Four Examples of Different Types of Open-Ended Questions That Can Be Posed to Students Using Learning Catalytics. The Larger View Shows the Instructor Control Panel View of the Question, with a Set of Sample Results, and the Smaller View Shows the Student Response View.

individual sketches; another version – designed for larger classes where it is not feasible to look at all student sketches at once – allows instructors to see a single "composite sketch" where all sketches are semi-transparently overlaid on top of one another. This latter mode is particularly useful for getting a sense of the common features of student sketches.

- *Highlighting* questions (lower left), where students highlight part of a text passage. Students might be asked to identify the part of the passage that indicates something in particular, to find a case of a particular literary structure, or simply to indicate what they find to be the most salient, interesting, or inspiring part of the text. The visual representation of student responses is a heat map where the brightness of each part of the text is in proportion to the number of students that highlighted it.
- *Word cloud* questions (lower right), where students enter a textual response and a word cloud is displayed where words are sized relative to their popularity in student responses. Word clouds such as these provide a

quick way to process textual responses in a large class where it is not feasible to read each individual student response.

Guiding Peer Discussions

As described previously, instructors can encourage more productive Peer Instruction discussions by automatically assigning students to groups for discussion. Our informal observations suggest that when students receive the grouping directions on their device (e.g., talk to Alice in front of you and Bob to your left), the social experience can be different from when the instructor gives generic instructions to "talk to your neighbor": providing explicit directions has the potential to break the ice for students who do not know each other and get students engaged in discussion quickly. In this way, the instructor obtains more control over the way groups are formed, because the grouping parameters are controlled by the instructor.

As a result, the instructor is freed up to use the time during Peer Instruction discussions for more interesting pedagogical purposes. The instructor can consult the graphical seating chart on their personal screen and note if there are clusters of students in certain areas of the room that all responded incorrectly before discussion; during discussion, the instructor can seek out those students or groups to listen in to their discussions to better understand student misconceptions – or to drop a hint or otherwise help guide the discussion.

The instructor can also ask the system to manage the time used for questioning. Normally, instructors and students are shown a timer on the projector screen that tracks how much time has already elapsed in that round of questioning; students are also shown a pie chart that tracks the fraction of class that has already responded to the question. If desired, Learning Catalytics can make use of a predictive model that watches the response data and at some point switches the count-up timer to a count-down timer; the amount of time initially shown is calculated based on the response pacing so that the remaining time should permit the vast majority of students to respond to the question. When the timer counts down to zero, students will either be automatically grouped for Peer Instruction or simply shown the results of the questioning, depending on parameters set by the instructor. In this way, instructors are freed from having to carefully monitor and manage the time, and can more productively take the time during student responding to go around the room and monitor student discussions or simply take a moment to think about how they want to structure the remainder of the class period.

Providing Actionable Data Analytics for Instructors

When instructors use Learning Catalytics, a large amount of formative assessment data is collected about students, both individually and as a whole. One focus of the design of Learning Catalytics is to make that data easily actionable by aggregating it in useful ways. In particular, it allows the instructor to easily browse through the data and take advantage of the hierarchical nature of the assessment measurements. Fig. 4 shows the course

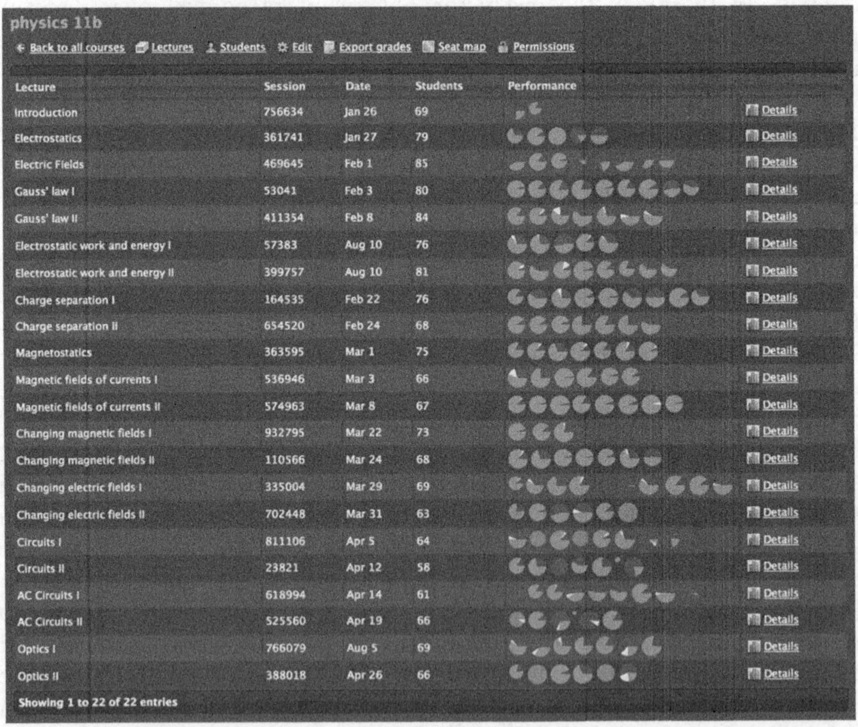

Lecture	Session	Date	Students	Performance	
Introduction	756634	Jan 26	69		Details
Electrostatics	361741	Jan 27	79		Details
Electric Fields	469645	Feb 1	85		Details
Gauss' law I	53041	Feb 3	80		Details
Gauss' law II	411354	Feb 8	84		Details
Electrostatic work and energy I	57383	Aug 10	76		Details
Electrostatic work and energy II	399757	Aug 10	81		Details
Charge separation I	164535	Feb 22	76		Details
Charge separation II	654520	Feb 24	68		Details
Magnetostatics	363595	Mar 1	75		Details
Magnetic fields of currents I	536946	Mar 3	66		Details
Magnetic fields of currents II	574963	Mar 8	67		Details
Changing magnetic fields I	932795	Mar 22	73		Details
Changing magnetic fields II	110566	Mar 24	68		Details
Changing electric fields I	335004	Mar 29	69		Details
Changing electric fields II	702448	Mar 31	63		Details
Circuits I	811106	Apr 5	64		Details
Circuits II	23821	Apr 12	58		Details
AC Circuits I	618994	Apr 14	61		Details
AC Circuits II	525560	Apr 19	66		Details
Optics I	766079	Aug 5	69		Details
Optics II	388018	Apr 26	66		Details

Fig. 4. The Course Dashboard. Each Row Represents a Class Session, and Each Small Pie Chart Represents a Question Asked During That Session.

dashboard for our pilot Learning Catalytics course; each row in the table corresponds to a class session. Each small pie chart represents a question that was asked during that lecture, with the size of the pie proportional to the number of students participating; if the question was asked twice with a Peer Instruction discussion in between, then the post-discussion results are shown. When it appears onscreen, green corresponds to students who answered the question correctly, red corresponds to students who answered incorrectly, yellow corresponds to students who answered incorrectly but subsequently pressed the "I get it now" button, and gray corresponds to questions where the response was not scored as correct or incorrect (questions where there is no right answer, or question formats where Learning Catalytics is not currently able to automatically score student responses).

By scanning the course dashboard, the instructor is quickly able to identify topics that students found particularly challenging or where the questions were simply particularly difficult (in this example, AC circuits), or whether there are trends in student participation over time. Hovering the mouse over any of the pie charts shows the question itself, and clicking on a pie chart allows the instructor to drill down into the individual student-level responses for the corresponding question. In this way, an instructor can review the course at a glance to help plan future instruction over the remainder of the semester, or to identify which topics would be ripe for review.

Similar dashboard functionality is available at the student level. An instructor can view a graphical display of an individual student's performance throughout the semester, and can use these data to zero in on the student's particular difficulties in the course, determine if there are performance or participation trends over time, and quickly and visually evaluate how well students work in Peer Instruction groups.

Using Learning Catalytics to Measure Learner Engagement

Typically, response technologies are used to measure student understanding (e.g., what misconceptions do students hold about this difficult idea?) or sentiment (e.g., what is the range of opinions in the class about this controversial topic?), and in the pilot physics course the former was the target of interest. However, we wanted to use the formative assessment data not just to understand student learning but also to begin to understand student engagement and metacognition. In this section we describe three ways that we can use the formative assessment data to start to illuminate these more elusive constructs.

Degree of Engagement

As a first pass at identifying low engagement, we examined student response times – the amount of time that elapses between the time a question is made available to students and the time a particular student actually responds to the question. Since in the pilot course students received participation credit for responding to the questions, we hypothesized that low-engagement students might simply respond to questions without putting a great deal of thought into them (e.g., randomly, or with only cursory reasoning). Such students might frequently enter a response only a few seconds after the question has been read – or wait until there are only a few seconds remaining to enter a response. In the pilot course, we measured for each student the average fraction of the available time that the student waited before responding. A value of 50% indicates that the student waited on average half the available time before responding, a value of 0% indicates that the student is always the first to respond, and a value of 100% indicates that the student is always the last to respond. Fig. 5 shows the distribution of average response waiting periods. Students at the tails of this distribution are unusually fast or slow to respond, which *may* suggest disengagement – although we were surprised to discover that in our pilot class the distribution is relatively smooth and no students in particular stand out.

Another possibility for measuring degree of engagement might be to compare responses to multiple-choice questions with responses to open-ended questions, to look for students that appear to be participating in multiple-choice questions but that do not give coherent responses to open-ended questions.

Knowing What You Don't Know

We can also use the data to identify (lack of) student metacognition. As Kruger and Dunning (1999) found in their classic study, people that are low-performing in a particular area often believe that they are higher performing than they are in reality. A Peer Instruction environment (Mazur, 1997) where students respond twice – and discuss their responses

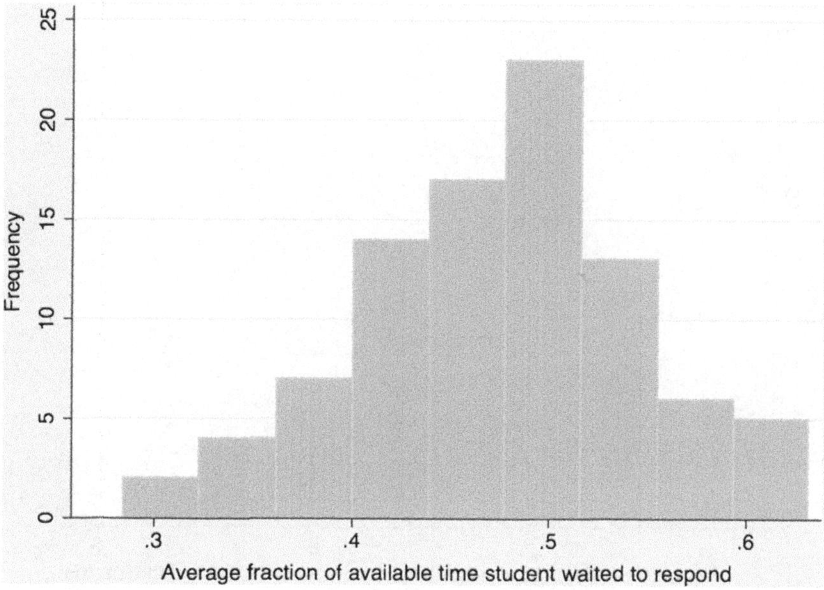

Fig. 5. Distribution of Average Waiting Periods (the Amount of Time Students Waited Before Responding to a Question) in Our Pilot Course.

with each other after their first response – provides a valuable opportunity to obtain a measurement of students' metacognition. In particular, we can identify rigid learners by finding students who frequently respond incorrectly twice even after having a discussion with another student who responded correctly. Fig. 6 plots a histogram of the proportion of the time that students fail to learn from a knowledgeable partner among the $N = 48$ students in the pilot class that responded incorrectly before discussion at least 10 times over the course of the semester. Using this metric, we can clearly identify a small number of students (5 out of the 48) that failed to learn from a more knowledgeable partner at least 50% of the time. This suggests that some small proportion of students fairly consistently do not recognize when their partner has the correct answer or reasoning. Of course, this is only a small part of a student's metacognitive toolset, but this metric could help identify a metacognitive deficiency in a rigid learner that is also performing poorly along traditional metrics (e.g., exam performance).

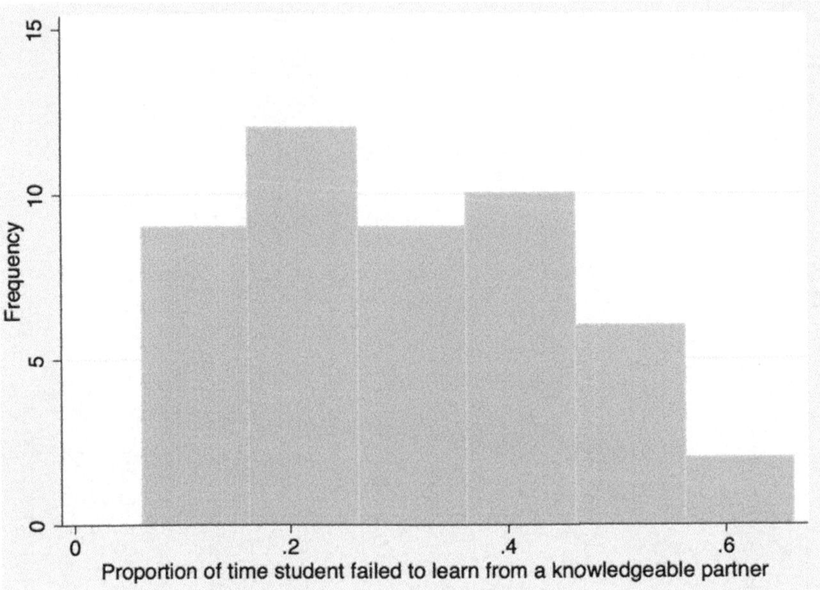

Fig. 6. Distribution of the Proportions of the Time That Students Failed to Learn from a Knowledgeable Partner in Our Pilot Course.

Natural Teachers

Some students, after responding correctly the first time, can fail to convince their discussion partner of their answer, while others are natural teachers who are consistently able to explain their answer cogently. It may be possible to identify these natural teachers through the Peer Instruction data: in our pilot class, we looked at all Peer Instruction sessions where a student has a discussion partner who answered incorrectly before discussion, and we measure the proportion of those occasions when the partner then answered correctly after discussion. Fig. 7 shows the distribution of this proportion across all students in the course. Interestingly, the distribution appears to be roughly normal, but with a fairly wide spread: on average, students' partners improve about half the time, but some students are able to get their partners to improve nearly 85% of the time and others are able to get their partners to improve only about 25% of the time. This is interesting as a phenomenon for further research, but could also be relevant as a measurement tool for a particular instructor: identifying the "natural

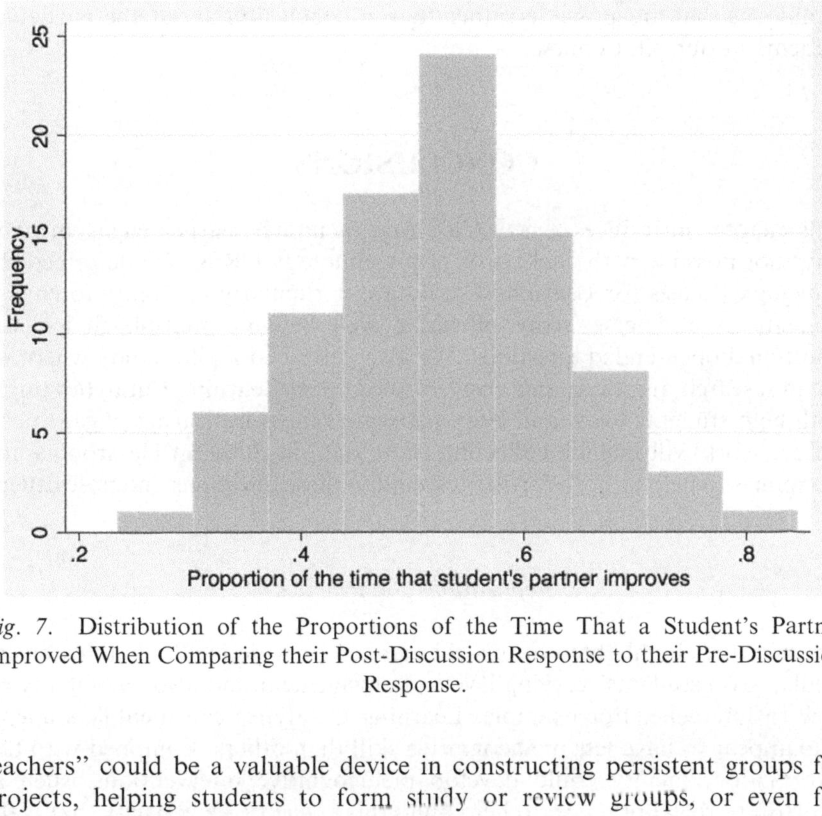

Fig. 7. Distribution of the Proportions of the Time That a Student's Partner Improved When Comparing their Post-Discussion Response to their Pre-Discussion Response.

teachers" could be a valuable device in constructing persistent groups for projects, helping students to form study or review groups, or even for advising students on potential career ideas.

A Limitation of the Pilot Course Data

We have observed that students sometimes fail to form the groups they are directed to form. In our pilot course, which used an early version of the platform, students were required to enter their seat number without the aid of a graphical seating map (Fig. 2), and students often did not enter the correct seat. As a result, students were sometimes assigned to groups with students that they were not actually sitting next to. Other times, students spoke with other adjacent students that were formally in another group, or students spoke with a member of the teaching staff. Therefore, the grouping data in our pilot course is extremely noisy, and the particular results we obtained above using this grouping data are intended to be illustrative of the techniques that are possible rather than a conclusion about the particular students in our pilot course.

CONCLUSIONS

This chapter introduces a new CRS that facilitates learner engagement in ways not possible with clickers or non-technology CRSs. We described the pedagogical basis for Learning Catalytics, particularly its ability to engage students in a diverse array of tasks, well beyond multiple-choice and traditional open-ended questions. We also described a pilot study where we posed research questions and answers about how Learning Catalytics might both help students learn and help instructors measure learner engagement. Future work will include collecting more data in different classrooms and disciplines to help us both further respond to these questions and pose others.

Implications for Practice

The measures highlighted in this chapter can provide faculty with extensive feedback on students' varying levels of engagement and also cue faculty on how to intervene. For example, Learning Catalytics can identify students who appear to have less metacognitive skill than others. Equipped with this information, faculty could develop metacognitive interventions, such as effortful retrieval practice, to help build this capacity – a capacity that is the mark of a master learner. Second, faculty can use Learning Catalytics to conduct fine-grained analysis on student learning and engagement. By making use of the formative assessment data provided by open-ended questions (e.g., the graphs students draw, the text they compose, or the passages they highlight), faculty can understand student learning at a deeper level and in ways that can enrich instruction.

As the use of older CRSs such as clickers continues to grow, so too will the awareness of their limitations. Learning Catalytics is already poised to offer a more robust, research-based instructional technology for driving learning and learner engagement in ways that no other technology currently can. The future of higher education will be shaped by faculty's willingness to turn their back on the time-honored lecture method and turn toward cutting-edge pedagogies and instructional technologies that arm them with strong and detailed data on students' levels of understanding and engagement, freeing instructors from ever having to experience the deadening silence that so often accompanies the question, *Any questions? Anybody?*

ACKNOWLEDGMENTS

We would like to recognize the significant work of several individuals who have contributed to the development of Learning Catalytics and the framework for this chapter: Learning Catalytics co-founder Gary King, members of the education subgroup of the Mazur Group at Harvard during the time of the pilot study (Ives Araujo, Jason Dowd, James Fraser, Jungsook Lee, Kelly Miller, Alvaro Neves, and Laura Tucker), and Alyssa Reinhart of the University of Texas at Austin.

REFERENCES

Ambrose, S., Bridges, M. W., Dipietro, M., Lovett, M. C., Norman, M. K., & Mayer, R. E. (2010). *How learning works: Seven research-based principles for smart teaching*. San Francisco, CA: Jossey-Bass.

Bjork, E. L., & Bjork, R. (2011). Making things hard on yourself, but in a good way: Creating desirable difficulties to enhance learning. In M. A. Gernsbacher, R. W. Pew, L. M. Hough & J. R. Pomerantz (Eds.), *Psychology and the real world: Essays illustrating fundamental contributions to society* (pp. 56–64). New York, NY: Worth Publishers.

Bonwell, C. C., & Elison, J. A. (1991). Active learning: Creating excitement in the classroom. ERIC Digests. Retrieved from http://www.oid.ucla.edu/about/units/tatp/old/lounge/pedagogy/downloads/active-learning-eric.pdf

Bransford, J. D., Brown, A. L., & Cocking, R. R. (Eds.). (2000). *How people learn: Brain, mind, experience, and school (expanded edition)*. Washington, DC: National Academy Press.

Bruff, D. (2009). *Teaching with classroom response systems: Creating active learning enviornments*. San Francisco, CA: Jossey-Bass.

Bruner, J. S. (1974). *Toward a theory of instruction*. Cambridge, MA: Harvard University Press.

Crouch, C. H., & Mazur, E. (2001). Peer Instruction: Ten years of experience and results. *American Journal of Physics*, *69*, 970–977. doi: 10.1119/1.1374249.

Duchastel, P. C. (1981). Retention of prose following testing with different types of test. *Contemporary Educational Psychology*, *6*, 217–226.

Epstein, M. L., Lazarus, A., Calvano, T., Matthews, K., Hendel, R., Epstein, B. B., & Brosvic, G. M. (2002). Immediate feedback assessment technique promotes learning and corrects inaccurate first responses. *Psychological Record*, *52*(2), 187–201.

Flavell, J. H. (1979). Metacognition and cognitive monitoring. *American Psychologist*, *34*(10), 906–911.

Glover, J. A. (1989). The "testing" phenomenon: Not gone but nearly forgotten. *Journal of Educational Psychology*, *81*, 392–399.

Hake, R. R. (1998). Interactive-engagement versus traditional methods: A six-thousand-student survey of mechanics test data for introductory physics courses. *American Journal of Physics*, *66*, 64–74.

Haladyna, T. M. (2004). *Developing and validating multiple-choice test items*. Mahwah, NJ: Lawrence Erlbaum.

Halpern, D. F., & Hakel, M. D. (2003). Applying the science of learning ot the university and beyond: Teaching for long-term retention and transfer. *Change*, *35*(4), 36–41.

Henderson, C., & Dancy, M. (2009). The impact of physics education research on the teaching of introductory quantitative physics in the United States. *Physical Review: Special Topics, Physics Education Research*, *5*, 020107-1–020107-9.

Heron, P., Shaffer, P. S., & McDermott, L. C. (n.d.). *Identifying and addressing student conceptual difficulties: An example from introductory physics*. Washington, DC: National Academy Press. Retrieved from http://www7.nationalacademies.org/bose/Heron_CommissionedPaper.pdf

Kang, S. H., McDermott, K. B., & Roediger, H. L. (2007). Test format and corrective feedback modulate the effect of testing on memory retention. *European Journal of Cognitive Psychology*, *19*, 528–558.

Kruger, J., & Dunning, D. (1999). Unskilled and unaware of it: How difficulties in recognizing one's own incompetence lead to inflated self-assessments. *Journal of Personality and Social Psychology*, *77*, 1121–1134. doi: 10.1037/0022-3514.77.6.1121

Lasry, N. (2008). Clickers or flashcards: Is there really a difference? *Physics Teacher*, *46*, 242–244.

Lasry, N., Charles, E., Whittaker, C., & Lautman, M. (2009). When talking is better than staying quiet. *AIP Conference Proceedings*, *1179*, 181–184.

Martinez, M. E. (1999). Cognition and the question of test item format. *Educational Psychologist*, *34*(4), 207–218.

Mazur, E. (1997). *Peer instruction: A user's manual*. Upper Saddle River, NJ: Prentice Hall.

Mazur, E. (2009). Farewell, lecture? *Science*, *323*(5910), 50–51.

McDaniel, M. A., Derbish, J. L., & Morrisette, N. (2007). Testing the testing effect in the classroom. *European Journal of Cognitive Psychology*, *19*, 494–513.

Miller, M. (2011). What college teachers should know about memory: A perspective from cognitive psychology. *College Teaching*, *59*(3), 117–122.

Palinscar, A., & Brown, A. L. (1984). Reciprocal teaching of comprehension-fostering and comprehension-monitoring activities. *Cognition and Instruction*, *1*, 117–175.

Piaget, J. (1985). *The equilibration of cognitive structures: The central problem of intellectual development*. Chicago, IL: University of Chicago Press.

Piaget, J., Green, D. R., Ford, M. P., & Flamer, G. B. (1971). The theory of stages in cognitive development. In D. R. Green, M. P. Ford & G. B. Flamer (Eds.), *Measurement and Piaget* (pp. 1–11). New York, NY: McGraw-Hill.

Posner, G. J., Strike, K. A., Hewson, P. W., & Gertzog, W. A. (1982). Accommodation of a scientific conception: Toward a theory of conceptual change. *Science Education*, *66*(2), 211–227.

Rieber, R. W. (Ed.). (1998). *The collected works of L. S. Vygotsky: (Vol. 5. Child Psychology)*. New York, NY: Plenum.

Schoenfeld, A. H. (1987). What's all the fuss about metacognition. In A. H. Schoenfeld (Ed.), *Cognitive science and mathematics education* (pp. 189–215). Hillsdale, NJ: Lawrence Erlbaum.

Schoenfeld, A. H. (2010). *How we think: A theory of goal-oriented decision making and its educational applications. Studies in mathematical thinking and learning series*. New York, NY: Routledge.

Smith, M. K., Wood, W. B., Adams, W. K., Wieman, C., Knight, J. K., Guild, N., & Su, T. T. (2009). Why peer discussion improves student performance on in-class concept questions. *Science, 323*(5910), 122–124. doi: 10.1126/science.1165919

TERC. (n.d.). *Wind on Oahu.* McDougal Littell. Retrieved from http://www.classzone.com/books/earth_science/terc/content/investigations/es1806/es1806page01.cfm

Watkins, J. E. (2010, May). *Examining issues of underrepresented minority students in introductory physics.* Cambridge, MA: Harvard University.

Wiggins, G. P., & McTighe, J. (2005). *Understanding by design.* Alexandria, VA: ASCD.

Zull, J. (2006). Key aspects of how the brain learns. *New Directors for Adult and Continuing Education, 110*, 3–9.

CREATING TECHNOLOGY RICH LEARNING ENVIRONMENTS FOR THE CLASSROOM

Robert Garrick, Larry Villasmil, Elizabeth Dell and Rhiannon Hart

ABSTRACT

This chapter reviews student engagement and learning over of a six year study period (>500 students) in a technology rich learning environment. The technology rich learning environment in this project consists of tablet PCs for each student (1:1 environment), visually immersive multiple projection screens, and collaborative digital inking software. This chapter reviews the education problem being addressed, and the learning theory used as a lens to focus specific active learning pedagogical techniques to address the educational problem. From this problem-based learning theory grounded approach, the features desired in a technology rich learning environment were developed. The approach is shared in this chapter with specific detailed examples to allow others to implement technology rich learning environments with active learning pedagogical approaches to address specific education problems in their institution. The technology rich learning environment implemented and studied includes multiple hardware/software pieces to create a system level solution versus a single device or single app solution.

Increasing Student Engagement and Retention using Classroom Technologies: Classroom Response Systems and Mediated Discourse Technologies
Cutting-edge Technologies in Higher Education, Volume 6E, 263–306

ISSN: 2044-9968/doi:10.1108/S2044-9968(2013)000006E012

INTRODUCTION

This chapter discusses an effort directed to increase engagement and retention while decreasing time to graduation of engineering students through the development and implementation of a technology rich interactive learning environment (TRiLE). Specifically, the chapter discusses in detail the following:

- The development of the TRiLE through a technology feature selection based on the pedagogical problem being addressed and desired learning outcomes.
- Specific examples in the TRiLE of how the technology features were utilized in the classroom.
- The results of a six year study period (>500 students) in this technology rich learning environment.
  - The experiment was structured as a quasi-experiment with the same instructors teaching both a control and treatment condition class during a term.
  - Student grades, student end of class surveys, pre-post technology attitude surveys, classroom observations, and video-taped focus groups were utilized to triangulate results with multiple qualitative and quantitative measures.

We use the term TRiLE (technology paired with interactive teaching approaches) to emphasize the necessary synchronization that must exist to balance and align the curriculum (content knowledge), instruction, and assessment (pedagogical knowledge) with the instructional technology features employed. If these components are not synchronized and evaluated with thoughtful attention paid to the educational objectives and principles of learning, the results can be less than effective. We also use the term TRiLE to emphasize a system approach to employing multiple technology components (hardware, software, immersive visual presentation) to build a technology rich environment that is built from learning and cognition knowledge bases in the science, technology, engineering, and math (STEM) education domain. With the recognition that there is no universal "best" teaching or assessment methods or "best" educational technology, we propose that the pedagogical approach and educational technology features be purposefully selected based on the pedagogical problem to be addressed and desired learning outcomes. While the specific technology hardware/software selected continues to change and evolve, we believe the educational technology features (e.g., classroom anonymity, digital collaboration, digital playback assessment, immersive visualization) will remain constant over a longer term.

This study set out to assess the impact of a technology rich learning environment on improvement in student engagement and retention in introductory engineering science/engineering technology courses, which have historically been proven to be challenging. The term *engineering* is used more broadly to encompass both engineering science and engineering technology courses/programs that exist in separate departments within our institution. With this objective in mind we also wanted to explore the following research questions:

1. What is the student's attitude toward using a technology rich learning environment?
2. How do students report that they prefer to learn new technology? (e.g., formal training, manuals)
3. How does the TRiLE affect student academic performance in the class? Specifically does the TRiLE decrease student D and F grades and those withdrawing from the class (W-grade) (DFW)?
4. Does the TRiLE improve academic performance, as measured by class grades, for those students that are not academically strong (grade point average (GPA) less than 3.0)?
5. Does the TRiLE improve academic performance for traditionally underrepresented groups in engineering programs?
6. What learning features of the TRiLE do students report a preference for?

The need for innovative teaching solutions around the world seems to be ever increasing in number and complexity. The motivation for this study arose with an understanding of these larger issues and the specific challenges and experiences of the research team in attracting and engaging engineering students in the engineering/engineering technology classroom. Significant resources and programs exist to attract students with a broad range of backgrounds, and interests into engineering science/engineering technology programs, but higher attrition rates and longer time to degree completion are still typical as compared to other programs (Borrego, Padilla, Zhang, Ohland, & Anderson, 2005; "Consortium for Student Retention Data Exchange – CSRDE"). This significant student attrition occurs during the first three years of the engineering programs as students struggle with challenging introductory classes (Borrego, et al., 2005). Marra and colleagues report that factors influencing students' decision to transfer out of engineering programs include "poor teaching and advising" and "engineering classes were unfriendly" (Marra, Rodgers, Shen, & Bogue, 2012). They also noted no difference between leavers and persisters in terms of academic success indicators (Marra et al., 2012). These students have the academic potential to succeed and have already chosen engineering as their initial field of interest, but still decide to leave engineering science or engineering technology programs. Unfortunately, five year graduation rates from engineering programs only range from 10% to 40% of the initial students entering the engineering cohort (Borrego, et al., 2005; Consortium for Student Retention Data Exchange – CSRDE). In other words, the majority of the students who have been recruited into engineering programs, 60–90%, do not graduate within a five year period. Engineering programs as compared to other programs have the longest time to completion across academic programs. These issues are especially troubling in light of the extensive admissions screening typical to engineering and engineering technology programs (Fortenberry, Sullivan, Jordan, & Knight, 2007; Lord et al., 2008; Seymour & Hewitt, 1997). In addition, once students leave the engineering program they are seldom replaced, as engineering programs have the lowest percentage of students transferring into the field (Ohland et al., 2008). Borrego et al. (2005) point out that the majority of this attrition occurs during the first three years of the engineering programs. Therefore, we focused on introductory engineering/engineering technology courses that were historically challenging to students. Sadly, studies have shown that a primary cause of the high attrition rates in engineering programs is the perception that the learning environment is often un-motivating and unwelcoming. The students' cognitive capabilities or their potential to perform well as engineers are not significant factors in determining their persistence. These negative perceptions about the learning environment are even more problematic in underrepresented populations (woman, and students of color) (Bergvall, Sorby, & Worthen, 1994; Busch-Vishniac & Jarosz, 2004; Harris et al., 2004; Salter, 2003; Sax, 1994; Vogt, 2007).

PROBLEM ADDRESSED

One of the problematic courses at the Rochester Institute of Technology (RIT) is Pneumatic and Hydraulic Systems, which is traditionally offered to second year students, having a significant rate of low grades and student withdrawals. The percent of students receiving a grade of D or F and withdrawing (DFW) from the class has averaged 22.8% over the last 10 times the class was taught (Fig. 1). A total of 504 students have taken the course over this period. In other words, approximately 115 students have

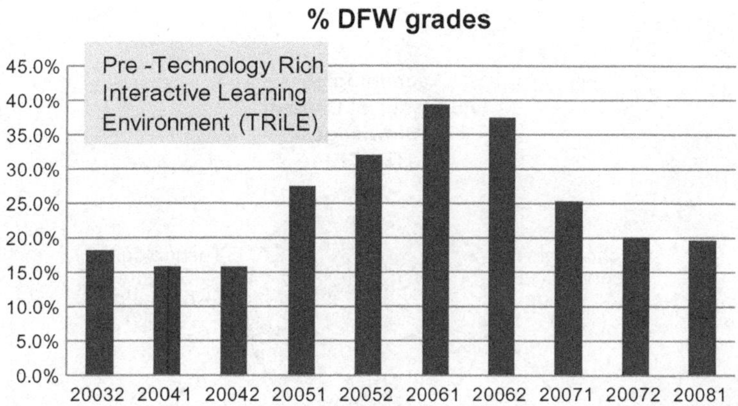

Fig. 1. Percentage of DFW Grades for Pneumatics and Hydraulics Class.

repeated the class or withdrawn from the program. This large number affects the department's retention rate and class scheduling. This DFW rate is similar to other engineering classes we have reviewed.

Theoretical Basis

We used as our conceptual framework for developing the technology rich learning environment the technological pedagogical content knowledge (TPACK) framework as proposed by Mishra and Koehler. This framework proposes how the knowledge of technology can be integrated with pedagogical and content knowledge to improve the learning environment (Fig. 2). The importance of not separating technology knowledge from the content and the specific pedagogical approaches has been noted by other researchers as critical for successful teaching (Margerum-Leys & Marx, 2002). As noted by Mishra and Koehler, "merely introducing technology to the educational process is not enough" (Mishra & Koehler, 2006).

Mishra and Koehler (2006) define technology knowledge as the skills required to understand and operate particular operating systems, hardware, and software tools. We would include in technology knowledge the vision and understanding of the technology possibilities to connect and move content and information in the learning environment. Technology will always continue to evolve and the technology knowledge component must also include the ability of the instructor to adapt, learn, and incorporate new

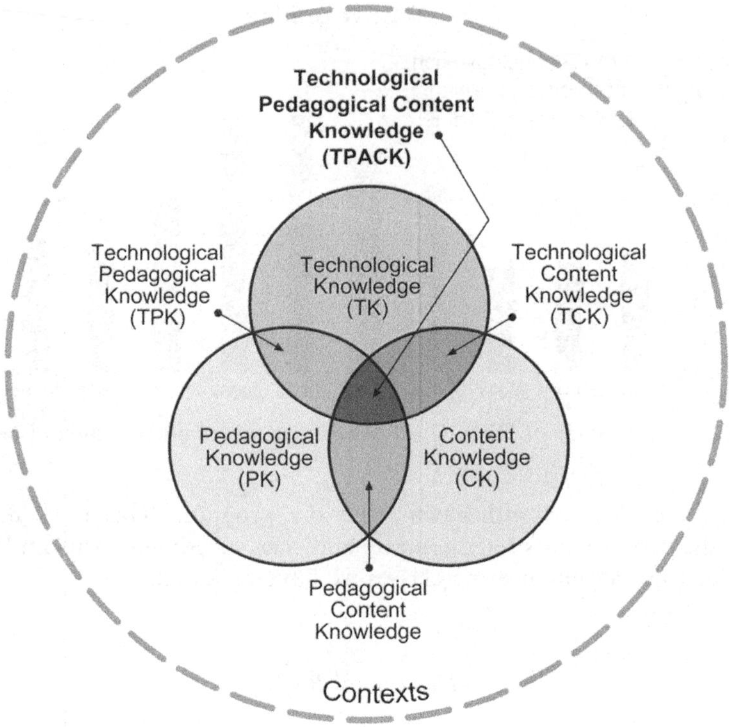

Fig. 2. Technological Pedagogical and Content Knowledge (TPACK) Reproduced by permission of the publisher, © 2012 by tpack.org; *Source*: http://tpack.org

technologies into both formal and informal learning opportunities. Shulman's formulation of pedagogical-content knowledge forms the basis for TPACK by defining content knowledge as the instructor's understanding of the subject, concepts, facts, theories, and approaches with the given field. Instructor content knowledge within the engineering discipline is critical to allow the instructor to clarify how an engineer approaches a problem and how this approach may differ from that of other STEM disciplines. Pedagogical knowledge involves a deep understanding of how students learn, the methods of teaching, the methods of assessment along with the overall educational aims and values. Pedagogical knowledge also includes an understanding of the theories of learning and assessment and how these can be applied to develop the learning environment. As we developed the technology rich learning environment, we used the *How People Learn* (*HPL*)

(Bransford, Brown, Cocking, Donovan, & Pelligrino, 2000) framework for designing the technology rich learning environment as our lens to highlight the aspects of instruction that could influence student learning and long-term retention. From the *HPL* perspective four interrelated items are key to designing an effective learning environment:

- Knowledge centeredness
- Assessment centeredness
- Learner centeredness
- Community centeredness

Knowledge centeredness focuses on the content taught and why the specific concepts are important. The knowledge centered view from *HPL* Chapter 3 advances the understanding of the student rather than memorization of disconnected facts and formulas. For the introductory engineering science/engineering technology classes we included cases, projects, authentic applications to include items beyond reading the text and solving typical textbook problems.

Assessment centeredness focuses on making the students' learning status visible to both the student and the instructor during the process of instruction. As noted by Pelligrino, frequent formative assessment allows the student to understand their level learning and gaps in understanding. For the technology-rich learning environment, we wanted to ensure that the instructor was able to incorporate frequent questions, polls, and student-solved examples into the lecture. The objective of the technology would be to ensure that the process of moving the information was effective and efficient.

Learner centeredness focuses on the student pre-knowledge, student learning goals, and cultural beliefs that they bring to the learning environment (Bransford et al., 2000). The more that the instructor is able to understand about each student, the better the instructor and adjust the pedagogical techniques and approaches to achieve the course learning outcomes. As noted in *HPL*, the learner centeredness and assessment centeredness overlap as the instructor queries the students to understand preconceptions and learning progress during the class.

Community centeredness is the fourth *HPL* focus in designing a successful learning environment. The community centeredness like the other three areas overlap and interact. The community view stresses the norms and connectedness of the learning environment. Our desire was for the technology to assist students to work in a collaborative manner and assist others in also succeeding in the class.

From the *HPL* knowledge, assessment, learner, and community areas, we outlined the following key pedagogical design principles for creating the technology rich learning environment:

- The ability to direct the learner's attention to the critical components in the new content to be learned
- Sufficient amount of student invention and practice with the new content to allow successful linkage and retrieval
- Timely, anonymous, and complete formative assessment feedback to both the instructor and student on their understanding of the content
- The ability to show concurrently different approaches, applications, and linkages to allow the student to make connections to the new content
- The ability to match the amount of content presented to not exceed the working memory load of the student with an ability of the student to proceed at their own pace
- A learning environment that emphasizes collaboration and values peer instruction.

From this learning theory-pedagogical knowledge viewpoint we determined what technology features were desired in the technology rich environment for the engineering content being delivered. In our case the technology rich environment needed to include the features linked to the desired pedagogical component as shown in Table 1.

The second key component to the TRiLE is the interactive/cooperative structure of the classroom. The interactive/cooperative structure as noted by Smith, Sheppard, Johnson, and Johnson (2005) is "the instructional use of small groups so that students work together to maximize their own and each others' learning." In analyzing over 150 rigorous education research studies that compared the efficacy of cooperative learning, Johnson, Johnson, and Smith report significant increases in student academic success with cooperative learning (Johnson, Johnson, & Smith, 1998a, 1998b). The relevant measures reviewed in the meta-analysis conducted by Johnson, Johnson, and Smith included knowledge acquisition, knowledge retention, higher level reasoning, and creativity in problem solving. They also found significant positive advantages with the use of cooperative learning for reading, writing, and student presentations, mathematical tasks, laboratory experiments, persistence, and transfer of learning from one situation to another (Johnson, et al., 1998a, 1998b). The significant positive results with cooperative learning are also correlated with a meta-analysis conducted by Springer, Stanne, and Donovan (1999). This meta-analysis focused on college introductory STEM courses from 39 rigorous education studies from 1980 or

Table 1. TRiLE – Pedagogical Component to Technology Feature Linkage.

Pedagogical Component	Technology Rich Learning Environment Feature
Ability to direct learner's attention to critical components	Digital inking of instructor projected live on student tablets Summary video lectures delivered prior to class and available after class Back-lit projection screens Ability to serve single slide, page at a time to students Students able to playback instructor digital inking
Sufficient amount of student invention and practice	Summary video lectures delivered prior to class to allow additional time for active learning activities (inverted or flipped classroom structure) Stylus digital inking interface for students Ability for individual or grouping of shared workspace
Timely, anonymous, and complete formative assessment feedback	Ability to retrieve and project student work (solved engineering problems/diagrams) anonymously live in class Ability to return student work electronically
The ability to show concurrently different approaches, applications, and linkages	Multiple (three) back-lit projection screens Ability to review and retrieve student solved problems that illustrate different approaches
The ability to match the amount of content presented to not exceed the working memory load of the student with an ability of the student to proceed at their own pace	Summary video lectures delivered prior to class and available after class to allow students to view, pause, rewind, or advance as needed Ability for students to save digitally inked notes and playback the digital inking as needed
A learning environment that emphasizes collaboration and values peer instruction	Cooperative learning pedagogical approach, group problem solving with the ability for students to work in a common digital environment

later. Synthesis publications summarizing the research on cooperative learning effects in chemistry include Bowen (2000) and in engineering Prince (2004). In a seminal study of over 6,000 students, Hake (1998) found a substantial improvement in conceptual understanding of physics principles using an interactive and engaging learning environment. Hake (1998) defined "interactive engagement" as "designed in part to promote conceptual understanding through interactive engagement of students in heads-on (always) and hands-on (usually) activities which yield immediate feedback through discussion with peers and/or instructors" (p. 65).

Creating an engaging and cooperative learning environment has been a key issue in engineering education for many decades (Smith & Goldstein, 1982; Smith, Johnson, & Johnson, 1981). In this timeframe, creating an engaging environment has been the focus of not only engineering education but also general higher education (Felder, 1995; Johnson, Johnson, & Smith, 1991; Johnson et al., 1998a; Johnson, Johnson, & Smith, 2007; MacGregor, Cooper, Smith, & Robinson, 2000; Millis & Cottell, 1997; Prince, 2004; Smith, Douglas, & Cox, 2009; Smith et al., 2005; Terenzini, Cabrera, Colbeck, Parente, & Bjorklund, 2001). Crouch and Mazur (2001) extensively documented the approach to interactive engagement over a 10 year period. The key elements include the following:

1. Cooperative learning activities
2. Group problem solving with the objective of improving problem-solving skills.

Learning Environment Design

The most common delivery method of classroom-based teaching and learning used in engineering education during the past 50 years (Smith et al., 2005) is one where the instructor stands up in front of a group of students to impart theoretical knowledge. This "chalk and talk" model or traditional approach to teaching is still of widespread use as current faculty was mostly taught under such environment (Nicholas, 2011). The model, graphically depicted in Fig. 3, is instructor-centered and presentation-based portrayed as such as one where "the information passes from the notes of the professor to the notes of the students without passing through the mind of either one." In the figure, we present a cycle that shows that students that are successful under the traditional method of teaching will most likely replicate that style of teaching if they become instructors once they graduate. Research Studies have long shown that this traditional approach where the instructor lectures the students being the centre of the activities occurring in the classroom is ineffective (Enriquez, 2009). Quantification into this lack of effectiveness is well summarized by Wirth and Perkins (2012) indicating that in most cases students pay attention to only 50% of the average lecture, recalling 42% of

Fig. 3. Traditional Class Delivery Method or "Pour It In," Modeled After Lila Smith (1975) (Smith et al., 2005).

the information immediately after a lecture, and remembering only 17% of the information one week later.

Prior to the implementation of the TRiLE approach, the delivery method for the course in reference followed more or less the traditional method described above. Regular lectures included some practice problems and once a week there was a practice lecture to use a computer for solving problems but always with the instructor at the center of the learning activities. In a process that started in 2007 (academic term 20062), the course curriculum has been improved by reorganizing topics, realigning the content to the hands-on laboratory activities, and embedding multiple practice problems within each class lecture. These improvements, carried out based on suggestions and comments from student's evaluations, led to significant increases in the grade averages and the students confidence level in applying the subject matter and the perceived course content coverage by the instructor (Fig. 4). In the figure, it can be observed that a downward trend in both grades and student confidence level preceded the academic term 20062 but shifted upward substantially in subsequent terms. Despite this level of relative success, some students in this sophomore course kept earning low grades ("D" and "F") and withdrawing ("W") from the class. As we already indicated, the

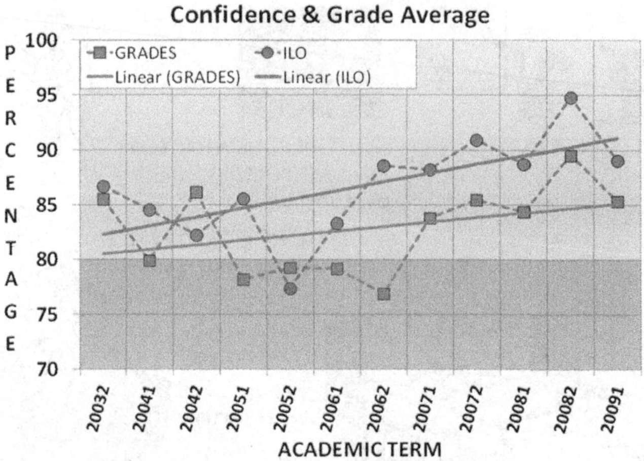

Fig. 4. Intended Learning Outcomes (ILOs) Student Confidence Average Scores.

historical rate of DFW is about 23% (Fig. 1) over the last 10 times the class has been taught, affecting the retention rate and class scheduling.

Facing the practical problem of having a high DFW rate among the students of the course, we as instructors asked ourselves the following two questions: Who is our target audience? How do we address their needs? (relationship between practical and research problems (Booth, Colomb, & Williams, 2003)). The students in the college classrooms today belong to the so-called millennial (Sweeney, 2005) or net (Tapscott, 2009) generation. Sweeny, conducting dozens of focus groups with college students in the United States and researching the vast literature concerning millennials, and Tapscott, leading teams to investigate and conduct qualitative research on the behavior of young people in several countries, concur in that the generation born after 1980, i.e., millennials are digital natives. In their words "they were born and grew up into an era in which digitally provided services were commonplace." Millennials love entertainment and as such enjoy gaming, the media, and the technology associated with it. Sweeny points out that by gaming, they learn by making mistakes with no long-term penalties for doing so. Millennials display a strong preference for experiential learning through trial and error. Millennials grew up in an environment where collaboration is present everywhere school work, sports, extracurricular activities, gaming, and personal lives. Tapscott emphasizes that millennials revel in the freedom that technology provides, a technology that allows them to interact with each other more often and in more depth than any generation before them. The millennials are a generation raised on immediate gratification grown up expecting instant access, more choices, and immediate feedback. Another key aspect on the millennials is their multitasking nature. While Sweeny calls it their preferred mode, a skill, and strength; Tapscott points to studies that show that our multitasking abilities are really limited but emphasizing that he sees a different picture when "observing Net Geners outside the laboratory." Tapscott also points out to the millennials norms of scrutiny, integrity, and innovation.

In summary, Sweeny and Tapscott coincide in that millennials

- are digital natives;
- love entertainment, enjoy games and media;
- are collaborative and effective at multitasking;
- learn experientially and continuously;
- expect more choices and selectivity;
- prefer customization and personalization;
- expect instant gratification and are impatient; and
- are achievement-oriented.

These main characteristics make the millennial generation clearly very distinct from previous generations of students at the same age. Certainly, they are not "wired" to thrive in a traditional classroom where the students have mostly a passive role. Therefore, it should not be a surprise that Oakley (Oakley, Hanna, Kuzmyn, & Felder, 2007) summarizes her work by indicating that there are compelling reasons for assigning students to work in teams on homework and projects with several well-known educational theories supporting the idea that students learn most effectively through interactions with others, pointing to cooperative learning as being more effective than competitive or individualistic learning that leads to significant gains in academic success, and concluding that working in teams was positively associated with students' self-assessed quality of learning. Similarly, Enriquez (2009) discusses that active participation with interactive and collaborative teaching and learning methods are more effective in science and engineering education, and that the use of technology has been found to be effective in enhancing the classroom experience to achieve a more interactive and collaborative environment.

The collaborative and experiential nature of the millennial student requires an alternative to the "chalk and talk" or "pour it in" traditional method of lecture delivery. It should involve cooperative and collaborative learning where information passes not only from faculty to students but also from students to faculty and among the students. This collaborative environment is illustrated as the "keep it flowing around" model (Smith et al., 2005) (Fig. 5). This model argues for balance between what the instructor does in

Fig. 5. Alternative (Cooperative) Class Delivery Method or "Keep It Flowing", Modeled After Lila Smith (1975) (Smith et al., 2005).

the classroom and the student contributions making the learning visible for all. It emphasizes that both interdependence and accountability are required for learning and essential for a student engagement instructional approach. As we outlined in the key pedagogical principles, the learning environment should be conducive to direct the student's attention to critical content components showing concurrently different approaches, applications, and linkages and provide timely formative assessment. In addition, this alternative environment should be rich in technology as the millennials are digital natives, enjoy games, and multimedia. The TRiLE is an approach intended to reinvent the traditional classroom transforming it into one where the combination of pedagogical techniques and the use of technology offers to the millennials the opportunity of being successful as students.

TRiLE Implementation

The TRiLE approach is a successful ongoing investigation and the product of multiple pilot studies. These pilot studies initiated in the spring of 2005 with an instructor using a single tablet PC to project notes on the classroom screen that were digitally captured by the tablet and made available to the students. In that way, students could focus on comprehension rather than copying the instructor's notes from the white board. This initial pilot study demonstrated that tablet PC based lectures helped to a greater extent students who had lower GPAs (Parthum, 2009). These academically challenged students benefited by receiving additional notes as a supplement to the general outline presentation. The pilot studies have evolved into redesigning the curriculum and using a specially designed classroom equipped with tablet PCs for each student, back-lit projectors for enhanced lecture presentations, and collaborative software that allows digital inking, note taking, hyperlinking, annotations, and in-class assessment among other features (Dell, Garrick, & Villasmil, 2011).

Course Redesign

In a comparable approach to Rawat, Elahi, and Massiha (2008), the inverted or flipped classroom (EDUCAUSE, 2012) pedagogical model has been adopted for redesigning and adapting the course. Like in the supplemental model where the lecture and reading material are available online in advance, in the flipped classroom model short video lectures are viewed by students before the class session. The course has been redesigned with the following goals in mind:

- Increase the availability of content to the students outside of the classroom via My Courses Management System.
- Present and embed video links of real applications within the context of the material presented in the classroom.
- Increase the use of interactive activities taking advantage of the technology available in the classroom to promote student participation, individual and group work, and student–student interactions.
- Create and administer immediate feedback assessment tools to better manage student-learning outcomes and encourage students to come prepare to class.
- Introduce activities that promote cooperative, collaborative, and problem/project-based learning.

TYPICAL SESSION

A typical classroom meeting session involves the following segments: (i) a brief discussion of schedule and reading and homework assignments for the week, (ii) a short quiz, (iii) a review section to solidify student preparation and correct misunderstanding, (iv) introduction of the objectives for the session, (v) an introductory video into the new material when appropriate, (vi) class polling for immediate feedback, (vii) 10–20 minute lecture, (viii) individual or collaborative activities, (ix) embedded videos/animations for concepts/principles reinforcement, (x) 10–20 minute lecture, (xi) individual or collaborative activities, (xii) a brief introduction to the laboratory session of the week, and an (xiii) end of class quiz.

(i) *Discussion of schedule and assignments for the week*

A 1–2 minute introduction to the meeting of the day checking on the status of the course, tracking the progress of the material covered according to the initial planning presented in the syllabus, and a reminder of the current and upcoming reading and homework assignments, including relevant due dates.

(ii) *Beginning of class short quiz*

When appropriate, a 5 minute one or two questions examination is administered to either check on the student understanding of the concepts discussed in the previous class or the student preparation for the day according to the reading assignments. These quizzes are completed digitally by the students on a tablet PC and submitted electronically via collaborative software, DyKnow®. The quizzes are graded also electronically after class and returned to the students "virtually" from the instructor office PC or any other computer where the software is properly installed. The quizzes provide formative assessment feedback to both the instructor and student on their understanding of the content (*HPL* key pedagogical design principle).

(iii) *A review section*

Five to 10 minutes are dedicated to review the most relevant principles and concepts of the previous class meeting. It allows addressing the misconceptions and mistakes observed in quizzes and engagement activities, and when considered relevant how they are interrelated to the material studied before. The review section provides continuity to the millennial student including some generic feedback.

(iv) *Introduction to the objectives of the day*

A 1–2 minute discussion on the content objectives to be covered, the two most important concepts students should be aware of – the engagement activities and assessment tools for the class meeting session.

(v) *Introductory videos*

The students have available short video lectures via Courses Management System that are encouraged to be viewed by students before the class meeting session, while significant in-class time is devoted to exercises, projects, or discussions, aka the inverted or "flipped" classroom structure (EDUCAUSE, 2012). In addition, a 2–3 minute web or DVD video is embedded within the context of each class meeting presenting current applications of the principles and components to be studied and analyzed when appropriate. This is particularly true at the beginning of the course and with the introduction of a new chapter (following the main textbook).

(vi) *Class polling for immediate feedback*

The collaborative software, DyKnow®, and the technology allow embedding polls within the PowerPoint presentation that can be administered as the class moves along. The polls are used to gather information about the student performance or opinions on a particular topic providing the instructor guidance on what concepts have been fully grasped and others that may require further dedication. Although similar in this regard to other technologies like clickers, results from the polls themselves in addition to any instructor note or written comments related to the polls can be embedded in the notebook of the class meeting session that every student is going to have available at the end of the class period (Fig. 6).

(vii) *10–20 minute lecture*

Following on the introductory short video corresponding to the day of the class meeting, the instructor presents the first series of principles and concepts of the particular topic to be studied laying the theory but making connections to the real applications and presenting components and parts where such principles are in play. Delivering the lecture, the instructor focuses on directing the student's attention to critical concepts showing concurrently different approaches, applications, and linkages (*HPL* key pedagogical design principles). The technology is used to target the millennial student nature by making the classroom enjoyable to attain a dual purpose to teach and entertain. Rather than one single screen or a white board, we have a layout of three back-lit projector screens and two white boards on the room side walls that allow presenting an instant connection between a formula and its real application, the use of a web resource with candor (on real-time), or even the traditional work write-out on the white board (millennial students expect more choices).

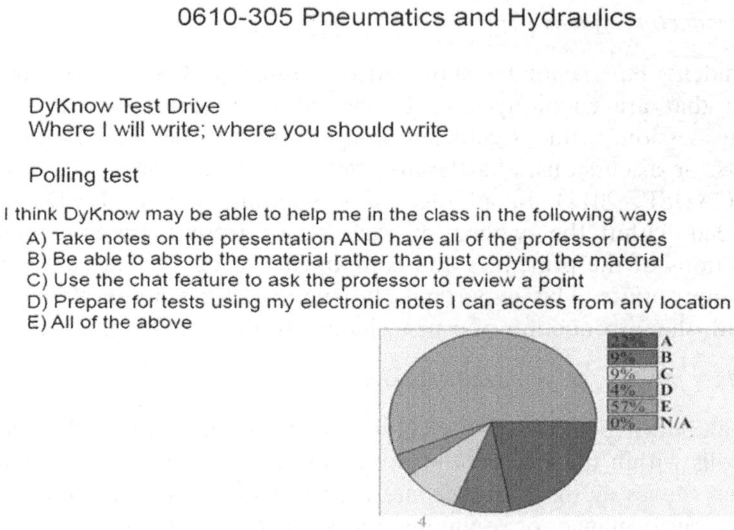

Fig. 6. Typical Polling Outcome. Student's Answers Collected and Shared with the Classroom.

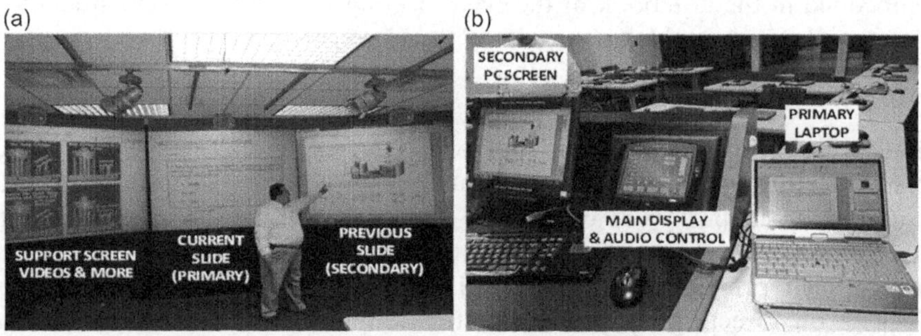

Fig. 7. TRiLE Classroom Projector Screens and Instructor Podium. (a) Projector Screens Arrangement. (b) Instructor Podium Arrangement.

Fig. 7 shows the actual configuration of the back-lit projector screens and the instructor podium in the TRiLE classroom. Fig. 7(a) presents the screen disposition for the lecture. The center screen displays the current slide of the PowerPoint of the meeting (as a DyKnow® notebook), the right screen displays the previous slide and the left screen is the support screen, i.e., videos, animations, Internet searches, part showings, etc. Showing the current and the previous slides simultaneously provides continuity in the flow of information particularly when directing the learner's attention to critical concepts and answering questions that frequently require go back in the presentation. In the specifics of the images displayed on the screens, the center screen contains a brief exercise with a multiple choice poll that students will answer once they solve the exercise while the right screen shows the principles and relations that relate to the question of the exercise posed in the poll. Fig. 7(b) shows the instructor podium. The instructor main computer is the primary laptop which has the current PowerPoint in the DyKnow® environment while linked to the secondary PC so the latter displays the slide flipped in the former. The main display and audio podium control allows to select multiple inputs for the back-lit screens. This arrangement clearly permits the instructor to simultaneously present animations, still images, text, formulas and even hand calculations, primary laptop, and secondary PC are both digital ink capable.

(viii) *Class group activities*

Providing short video lecture content online frees class time (Rawat et al., 2008), so a larger portion of the meeting is dedicated to interactive learning and class discussion/collaborative activities targeting the development of critical thinking and problem-solving skills fomenting student invention and practice (*HPL* key pedagogical design principle). In this regard, the tablets are an invaluable resource in the implementation of interactive group learning activities. The tablets' inking capability coupled with the DyKnow® software collaborative nature makes the management of students' group activities and the direction of classroom discussions straightforward. For instance, when new topics are introduced access to the Internet allows setting general discussions by leading the students to search for new concepts in a group manner and after few minutes the instructor could proceed to display the student findings "live" on the main screen to ensue discourse (Fig. 8(a)).

Fig. 8(b) shows the panel submission of a group assignment (groups of two students) that was properly solved. Such panels are based directly on class content and students can generate them from class discussions, case studies, and interactive activities, or in this case a practice problem. The submitted panels can be transferred to the instructor PowerPoint (DyKnow® notebook) of the current class meeting so that all students will have them visible and available in their tablets and able to reference them when they save their notebook at the end of the class session. Based on

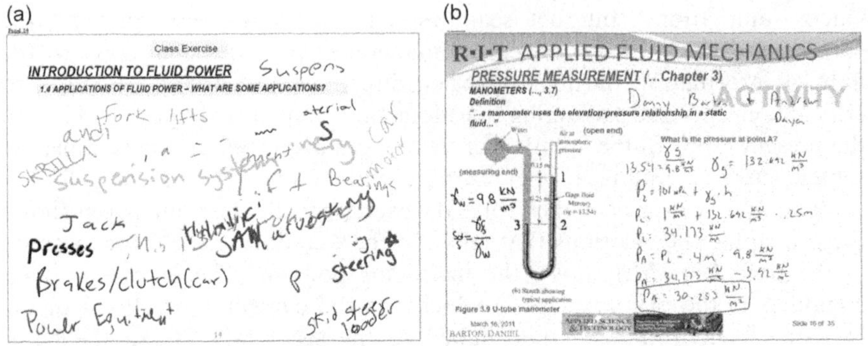

Fig. 8. Typical Group Activities: Students Sharing the Main Screen and Instructor Assisted Discussion. (a) Class Exercise "Live" Panel Display. (b) Group Activity Panel Submission.

anecdotal evidence, when working in groups the students normally prefer to work side by side although the tablet DyKnow® software combination allows creating virtual groups so students sitting across the room could work together communicating via chat. Most students fit the millennial norm of being collaborative.

(ix) *Videos/Animations*

Appealing to the digital nature of the millennials and the hands-on disposition of the engineering technology students, short videos and animations are presented to show simple applications of the main concepts and principles presented in class in the real world. They act as content reinforcement. Fig. 9(a) shows a panel of the DyKnow® notebook with a "flat" image of the animation and the hyperlink embedded in it connecting to the website hosting the animation to be displayed in the left screen of the classroom. In contrast, Fig. 9(b) shows a panel presenting the components of a system that is being discussed and analyzed after the principles of operation were introduced. In this case the animations linked in the panel are complementary information.

(x) *10–20 minute lecture*

A second short lecture as described in point (vi) follows after several student exercise to complete the instructor presentation of principles and concepts of the particular topic or topics for the class meeting session.

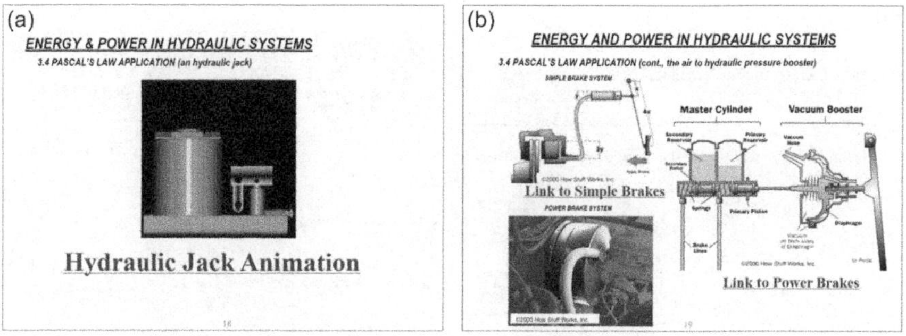

Fig. 9. Embedding Links to Videos and Animation Within the Lecture Notebook. (a) Slide with a Link to a Video Animation. (b) Slide with Two Links to Two Java Apps.

(xi) *Individual exercises/Polling*

Like with group exercises, the technology allows the instructor to be creative in the way individual assignments are given. Fig. 10(a) shows a panel containing an individual exercise assigned as a multiple-choice poll question including the digital ink with the instructor solution. In addition to choosing their answers which will give the instructor an immediate assessment on the student learning, the students can submit their panel that can then be displayed on the main screen and discussed by the instructor. Although only selected student panels can be discussed in large classes, this approach has proven to be very valuable for the students in providing immediate formative assessment feedback (*HPL* key pedagogical design principle).

In contrast, Fig. 10(b) shows the panel submission of an individual assignment properly solved where the instructor led the simplification of the main formula required to solve the problem. The technology in the case of this practice problem allows the dedication of one "blank" panel to the solving of the problem projected on the main or center screen while the problem itself is being displayed in the previous or right screen of the classroom (see insert in Fig. 10(b)). In this way, the students can concentrate in the problem solving in their own tablet PC screens while observing the problem statement including any clarification notes from the instructor in the classroom complementary or left screen and sidewall whiteboards.

(xii) *Introduction to the weekly laboratory session*

When new components are going to be used in the weekly laboratory session, the last 10–15 minutes of the class meeting session are dedicated to

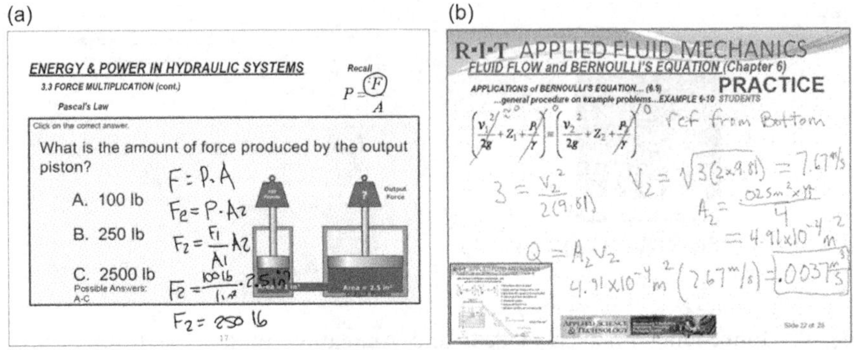

Fig. 10. Typical Individual Activities Combined with Polling or Standalone. Instructor's Notes are Shown. (a) Combined Poll/Individual Exercise. (b) Individual Practice Exercise.

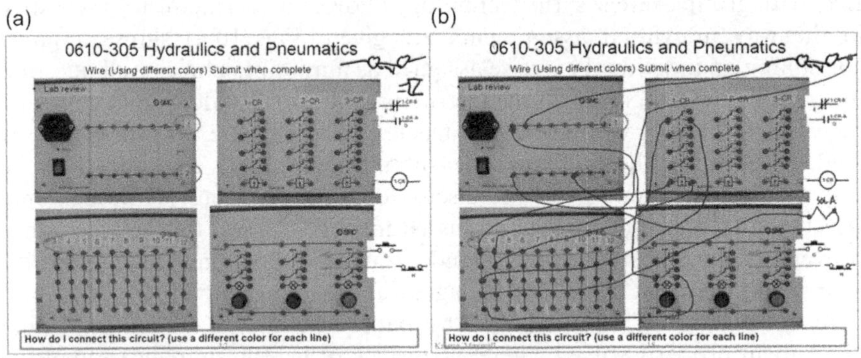

Fig. 11. Panels of the Laboratory Review Section of a Typical Lecture. (a) Original Panel. (b) Retrieved Student Panel.

describe briefly those components. Then, pictures of the actual components are laid out in a panel with a small ISO circuit attached to it. The students are asked to work in groups to draw the connections between the components following the circuit to mimic the activities they would do in the actual experiments of the weekly laboratory session (Fig. 11). To provide immediate feedback to the students, few student panels with their attempts to "build" the circuits are retrieved and reviewed and discussed with the students. Although the instructor might lead the discussion, students are encouraged to participate and "defend" their decision in "constructing" the circuits.

(xiii) *End of class meeting quizzes*

Typically, at the end of the class meeting or sometimes within the class period short quizzes are administered. In addition to being a direct assessment tool that will be graded, they provide instant feedback on the effectiveness of class activities and previous discussions. Quizzes administered within the class period are immediately discussed projecting on the screen selected panel submissions providing "real-time" feedback to the students who are also exposed to alternate solutions and approaches for a given problem (*HPL* key pedagogical design principles). Quizzes administered at the end of the class period are graded after the class and returned electronically the same day or the day after. The results are available for review by the next class and the instructor will be able to cover in the review portion of the class meeting those concepts that the students appear not to fully grasp.

From a student perspective, this approach caters to their perceived need for immediate gratification, the millennials generation (Sweeney, 2005), when they expect instant access to information and immediate feedback. Fig. 12 includes a couple of quizzes that features the input options for the students. Fig. 12(a) shows a student solution where the input was text via the tablet keyboard. In contrast, Fig. 12(b) shows a student solution where the input was digital ink via the tablet pen.

We have outlined above all the activities that we have developed over the course of the pilot studies for the Pneumatics and Hydraulics Systems course as well as we are going to describe a couple below of most recent introduction. The layout of the typical session has been refined from academic term to academic term based on the pedagogical knowledge outlined in the theoretical section targeting the nature of the millennial

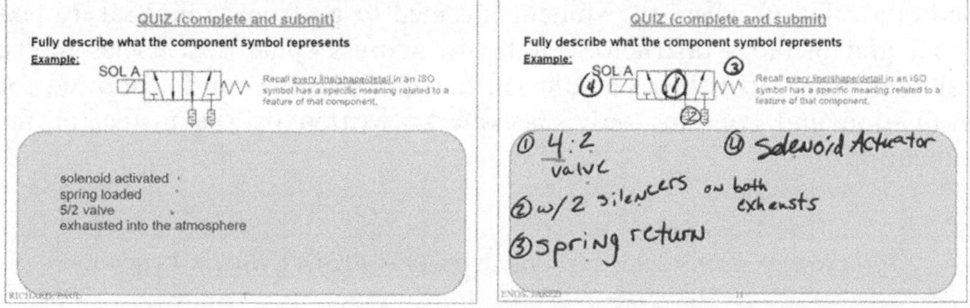

Fig. 12. A Within Class Quiz Comparing Student Input Methods, Keyboard versus Digital Pen. (a) Quiz Completed with Text as Input. (b) Quiz Completed with Digital Ink.

generation. By no means, are we implying that all college students conform to the digital native norms we have summarized such as enjoying gaming, media, and the need for collaboration. As we are going to present in the results section, our students seem to have responded well to these changes, but as other authors recommend, applying digital native generalizations should be approached with caution (Selwyn, 2009).

COURSE COMPLEMENTARY ACTIVITIES

Midterm Tests and Final Examination Review Sessions

One engagement activity that seems to have really fit well with the students is to perform review sessions as a way to prepare to midterms and particularly the final exam. The flexible seating allows setting the classroom into two opposing teams that compete for bonus points while solving practice problems. To cover the entire material, the two teams are divided into multiple groups and each group solves a problem of a different topic. Five or six rounds of problems are assembled. At the end of each round, all groups of both teams submit their panels and students themselves grade their work following a rubric. The instructor mainly acts as a facilitator and a judge. The instructor assumes the teaching role only when the two groups in both teams solving the same problem struggle with main or concepts have difficulty in solving it properly. The session is entirely student driven and the approach allows them to practice and be exposed to all the applicable content. This activity provides a learning environment that emphasizes collaboration and values peer-to-peer instruction; there is timely and complete formative assessment feedback with sufficient amount of student practice (*HPL* key pedagogical design principles). Fig. 13 presents the comparison between submissions of the same problem of two groups in opposing teams. Fig. 13(a) shows a solution where the students decided to go from digital ink to text input and includes instructor's notes to address some deficiencies in the solution. Fig. 13(b) shows a solution that fits well the rubric followed for evaluation and contains only checkmarks written by the instructor for validation.

Integrating Experience: Cooperative and Project-Based Learning

Regarding cooperative learning, millennials are collaborative, Oakley et al. (2007) summarized well that there are compelling reasons for assigning

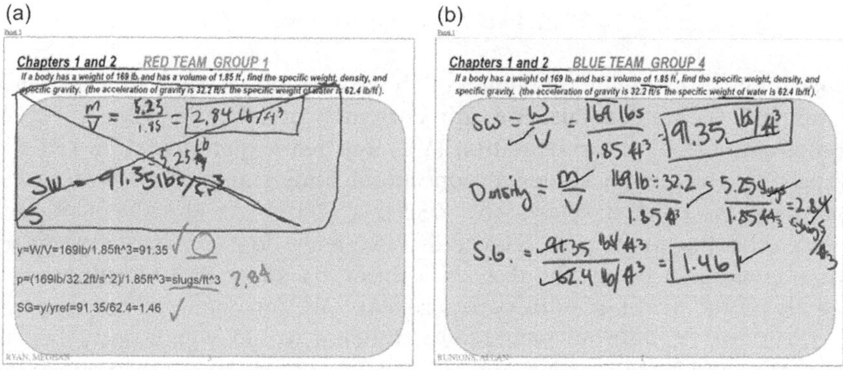

Fig. 13. Student Panel Submissions in a Final Examination Typical Review Session. (a) Panel with Instructor Notes. (b) Panel with Instructor Checkmarks.

students to work in teams on projects, with several well-known educational theories supporting the idea that students learn most effectively through interactions with others. As we already have discussed, an idea that hundreds of empirical research studies have confirmed, according to Smith et al. (2005) who found that cooperative learning leads to significant gains in academic success, quality of interactions with both classmates and faculty members, and attitudes toward the college experience when comparing the relative efficacy of cooperative, competitive, and individualistic learning.

In reference to project-based learning, millennials learn experientially and continuously, future engineers need to be adept communicators, good team members, and lifelong learners (Dym, Agogino, Eris, Frey, & Leifer, 2005). To complement the use of technology in the classroom and provide a beyond the textbook and authentic real-life experience, we introduced in the class a design project based on the renewed interest on fluid power technology particularly on transportation applications due to the fact that hydraulic hybrids can be cost-effective, achieve high fuel efficiency with low carbon emissions and can store and discharge energy much faster than electric batteries when compared to gas-electric hybrid systems. The objective of the project was to apply basic principles of fluid power technology to the control and propulsion of light-weight vehicles generating design specifications of the components of a fluid powered vehicle to compete in an institute-wide sanctioned green race challenge. The overarching goal of assigning the design project to the class is to guide the students into developing the ability to use what has been learned in the context of the classroom to a real-life application addressing one of the key issues in the cognitive sciences, transfer (Dym et al., 2005).

Virtual Experimentation

Appealing to the digital, gaming, collaborative, and learning by experience nature of the millennials, we are currently investigating the value of combining virtual experimentation (VE) and real experimentation (RE) in respect to changes in students' conceptual understanding of fluid power following the work developed by Zacharia (2007). As already mentioned above, the Pneumatic and Hydraulics Systems course has a laboratory component and being an abstract subject its successful teaching relies heavily on the use of laboratory experiments. We formulated the hypothesis that current engineering technology students would significantly benefit from the combination of VE and RE, allowing them to see the connection between abstract principles, equations, and the real-world applications in a collaborative manner.

To perform the laboratory activities, the students have at hand a manual containing a guide for each week session. As preparation for the laboratory session, we are requesting students to construct the circuits in Automation Studio™ (ASTM) and bring a print out with a brief explanation of how the circuits should work as a way to implement the combination of virtual and real experimentation. Preliminary results (Villasmil & Garrick, 2012) in comparing student skills in pre-lab preparation, laboratory report grades, and student survey indicate that incorporating a virtual experiment in conjunction with a real physical experiment appeared to be advantageous to student preparedness and the student's understanding of the course material. Fig. 14 presents a comparison between an early pre-lab of a simple circuit built by a single student that operates with some limitations in its intended objective with a complex circuit that perform flawlessly in compliance with the intended operation built by a group of students as the final laboratory of the course (bonus project).

THE CLASSROOM FACILITIES

To implement and evaluate the major features of the TRiLE holistic approach, a special conditioned classroom was used where the following needs are met:

- Student-instructor, student-student, student-note taker collaborative software to allow live document collaboration and information to be

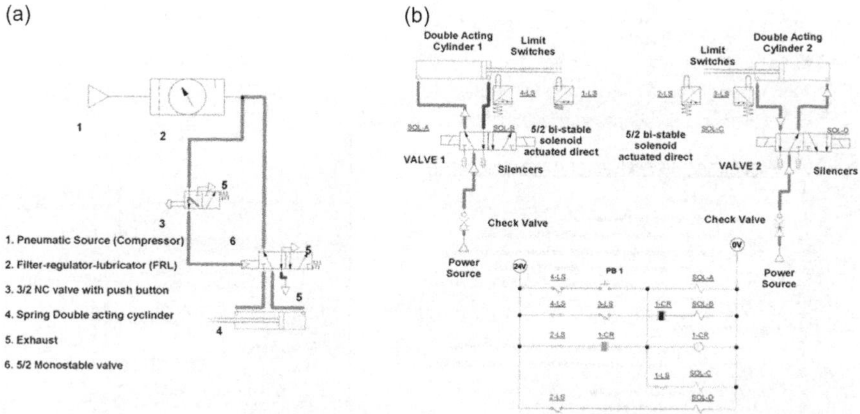

Fig. 14. Virtual Experimentation Pre-Lab Circuits. (a) Simple AS™ Circuit. (b) Complex AS™ Circuit.

easily pushed/pulled across a student 1:1 mobile computing environment, with the option of anonymous student request for feedback, flagging, and chat features. Currently DyKnow® class management software is being used (Fig. 15).

- A rich (more than multiple choice) student response system for formative assessment with immediate feedback that supports "just in time teaching." Currently DyKnow® class management software is being used.
- A mobile computing environment for integration of e-texts, notes, instructor presentation, videos, pictures, diagrams, digital inking into one file save in one "cloud" space. Currently tablets are being used, with note files saved in a personal student worldwide accessible server space. New slates are being evaluated as replacements (Fig. 16). The use of a tablet PC lecture environment has been reported to increase student interest and involvement (Berque, Johnson, & Jovanovic, 2001; Birmingham, DiStasi, & Welton, 2009; Chidanandan et al., 2007, 2008; Johri & Lohani, 2008; Lohani, Castles, Johri, Spangler, & Kibler, 2008; Sneller, 2007; Stanton, 2008).
- A visually immersive three projection screens for rich visual presentation of material (video, simulations, virtual experiments, remote experiments, video guest speakers to integrate engineering epistemology into the classroom). Fig. 17 presents the current back-lit projecting screen layout of the classroom.

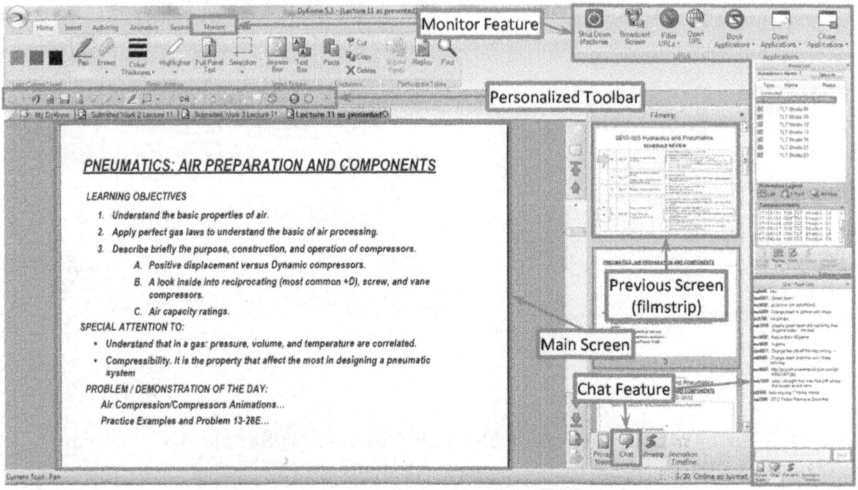

Fig. 15. The DyKnow® Environment.

Fig. 16. The Mobile Computing Environment. (a) Current Convertible Tablets. (b) Slates Currently Under Evaluation.

- Multiple input hardware sources, podium tablet and PC computers, document camera, DVD, VCR, auxiliary video (i.e., V-iPod), TV tuner, in-room cameras, campus video feeds, and Matrox feed with a touch-panel system able to mix, match, and compare any of these sources.

Fig. 17. Back-Lit Projector Screens Layout.

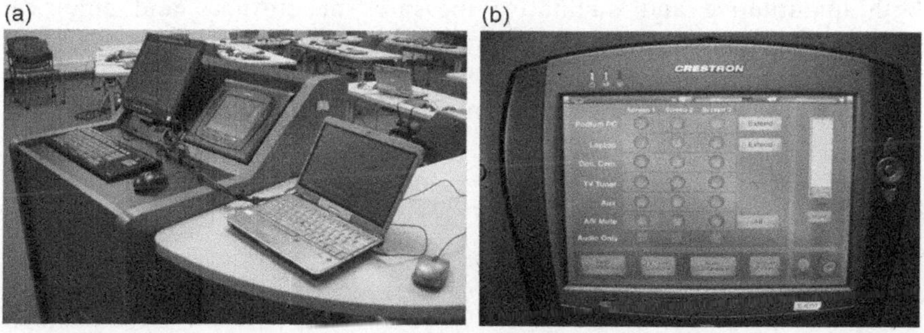

Fig. 18. Instructor Podium and Classroom Technology Control System. (a) Instructor Podium: Main Tablet and Auxiliary PC. (b) Creston Wireless Capable Control System.

Fig. 18 presents the classroom podium and a close-up of the audio and video wireless capable control system.

RESULTS

Data collection and subsequent analysis were guided by the project's research questions.

1. What is the student's attitude toward using a technology rich learning environment?
2. How do students report that they prefer to learn new technology (e.g., formal training and manuals)?
3. How does the TRiLE affect student academic performance in the class? Specifically does the TRiLE decrease student D and F grades and those withdrawing from the class (W-grade) (DFW)?
4. Does the TRiLE improve academic performance, as measured by class grades, for those students that are not academically strong (GPA less than 3.0)?
5. Does the TRiLE improve academic performance for traditionally underrepresented groups in engineering programs?
6. What learning features of the TRiLE do students report a preference for?

A uniform assessment approach was applied to both the control and experimental sections. This method of analysis included multiple examples, both quantitative and qualitative measures of attitudes and empirical success. The use of sometimes redundant measures in multiple analytical forms allows for a much more complete picture of the successes and limitations of the present research model. Comparative assessment data is composed of the following:

- Pre- and post-class technology surveys
- Student grades
- End of class TRiLE surveys
- End of class focus groups.

For each course, control and experimental sections with comparable student demographic (incoming GPA, ethnicity, and gender) were included in the assessment. Control and treatment groups were taught by the same professors. Prior to and after participation, quantitative surveys of students' experiences with and attitudes regarding technology were conducted. These surveys assessed students' preferences, comfort with, and engagement in, the technology rich environment, as well as selected learning-related characteristics, e.g., self-efficacy, confidence. The data was analyzed using appropriate parametric and non-parametric statistics. The key function of the self-report aspect of this intervention is to understand how the users of the tablet PC technology view their experiences; indeed, the potential usefulness of this technology as a meaningful pedagogical tool is mediated in part by the experiences and attitudes of the students involved.

Student grades were considered, specifically comparing outcomes for students in the experimental versus control settings. Comparisons were made overall, as well as considering individual subgroups that might have been differentially affected. Examples of these subgroups include racial and ethnic categorization, age, gender, year in school, etc.

At the end of the term, students in both experimental and control classes were surveyed as to their experiences in their classes. Those in the experimental classes were asked about the specific interventions used, their sense of effectiveness, and preference for those technologies in this and other related classes.

At the end of each course, focus groups were held with the students who participated in the treatment classes. (Focus groups were also held with students who participated in the control classes, but given their lack of experience with the experimental interventions, their responses did not include information about the TRiLE, and thus their focus group responses are not included here.) Students were invited to participate in the focus group during the last class period. Their participation was incentivized by providing pizza and soda. With signed student releases, the focus groups were videotaped to allow independent qualitative analysis of the groups by the research team. The focus groups followed up on questions raised by the survey and explored students' perceptions and experiences of the technology rich learning environment. Focus group transcripts and video were analyzed qualitatively using conventional content analysis (Hsieh & Shannon, 2005), as well as analytic induction (Erickson, 1986). The results of the focus group provided important contextual information to the research team so that they may revise and adjust the curriculum and pedagogical techniques used in the technology rich learning environment. Key issues considered were perceptions of the usability, subjective beliefs about the academic effects, and the level of interest in extending the use of the technology rich environment in both similar and more diverse settings

Pre- and Post-Class Technology Surveys

Pre- and post-surveys were given to assess the students' attitude toward technology and its use in the classroom. This survey was developed and used for a project at Concordia University that studied the impact of using tablet PCs on student participation and feedback (Stevenson, 2006). Students in all classes (both experimental and control) were assessed using these surveys. Participants (in both control and treatment groups) reported that they felt comfortable learning about computer technology (99% agreed or strongly agreed), 77% agreed or strongly agreed that they enjoyed using computer technology in their classes, and 72% agreed or strongly agreed that using a computer makes tasks more interesting. Although the majority of the students did not feel anxious when using computer technology, 20% did indicate that using computer technology results in some anxiety.

In the post-survey given to the treatment condition group, 90% indicated that they enjoyed learning about how computer technology can be used within their major compared to 83% in the pre-survey. The findings of the technology survey support that the students in this study were generally open to technology and using technology in the classroom.

Additionally, the survey included questions to determine the way students best learn computer applications. Being required to complete a task using an application, taking a workshop on the application and playing around with the application were most often cited as the way the students best learn a computer application. They were less likely to read the application manual, get one-on-one assistance from an expert, and use online help and tutorials. "Playing around with" an application was one of the most highly used methods reported by the students (44% agreed or strongly agreed).

The survey included an open ended response question that asked if the students had any additional comments related to the use of technology in the classroom. Sample comments included:

> I've used the computers in the (Teaching and Learning Technology) TLT Studio before and it is a great enhancement to learning.

> I really enjoy the use of computer (in class) because that way the entire class can work together in solving problems. I feel like I learn better.

Student Grades

The first quarter when the TRiLE approach was utilized, student performance was assessed by administering similar test questions, homework assignments, and quizzes and comparing the results to students in the previous classes. All students in the first class using the TRiLE approach ($n = 27$) achieved an A, B, or C grade, and none of the students received a D or F, and there were no student withdrawals. Using a Poisson distribution, we have a 99% level of confidence that this experiment sample is different from the previous population in terms of overall class performance.

One of the evaluation techniques used in study reviewed student DFW rates prior to the TRiLE and after the implementation of the TRiLE. Similar

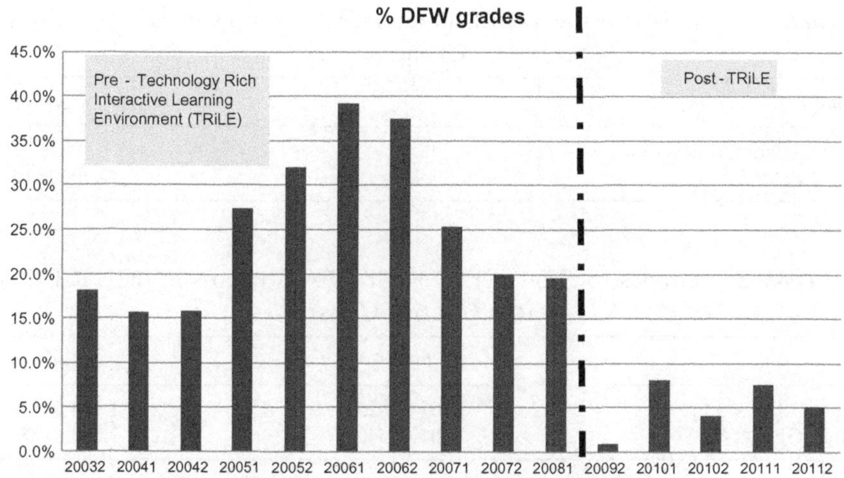

Fig. 19. Second Year Fluid Power Historical DFW Rates.

to the initial study we saw a decrease in DFW rates (Fig. 19) with particular benefit to academically at-risk students GPA > 2.0, but < 3.0 (Fig. 19).

Analysis of DFW rates for control versus treatment groups for the TRiLE project have shown rates of 22.6% for the control groups versus 9% for the treatment group. Using a hypothesis test between the differences in proportions in DFW rate, the difference in DFWs from the control to the treatment sample is statistically significant ($Z = 2.33$ versus a critical $z = 1.96$ (95% confidence)). The decrease in DFW is evidenced over time, with different instructors and different courses. These results support that the TRiLE approach is effective in lowering DFWs which research has shown to correlate with improved retention in engineering programs.

A significant difference in grades was found between the treatment (TRiLE) and control groups ($t(316) = 6.587$, $p < .001$). The treatment grades were higher than control grades as shown in Table 2.

Grades were also analyzed for minority African American, Latin American, Native American (AALANA) and deaf/hard of hearing students with no significant difference in the mean. The analyses of grades suggest higher grades and bigger difference for students with lower GPA (below a 3.0), but that may be due to a ceiling effect as shown in Table 3.

Table 4 displays the findings that higher grades for students who are in their third or higher year were noted, but a bigger difference in grades for second year students.

Table 2. Grades for the TRiLE (Treatment) Group versus the Control Group.

TRiLE	Control
Mean (standard deviation)	
3.192 (0.8500)	2.500 (1.014)

Table 3. Grades for Low versus High GPA Students in the TRiLE versus Control Classes.

	TRiLE	Control
Low GPA (<3.0)	2.507 (0.8259)	1.904 (0.8687)
High GPA (>3.0)	3.607 (0.5407)	3.263 (0.5833)

Table 4. Grades for Second Year Students versus Students in Year 3 or Above in the TRiLE versus Control Classes.

	TRiLE	Control
Second year	3.116 (0.9312)	2.343 (1.0831)
Third year or higher	3.214 (0.6118)	2.558 (0.9862)

Initial data shows that women received higher grades than men in the TRiLE classes, while in the control classes, women's grades were lower and were more broadly distributed. With a sample size of only 38 women, this is considered a preliminary finding and not significant, but is a trend the team will continue to monitor (Table 5).

End of Class TRiLE Survey Findings

At the end of all the classes, students were surveyed ($n=525$) to evaluate their preferences, interaction, and engagement in the class and conducted videotaped focus groups. Both control and treatment groups were included in the focus groups. The demographics of the students surveyed are shown in Table 6. No first year student classes were included in the study due to the focus on historically difficult engineering technology classes which typically

Table 5. Grades for Men versus Women in the TRiLE versus Control Classes.

	TRiLE	Control
Male	3.160 (0.8684)	2.568 (0.9966)
Female	3.474 (0.6118)	2.105 (1.0485)

Table 6. Student Demographics in Study.

Academic Year Distribution	
First year	0%
Second year	38%
Third year	31%
Fourth year	10%
Fifth year	21%
Entering Class GPA Distribution	
2.0–2.5	11%
2.5–3.0	36%
3.0–3.5	36%
3.5–4.0	17%

occur during the second, third, and fourth years. RIT has a cooperative education program with students working in the engineering field during their fourth and fifth years for a total of one year of employment. Therefore, fourth and fifth year students are similar to a senior (fourth year) class academically at a traditional university.

The student's GPAs ranged from 2.0 to 4.0 on a 4.0 scale as shown in Table 2. The entering grade distribution was close to a normal distribution. All of the students were full time students. The majority of students were between 18 and 22 years of age with only 3.7% "non-traditional" students who ranged in age from 23 to 40 years old. Before taking the class in the technology rich learning environment, 83% reported that they usually took notes by hand. Eight percent reported that they usually took notes using a laptop or desktop computer during class lectures and 14% reported that they usually do not take notes during lectures.

From both the treatment and control groups, only 15% of the students preferred or strongly preferred a standard lecture learning environment, with only 9% strongly preferring standard lecture. In the survey, the "standard environment" was defined as involving instructors talking to the students and no classroom technology. In contrast, 66% of the students in the treatment sections reported to prefer or strongly prefer the TRiLE classroom environment: lecture with DyKnow, tablet PCs, and PowerPoint lectures with animations and videos. Twenty-seven percent strongly preferred this environment. The students from the TRiLE group preferred or strongly preferred lecture environments that involved the following features (% of preferred/strongly preferred):

- Instructor's notes directly over the presented PowerPoint during lecture (77%)
- Animations or videos incorporated into the PowerPoint lecture (73%)
- The technology rich learning environment features (tablets, collaboration, multi-screen projection) (66%)
- Real-time integration of lecture notes and student's personal notes into one document (71%).

Students from both the treatment and control groups indicated that they preferred/strongly preferred the following:

- Group problem solving work (74%)
- Example problems completed by the instructor (74%).

All of the students who rated that they "preferred/strongly preferred" lecture environment features were consistent over the academic year of the students except for the preference for the technology rich learning environment which increased with student academic year.

Students in the treatment group responded that they were more likely to take notes in the technology rich lecture environment. The second year students reported a lower agreestrongly agree than third, fourth, or fifth year students on this issue. Students with the lowest GPA entering the class (2.02.5 GPA) reported with a greater likelihood to take notes in the technology rich environment as compared to the higher GPA groups.

Students in the treatment group also reported that they were more likely to use these notes for both homework and pre-test reviews, with the upper-class students reporting a greater agreement level. They indicated the notes taken in this lecture environment were more thorough and helped them better comprehend the material. The students with the lowest GPA entering the class (2.0 to 2.5 GPA) had a greater agree-strongly agree reported than the other higher GPA groups (3.0-4.0 GPA) for each of these measures: more likely to use notes for homework, more likely to use notes for tests, more thorough notes, and improved comprehension due to notes in technology rich environment. This was especially true for the reported improved comprehension of the material. Students reported that the ability to store a single comprehensive file made it advantageous rather than having written notes separate from the instructor's presentation material and annotations (Garrick & Koon, 2010a, 2010b). We also found that deaf and hard of hearing students taking the class also benefited considerably from the multi-screen visual presentation and the ability to see the instructor's and the note taker's annotations simultaneously with the interpreter.

Students in the treatment group preferred solving problems in class using the technology rich environment. They felt that completing exercises both individually (76% agree-strongly agree) and in group format (74% agree-strongly agree) helped them learn the material better than just watching the instructor complete problems. They overwhelmingly agreed that working virtually in groups was an effective method to do in-class problem solving. From the focus groups, several students said that group problem solving was the "best way" to learn. The ability to make corrections seeing them immediately and the ability to watch the process were the most common positive comments. Overall, 73% of the students said they would recommend the use of the TRiLE environment for their engineering technology classes.

End of Class Focus Groups

The end of class focus group followed up on questions raised by the survey and explored students' perceptions and experiences of the technology rich learning environment. Consideration was given to the students' perceptions of the usability, subjective beliefs about the academic effects, and the level of interest in extending the use of the technology rich environment in both similar and more diverse settings. The group facilitator asked questions about the use of the tablet PCs, group work, note taking, preparation for tests, and overall learning. An independent evaluator reviewed video recordings of the focus groups and scored each student remark as positive or negative in one of several categories. Table 7 shows a summary of responses.

The summary of focus group comments is from both the treatment and control groups except for statements directly relating to the technology rich classroom.

- *Active learning* – Comments were considered to address active learning if they mentioned participation, being more interesting or enjoyable. All comments about active learning were positive, e.g., "I really felt involved

Table 7. Focus Group Response Summary.

Focus Group Comments	Proportion Positive
Active learning	100.0%
Learning	100.0%
Engagement	93.3%
Preparation for tests	80.0%
Note taking	71.4%
Group work	70.0%
Involvement in process	50.0%

in the class." Students also said the use of the PC and the ability to watch the process on the screen allowed them to "immerse in the material" and do less note writing. Other said seeing mistakes on the screen and reacting immediately were beneficial.

- *Learning* – Learning comments were direct statements about how much was learned rather than the process. Though there were fewer comments on this dynamic, all of them were positive.
- *Engagement* – Student comments related to being actively involved in the classroom process were considered measures of engagement. These comments were distinguished from active learning in that they were more directly about process. All but one student comment (93.3%) in this area supported the use of technology rich environment in increasing engagement.
- *Preparation for tests* – Comments related to the usefulness of the technology rich environment in preparing for tests were mostly positive (80.0%), though only five students made comments on this topic.
- *Note taking* – Using technology rich environment to take notes was the subject of many comments and most were positive (71.4%). Students who did not feel the technology rich environment were helpful generally compared them to paper and pencil and said they still preferred to have their notes in a notebook. The positive comments reflected the value of later access via the Internet and being able to see corrected notes resulting from the professor's comments, class discussion, or workgroup process.
- *Group work* – One of the primary functions of the technology rich environment is the use in group work. This area received the most comments with more than two thirds being positive. Several students said that group problem solving was the "best way" to learn. The ability to make corrections and see them immediately and the ability to watch the

process were the most common positive comments. One student felt that group work reduced the incentive to do work and two students felt it was impersonal.

- *Involvement in process* – Being involved in the process was reflected in comments directly related to what happened in classroom rather than the result. These comments were generally in the form of concrete suggestions such as using two slides, one reflecting their own work and one reflecting the group or the professor's work. Half of the comments about process were generally supportive of the way the technology rich environment was used.

Several students felt that assigning roles in groups, e.g., leader, scribe, did not work, and that groups did not adhere to roles. Most students commented they really felt involved in the class. Students also said the use of the technology rich environment together with the ability to watch the process on the screen allowed them to "immerse in the material" and do less note writing. Other said seeing mistakes on the screen and reacting immediately was beneficial.

Several students in the non-technology rich environment group (control group) said they were aware of the technology rich environment and would like to have access to that setting. Of the students in the non-technology rich environment, only 36.8% of the comments about group work were positive as compared to 70% in the technology rich environment. Negative comments reflected dissatisfaction with trying to work within group roles and with the logistics of working on large sheets of paper. One of the "control groups" included the use of active learning techniques but did not involve the use of technology (tablet PC's, software, etc ...). This group used large tablets of paper for group work in class. Students felt that making corrections was cumbersome and messy on paper.

CONCLUSIONS

The TRiLE approach in the classroom helps students succeed in engineering classes. The traditional lecture "stand and deliver" or "teaching by telling" approach, while commonly used in engineering classes, needs to be re-examined as a method for introductory engineering courses. These traditional teaching methods do not take advantage of current technology available to help students construct and internalize accurate understandings of fundamental engineering concepts through actively engaging those concepts.

Overall, the students with a lower GPA entering the courses perceived a greater benefit from this learning environment and recommended using the technology rich lecture environment. These results appear in agreement with those found in the larger work of Hake and others that an interactive and engaging learning environment can result in improved student learning of the material (Felder, 1995; Hake, 1998; Johnson et al., 1998b; Terenzini et al., 2001). The technology rich environment allows the instructor to implement an interactive and engaging learning environment within the digital media of tablet PCs and collaborative (DyKnow) software. This environment also increases student likelihood of note taking and using these notes especially for the attrition vulnerable population with lower GPAs.

The technology rich environment used in this study addresses the experiential and exploratory nature of the students currently enrolling in colleges across the world, the millennial generation (Sweeny, 2008), who get lots of interactivity and feedback about what works and what does not. In this study, student interactions seemed very positive and the faculty felt that the students were more engaged. Nevertheless, we were unable to unequivocally demonstrate these effects. In addition, the engineering faculty was unable to construct an instrument for students where they would rate their own sense of engagement and learning ability, and develop an overall understanding of their objective level of comprehension.

This project's findings are in agreement with other studies that involved tablet PCs only or tablet PCs and collaborative software (Berque et al., 2001; Birmingham et al., 2009; Chidanandan et al., 2007; Chidanandan et al., 2008; Johri & Lohani, 2008; Lohani et al., 2008; Sneller, 2007; Stanton, 2008). These studies also showed increased student interest and involvement in engineering and science classroom studies. This material is based upon work supported by the National Science Foundation under Grant No. 1137106.

REFERENCES

Bergvall, V. L., Sorby, S. A., & Worthen, J. B. (1994). Thawing the freezing climate for woman: Views from both sides of the desk. *Journal of Woman and Minorities in Science and Engineering*, *1*(4), 323–346.

Berque, D., Johnson, D. K., & Jovanovic, L. (2001). *Teaching theory of computation using pen-based computers and an electronic whiteboard.* Paper presented at the Proceedings of the

6th Annual SIGCSE Conference on Innovation and Technology in Computer Science Education, June 25, 2001–June 27, 2001, Cantenbury, UK.

Birmingham, W., DiStasi, V., & Welton, G. (2009). *Learning style, student motivation, and active learning*. Paper presented at the 2009 ASEE Annual Conference and Exposition, June 14, 2009–June 17, 2009, Austin, TX, USA.

Booth, W. C., Colomb, G. G., & Williams, J. M. (2003). *The craft of research*. Chicago, IL: University of Chicago press.

Borrego, M. J., Padilla, M. A., Zhang, G., Ohland, M. W., & Anderson, T. J. (2005). *Graduation rates, grade-point average, and changes of major of female and minority students entering engineering*. Paper presented at the Frontiers in Education – 35th Annual Conference 2005, FIE' 05, October 19, 2005–October 22, 2005, Indianapolis, IN, USA.

Bowen, C. W. (2000). A quantitative literature review of cooperative learning effects on high school and college. *Journal of Chemical Education*, *77*(1), 116–119.

Bransford, J. D., Brown, A. L., Cocking, S., Donovan, S., & Pelligrino, J. (2000). *How people learn: Brain, mind, experience, and school*. Washington, DC: National Academies Press.

Busch-Vishniac, I. J., & Jarosz, J. P. (2004). Can diversity in the undergraduate engineering population be enhanced through curricular change? *Journal of Woman and Minorities in Science and Engineering*, *10*(3), 255–282.

Chidanandan, A., DeVasher, R., Ferro, P., Fisher, D., Mitra-Kirtley, S., Merkle, L., … Williams, J. M. (2007). Work in progress – Assessing the impact of penbased computing and collaboration-facilitating software in the classroom. In *37th ASEE/IEEE Frontiers in Education Conference, FIE 2007*, Milwaukee, WI (pp. T1G17–T1G18).

Chidanandan, A., Ferro, P., Frolik, J., Hirotani, M., Schmidt, K., Walter, D., & Williams, J. (2008). Panel session-pen-based computing in the engineering and science classroom: Implementation scenarios from three institutions. In *38th ASEE/IEEE Frontiers in Education Conference, FIE 2008*, Saratoga Springs, NY (pp. F4G1–F4G2).

Consortium for Student Retention Data Exchange – CSRDE.

Crouch, C. H., & Mazur, E. (2001). Peer instruction: Ten years of experience and results. *American Journal of Physics*, *69*(9), 970–977.

Dell, E. M., Garrick, R. D., & Villasmil, L. A. (2011). The impact of the use of tablet PCs paired with active learning techniques on engineering education. *Journal of Applications and Practices in Engineering Education*, *2*(2), 66–76.

Dym, C. L., Agogino, A. M., Eris, O., Frey, D. D., & Leifer, L. J. (2005). Engineering design thinking, teaching, and learning. *Journal of Engineering Education*, *94*(1), 103–120.

EDUCAUSE. (2012). Flipped classrooms. 7 Things you should know about …™. *EDUCAUSE*. Retrieved from http://www.educause.edu/library/resources/7-things-you-should-know-about-flipped-classrooms. Accessed on February 7, 2012.

Enriquez, A. (2009). Using tablet pcs to enhance student performance in an introductory circuits course. In *Proceedings: 2009 American Society of Engineering Education/Pacific Southwest Section Conference*, San Diego, CA (pp. 19–20).

Erickson, F. (1986). *Qualitative methods in research on teaching* (3rd ed.). New York, NY: Macmillan.

Felder, R. M. (1995). A longitudinal study of engineering student performance and retention. IV. Instructional methods and student responses to them. *Journal of Engineering Education*, *84*(4), 361–367.

Fortenberry, N. L., Sullivan, J. F., Jordan, P. N., & Knight, D. W. (2007). Engineering Education Research Aids Instruction. *Science*, *317*(5842), 1175–1176.

Garrick, R. D., & Koon, M. (2010a). *A mixed-method comparison evaluation on the impact of tablet PCs and pen-based technology for a pneumatics and hydraulics class*. Paper presented at the American Society for Engineering Education, St. Lawrence Section 2010 Meeting.

Garrick, R. D., & Koon, M. (2010b). Using tablet PCs and pen-based technology to address poor student performance in an engineering technology class. In R. H. Reed & D. A. Berque (Eds.), *The impact of tablet PCs and pen-based technology on education: Going mainstream* (p. 176). West Lafayette, IN: Purdue University Press.

Hake, R. R. (1998). Interactive-engagement versus traditional methods: A six-thousand-student survey of mechanics test data for introductory physics courses. *American Journal of Physics*, *66*(1), 64–74.

Harris, B. J., Rhoads, T. R., Walden, S. E., Murphy, T. J., Meissler, R., & Reynolds, A. (2004). Gender equity in industrial engineering: A pilot study. *NWSA Journal*, *16*(1), 186–193.

Hsieh, H., & Shannon, S. E. (2005). Three approaches to qualitative content analysis. *Qualitative Health Research*, *15*, 1277–1288.

Johnson, D. W., Johnson, R. T., & Smith, K. A. (1991). *Cooperative learning: Increasing college faculty instructional productivity*. ASHE-ERIC Report No. 4. The George Washington University School of Education and Human Development.

Johnson, D. W., Johnson, R. T., & Smith, K. A. (1998a). *Active learning: Cooperation in the college classroom*.

Johnson, D. W., Johnson, R. T., & Smith, K. A. (1998b). Cooperative learning returns to college: What evidence is there that it works? *Change 30*, 26–35.

Johnson, D. W., Johnson, R. T., & Smith, K. A. (2007). The state of cooperative learning in postsecondary and professional settings. *Educational Psychology Review*, 19, 15–29.

Johri, A., & Lohani, V. (2008). *Representational literacy and participatory learning in large engineering classes using pen-based computing*. Paper presented at the 2008 IEEE Frontiers in Education Conference, October 22–25, 2008, Piscataway, NJ, USA.

Lohani, V., Castles, R., Johri, A., Spangler, D., & Kibler, D. (2008). *Analysis of tablet PC based learning experiences in freshman to junior level engineering courses*. Paper presented at the 2008 ASEE Annual Conference and Exposition, June 22, 2008–June 24, 2008, Pittsburg, PA, USA.

Lord, S. M., Brawner, C. E., Camacho, M. M., Layton, R. A., Long, R. A., Ohland, M. W., & Wasburn, M. H. (2008). *Work in progress – Effect of climate and pedagogy on persistence of women in engineering programs*. Paper presented at the 38th ASEE/IEEE Frontiers in Education Conference, FIE 2008, October 22, 2008–October 25, 2008, Saratoga Springs, NY, USA.

MacGregor, J., Cooper, J., Smith, K. A., & Robinson, P. (2000). *Strategies for energizing large classes: From small groups to learning communities*. San Francisco, CA: Jossey-Bass.

Margerum-Leys, J., & Marx, R. W. (2002). Teacher knowledge of educational technology: A case study of student/mentor teacher pairs. *Journal of Educational Computing Research*, *26*(4), 427–462.

Marra, R. M., Rodgers, K. A., Shen, D. M., & Bogue, B. (2012). Leaving engineering: A multi-year single institution study. *Journal of Engineering Education*, *101*(1), 6–27.

Millis, B. J., & Cottell, P. G. (1997). *Cooperative learning for higher education faculty*. Phoenix, AZ: Oryx Press.

Mishra, P., & Koehler, M. J. (2006). Technological pedagogical content knowledge: A framework for teacher knowledge. *Teachers College Record*, *108*(6), 1017–1054.

Nicholas, J. B. (2011). *Investigating engineering educators' views on the use of educational technology: A Q methodology study*. ProQuest Dissertations and Theses.

Oakley, B. A., Hanna, D. M., Kuzmyn, Z., & Felder, R. M. (2007). Best practices involving teamwork in the classroom: Results from a survey of 6435 engineering student respondents. *IEEE Transactions on Education*, *50*(3), 266–272.

Ohland, M. W., Sheppard, S. D., Lichtenstein, G., Eris, O., Chachra, D., & Layton, R. A. (2008). Persistence, engagement, and migration in engineering programs. *Journal of Engineering Education*, *97*(Compendex), 259–278.

Parthum, M. (2009). *Teaching with a tablet PC, a new technology for the classroom and academic usage*. Paper presented at the 2009 ASEE Annual Conference and Exposition, June 14, 2009–June 17, 2009, Austin, TX, USA.

Prince, M. (2004). Does active learning work? A review of the research. *Journal of Engineering Education*, *93*(Compendex), 223–231.

Rawat, K. S., Elahi, M., & Massiha, G. H. (2008). *A pilot project in evaluating the use of tablet PCs and supporting technologies in sophomore electronic technology courses*. Paper presented at the IAJC-IJME International Conference on Engineering & Technology, Nashville, TN, USA.

Salter, D. W. (2003). Women's views of the factors that encourage and discourage classroom participation. *Journal of College Student Development*, *44*(6), 831–844.

Sax, L. J. (1994). Mathematical self-concept: How college reinforces the gender gap. *Research in Higher Education*, *35*(2), 141.

Selwyn, N. (2009). The digital native-Myth and reality. *Aslib Proceedings*, *61*(4), 364–379.

Seymour, E., & Hewitt, N. (1997). *Talking about leaving: Why undergraduates leave the sciences*. Boulder, CO: Westview Press.

Smith, K. A., Douglas, T. C., & Cox, M. F. (2009). Supportive teaching and learning strategies in STEM education. In R. Baldwin (Ed.), *Creating a culture/climate that supports undergraduate teaching and learning in STEM*. Vol. 117. (pp. 19–32). New Directions for Teaching and Learning. San Francisco, CA: Jossey-Bass.

Smith, K. A., & Goldstein, H. (1982). *Cooperative learning in engineering workshop*. Paper presented at the Proceedings-1982 Frontiers in Education Conference., Columbia, SC, USA.

Smith, K. A., Johnson, D. W., & Johnson, R. T. (1981). Structuring learning goals to meet the goals of engineering education. *Engineering Education*, *72*(Compendex), 221–226.

Smith, K. A., Sheppard, S. D., Johnson, D. W., & Johnson, R. T. (2005). Pedagogies of Engagement: Classroom-Based Practices. *Journal of Engineering Education*, *94*(1), 87–101.

Sneller, J. (2007). *The tablet PC classroom: Erasing borders, stimulating activity, enhancing communication*. Paper presented at the 2007 37th Annual Frontiers in Education Conference-Global Engineering: Knowledge Without Borders, Opportunities Without Passports, October 10–13, 2007, Piscataway, NJ, USA.

Springer, L., Stanne, M. E., & Donovan, S. S. (1999). Effects of small-group learning on undergraduates in science, mathematics, engineering, and technology: A meta-analysis. *Review of Educational Research*, *69*(1), 21.

Stanton, K. (2008). *Work in progress – Enhancement of problem solving techniques with tablet PC-based learning technologies*. Paper presented at the 38th ASEE/IEEE Frontiers in

Education Conference, FIE 2008, October 22, 2008–October 25, 2008, Saratoga Springs, NY, USA.

Stevenson, J. (2006). Using tablet PCs to enhance student participation and feedback. Retrieved from http://faculty.concordia.edu/jims/Technology_for_Teaching/HPTechnologyforTeaching-ProjectUpdate-CUA.htm#Impactstudent. Accessed on March 29, 2012.

Sweeny, R. (2008). *Are engineering students typical millennials? A live focus group.* Paper presented at the American Society for Engineering Education, Pittsburgh, PA, USA.

Sweeney, R. T. (2005). Reinventing library buildings and services for the millennial generation. *Library Administration & Management*, *19*(4), 165–175.

Tapscott, D. (2009). *Grown up digital: How the net generation is changing your world.* New York, NY: McGraw-Hill.

Terenzini, P. T., Cabrera, A. F., Colbeck, C. L., Parente, J. M., & Bjorklund, S. A. (2001). Collaborative learning vs. lecture/discussion: Students' reported learning gains. *Journal of Engineering Education*, *90*(1), 123–130.

Villasmil, L. A., & Garrick, R. D. (2012). Implementing a virtual laboratory for a directed and synchronous student learning experience in fluid power. In *119th Annual Conference and Exposition of the American Society for Engineering Education* (ASEE 2012).

Vogt, C. M. (2007). Social cognitive construct validation. *Determining Women's and Men's Success in Engineering Programs*, *78*(3), 337–364.

Wirth, K. R., & Perkins, D. (2012). *Learning to learn.* Retrieved from http://www.macalester.edu/geology/wirth/learning.doc. Accessed in April 2012.

Zacharia, Z. C. (2007). Comparing and combining real and virtual experimentation: An effort to enhance students' conceptual understanding of electric circuits. *Journal of Computer Assisted Learning*, *23*(2), 120–132.

LEARNING TOOL OR DISTRACTION: STUDENT RESPONSES TO THE USE OF iOS DEVICES

Lauren Miller Griffith and Brian A. Roberts

ABSTRACT

Using a navigational metaphor, this chapter introduces readers to the sometimes stormy seas of implementing new learning technologies into a course, especially those that have pre-existing design flaws (lack of rigor, accountability, content and time constraints, etc.). In addition to presenting what we feel are some best practices in using iOS devices, we analyze nearly 600 students' reactions to these devices related to how they were used in a 100 level survey style course. For every student who told us that they were "awesome" or helped them "learn and discover new things through [the] course," there were multiple students who felt that "they are damaging [the] learning experience because they are distracting." The central argument of this chapter is that without engaging in a dialectic course (re)design process that puts the affordances of the learning technology in conversation with classic principles of instructional design, the utility of adding iOS devices will be limited at

Increasing Student Engagement and Retention using Classroom Technologies: Classroom Response Systems and Mediated Discourse Technologies
Cutting-edge Technologies in Higher Education, Volume 6E, 307–336

ISSN: 2044-9968/doi:10.1108/S2044-9968(2013)000006E013

best and distracting at worst. The instructors in the course described here did use the devices in a variety of ways and many students were satisfied with the learning experience. However, for others, the combination of the course being too easy and too forgiving along with putting the Internet into students' hands was a recipe for incivility and off-task uses of technology.

INTRODUCTION

Uncharted waters can be scary to both experienced and unsalted sailors alike. The same idea applies to faculty as they attempt to make a change in their course, even more so if it involves learning new technologies. Working in faculty development, the authors are not the captains of the ship described here, but rather seasoned crewmembers that assist the faculty in a variety of roles including as navigators, deck hands, and more. In this chapter, we intend to make these uncharted waters somewhat more navigable for those brave enough to head out into new territory by sharing our experiences, observations, insights, findings, and recommendations. This chapter reflects our years of firsthand experience in supporting multiple teams of faculty members in the classroom, extensive classroom observations, student surveys, and focus groups in the Fall 2011 semester sections of the course discussed here.

We argue that implementing educational technology hardware and software can only be effective and beneficial to the learning environment if the faculty and administration are willing to work through a process of self-assessment and course (re)design. This necessary process includes, at minimum, the following steps:

1. Identify the issues of concern from all perspectives. If there is not a problem to solve, consider what it is that you wish to accomplish via the incorporation of a new technology. Ask yourself why you are considering changing the techniques that you are currently using.
2. Research both traditional (no tech) and technology-based potential solutions to the problem identified in step one while always keeping financial considerations in mind.
3. Identify support resources that are available to work with to implement the potential solutions. This could include help desk staff, instructional designers, instructional technologists, colleagues, the Internet, vendor resources, training opportunities, and more.

4. Evaluate your comfort level with changing the way you are going to deliver content, especially if it is going to require technology.
5. Dedicate yourself to learning and truly understanding how the method or technology works in order to be able to use it as effectively as possible. Consider others' success, failures, and best practices.
6. Be willing to (re)design your course with an eye toward rigor and accountability to ensure that your students are benefiting from the new method or technology that you choose to implement.
7. Develop a multi-staged implementation plan that includes evaluation of effectiveness from day one.

Without addressing each of these steps, the likelihood of a successful implementation will be low. Further, we argue that if not properly planned and executed, the use of the device will impact the learning environment and student experience in a negative manner as this case will demonstrate.

The remainder of this chapter will introduce readers to the history of the course including the rationale for adding iOS devices as well as the tools that have been used in this course and an explanation of how the technologies were used. We also offer personal experiences and scholarly literature in support of the utility of these tools, present the results of our research in this course, and make recommendations for using these devices to construct the best possible learning environment and experience for everyone involved.

ABOUT THE COURSE

The course from which we draw these conclusions is a 16 week survey course at the 100 level offered to more than 600 students each semester, the majority of whom are freshmen. Students must perform at a satisfactory level in this course before they are accepted into the related program of study. In short, it is a gateway course designed to introduce students to their potential future profession and help them decide if this course of study is truly something they want to pursue. In our sample, roughly 90% of the students determined that they still want to pursue this program upon the completion of the course.

The course has historically been team-taught by three faculty members with the assistance of one graduate student. Prior to 2009, there were only two learning technologies being utilized in the course: a learning management system (LMS) and a radio frequency classroom response system ("clickers"). The trio of faculty teaching during this timeframe, now retired, relied heavily upon the use of clickers to encourage discussion as well as to monitor student attendance in the course. The LMS was used to deliver course information and documents, host asynchronous discussions, monitor grades, and simplify communication.

Nearing the end of their careers, the previous instructors recognized mobile learning as an emerging trend within higher education. Via the combined efforts of the faculty, administrators and various campus resources, the decision was made to use iOS devices in the course to align with this trend. Because the cost of the iOS device was far greater than that of a simple radio frequency clicker, the parties involved determined that they would need to intensify their utilization of the iOS devices to justify the more expensive hardware.

The resultant plan for using the iOS devices was to incorporate a variety of learning technologies and mobile learning scenarios into the course, program, and university as a whole. Each student in this course was and still is required to obtain an iOS device (minimum iPod touch) to use throughout the semester. In order to defer the increased cost of this far more advanced device, students were given the option to either use an iOS device that they already owned, purchase one, or rent one from the campus bookstore for an amount equivalent to that of the basic clickers that had been used in previous semesters. Intended uses of the device were for student engagement via interaction primarily with the following systems: clickers, podcasting, backchanneling, and the LMS. Their goal was to increase students' engagement in the course both in and out of the classroom while also encouraging them to become more literate in a variety of learning technologies that may serve them well in their future educational and professional endeavors. After two semesters of using the iOS devices, the original trio chose to retire, thus passing the technology-enhanced course to the current trio of faculty and a new graduate assistant.

Each member of this new team is assigned one of the four back-to-back face-to-face sections that are offered 3 days per week, Mondays, Wednesdays, and Fridays at 8:00, 9:00, 10:00 and 11:00 a.m. Each of the instructors brings decades of experience working in the profession into the university classroom setting. This teaching team has been involved in the planning, content creation, presentation, and assessment of each of the sections for two semesters prior to the one in which we carried out our observations, surveys, and focus groups. This chapter is based upon the trio's third semester of teaching the course together.

IDENTIFYING THE KEY ISSUES

In order to gain a well-rounded understanding of the current successes and challenges within this course, we were granted permission by the current trio of faculty to enter their classroom throughout the semester to observe, interact with, survey the students using a classroom response system, and conduct focus groups with a sample of randomly chosen students. Throughout this chapter, we highlight the students' experiences because their attainment of the learning objectives motivates our work as instructional designers/technologists. While this was a positive learning experience for many students, our research shows there to be four issues that contribute to other students' discontent with this particular course.

First, a lack of student engagement has been a chronic problem in this course for several years. The problem is recognized by students, faculty, and administrators and has persisted despite two separate cohorts of faculty taking ownership of the team-taught course. Bruff defines engaged students as "those who actively and intentionally participate during class, giving serious thought to the topics discussed" (Bruff, 2009, p. xiv). Although the iOS devices were originally incorporated into the course to make use of mobile learning opportunities, we argue that effective use of the devices can also improve in-class engagement by encouraging active learning even within large sections such as these. Underutilizing the devices, as occurred in this class, tends to promote disengagement and frustration.

A second issue has been the fact that at no time has the course ever been completely overhauled or redesigned to assure that course objectives align with the use of the learning technologies that have been added into the course. The iOS devices were incorporated into the course, ostensibly to encourage mobile learning, but without rethinking what made sense to present in the in-class versus out-of-class environments. Furthermore, having these devices in class presents new opportunities for students to make use of just-in-time resources found online, but the course has not been restructured to take advantage of these capabilities.

Third, throughout the semester the majority of students expressed the opinion that the uses of the iOS devices did not justify the cost. Thus, demonstrating value in terms of student learning is a key challenge within this course. Many of our students today are "bringing to higher education exactly the same consumer demands they have for every other commercial enterprise with which they do business. They believe that since they are paying for college, their schools and their professors should give them what they want" (Levine, 2005, p. 158). But education is not like every other institution or business with which students interact. As educators, one of our main focuses should be to move students along their own paths of intellectual development toward a goal that may or may not yet be identified.

Although somewhat outside of the scope of this chapter's focus, another obstacle is that none of the trio have either full time or tenured status, which increases the likelihood of faculty turnover from semester to semester. Time and financial constraints make it difficult to keep the team abreast of the technical and pedagogical skills and knowledge that they need in order to assure success when utilizing the various learning technologies and strategies involved. There is also an issue of how much time and energy adjunct faculty can afford to dedicate to a course when universities offer them less job security, support, and benefits than their tenured and tenure-track counterparts (Kirp, 2005, p. 123). This issue is indicative of the current state of higher education in the United States and should be taken into consideration by administrators wishing to infuse their courses with any new pedagogy or technology. The need for a master syllabus, collection of lesson plans and teaching materials, and training is imperative if the course is to be taught with the same heavy focus on technology from semester to semester regardless of the faculty teaching the course.

These issues are complex and multi-stranded. Our purpose here is not to blame any single party. Rather, we see this as indicative of the general state of higher education. We hope that in the process of untangling the various causes of students' dissatisfaction with the iOS devices, we can shed some light on how we might progress beyond the obvious obstacles of our current system and make use of various learning technologies, as appropriate, to improve the impact on the future of academia as a whole.

RESEARCH METHODS

This study benefits from the triangulation of three different methods: observation, surveys, and focus groups. The authors, primarily Lauren Miller Griffith (LMG), conducted classroom observations throughout the 16 week duration of the course. A total of 20 observations were completed across the four sections. LMG compiled detailed reports for the teaching team following each observation. The reports were sometimes discussed during weekly meetings that were held to assist the faculty in any way possible with their course. At least one of the authors was present in each of these weekly meetings.

Three surveys were conducted during regular class sessions throughout the semester. The first occurred during the fifth week after each of the students were fully registered into each of the learning technology systems that were going to be utilized in the course ($n = 613$), the second during the 10th week ($n = 501$), and the third during the 15th week of the semester ($n = 442$). These Likert-scale and true/false questions asked students to reflect on their perceptions of the efficacy of various pedagogies and how the use of the iOS devices influenced their learning. One open-ended question asked them to articulate the ways in which they were using the devices above and beyond what was asked of them by the teachers. Because each of the surveys was composed of the exact same questions and answer choices, it allowed for a comparison of student perceptions at three key points in the semester.

The focus groups were held during the 15th week of the semester ($n = 9$).[1] Brian A. Roberts (BAR) and LMG conducted these sessions in an informal manner without the presence or involvement of the faculty so that students could be open and honest in regards to their personal experiences with the course, the technology, and more. The focus groups were designed to be an open-ended dialogue in which we asked them about their general impressions of the course, how the iOS devices influenced their learning, and what suggestions they might make for improving the use of these devices in the future. This interaction also allowed students to expand upon the answers they gave during the in-class surveys.

COURSE MAP AND TOOLBOX

To better understand the potential benefits of these technologies as well as their limitations, this section paints a picture of the ways in which the iOS devices were used in this classroom on a day-to-day basis. We first offer a generic description of the tool used (i.e., iOS devices used as "clickers," used for backchanneling), followed by a more specific explanation of how it was used in this particular course. We round out each subsection by describing the benefits and drawbacks of using the tool in this way as well as recommendations for more effective utilization of the technology. Each is discussed in order of the frequency with which it was used. Subsequent sections will provide more general advice regarding logistical challenges that you may encounter when incorporating mobile devices into your learning environment.

Classroom Response System ("Clickers")

This course made extensive use of a classroom response system implemented on an iOS device, through which students were able to respond to polls posed to them by the instructors. In theory, using the iOS devices and clicker "app" to poll students during class should improve student engagement because "[c]licker technology makes the use of [peer instruction and other active learning strategies] feasible and manageable, even for large classes" (Zhu, 2007, p. 2). This is particularly likely when the students' responses are used in conjunction with discussion. The hardware devices typically referred to as "clickers" only allow students to respond to multiple-choice questions. The iOS device allows for text entry, which makes it possible for students to respond to fill in the blank, short answer and numeric response questions.

Because the students in this class owned or rented their devices for the duration of the semester, the instructors were able to attach points/grades to individual student responses. The clicker slides utilized in this course included opinion polls, monitoring questions, and information recall. While not phrased in these terms to the students, oftentimes the slides used appeared to be aimed more at the managerial function of taking attendance or recording participation than of assessing learning. A minimum of one clicker slide was used each day.

Our observations confirmed that the faculty used the iOS devices regularly, but generally used them to either ask students' opinions on an issue or to ask factual questions at a very low level on Bloom's Taxonomy of Learning. The latter set of questions generally required little more than basic recall of information and the facts/statements they were being asked to recall were so easy, most students could deduce the right answer without having completed their reading assignments. When the questions did have a right/wrong answer, the percentage of students getting the answer correct often hovered in the 75–90% range. Only on rare occasions were students asked to demonstrate understanding, application, synthesis, or evaluation.

The iOS devices as clickers were most effective in this class when used in concert with follow-up discussion. When students were asked to respond to a clicker poll related to a difficult or controversial subject, it increased their interest and willingness to participate. Students exhibited high levels of engagement and often referenced personal experiences to help buttress their arguments. Eventually, we would like students to use scholarly evidence to support their arguments, but discussions such as these that introduce students to their peers' diverse perspectives in the context of ambiguous scenarios are useful in moving students to more advanced stages of intellectual development (Kloss, 1994).

Another strength of this tool is the immediacy with which poll results can be visually displayed to students. Throughout the course of our observations, when the graphical results of students' responses were particularly dramatic, showing large discrepancies in views or in what students perceive to be the correct answer, students gave verbal indications of their interest. Sitting in the classroom, one could hear waves of "hmm," "wow," and "oooh." Students in our focus groups confirmed that bar graphs were useful in appreciating their peers' opinions on issues and prompted further discussion. It is our experience that when students realize that others share their same opinion, they tend to be more willing to participate in discussion. However, in this study two students confirmed that when their opinion was in the minority, they were particularly likely to stand up and defend it because they wanted those opinions to be heard. As these students' actions suggest, clickers can give voice to otherwise underrepresented positions (Zhu, 2007)

Another effective use of iOS devices that we occasionally witnessed was in helping students create cognitive bridges between different segments of the class. This is important and should be done more extensively in survey classes that take a scattershot approach to "covering the content." For example, during one class the teachers gave a micro-lecture followed by several multiple-choice questions that required students to apply what they had just learned about various industry-specific philosophies. This prepared them for the next activity in which they would have to watch short video clips, determine which philosophy motivated the central character's actions, and record evidence of how the character enacted that philosophy. Put more generally, well-timed clicker questions can be used to help scaffold students' ability to work with content at advanced levels. They might be used to test recall before asking students to understand a concept or they might be used to see if students can apply a theory before being asked to evaluate its uses in a particular case.

The polling questions were also used to gather information that could inform the teachers' performance in the classroom. For example, one question asked students to rate how successful or unsuccessful a particular web-based assignment had been in answering their questions about the degree program. This kind of information can be used to inform future iterations of the assignment; however, the impact is limited unless the faculty asks students to also provide examples of what worked and what did not as well as how the assignment could be improved.

In addition to the successful uses of iOS devices as clickers described above, there is a wealth of opportunity to further develop meaningful uses of the system. According to our surveys, knowing that they would have to answer "clicker questions" in class had a minimal effect on students' pre-class preparation. At the beginning of the semester, as many as 30% of students in one section reported that they were more likely to prepare as a result of the questions, but this number quickly dropped off as the semester progressed. By the end of the term, only 17% of the students in our sample reported preparing more than they would otherwise because of these questions. So while these questions had a positive effect on a small group of students' preparation and a negative effect on an even smaller subset of the students (less than 10%), the majority of students in all sections did nothing different in terms of preparation because of these questions. This stands in contrast to a study conducted at the University of Michigan in 2006 and 2007, which indicated that students prepared more for class because they knew they would be answering questions with clickers (Zhu, 2007). We do not have data to explain this discrepancy, though it may be related to the point system used. Students in the course reviewed here were awarded full credit regardless of whether or not they answered questions correctly. Thus, more emphasis was placed on attendance and participation than on preparation and accurate recall.

Students voiced frustration that the instructors used questions that did not prompt enough critical thinking, nor help them assess their knowledge of course content. Students saw some of the iOS questions as "random" or as a more convenient way to collect attendance data. During the focus groups, one student said she was initially "bitter" toward having to have the iOS device in part because she felt like they were just being used to assign points for daily attendance. In retrospect she saw that "it served some purpose," but she was still not overly positive about using the devices. Another student remarked that the questions were too simple and did not "teach" the students anything about the material, which led some students in our focus groups to conclude that it was an "opinions course." When using clickers to generate in-class discussion, instructors can use questions that would be unfairly ambiguous to include on an exam because "it creates the opportunity for students to share and discuss the reasons they have for selecting particular answer choices, thereby encouraging critical thinking" (Bruff, 2009, p. 8).

This is not to say, however, that student opinions have no place in the classroom. For the most part, students seemed to enjoy the discussions that were prompted by opinion polls and many of those who participated in our focus groups would like more follow-up discussion. In several instances, the faculty cut discussion short because they felt compelled to "cover the content," which is a familiar faculty lament about survey courses. But because students need time to process the information being presented and assimilate it into their mental schema, additional time spent on discussion may be worth the cost in terms of coverage.

Our recommendations for more effective utilization of iOS devices as clickers come from our research with this course as well as the literature on classroom response systems. Our strongest recommendation is to be very intentional when selecting the questions as the results of using clickers will rely upon the quality of the question asked. Repeatedly throughout the semester we encountered evidence to suggest that the material was not sufficiently difficult to prompt student growth. In fact, during the focus groups, one student said that she and her peers were just "idling" through the course. The faculty most often asked opinion poll questions, but on the occasions that the instructors used clicker questions with correct and incorrect answers, the high percentage of students who were able to answer the question correctly on the first try indicates that the questions were too easy. Using these questions gave us as observers the impression that the questions were being used merely as a way to collect attendance, which we know has the tendency to alienate and even anger students (Bruff, 2009; Zhu, 2007).

Increasing the diversity and difficulty level of the questions asked could spark more informed discussion among students as stronger questions tend to "ensure a closer connection between clicker questions and course learning objectives" (Zhu, 2007, p. 5). However, this will be most successful when the students know they are being held accountable for knowing the correct answers either individually or in teams. We would recommend in this case that faculty get creative in their assignment of points for participation rather than telling students which questions are worth points or not and which one holds them accountable for being in the room.

Immediate feedback is one of the biggest advantages offered by classroom response systems because students are made aware of the areas in which they could use additional review or feedback (Bruff, 2009; Zhu, 2007). One of our focus group participants said that she would have appreciated more critical thinking questions, and some with a correct/incorrect answer that not everyone got correct. Classroom response technology can be a great asset in letting us know when we need to push for more critical engagement. For example, if students perform significantly worse on a particular question than the class average, this is probably an opportunity for more engagement with students' responses; however, this cue was unheeded in this particular class.

Being responsive to the students' needs, based on their answers to challenging clicker questions, necessitates instructional flexibility (Zhu, 2007). Using the classroom response system introduces a bit of uncertainty into the classroom experience. It is difficult to predict how students will answer the questions and whether or not a particular prompt will lead to a productive discussion. Adopting the iOS devices, like any classroom response system, demands enough flexibility to let a student-led discussion run its course before moving on to another topic. However, it is also important to not let discussion drag on too long, which can happen when underprepared students need remedial attention (Dufresne, Gerace, Leonard, Mestre, & Wenk, 1996). To balance these two demands, faculty may wish to announce to their students how much time is allocated for each discussion and post a countdown clock on the screen so everyone knows when it is time to move on to the next topic.

The following is an extensive, but certainly not all-inclusive, list of ways that we recommend that faculty consider using classroom response systems to increase student engagement and interaction in their face-to-face courses:

- Use polls to drive discussion
- Engage students in peer instruction (i.e., Think-Pair-Share)
- Offer monitoring questions (academic housekeeping questions such as, "Has your group met yet?" or "We are over half way through the semester. Have you started your final project?")
- Pose scenario-based application questions
- Gather student perspectives and opinions anonymously
- Poll students regarding sensitive subject matter
- Personalize statistics to the immediate audience (i.e., anonymously asking how many students have ever had a sexually transmitted disease before showing the national statistics)
- Identify and overcome misconceptions
- Check for understanding
- Assess prior knowledge
- Scaffold exercises
- Create a time for telling (i.e., build anticipation for what should be learned from the activity)
- Ask confidence level questions
- Spark competition
- Poll spontaneously based on topics that arise from discussion

- Make demographic comparisons
- Conduct survey-based research in the classroom
- Assess pre and post knowledge
- Solicit response to current events
- Peer assessment of group projects and presentations.

Many classroom response systems offer the option to link polls with points that can in turn calculate students' grades based upon their participation, attendance, and assessment performance. This option, however, generally means that students would be required to own and register a device of their own.

Backchanneling

If we consider the primary instructional activity taking place at a given moment (i.e., the lecture, demonstration, film, etc.) to be the frontchannel, then any communication taking place within the learning environment simultaneously can be considered the backchannel. This may be as low tech as students passing notes or whispering, or as high tech as a twitter feed. This backchannel offers students the opportunity to interact with the professor, the presentation, and each other (Yardi, 2008). This interaction may include comments, questions, clarifications, or responses related to the content being offered by the professor in the frontchannel. Its instructional benefit comes from being directly influenced by action in the frontchannel (Rothenberg & King, 2006). There are many technological solutions available that can be used as a backchannel such as an instant messaging/chat software, twitter, or other dedicated tools. This simple method of communication can be implemented in a classroom setting in a variety of ways, both publicly and privately depending upon the system that is being used, either with or without the instructor's knowledge or involvement. It is our recommendation that faculty and students consider creating a separate account solely to be used for their educational endeavors so as to avoid inundating their personal social media accounts with course related activity.

This course utilized a free backchanneling tool that was developed and made publicly available by another university. Primary use in this course included asking individual students to submit questions and comments during selected frontchannel presentations, which students may or may not have been likely to ask during a traditional verbal discussion. This communication technique was used both during faculty-led lectures and during guest presentations. The faculty also used the backchannel as a means for reporting the outcomes of small group work. Whenever backchanneling was used in this course, it was monitored by one of the faculty or the graduate student.

Students' initial reactions to backchanneling were extremely positive. In the first survey, two-thirds of students in our overall sample reported that it had had a positive influence on their learning. The highest praise came from the 10 a.m. section, in which 75% of students gave this response. We believe their ratings of this technique are high because it fosters peer-to-peer interaction in a large lecture hall that might otherwise leave students feeling isolated and anonymous. This correlates with other survey questions showing that in both this course and others at the same institution, students report peer-to-peer learning as a highly engaging activity. This supports our goal of fostering active learning because peer-to-peer interactions encourage a constructivist mode of learning, which is "organic rather than static" (Yardi, 2008, p. 149).

Backchanneling can be used to prioritize students' questions or concerns during a presentation. By voting on a question/concern that has already been posted, students see that their thought is not unique. This reinforces the urgency to solicit a response. In a similar vein, the instructors in this course occasionally asked groups of students to define a concept, post it through the backchannel, and vote on which group had written the best definition. Both of these applications encourage peer-to-peer interaction.

Another benefit of backchanneling is that it allows students to anonymously voice their opinion or ask a question without the fear of appearing unintelligent in front of their peers (Nobarany, Haraty, Fels, & Fisher, 2011). It also provides "a quick casual way to get multiple perspectives" about an issue (Rothenberg & King, 2006, p. 17). Students who are shy or inhibited in the physical classroom may feel more inclined to express themselves in the backchannel (Yardi, 2008). The backchannel can become a "testing ground for ideas or comments that [students are] uncertain about sharing out loud in the class" (Rothenberg & King, 2006, pp. 27, 28). Granted, the perceived utility of this tool may be related to an individual's proclivity to ask sensitive questions in a public forum. One student in our focus groups said she would ask pretty much anything in class, but recognized it would be helpful for people who are more intimidated by talking in large groups.

While the students' reaction to the backchannel function was initially positive, when they were surveyed in September, the popularity of this tool had dipped by the middle of the semester. When surveyed in October, only

38% of our sample was willing to give it a positive rating. The remaining students were split between assessing it negatively (32%) and being undecided (29%). However, by the end of the semester, 54% of students in the sample reported that it had made a positive difference in their learning. We imagine part of this ebb and flow is related to the infrequency with which the backchanneling technique was used.

We also recommend seeking a balance in terms of how instructors use the backchannel system. In this course, students' comments and queries were always posted on the projection screen for all, including the frontchannel presenter, to see. However, it would also be possible to enable peer-to-peer engagement via the backchannel without projecting it on screen. In this case, a second faculty member or graduate teaching assistant might monitor and respond to students' posts. Keep in mind, however, that students may change their behavior if the instructor or an assistant was participating in the backchannel (Rothenberg & King, 2006). Therefore, it might be beneficial to leave some conversations unmonitored from time to time.

We offer the following ideas for utilizing the power of backchanneling in your classrooms:

- Encourage monitored or unmonitored peer interaction
- Foster synchronous on-topic peer discussion in the classroom
- Conduct synchronous topic-specific discussion outside of the classroom (via sort and search options)
- Clarify frontchannel content
- Vote
- Share information and resources
- Facilitate communication between faculty members and students during classroom presentations
- Submit questions
- Submit group work following an activity
- Reflect on content presented
- Summarize the topic at hand.

Learning Management System

The university where this course is taught utilizes a robust LMS that offers a wide variety of tools within it including a document repository, discussion boards, and assessment and communication tools to name a few. The students in this course were expected to log into the LMS using their iOS device to interact with the instructors and their peers regularly throughout the semester both in and out of the classroom. For example, students completed individual quizzes on their own time and group quizzes during the class period.

One of the benefits of using the iOS devices in conjunction with an LMS is that students can have access to their assignments, grade, and course documents while the professors are discussing them in class. In the open-ended portion of the survey, one student wrote, "I've installed the [LMS] application to see what homework the professors are talking about or to follow along with a file they're discussing in class." It also makes it easier for students to monitor their progress within the course. In the survey, another student wrote, "I used this device to go on [the LMS] to check on how I am doing in my classes." Timely feedback on learning is one of the principles of good teaching (Chickering & Gamson, 1987). Using the LMS to complete in-class assessments electronically, students are given the opportunity for immediate feedback once they have submitted their answers.

Although there are some clear benefits to using the LMS in conjunction with the iOS devices, students' reactions were not uniformly positive. In the open-ended portion of our survey, the most pronounced change in what students reported doing with their iOS devices has to do with the LMS. The number of references to the use of the LMS was much higher during the first survey. Mention of this application declines significantly over the course of the three surveys. The average across all four sections at the time of the first survey was 65 whereas it had dropped to 15 by the final survey. With the data available, it is unclear whether students had stopped using their iOS devices to access the LMS or if they simply opted not to enter this information in later surveys.

In the open-ended portion of our survey, some students reported frustration when trying to run the LMS through the built in browser on their iOS devices. One student wrote, "I tried to use it [the LMS] but it doesn't work well with [the iOS device]." To remedy this situation, instructors might want to alert their students to the existence of specific LMS "apps" when available. This aligns with our overall recommendation below to coach students in appropriate uses of the iOS device for both the in and out of class environments.

The ability to view and download documents from the LMS has a number of affordances. For one, in a large class such as this, it is expensive and time consuming to print and distribute handouts for each student. Using the LMS, on the other hand, faculty can prepare documents ahead of time and have students view or download them to their devices as needed. Taking this principle one step further, students may find it beneficial to combine this view/download capability with other "apps" to take notes, make changes, and share the documents with others during class and outside of the classroom. This would necessitate either faculty recommended or a self-generated list of "apps" that would work to do this. The following is a list of ways to consider utilizing the LMS.

- Share documents (assignments, syllabus, etc.)
- Post and check grades in the LMS
- Use calendaring "apps" for time management
- Communicate (announcements, email, blog, discussion boards, etc.)
- Wiki interaction
- Deliver media
- Access link repositories
- Assess learning with practice quizzes, formal quizzes, and exams.

Internet Access

Whether you love it or hate it, we're pretty convinced that the Internet is here to stay. Considering the use of iOS devices literally means that the students have the world (wide web) in their hands, the impact can be either a benefit or a distraction depending upon how the device and tools are being used. Much of what has been previously described in this chapter hinges upon the fact that each student had a device and wireless access to the Internet. The instructors capitalized upon this by both directing students to specific course-related web resources as well as encouraging them to utilize just-in-time learning methods on their own. Examples of this included on-the-spot research, obtaining definitions of unknown vocabulary, identification of current events, and hot topics within the field of study.

Over the course of the semester, students became more adept at using their iOS devices to research websites related to the course content. During our first survey, students were either not using their devices to access web-related content or were unable to recognize the value of visiting subject-related websites. At that time, only 11 students from the entire sample mentioned this use of their devices. However, by the end of the semester, 92 students in the sample reported using their devices for this purpose.

There was also a sharp increase in the use of the iOS devices to access just-in-time resources. By this we mean web searches for information that aids discussion, clarifies topics introduces by the instructor, or answers questions individuals have during the course of an in-class assignment or quiz. During the first survey, only 18 students in the entire sample mentioned this use. By the second survey it had increased to 120 and by the third survey, the number of students mentioning this use of the iOS devices stood at 137. One student in particular found this function to be extremely valuable. The student wrote, "[h]aving the Internet in a mobile device is awesome!! It's like ultimate access to information. If I ever have a question, the device will have an answer for it 99% of the time."

Having the world in their hands also means they have an increased likelihood to engage with Internet content in off-task manners. This could include a wide range of activities. For example, one student wrote that he or she uses the iOS device for "[e]verything under the sun. I use my email, Facebook, and twitter constantly." And while the latter two uses could have educational applications, they are more often used to communicate with friends about non-educational topics. Another student wrote, "I do not like using [the devices] and I feel that they are damaging my learning experience because they are distracting – even if I'm not messing around [with] my device, I can see the others in front of me messing around." This fits with the way that today's students have sometimes been described as an "always on" population that is constantly engaged with technology (Yardi, 2008).

The frequency with which students are accessing social media sites such as Facebook and Twitter for off-task uses during class is cause for concern. The average number of students per section who report using their iOS devices for social media was 10 during the first survey, 13 during the second survey, and 12 during the third survey. Our observations however suggest that this frequency is much higher. Also discouraging is the frequency with which students are using their iOS devices to pass time during class. Items from the open-ended portion of our survey coded as "pastimes" include games, general web surfing, checking sports scores, etc. During our first survey, an average of nine students per section referenced this theme, but during the final survey, this average had soared to 19 students per section. Of course, having distractions in the classroom is nothing new (Yardi, 2008). There were distractions in the classroom long before electronics found their way into the room. The student that you had a crush on, birds outside the window, and doodling in your notebook were the original distractions (e.g., Thornton, 2011). Adding the iOS devices to the classroom broadens the scope of potential distractions.

In addition to being a distraction, however, surfing the Internet can pose other problems for a class using some of the previously mentioned tools such as classroom response systems that rely upon having sufficient bandwidth to interact via Wi-Fi. This is particularly important in large lecture halls such as the one in which this course took place. Some students in this course were occasionally unable to submit their clicker poll responses because they had not connected to or had been disconnected from the wireless network due to bandwidth constraints. Despite experts coming to the classroom with sophisticated equipment designed to test the strength of a wireless signal, we were unable to determine the cause of students being kicked off the network. We have a strong assumption that off-task uses of devices (social media, YouTube, checking sports scores, texting, instant messaging, etc.) may have used so much bandwidth that some students were occasionally unable to connect.

The Internet has the potential to provide as many benefits as it does pitfalls, but the determining factor may be how well the instructor frames Internet use within the classroom culture. It may be that web browsing capabilities are not inherently distracting, rather many faculty work against them instead of using them as a tool (Yardi, 2008). Considering how many students eventually came to value the just-in-time affordances of their devices, we recommend that faculty give their students explicit instruction on how they might take advantage of these resources during class time. Furthermore, if an instructor wants to direct his or her students to a specific website, it is recommended that he or she first ensure that the site is mobile friendly. One of the students in our sample wrote, "[i]n class, the professors will tell us to go to an educational website on our iOS devices but I usually just use my laptop."

Regardless of the type of devices being used, we hear all too often that faculty get discouraged by the amount of off-task use of mobile Internet capable devices can be in the classroom, but we encourage you and your students to find on-task course-related reasons for students to use their devices. The following is a shortlist of ways to encourage students to use their devices on-task:

- Take and share notes
- Record classroom presentations
- Capture key moment and content with photos
- Locate and view web resources
- Access and share documents
- Look up vocabulary
- Utilize time management and calendaring resources
- Add content to blogs and wikis

- Communicate (email, discussion boards, instant messaging, etc.)
- Use social media as it relates to course content
- Read electronic textbooks
- Create documents
- Access LMS
- Create note cards.

Podcasting

When iOS devices were first introduced into this course, it was done with the intention of promoting mobile learning through the use of podcasting. However, by the time we conducted this study in the Fall of 2011, podcasting was no longer being utilized. Even without data from these students, we present it here as another effective use of the iOS devices. Any content that you create and deliver can benefit your course in the future because the learning objects are reusable. With the craze of flipping classrooms gaining momentum every day, there are countless ways to consider using podcasting in and out of the classroom. A few ideas to get you started are as follows:

- Capture, deliver, and store classroom presentations
- Deliver mini-lectures prior to class in order to dedicate classroom time to active learning and application of concepts (flipped classroom)
- Provide software, interface, and system tutorials
- Clarify content outside of class
- Create and view presentations by students
- Take virtual field trips
- Deliver multimedia-based announcements
- Deliver content in professor's absence
- Feature guest speakers that may not be able to visit the physical classroom.

SINGLE REQUIRED DEVICE (iOS) VS. BRING YOUR OWN DEVICE (BYOD)

A clear theme that emerged from the analysis of our data showed that students would prefer to be able to use a device that they may already own versus having to obtain a specific single device mandated by the individual instructors or the institution. We believe that this may be attributable to the students' view that they did not see the educational value in using the device in comparison to the cost of obtaining it.

Students by and large did not think that the use of technology in this course justified the expense of the devices used. At no point during the semester did the percentage of students in our overall sample who believed the use *did* justify the device reach 25%. When students were asked this question at the midterm, 65% of our overall sample believed that the use did *not* justify the cost. Student opinion rebounded slightly toward the end of the semester, perhaps because the teachers had started to develop more provocative questions. However, they were unable to return to the initial peak in September at which time 54% of students discounted the value of the devices. While some of this dissatisfaction could be lessened if faculty used a "Bring Your Own Device" (BYOD) model, it is also likely that students would better appreciate the value of the devices if they were used in more rigorous and pedagogically sound ways that align with their pre-existing practices.

Some students in our focus groups were frustrated that they had to use iOS devices rather than their own laptops. While the cost of a laptop might be seen as an argument against its inclusion in the classroom, one student told us that among his friends, "everyone has a laptop. Every single person has a laptop." Despite this student's conviction, it bears keeping in mind that requiring such an expensive device might disadvantage students from lower socioeconomic classes. One safeguard against this might be finding ways to use mobile devices that students already own (Deubel, 2009). The cell phones many students own are powerful computing devices that instructors can utilize in the classroom (Prensky, 2004). Faculty should consider whether or not cell phones and laptops could be included in the list of devices from which students may choose. However, a BYOD model would necessitate a great deal of familiarity on the part of the faculty and tech-support staff in supporting a wide array of devices.

There are also some drawbacks to using a single device. For example, it might limit the potential use of new applications that are developed for devices other than the one selected. After making the initial investment in the technology, faculty and students are more or less "locked-in" to using that device for the foreseeable future. Instructors may also encounter some initial student resistance to being asked to obtain a new device, especially if they already own a laptop, smartphone, or other device with similar wireless capabilities. Based on our survey and focus group data, the stakes for proving the device's value are highest when students are required to have a single device.

Although proving value is of concern no matter what device they use, there are some benefits to having all students use the same device. Having students use the same device supports inclusive teaching practices, as a student's socioeconomic background will not unfairly advantage or disadvantage him or her based on the quality of device that he or she can afford. Nonetheless, we recognize that one's economic background may influence the pre-existing skills he or she brings to the use of technology. Also, while using the same device means that students would have access to the same pool of "apps," students from different socioeconomic backgrounds may or may not be able to afford the same extra costs which would have to be identified and required upfront.

From a support standpoint, the obvious benefits for tech-support staff would include the ability to create a single set of tutorials. Furthermore, the use of a single device reduces the number of potential pitfalls that students may encounter. As such the support staff would be able to more easily troubleshoot these issues. Using a single device may also allow for bulk purchases which may reduce the bottom line for students, whether they are purchasing the devices or renting them from the institution.

We recommend that faculty carefully consider their intended uses of the devices as well as their student population before determining whether they will require a single device or allow students to choose their own devices. If the former option is chosen, faculty may wish to consider which device allows for the greatest number of relevant, free or low-cost "apps" to ensure that they keep the playing field level for students of different socioeconomic backgrounds. If the latter option is chosen, faculty should define a minimum set of criteria on an annual basis as to what devices the students can use in the course. Furthermore, faculty must agree to follow a 4 or 5 year progression in which they continue to support older devices with lesser capabilities in upper level courses.

We also recommend consistency with use and an agreement between various university colleges and departments to use certain "apps" and systems. A unified implementation on a university or, at least, college level in which faculty collaborate to identify and share resources, uses, and outcomes with one another will benefit everyone in the end. Students should also be brought into these discussions in order that their experiences, thoughts, and feelings are considered in the decision-making process in order to avoid solely top down administrative decisions. Without this communication, the decisions of one college, department or individual faculty member can greatly influence the students' campus-wide experiences and costs. When different groups make individual technology choices on their own, students could be required to obtain multiple redundant devices (e.g., different classroom response/clicker devices and different models of the same device).

RECOMMENDATIONS FOR MEETING THIS (AND ANY) COURSE'S KEY CHALLENGES

Having described the ways in which the faculty utilized the iOS devices in this particular course as well as the students' responses to those uses, we now return to the key issues identified at the outset of this paper. Because the learning outcomes associated with any technology are dependent upon the ways in which the technology is used (e.g., Bruff, 2009), we now offer several over-arching recommendations for how the iOS devices can be employed to (1) increase student engagement, (2) add value to the course, and (3) align with the overall design of the course.

Student Engagement

Using a unidirectional mode of instruction like traditional lecture "assumes that students are able to assimilate the information and integrate it into their existing understanding of a topic and are also able to adjust their understanding of related concepts" (Preszler, Dawe, Chuster, & Shuster, 2007, p. 29). However, this is not effective for the majority of students. Nonetheless, many students today are accustomed to passively sitting through lectures. A constructivist notion of learning demands a much more active approach (Dufresne et al., 1996). But adding an interactive technology to the classroom means that students will need some support as they adjust to their new role in the active classroom. Student buy-in will be more likely when the instructor is transparent about the rationale for using the new technology (Zhu, 2007). Engagement will also be improved by incorporating tools, like backchanneling, that encourage sustained rather than sporadic attention (Yardi, 2006).

While each of the tools and methods that have been described can add benefit to the classroom environment in their own way, if used effectively, we caution against using them as replacements for traditional classroom methods such as discussion and interaction. In discussing some of these applications, a faculty member once said to BAR, "I miss hearing them talk." In response to this, we recommend that faculty strive for a balance between using these technologies and encouraging traditional interpersonal communication. In the open-ended portion of our survey, one of the students in this course wrote, "if I wanted a class where I never had to talk to the teacher, I would have taken an Internet course." The technological applications described here are most effective when used to spark student discussion and lively engagement in the service of the learning objectives.

As with all technological tools, we recommend seeking a balance of technological engagement and interpersonal engagement with students. Bruff writes that "[t]here is something about pressing a button on a clicker that lowers the barrier between students and instructor" (2009, p. 198). We were therefore surprised to read one student's survey response that said using the iOS device "has taken away from the student teacher relationship." Several students voiced a preference for what they called "old school" teaching methods. As one student from our focus groups said, "I'm old school, I like those teaching techniques." Another student told us that if he were a teacher, he would not want his students to be "staring at a screen"; he wants them being vocal. Though not voiced in these terms, this student's concerns also raise the question of whether or not "staring at a screen" is distracting. We recommend instructors help students think about using the iOS devices selectively so as "not to lose track of the primary flow of information" (Nobarany et al., 2011, p. 1583).

Demonstrating Value

The more courses in which students can use their device, the lower the stakes are for any one instructor to shoulder the burden of providing hundreds of dollars worth of value within a single semester. Students will grumble at the cost of buying/renting new hardware for a course if the only, or primary, purpose is to make the instructor's job easier with tasks such as automatic grading. However, if the students perceive value in the devices, they will be less resistant (e.g., Bruff, 2009). Students have to see the value of using the devices in order for faculty to gain their collusion in the instructional practice. To get the most value for their investment, the curriculum of any program seriously considering the incorporation of iOS or other similar devices should include "mobile literacy" (Deubel, 2009). Additionally, many students appear to be using trial and error methods of searching for information, so their use of iOS devices to access just-in-time resources would be greatly facilitated by instruction in this area (Conole, de Laat, Dillon, & Darby, 2008).

When students begin using the devices in non-requisite ways that grow out of their own individual learning needs, they often do see this value. For example, one student wrote, "having mobile web on my phone and being allowed to use it in class has helped me learn and discover new things through this course." Other student-generated uses of the devices included taking photos as a record of what occurred during the classroom, using the audio and video recording features to capture the lectures and review at a later date, note-taking, and time management.

Course Design

Technology itself cannot improve instruction, but it can enhance the effectiveness of good instructional design (Yardi, 2008). When conceived as an integral part of the course design, a new technology can transform the way one teaches. One study found that when clickers were incorporated into instruction, the time devoted to lecture decreased and the time devoted to students' understanding increased because the instructor's role changed from being a sage on the stage to a guide on the side (Dufresne et al., 1996). But the utility of any new tool hinges upon whether it and associated pedagogies are being used in a manner that aligns with the learning objectives (Dufresne et al., 1996). We recommend against using technology for the sake of technology, but rather use a technology to enhance the quality of the learning experience.

As with any instructional design project, it is advisable to first identify how the students should be different as a result of having taken the course. Using backwards design helps an instructor identify the key knowledge and skills that students need to learn in order to begin asking "essential questions" and developing "enduring understandings" within a discipline (Wiggins & McTighe, 2005). After an instructor uses this process to identify learning goals and winnow down the content to the most important elements, he or she is in a better position to use technology in alignment with the courses' objectives. For example, instructors might use podcasting to deliver content that is "worth being familiar with" but does not fall into the domain of "big ideas and core tasks" (Wiggins & McTighe, 2005, p. 71). In-class time, then, can be spent engaging students in both traditional and technology enhanced active learning strategies geared toward helping them construct these enduring understandings.

In thinking about course design, it is tempting to think that if we build it, they will learn. However, without sufficient accountability structures in place, even otherwise well designed courses will have little influence on student learning. For example, early in the semester the instructors used the classroom response system to ask students whether or not they had accessed the online materials associated with the text, 96% of them reported that they had not done so. This provided much needed information to the instructors who then spent the next few minutes explaining the benefits of the resources. But without accountability structures in place to ensure that students would begin using the resources, the instructors' admonitions were largely unheeded.

The degree of accountability must be even higher in courses where students' intrinsic motivation to excel seems lacking. Take, for instance, the example of a student in our focus groups who told us that she wanted to "be a good student this semester" but because quizzes can be taken multiple times she ultimately resorted to skimming the book for answers while taking the quiz. In the words of another focus group participant, these structures were "too forgiving" to encourage much studying. In addition to encouraging compliance with the learning task, asking students to produce some sort of evidence of their learning tends to increase their engagement (Bruff, 2009). In a best case scenario, students begin holding themselves accountable for excellence to the degree that the instructor-student relationship becomes less authoritarian and more egalitarian (e.g., Barr & Tagg, 1995).

Students will resist the use of a technology if they believe that its only purpose is to make the instructor's job easier. As one particularly frustrated student wrote for the open-ended survey question, some students perceived that the instructors mandated the use of iOS devices because "they are just too lazy to take attendance." With this in mind, it is important to make sure that the questions asked and tasks assigned on the devices are sufficiently rigorous for students to see the benefit of these devices in terms of their learning.

Several issues contributed to a relatively low level of academic rigor in this course. That the faculty members did not make the course more rigorous was due to their reservations about how much the students could handle. The instructors also appeared hamstrung by the fact that the course was intended to be a survey style overview of the profession and did not feel as if they could go into sufficient depth on any one topic that would allow students to engage in sophisticated discussion of the topic.

During our focus groups, one student countered her peers' claims that the course was too easy by reminding them that the class was designed to teach them what the profession is all about so they could make informed decisions about whether or not they want to continue in the field. This student thought the course could be made a little harder but insisted that it was not a class made to push the envelope. We found this comment rather unsatisfying and recommend using technological capabilities such as podcasting and just-in-time web resources to provide students with the additional information they need to engage in intellectually rigorous discussions of the subject without unduly adding to the course content.

We also recommend that instructors evaluate students' progress immediately and regularly. For example, instructors might use clickers to assess students' incoming knowledge about a topic, which is useful for identifying misconception and for determining how much time needs to be devoted to a particular topic (Zhu, 2007). In the case of this course, doing so might have countered many students' assumptions that this was "an opinion's course." We have long known that giving prompt feedback on learning is an effective practice of undergraduate education (Chickering & Gamson, 1987), but it often seems difficult in large classes. The size of one's course will likely remain outside of the instructor's control, but new technological tools such as those described in this chapter can make it more feasible to continue these time-tested best practices in undergraduate education even in large sections (e.g., Zhu, 2007)

CONCLUSION

Academia has come under fire for allowing students and faculty to be adrift in the uncertain seas of higher education (Arum & Roksa, 2011). Questions about the purpose of higher education, the standards to which we hold our students, and the adequacy of our students' preparation for higher education are even further complicated by the proliferation of new learning technologies. These new technologies hold great potential for transforming the learning environment in which our students are situated; however, without careful consideration of why and how we are using them, their impact will be limited at best and counterproductive at worst. Our intent in writing this chapter was to provide a map of what did and did not work for a particular set of faculty as well as offer some recommendations based upon our research. We hope that by sharing this journey, others wishing to embark on similar paths are able to do so on calmer seas.

These instructors used the iOS devices in several significant ways such as prompting discussion with clicker questions, sustaining engagement throughout the class sessions by promoting the use of backchanneling, using an LMS, etc. They sought to get on board with mobile learning, but did so without any true (re)design. As such, students did not see the value of the devices and continued to exhibit the same disengagement and frustration with the course as had previous students in this course. This course's inherent flaws (lack of rigor and accountability) continued to promote disengagement despite the faculty's implementation of the iOS devices into the classroom. These flaws combined with the presence of iOS devices that have access to the Internet is a sure fire recipe for incivility and off-task use of the technology. Rather than solving the problem of disengagement as they intended to do, the iOS devices became fuel for the fire. It is our belief that in order to assure that the devices are being used effectively and that students are getting both a substantial educational and monetary value out of their devices that faculty must work to (re)design their course with the devices and technologies in mind from start to finish.

We cannot stress strongly enough the importance that all stakeholders begin their journey by evaluating the existing course or program and the primary goals regarding the implementation of new learning technologies. Once these key factors have been considered, faculty, staff, and any other individuals involved can then identify the appropriate learning technologies and hardware (single or BYOD model) that will suit their needs. Throughout this process, the stakeholders should identify resources that can assist with pre-implementation planning, technical training, and pedagogically sound practices. This process will ultimately lead to far smoother sailing for all during the semester. Any implementation plan needs to include constant and consistent evaluation of the technology's effectiveness and value in terms of student learning. Finally, faculty should always consider how their individual decisions may impact the overall program and university as a whole.

NOTE

1. We had originally intended to use a simple random sample to form our focus groups; however, there were a number of confounding factors that made this difficult. In particular, because we were asking students to meet with us outside of normal class hours during the last week of the semester, we had difficulties recruiting them. Therefore, it is not as representative as we had hoped, but the alignment between their responses and the survey responses increases our confidence in the reliability of their comments.

REFERENCES

Arum, R., & Roksa, J. (2011). *Academically adrift: Limited learning on college campuses*. Chicago, IL: Univeristy of Chicago Press.

Barr, R., & Tagg, J. (1995, November/December). From teaching to learning-A new paradigm for undergraduate education. *Change, 27*(6), 13–25.

Bruff, D. (2009). *Teaching with classroom response systems: Creating active learning environments*. San Francisco, CA: Jossey-Bass.

Chickering, A. W., & Gamson, Z. F. (1987). Seven principles for good practice in undergraduate education. *AAHE Bulletin, 39*(7), 3–7.

Conole, G., de Laat, M., Dillon, T., & Darby, J. (2008). "Disruptive technologies", "pedagogical innovation": What's new? Findings from an in-depth study of students' use and perception of technology. *Computers & Education, 50*(2), 511–524.

Deubel, P. (2009, March 19). Mobile devices: Facing challenges and opportunities for learning. *THE Journal (Transforming Education Through Technology)*. Retrieved from http://thejournal.com/articles/2009/03/19/mobile-devices-facing-challenges-and-opportunities-for-learning.aspx

Dufresne, R. J., Gerace, W. J., Leonard, W. J., Mestre, J. P., & Wenk, L. (1996). Classtalk: A classroom communication system for active learning. *Journal of Computing in Higher Education, 7*, 3–47.

Kirp, D. L. (2005). This little student went to market. In R. H. Hersh & J. Merrow (Eds.), *Declining by degrees: Higher education at risk* (pp. 113–130). New York, NY: Palgrave Macmillan.

Kloss, R. J. (1994). A nudge is best: Helping students through the Perry scheme of intellectual development. *College Teaching, 42*(4), 151–158.

Levine, A. (2005). Worlds apart: Disconnects between students and their colleges. In R. H. Hersh & J. Merrow (Eds.), *Declining by degrees: Higher education at risk* (pp. 155–168). New York, NY: Palgrave Macmillan.

Nobarany, S., Haraty, M., Fels, S.S., & Fisher, B.D. (2011). Leveraging trust relationships in digital backchannel communications. In S. A. Barab, K. E. Hay & D. T. Hickey (Eds.), *CHI EA '11 proceedings of the 2011 annual conference extended abstracts on human factors in computing systems* (pp. 1579–1584). New York, NY: ACM.

Prensky, M. (2004). What can you learn from a cell phone? Almost anything! *Innovate*, 1(5). Retrieved from http://innovateonline.info/pdf/vol1_issue5/What_Can_You_Learn_from_a_Cell_Phone__Almost_Anything!.pdf

Preszler, R. W., Dawe, A., Chuster, C. B., & Shuster, M. (2007). Assessment of the effects of student response systems on student learning and attitudes over a broad range of biology courses. *Life Sciences Education, 6*, 29–41.

Rothenberg, M., & King, J. (2006, May). *Social uses of communication backchannels in a shared physical environment*. Retrieved from: http://groups.ischool.berkeley.edu/backchannel/downloads/backchannel.pdf

Thornton, B. (2011, April). Personal technology in the classroom. *eLearn Magazine*. Retrieved from http://elearnmag.acm.org/archive.cfm?aid = 1999649

Wiggins, G., & McTighe, J. (2005). *Understanding by design* (2nd ed.). Columbus, OH: Pearson.

Yardi, S. (2006). The role of backchannel in collaborative learning environments. In S. A. Barab, K. E. Hay & D. T. Hickey (Eds.), *ICLS '06 proceedings of the 7th international conference on learning sciences* (pp. 852–858). International Society of the Learning Sciences.

Yardi, S. (2008). Whispers in the classroom. In T. McPherson (Ed.), *Digital youth, innovation, and the unexpected* (pp. 143–164). Cambridge, MA: MIT Press.

Zhu, E. (2007). Teaching with clickers. *Center for Research on Learning and Teaching Occasional Papers, 22*. Retrieved from http://www.crlt.umich.edu/publinks/CRLT_no22.pdf

ABOUT THE AUTHORS

Anthony 'Skip' Basiel has been involved in e-learning in the United Kingdom for almost two decades. His work with the British Council in 2004 won him eTutor of the Year Award with the Higher Education Academy. As an Adobe International Education Leader he has expertise in new media and web video conferencing consulting organizations such as Oxford University. He is an Adobe Certified Associate in Web Communication (2010).

Patrick Blessinger is the founder and executive director of the International Higher Education Teaching and Learning Association and a research fellow at the School of Education at St. John's University in Queens, New York, USA. He has taught over 150 college and university courses and he has served as a program chair at colleges and universities in the United States and European Union. He consults with HE institutions in the areas of technology innovation and internationalization and serves as an academic and accreditation advisor for HE institutions. He is the co-founder and co-director of the Institute for Meaning-Centered Education. He is the founder and editor of the *International HETL Review* and co-editor of the *Journal of Applied Research in Higher Education*. He is co-editor of several volumes within the *Cutting-edge Technologies in Higher Education* book series (Emerald) and co-editor of the book, *Meaning-Centered Education: International Perspectives and Explorations in Higher Education* (Routledge). He attended Auburn University, Georgia Tech, and the University of Georgia. He is a peer-recognized expert and thought leader in the field of teaching and learning and he has received several academic awards including a Fulbright Scholarship from the U.S. Department of State and a Governor's Teaching Fellowship from the State of Georgia, USA.

Leonardo Caporarello has earned his Ph.D. in Management Information Systems at the LUISS University in Rome (Italy), and the M.A. in Business Administration and Law at Bocconi University in Milano. He is professor of Leadership and Organization at SDA Bocconi School of Management, where he is also the director of the Learning Lab. The SDA Bocconi Learning Lab aims at research and development of technology-based innovation for enhancing managerial learning processes. Moreover, the

Learning Lab facilitates and supports faculty members in designing courses, at master and executive levels, which use technology for enhancing and augmenting the learning experience. He is involved in teaching and research projects at both national and international levels. He has been visiting professor at the Keyo University (Tokyo, Japan), and visiting scholar at the Michigan State University (USA). Moreover, Dr. Caporarello has been involved in a number of professional experiences in managing organizations, and in consultancy projects in IT and organization fields. He teaches Change Management at graduate level, Organization Behavior and Design in Executive and MBA programs. His research and professional interests include organizational and team behavior; project and change management; blended learning methodologies; designing of web-based management simulations; organizational integration governance and mechanisms; and IT adoption processes.

Marija Cubric is a reader in e-learning and a principal lecturer at University of Hertfordshire Business School, UK, where she teaches information systems and project management related subjects. Before joining academia in September 2004, she worked on system and software development for telecommunication industry in the United Kingdom and Canada. Marija holds a Ph.D. degree in Computer Science (1994) from Concordia University in Montreal, Canada, M.A. in Learning and Teaching in Higher Education from University of Hertfordshire (2007), and M.Sc. in Mathematics with Informatics from University of Belgrade (1989). She is a fellow and chartered IT professional of British Computer Society and fellow of Higher Education Academy. Her research interests are agile and innovative learning designs, application, and evaluation of educational technologies.

Elizabeth Dell is associate professor of Manufacturing and Mechanical Engineering Technology and the Miller Endowed Professor at the Rochester Institute of Technology. She is the Program Chair for Undeclared Engineering Technology and serves as the director of Women in Technology. Her primary teaching responsibilities include introductory and advanced courses in Materials Technology and Polymer Engineering and their associated laboratories. Dell received degrees in Mechanical Engineering from Kettering University and Macromolecular Science and Engineering from the University of Michigan. Research interests include engineering technology education, sustainable materials development (selection and characterization), and increasing the diversity of the engineering workforce. She is part of a team that is studying the impact of the use of technology paired with active learning on student learning. She is interested in the impact this pedagogical approach has on underrepresented groups in engineering, such as women and deaf and hard or hearing students. In her role as the director of Women in Technology, she leads recruitment and retention efforts to promote gender diversity. She is active in the Society of Women Engineers serving as the Outreach Chairperson for the Rochester NY section and serves on the Professional Development Committee of the Women in Engineering Pro Advocates Network (WEPAN). Prior to her academic appointment, Elizabeth worked in automotive material and product design at Toyota and General Motors.

Antonella Esposito has been e-learning practitioner since 1996. She led the CTU (e-learning university center) of the University of Milan, Italy, for 7 years. Currently she is a Ph.D. candidate in the e-learning program, Open University of Catalonia, working on a project focusing on doctoral e-researchers and new forms of research apprenticeship. In 2011, she was awarded the M.Res. in Educational and Social Research (Institute of Education, University of London), by submitting a dissertation on the interplay of digital scholarship and open scholarship practices of researchers in an Italian university. Her main research interests refer to social media in higher education, research ethics in online settings, issues related to emerging forms of academic scholarship, and innovation in doctoral pedagogy.

Iris Fischlmayr is associate professor at the Department of International Management, Johannes Kepler University Linz, Linz, Austria. She received her master's degree in International Trade and Commerce and her doctorate in Economic and Social Sciences at the Johannes Kepler University. In 2010, she has received her venia docendi (habilitation) for Business Administration. Her research and teaching are in the field of cross-cultural management and international human resource management, with special interest on expatriation, alternative forms of international work, female expatriates, virtual multicultural teams, and virtual collaboration. Her research is published in highly ranked journals (e.g., *Journal of International Human Resource Management*, *International Studies of Management and Organization*, *Management International Review*) and presented at international conferences (e.g. Academy of Management, European Group for Organizational Studies). Dr. Fischlmayr is involved in international teaching, research, and consulting projects with partner universities and multinational corporations. She is also co-author of a recently published book in professional expatriation management, which is targeted to HR managers and CEOs of international companies.

Robert Garrick, Ph.D., P.E., is associate professor in the Department of Manufacturing and Mechanical Engineering Technology and Packaging Sciences of the College of Applied Science and Technology at the Rochester Institute of Technology (RIT), USA. Robert is the Thermo-Fluids curriculum co-chair for the department. He worked for 25 years in automotive engineering research and holds seven U.S. patents. Since joining RIT in 2008, he has made a number of key contributions to educational excellence, including developing technology rich learning environments to enrich STEM education through his department and college. Nominated by his students to receive RIT's highest award for teaching, he was the sole recipient of the Eisenhart Provost's Award for Excellence in 2010 and became recognized as model for excellence in teaching. Garrick is the principal investigator of a current National Science Foundation (NSF) project in researching the technology rich interactive learning environment (TRiLE) with "barrier" engineering classes.

Sarah Gilbert has a masters in Library and Information Studies from Dalhousie University and is the research assistant with Faculty of Management. For her master's thesis, Sarah looked at *Supporting the Student Research-Paper Writing Process: Activities, Technologies, and Sources*. Her research interests encompass information seeking and retrieval activities, and investigating the integration of tools and technologies in student learning processes. She will shortly begin pursuing her doctoral studies.

Lauren Miller Griffith, Ph.D., is an instructional designer in the Faculty Center for Innovative Teaching at Central Michigan University. In this capacity, she uses her skills as an applied anthropologist to observe, analyze, and develop plans for improving education at the local level. She also works extensively with graduate students to support their development as teaching assistants and as future faculty. Lauren makes inclusive teaching a priority and has worked on various committees and initiatives to promote greater understanding of diversity among Central Michigan's faculty. Prior to her work at Central Michigan, she taught anthropology at Northern Arizona University. Lauren completed her doctorate and master's degrees in cultural anthropology at Indiana University where she was also fortunate enough to learn about the field of instructional consultation and design. Her development as an instructional designer was shaped in no small part by her participation in the Teagle Collegium on Inquiry in Action at Indiana University. Her anthropological research is focused on the intersections of tourism, performance, and education. More specifically, she is interested in populations that engage in apprenticeship pilgrimage as a means of augmenting their legitimacy within a performance genre that is not native to their own culture milieu. Her instructional design research includes collaborative learning, metacognition, and intellectual development.

Mark J. Hager is an associate professor of Psychology at Menlo College in Atherton, California. He earned his B.A. from Golden Gate University, his Ed.M. from Harvard University, and his Ph.D. in Education and Psychology from the University of Michigan. Dr. Hager's research has two streams: faculty development for e-learning and mentoring relationships in educational and professional development settings. Dr. Hager received a Harris Manchester Summer Research Institute Fellowship for 2010, during which he elaborated his research on faculty and student engagement with e-learning technologies. The research he initiated at Oxford formed the theoretical foundation for this case study analyzing technologically enhanced teaching and learning activities. Dr. Hager's other stream of research focuses on social-psychological influences on faculty teaching and student learning, particularly the role of mentoring and developmental relationships in educational and training settings. His recent publications include a chapter on holistic student development in *Advances in Motivation and Achievement*, Vol. 14. He is co-author (with Adrian Burgos and Jayne London) of the very successful University of Michigan handbooks on mentoring in graduate education now used throughout the United States. He has presented his research on graduate education in London to the UK Council, and in Berlin at the International Congress of Psychology. He is a regular speaker at the American Educational Research Association on diversity in mentoring relationships and faculty and student development.

Rhiannon Hart, Ph.D., is assistant professor of Psychology and a cognitive psychologist. Hart has conducted research on the cognitive processes underlying learning, and the effect of executive control on long-term memory. The eventual applications of this research extend to educational environments, potentially providing a means for students both with and without attentional difficulties to optimize learning.

Michael Howarth is making a range of e-learning video resources for the Teaching in Higher Education (TiHE) course that set a new standard for postgraduate teaching assistants and staff as part of the new higher education teaching strategy for University College London, UK.

Amanda Jefferies is a reader in Technology Enhanced Learning at the University of Hertfordshire, UK, where she is based in the School of Computer Science and leads the Technology Supported Learning Research group. She was seconded to the university's nationally funded Centre for Excellence, the Blended Learning Unit (BLU) for 5 years from 2005, where she led the Evaluation, Research and Scholarship strand of the work. She was awarded a UK National Teaching Fellowship in October 2011 in recognition of her long-standing commitment to promote an excellent student experience and her research into using technology to support HE student learning. Amanda is well-known for leading innovative research into understanding the student experience through using student constructed reflective video and audio diaries, a technique she refined when she directed the JISC-supported "Learner Journeys" STROLL project from 2007 to 2009 as part of the JISC funding for its E-Learning Programme.

Tine Köhler is a lecturer for International Business in the Department of Management and Marketing at the University of Melbourne, Australia. Her research focuses on Global Teamwork, Research Methods and Statistics. Her main research interests are in the area of cross-cultural management, cross-cultural communication and coordination, group processes, trust, and motivation, qualitative research methods, meta-analysis, and regression. She received her Pre-Diploma from the Philipps-University Marburg in Germany and her M.A. and Ph.D. degrees from George Mason University in the United States. Before joining the University of Melbourne, she worked at the International Finance Corporation (World Bank Group, USA) as a consultant for leadership development. Dr. Köhler is an editorial board member of *Organizational Research Methods*, *Academy of Management Learning and Education Small Group Research*, and the *Journal of Management Studies*. She further reviews for the *Academy of Management Journal*, *Journal of Organizational Behavior*, and the *Canadian Journal of Administrative Science*. She has published her work in *Organizational Research Methods, Small Group Research*, and in book chapters and conference proceedings. Dr. Köhler serves on the International Advisory Board of the Consortium for the Advancement of Research Methods and Analysis (CARMA) and is a member of the Melbourne International Business Research Unit (MIBRU).

Timo Lainema, Ph.D., is adjunct professor, Turku School of Economics (TSE), Turku, Finland. He holds a Ph.D. and a master's degree in Economics and Business Administration (with an emphasis on Information Management) from TSE. His Ph.D. thesis (2003) focused on the use of business simulation games in business process education. He constructed his first business simulation game in 1987 and since then he has applied simulation games in business education, in universities, executive education and in-house management development programs. His research interests are learning through simulation gaming, knowledge sharing in virtual working contexts, and decision making in time intensive environments. He is especially interested in modern conceptions of learning and how they relate to computer-based education, and holds an adjunct professorship in Education. He has participated in several projects related to innovative use of IT in management education. He has published articles, e.g., in *Computers and Education*, *Simulation & Gaming*, *Journal of Information Technology Education*, *Journal of Research on Technology in Education*, *Journal of Interactive Learning Research*, and *International Journal of Advanced Technology for Learning on Games-Based Learning*.

Brian Lukoff is a postdoctoral fellow in Technology and Education at the Harvard University School of Engineering and Applied Sciences. Dr. Lukoff's research is on the development of technology to drive formative assessment and student engagement, particularly in large lecture classes. He received his Ph.D. from the Stanford University School of Education. His dissertation focused on the development and validation of an automated methodology for scoring responses to "graphical response" test questions, and received the 2011 Brenda H. Loyd Outstanding Dissertation Award from the National Council on Measurement in Education. He also holds a M.S. in Statistics from Stanford University and a B.A. in Mathematics from Cornell University. Dr. Lukoff is also the CEO and co-founder of Learning Catalytics, a company that is commercializing the interactive teaching technology and making it available to teachers at the primary, secondary, and postsecondary levels.

Eric Mazur is the Balkanski Professor of Physics and Applied Physics at Harvard University and the area dean of Applied Physics. He holds a Ph.D. degree in experimental physics from the University of Leiden in the Netherlands. Dr. Mazur is author or co-author of 247 scientific publications and 12 patents. He developed the Peer Instruction method in the 1990s and writes and speaks extensively on education. His articles and book on *Peer*

Instruction have been widely referenced in a large array of peer-reviewed journals. Dr. Mazur is a co-founder of Learning Catalytics.

Ferdinando Pennarola is associate professor of Organization and Management Information Systems at Bocconi University, Milano (Italy). He has earned his doctoral degree in Business Administration at Bocconi University, where he joined the faculty in 1986. He gained the Full Professorship qualification in 2006. He is delegate rector for Technology Enhanced Learning at Bocconi since 2005. He teaches three major topics: Management Information Systems, Change Management, and Management Consultancy in both graduate and undergraduate programs at Bocconi University and in several executive education initiatives. His research appeared in top-rated international journals like *Review of Managerial Science*, *Journal of Management Education*, *International Journal of Information Management*, *Information Systems and E-Business Management*, and in books and chapters published by Pearson, Gower, and Springer. At Bocconi School of Management (SDA Bocconi), in 1992 he established the laboratory for advanced learning processes (TED) that he chaired for 12 years. TED has been the innovation unit of Bocconi School of Management in fields like e-learning, technology-mediated learning processes, simulation, and business gaming, leading a number of projects every year that involved a wide part of Bocconi Faculty. From January 2005 Dr. Pennarola is chairman of the Board of ISBM (International Schools of Business Management), based in London, UK, an international consortia of 11 business schools that run the ITP (International Teachers Programme) since the 1970s. He is a member of the editorial board of *Organization* (1994–2009), and the *Journal of E-Business Management* (since 2008 to today), leading scientific publications by Sage and Springer, respectively.

Brian A. Roberts wears a lot of different hats in his role as an instructional technologist in Central Michigan University's Faculty Center for Innovative Teaching: evangelist, trainer, developer, cheerleader, techy, fire fighter, consultant, and all-around friend to faculty, staff, and students. He is well versed in a wide variety of instructional and multimedia technologies including photography, digital imaging, classroom response systems, web development, podcasting, screen recording, presentation tools, social media, backchanneling, mobile learning, and much more. Brian's favorite part of his job is that he gets to interact with faculty and students from a wide variety of disciplines throughout the university community and learn a little bit about a lot of things. This makes him dangerous at cocktail parties. As an instructional technologist, he has long been called upon to assist faculty in delivering course content in new and innovative ways. After a lengthy hiatus, Roberts has recently returned to university life in the role of student. This new role has renewed his desire to assure that the use of any instructional technology is done so with a solid connection between the tech and effective instructional design.

Cristina Rubino, Ph.D., is assistant professor in Management at California State University, Northridge. Her major research interests include employee health and well-being, employee development (e.g., training, mentoring), and diversity. She has published academic articles in journals such as *Journal of Occupational Health Psychology, Stress & Health,* and *International Journal of Selection and Assessment.* Through the collaboration between ExxonMobil and the University of Houston, Dr. Rubino has contributed extensively to several job and training needs analysis projects, and to the development of training and mentoring program and mentor assessment system. In addition to working in Houston, she has also developed training and mentoring programs in Angola and Saudi Arabia. Dr. Rubino has presented her research at the top conferences in psychology, including the Society of Industrial and Organizational Psychology and Academy of Management annual meetings.

Mark Russell is an engineer by background with disciplinary interests in the thermal and fluid sciences. This area of interest includes simulations and computer programming. In addition to his subject-related interests and interests relating to engineering education, Mark has developed expertise relating to learning and assessment. Mark's Ph.D. was in the area of technology-enhanced educative assessment. Mark won the Times Higher E-tutor of the Year (2003), is a National Teaching Fellow (2005), and directed the JISC funded "Effecting Sustainable Change in Assessment Practice and Experience" (ESCAPE) project and the JISC funded "Integrating Technology-Enhanced Assessment Methods" (ITEAM) Project. Mark was the director of the University of Hertfordshire's Assessment and Feedback Project of the University of Hertfordshire, UK. Mark has moved from the University of Hertfordshire and is now the director of Technology Enhanced Learning and head of the Centre for Technology Enhanced Learning at King's College London.

Eeli Saarinen, M.Sc. (Economics and Business Administration), is a researcher at Turku School of Economics (TSE), Turku, Finland. He is currently positioned at the department of Management and Organization in Turku School of Economics where he is finishing his doctoral dissertation about leadership processes in virtual organizations. He has an active role in executive training programs. He also works for different state-owned programs as an expert of new leadership and innovation policy. For the past years he has been closely involved with simulation game trainings and published several articles based on the data from these trainings. His research interests include leadership, global virtual teams, cross-cultural communication, trust, learning in virtual environments, knowledge sharing in virtual contexts, team dynamics, networks, and virtual organizations.

Julie Schell is a research associate within the Mazur Group of the School of Engineering and Applied Sciences at Harvard University and an instructional designer at the University of Texas, Austin. She studies the diffusion and uptake of pedagogical innovation and is an expert in Peer Instruction (PI), an innovative teaching method developed by Eric Mazur. She co-founded PI Network, a global community of and for PI users. She also authors the official Peer Instruction Blog, *Turn to Your Neighbor*. She received her doctorate in May of 2009 from Teachers College, Columbia University and her M.S. in Counseling and Educational Psychology, with an emphasis in Instructional Technology from the University of Nevada, Reno in 2000. Her dissertation, *Venturing Toward Better Teaching: S.T.E.M. Professors' Efforts to Improve Their Introductory Undergraduate Pedagogy at Major Research Universities*, was selected as the 2009 Dissertation of the Year from the American Educational Research Association, Postsecondary Education Division.

Lorn Sheehan is associate professor and associate director at School of Business Administration, Dalhousie University, Canada. Lorn's research is related to tourism destination management and stakeholder management. He teaches in the areas of strategic management and tourism management and has published in leading journals in the tourism field and delivered numerous conference presentations related to his research. Lorn has served on boards of various industry and educational organizations including Tourism Calgary (as chair); Calgary Tourism Education Consortium (as chair); Calgary Chamber of Commerce on the Tourism Committee (as chair); Environment Committee, Tax and Economic Affairs Committee; Alberta Chamber of Commerce Policy Committee; Calgary and Area Tourism Destination Region (as vice-chair); and the Travel and Tourism Research Association.

Lois M. Shelton earned a Ph.D. in Business Economics from Harvard University and is an associate professor in the Department of Management at California State University, Northridge. A former business executive with nearly 10 years of experience in management consulting and real estate development, her diverse research interests include entrepreneurship, industry and social structure, the work/non-work interface, and role theory. In addition to a number of book chapters published in the both U.S. and abroad, her work has appeared in leading journals such as the *Strategic Management Journal, Entrepreneurship, Theory & Practice, Journal of Small Business Management,* and *Journal of Developmental Entrepreneurship.* She teaches strategy, management, and organizational behavior, and international business courses in the undergraduate and MBA programs and quantitative methods in the Grenoble Ecole de Management DBA program (France).

Binod Sundararajan is assistant professor at the School of Business Administration, Dalhousie University, Canada. Binod's interests lie in organizational, professional, and business communication; computer-mediated communication; computer-supported collaborative learning (CSCL), computer-supported cooperative work (CSCW) and social network analysis. He conducts research in business and professional communication practices, adoption and diffusion of mediated technologies, use of CMC in such diverse areas as immigrant entrepreneurship, justice, teaching, collaborative work, and learning. He also has a parallel stream of research where he has mapped the social structures and networks of important actors in the Underground Railroad Movement and is also working on the networks of Irish immigrants to Halifax, Nova Scotia.

Larry Villasmil, M.Sc., Ph.D., is assistant professor in the Department of Manufacturing and Mechanical Engineering Technology and Packaging Sciences of the College of Applied Science and Technology. Before joining the RIT faculty, Dr. Villasmil accumulated 5 years of research experience, was a graduate teaching assistant and a fellow of the Graduate Teaching Academy sponsored by the Center of Teaching Excellence at Texas A&M University. Prior to his enrollment at Texas A&M, he worked in the Exploration and Production division of one of the largest state owned oil corporations for 12 years as conceptual engineering leader and rotating equipment and machinery advisor, while serving as instructor for the international educational branch and content specialist to periodically revise and update the Standards and Design Engineering Manual. Dr. Villasmil has been able to bring this extensive industrial experience to his classroom and curriculum development activities. Larry's current areas of research include computational fluid dynamics and turbulence modeling and its application to multiphase flow and internal combustion engines; wind power as alternative energy; fluid power; and the use of technology in the classroom as he is currently collaborating in evaluating the impact of tablet PCs and collaborative software on improving learning in sophomore classes. He has mentored undergraduate students so they engage in research activities and their work has been published in venues like ASEE and SAE. He is a member of the department curriculum committee and serves as "Thermo-fluids Area Curriculum Co-Champion" leading curriculum development efforts for related courses in the Mechanical and Electro-Mechanical Engineering and Technology programs.

Charles Wankel, professor of Management at St. John's University, New York, earned his doctorate from New York University. Charles is on the Rotterdam School of Management Dissertation Committee and is honorary vice rector of the Poznań University of Business. He has authored and edited about 46 books including the bestselling *Management*, 3rd ed. (Prentice-Hall, 1986), 11 volumes in the IAP series Research in Management Education and Development, the *Handbook of 21st Century Management* (Sage, 2008), and the *Encyclopedia of Business in Today's World* (Sage, 2009), which received the American Library Association's Outstanding Business Reference Source Award. He is the leading founder and director of scholarly virtual communities for management professors, currently directing eight with thousands of participants in more than 90 nations. He has been a visiting professor in Lithuania at the Kaunas University of Technology (Fulbright Fellowship) and the University of Vilnius (United Nations Development Program and Soros Open Society Foundation funding). Fortune 50 consulting clients include McDonald's Corporation's Hamburger University and IBM Learning Services. International consulting includes TNK-Nizhnevartovsk (former ChernogorNeft) Oil Company, Siberia.

Christa L. Wilkin, Ph.D., is assistant professor of Management at California State University, Northridge. She received her Ph.D. from McMaster University in Hamilton, Canada. Her primary research interests include organizational justice in employment relationships and various kinds of non-standard work arrangements such as temporary workers and volunteers. Her research is published in the *Journal of Organizational Behavior*,

International Journal of Selection and Assessment, International Journal of Human Resource Management, and two edited volumes. Her work has been presented at several international conferences such as the Academy of Management Annual Meeting, Society for Industrial Organizational Psychology Annual Meeting, and the International Industrial Relations Association (IIRA) African Regional Congress. She has worked in human resources as a volunteer intern in Botswana, Africa and as a human resources assistant at a non-profit organization. She has also worked in various managerial capacities in the health care and food service industries. She is a Certified Human Resources Professional (CHRP).

Deone Zell, Ph.D., is the director of the Faculty Technology Center at California State University, Northridge (CSUN), where she leads initiatives that help faculty improve teaching and learning through technology. Prior she served as interim director of Graduate Programs in the College of Business and Economics, and for 12 years as professor of Management where she taught classes in Management and Organizational Behavior, Organization Theory and Change, and Innovation. She received her Ph.D. at UCLA. She is the author or co-author of three scholarly books on the topics of organizational innovation and strategic planning: *Thinking Strategically in Turbulent Times* (M.E. Sharpe, 2005); *Awakening the Academy* (Anker Publishing Company, 2002); and *Changing by Design* (Cornell University Press, 1997). She has authored articles on topics of innovation and organizational change in journals such as the *MIT Sloan Management Review, Organizational Dynamics, Academy of Management Learning & Education, Journal of Applied Behavioral Science, Business & Society, Journal of Management Inquiry,* and *International Journal of Organizational Analysis.* For 3 years, she managed a large-scale research project funded by the Alfred P. Sloan Foundation that investigated organizational transformation in higher education. Originally trained as an industrial anthropologist, she also worked on research projects in private sector companies such as Hewlett-Packard and Toyota Motor Company to understand how technology and high-engagement management techniques lead to superior performance. Her research interests include organizational evolution and change, social networks, the diffusion of innovations, technology evolution, and the transition to an environmentally sustainable economy.

Tarek Zoubir a tutor for teacher training at the School of Education Middlesex University, UK, and until recently a program adviser for postgraduate and undergraduate students at the Institute for Work Based Learning at Middlesex University. During the 6 years as an adviser he has been an online tutor for undergraduate and postgraduate students supporting their work-based projects. He has been part of the education department at Middlesex University since 2010. As an Academic Assistant he provides direct support to directors of programs, academics, and general advice to undergraduate as well as postgraduate students. The focus of his work has been to better incorporate technology in existing blended learning designs to enhance teaching and learning. Among other things this has included the use of wikis to address government and institutional priorities and the use of video to capture M.A. Education seminars to meet students' requests. To date he has facilitated teaching and learning across a number of online platforms that include Blackboard, wikis, CMS systems such as Plone, and social media tools. Tarek currently works across education department directorates using a variety of technologies and crosses boundaries to act as a broker receiving, achieving, and sharing good practice. Tarek qualified with a B.Sc. Psychology with Criminology from Middlesex University and a M.A. in Education, Leadership, Management and Change from the same institute. He also holds a Certificate of English Language Teaching to Adults (CELTA) accredited by Cambridge University. Prior to his work with the university, Tarek worked as a Summer School and college level teacher of English as a Second/Foreign Language. In addition, he has created e-learning resources for the Institute, CDs, the *Institute's Wednesday's Webcasts,* and Adobe Acrobat PDF form technology for online use. For the last 2 years he has had responsibility for interviewing managers, business leaders, and employees to create video materials (approximately 200 hours) for staff and for students, aimed to provide the professional face of the institute to the business community. He is an Adobe Education Leader. He is currently developing his view of education as a "hands-on thinker," with one foot in the academic world and another in the practical activity of the business environment. Tarek is familiar and comfortable with managers and employees through work as a senior BBC education producer, broadcaster, and commissioning editor on location in Britain and abroad.

AUTHOR INDEX

SUBJECT INDEX